RESEARCH HANDBOOK ON KNOWLEDGE TRANSFER AND INTERNATIONAL BUSINESS

Research Handbook on Knowledge Transfer and International Business

Edited by

Zaheer Khan
Professor in Strategy and International Business, Business School, University of Aberdeen, UK

Smitha R. Nair
Formerly Professor of Strategy and International Business, Amrita School of Business, Amrita Vishwa Vidyapeetham, Coimbatore, India

Yong Kyu Lew
Professor of International Business, HUFS Business School, Hankuk University of Foreign Studies, Seoul, South Korea

EE Edward **Elgar**
PUBLISHING

Cheltenham, UK • Northampton, MA, USA

Published by
Edward Elgar Publishing Limited
The Lypiatts
15 Lansdown Road
Cheltenham
Glos GL50 2JA
UK

Edward Elgar Publishing, Inc.
William Pratt House
9 Dewey Court
Northampton
Massachusetts 01060
USA

Paperback edition 2023

A catalogue record for this book
is available from the British Library

Library of Congress Control Number: 2021949001

This book is available electronically in the **Elgar**online
Business subject collection
http://dx.doi.org/10.4337/9781788976114

MIX
Paper | Supporting responsible forestry
FSC
www.fsc.org   FSC® C013604

ISBN 978 1 78897 610 7 (Hardback)
ISBN 978 1 78897 611 4 (eBook)
ISBN 978 1 03532 204 6 (Paperback)

Printed and bound by CPI Group (UK) Ltd, Croydon, CR0 4YY

Contents

v

Contributors

Ahmad Arslan is currently working as an Associate Professor at the Department of Marketing, Management and International Business, Oulu Business School, University of Oulu, Finland. Previously, he has worked in academia in different universities in the UK and Finland. His earlier research has been published in prestigious academic journals such as *British Journal of Management, International Business Review, International Marketing Review, International Journal of Organizational Analysis, Journal of Business Research, Scandinavian Journal of Management, Journal of Strategic Marketing, Journal of Knowledge Management, Journal of Organizational Change Management, Production Planning & Control,* and *Technological Forecasting and Social Change* among others. Moreover, he has also contributed book chapters to several edited handbooks addressing different management related topics. Finally, he holds several editorial board memberships and is currently a Senior Editor of *International Journal of Emerging Markets (Emerald)*.

Deborah Callaghan is a Senior Lecturer in Human Resource Management and Organisational Behaviour at Liverpool Business School, Liverpool John Moores University. Deborah has taught across a broad range of undergraduate and postgraduate programmes in international business strategy, social responsibility, organisational behaviour and human resource management programmes which are CIPD accredited in the UK and international market. Deborah has extensive industry experience in project management and learning and development in both the public and private sectors. She was awarded her PhD at the University of Liverpool in 2019. Her research interests include how policy and process is enacted in organisational contexts, gender inequality at work, employee voice, workplace bullying and harassment, in particular the challenge of implementing anti-bullying intervention strategies, and contemporary changes in the labour market.

Nigel Driffield is Deputy Pro Vice Chancellor for regional engagement and also Professor of International Business at Warwick Business School, having held a similar post at Aston Business School for 10 years. He has a PhD from Reading University. He is the Midlands Lead for the ESRC Productivity Institute. He also holds a £1 million investment from ESRC looking at productivity in the West Midlands, "From Productivity to Prosperity". He recently held a prestigious Leverhulme Fellowship, investigating the impact of internationally mobile capital on both home and source countries, particularly in terms of competitiveness and labour markets. More generally, he is currently an advisor to the BEIS Select Committee, and the Department of International Trade, with a focus on inward investment. He has carried out research and consultancy projects for UNCTAD, World Bank, European Commission, OECD, and in the UK several government departments and local regional development bodies. He is on the editorial review board of the *Journal of International Business Studies*, as well as the *Journal of World Business* and the *Global Strategy Journal*.

Ismail Gölgeci is an Associate Professor at Aarhus University, Herning, Denmark. His research has been published in *Journal of International Business Studies, Human Relations, Industrial Marketing Management, Journal of Business Research, International Business*

Review, International Small Business Journal, International Marketing Review, Journal of International Management, Supply Chain Management: An International Journal, Production Planning & Control, Journal of Knowledge Management amongst others. He is an editorial review board member of *Journal of Business Research* and *Review of International Business and Strategy* and guest editor at *Industrial Marketing Management, Journal of Business Research, International Journal of Physical Distribution & Logistics Management* and *European Journal of Marketing.*

Lamia Ben Hamida is a Professor at la Haute école de gestion Arc of the University of Applied Sciences and Arts Western Switzerland/HES-SO. She has a PhD in Economics, titled: "Inward Foreign Direct Investment and Intra-Industry Spillovers: The Swiss Case". Her thesis analyses the main key factors determining FDI intra-industry spillover effects. She also studied the effect of outward FDI spillovers on the home economy, the role of southern MNCs on the economic development of European countries. Her research interests focus on: multinational corporations and Foreign Direct Investment (FDI), innovation activity and knowledge transfer, FDI and export spillovers, learning processes and technological change. She has published her research in many journals, such as *Journal of Contemporary Management, International Business Review*, and *International Journal of Export Marketing.*

Shuna Shu Ham Ho is currently a Lecturer in the Strategy and International Business area group at Rowe School of Business, Faculty of Management, Dalhousie University. She is also a PhD Candidate in International Business and Strategy at Beedie School of Business, Simon Fraser University. Her research generally focuses on the socio-spatial environments of international business. Her recent research interests include such non-market strategies as the corporate social responsibility of multinational enterprises for attaining social license as well as their corporate political activities for obtaining legal license under the hybrid governance among civil society, the state, and the market. Her quantitative research work frequently combines spatial analytics and data-mining methods with econometric techniques. The adoption of these research methods was inspired by her educational background in Geo-Information Science and Information Engineering.

Pia Hurmelinna-Laukkanen is Professor of Marketing, especially International Business at the Oulu Business School, University of Oulu, and Adjunct Professor (Knowledge Management) at the LUT University, School of Business and Management. She has published about 75 refereed articles in journals such as *Journal of Product Innovation Management, Industrial and Corporate Change, International Business Review*, and *Industrial Marketing Management*, and over 200 other scientific and managerial publications in the field of innovation management.

Zaheer Khan is a Professor in Strategy & International Business at Aberdeen University Business School, University of Aberdeen, UK. He is a Senior Fellow of the Higher Education Academy, and an elected Fellow of the Academy of Social Sciences. He sits on the editorial boards of *British Journal of Management, Journal of World Business, Multinational Business Review*, and *Journal of Knowledge Management*. His research focuses on global technology management, alliances and internationalization of emerging markets' firms. His work has appeared in the *Journal of International Business Studies, International Business Review*,

Human Relations, *Journal of World Business*, *Global Strategy Journal*, *British Journal of Management*, and *International Journal of Management Reviews*, among others.

Minnie Kontkanen is a Programme Manager of the Master's Degree Programme in International Business at the University of Vaasa. She has long-term teaching experience in the areas of international marketing, entry strategies and internationalization behaviour. Her research areas of interest include international marketing strategies, uncertainty and risk in internationalization strategies, and sustainability. Her studies have been published in edited books and in journals such as *Technological Forecasting & Social Change*, *Journal of Transnational Management* and *Journal of Strategic Marketing*.

Olli Kuivalainen is Professor of International Marketing and Entrepreneurship at LUT University, School of Business and Management, Finland. His expertise covers broad areas of international business, marketing and entrepreneurship and their interplay. His current research topics are, for example, in the domain of international entrepreneurship (international new ventures and born globals and how they organise themselves and what role digitalization has in internationalisation), and decision-making in internationalisation (decision-making logics, international opportunities, heuristics and biases, entry mode and market choice). His academic work has been published in journals such as *Journal of International Business Studies*, *Journal of World Business*, *International Business Review*, *International Marketing Review*, *Journal of International Marketing*, *Industrial Marketing Management*, *Technovation*, and *International Small Business Journal*.

Jae Eun Lee is Professor of Department of International Trade at Sunchon National University (SCNU), Suncheon, South Korea. He is also the Chairperson of Division of Economics and International Trade as well as the head of the Department International Trade of SCNU. Previously, he served as Director of Start-up PLUS Center and Start-up Education Center of SCNU. He majored in international business, and his minor is organizational theory. He completed his PhD at School of Business, Yonsei University, Seoul, South Korea. His research interests are in global strategy of MNEs and SMEs, global strategic alliance, and global entrepreneurship. He has won many academic awards and government commendations including Commendation by the Minister for MOTIE (Ministry of Trade, Industry and Energy) of the Korean Government and Best Doctoral Dissertation Award in the Korean Academy of International Business. He has published journal articles in international journals including SSCI and KCI journals.

Jong Min Lee is a Lecturer (Assistant Professor) in International Business and Strategy at Henley Business School, University of Reading, UK. His main research interests sit at the intersection between international business and global strategic management. His current research focuses on global staffing strategies, knowledge management, dynamic capabilities, and strategic changes in the context of multinational firms. His research has been published in leading academic journals (including *Journal of International Business Studies*, *Journal of World Business*, *Journal of International Management*, and *Journal of Business Ethics*, among others) and recognized by multiple awards from various international conferences. He currently serves on the editorial review board of the *Journal of International Business Studies* and works as a reviewing editor of *Asian Business & Management*.

Tiina Leposky is an Assistant Professor at the University of Vaasa, Finland, in the School of Marketing and Communication within the International Business and Marketing Strategies research group. Her research areas include servitization and digitalization of international companies, customer value creation in sales relationships across borders, divestments and exits of international companies, and value co-creation and service provision with impoverished people. Her research has been published in, among others, the *Journal of Strategic Marketing* and *Journal of Transnational Management.*

Yong Kyu Lew is Professor of International Business at Hankuk University of Foreign Studies (HUFS), Seoul, South Korea. He completed his PhD at Manchester Business School, UK. Previously he held faculty positions at the University of Hull and the University of Manchester in the UK. He sits on the editorial boards of *Asia Pacific Journal of Management*, *Multinational Business Review*, and *critical perspectives on international business*. He has published journal articles in mainstream journals, including *Journal of International Business Studie*s, *Long Range Planning*, *Sustainable Development*, *Global Strategy Journal*, *International Business Review*, *Management International Review*, *Journal of International Management*, *Journal of Business Research*, *International Small Business Journal*, *R&D Management*, and *Industry and Innovation*, among others.

James H. Love is Professor of International Business at Leeds University Business School. He previously held chairs in international business and economics at Aston, Birmingham and Warwick Universities, and earlier worked in the economics department at Strathclyde University. His background is in applied microeconomics, principally in the fields of international business and innovation. He is also an associate at the Enterprise Research Centre, an independent research organization which conducts policy-relevant research on SME growth and development, and a visiting Professor at the University of Tartu, Estonia. He has acted as a consultant on aspects of inward investment and innovation policy for a number of organizations including the OECD, UK Trade and Investment (UKTI), Advantage West Midlands, the Manchester Independent Economic Review, the Scottish Executive, Scottish Enterprise, Invest Northern Ireland, and Forfas (Dublin). He has also held visiting chairs and fellowships at Copenhagen Business School and Wolfson College, Cambridge. He is a Fellow of the Academy of Social Sciences and of the Higher Education Academy.

Stefano Menghinello works at the Istituto nazionale di statistica (ISTAT) Direzione centrale per la raccolta dati (DCRD), Italy. He holds a PhD from the University of Birmingham. His main research interests focus on multinational firms, business clusters and regional development.

Smitha R. Nair is Professor of Strategy & International Business, Amrita School of Business, India. She has served as faculty at the Management School, University of Sheffield (UK) and University of East Anglia (UK). Her research interests include cross-border knowledge flows in multinationals, organizational innovation and internationalization patterns of emerging market firms. She has authored/co-authored book chapters and scholarly articles in leading journals such as *British Journal of Management*, *International Business Review*, *Management International Review*, *International Journal of Management Reviews*, *Journal of Business Research*, *European Journal of Marketing*, and *Journal of Knowledge Management*.

Chang Hoon Oh is William and Judy Docking Professor of Strategy in the School of Business, University of Kansas. He previously was William Saywell Professor of Asian Pacific Studies in Beedie School of Business, Simon Fraser University. His research centers on non-market strategy in challenging environments, business continuity and sustainability, and globalization versus regionalization. He also contributes to interdisciplinary works and bridges the gap between business and economics, and between business and political science. He is co-editor-in-chief of *Multinational Business Review*, and serves as a member of the editorial review board for the *Journal of International Business Studies*, *Journal of World Business*, and *Journal of International Business Policy*. He has published more than 45 papers in peer reviewed journals

Jan-Tore Øian is a Partner/Senior Broker at Fram Insurance Brokers AS in Oslo, Norway. The niche firm specializes in placing and facilitating marine insurance products for commercial vessels with risk carriers across the world. His expertise is in property & casualty, third party liability and war risk insurances within the maritime sector. One of his main responsibilities is to establish and maintain relationships with clients and insurers for the firm around the globe. He holds an MSc in International Business and Management from Alliance Manchester Business School where he graduated with distinction and wrote his dissertation in the domain of knowledge transfer and absorptive capacity in born global firms. Prior to that he served in the Norwegian Armed Forces as a Non-Commissioned officer both domestically and abroad as part of NATO.

Byung Il Park is currently a Professor in International Business at the College of Business, Hankuk University of Foreign Studies, South Korea. His research focuses on Asian emerging-market MNCs, MNC strategy and corporate social responsibility of MNCs, and MNC corruptions. He has published in such journals as the *Journal of World Business*, *Journal of International Management*, *Management International Review*, *International Business Review*, *International Marketing Review*, *Corporate Governance: An International Review*, *International Small Business Journal* and *Asia Pacific Journal of Management*. In addition, he is Editor-in-Chief of *International Journal of Multinational Corporation Strategy* and has also handled special issues for *Journal of World Business*, *Journal of Business Research*, *International Marketing Review*, *Thunderbird International Business Review*, *Canadian Journal of Administrative Sciences*, and *European Journal of International Management*.

Matti Saari is a PhD student at School of Marketing and Communication, University of Vaasa, Finland. His research interests focus on the internationalization of small and medium-sized enterprises and information and communication technology (ICT) with specific emphasis on the digital platforms and big data.

Mayumi Tabata is a Professor in the School of Commerce at Senshu University, Tokyo, Japan. She was born and brought up in Tokyo and moved to Taiwan in 1995 after earning a master's degree of political economy in Japan. She received her PhD in Sociology from National Taiwan University in 2007 and worked in the Department of Sociology in National Dong Hwa University and National Taipei University as an Associate Professor for over 10 years. Her main research interests include Asian capitalism and the global production network, global talent mobility in the East Asian high-tech industry, and the impact of the student movement on the development of social enterprise in Taiwan. Her research has appeared in

Asian Survey, East Asian Science, Technology and Society: An International Journal (EASTS), *Evolutionary and Institutional Economics Review*, and others.

Heini Vanninen, DS. (Econ. and Business Administration), is a Postdoctoral researcher at LUT University, School of Business and Management. Her research interests are interdisciplinary, covering areas related to, for example, the digitalization of international business, digital marketing (social media, influencer marketing) and organizing in the digital era. Her academic work has been published in, for example, *International Business Review*.

Jerra Veeger is an alumna of the University of Amsterdam Business School, graduating cum laude with a Masters in Business Administration concentrating on International Management. Her studies centered on innovation and sustainability in the international retail environment with a key focus on the Sustainable Development Goals and their implementation in business. The cases analyzed here are drawn from her Master's thesis, which considers how knowledge can best be transferred between stakeholders from various sectors (public, private, government, non-profit) in order to reach their common goals. Currently, she works on sustainable supply chain development and social compliance issues for a Dutch retail chain.

Michelle Westermann-Behaylo (J.D. Vanderbilt University; PhD George Washington University) is Assistant Professor of International Management and Co-Director of the Sustainability Initiative at the University of Amsterdam Business School. Her research explores the social and environmental impacts of business, particularly on the most vulnerable stakeholders. She writes about the role of business in respecting human dignity and human rights, and engaging with the Sustainable Development Goals. Her latest project considers how information and communication technology and digital platforms can amplify stakeholder voices. Her work has been published in *Strategic Organization, Academy of Management Perspectives, Business & Society, Business Ethics Quarterly, American Business Law Journal*, and *Journal of Business Ethics*. Her research has received financial support from, among others, the Netherlands Organization for Scientific Research, the Aspen Institute, the Institute for Economics and Peace, and the One Earth Future Foundation.

Jie Wu is Professor in Strategy & Entrepreneurship at University of Aberdeen Business School, University of Aberdeen, UK. His work has appeared in some of the leading strategy/international business, and interdisciplinary business management journals including *Strategic Management Journal, Journal of International Business Studies, Research Policy, Strategic Entrepreneurship Journal, British Journal of Management, Harvard Business Review, Journal of World Business, Global Strategy Journal, Journal of Business Ethics, International Journal of Research in Marketing*.

Introduction to *Research Handbook on Knowledge Transfer and International Business*

The Context

The latter half of the 20th century witnessed a shift in the economic activity from manufacturing to services. As a consequence of this shift, we saw the emergence of a knowledge-based economy, where the reliance on knowledge to build capabilities and competencies took precedence. It thus became vital for organizations to focus on the production, communication and consumption of knowledge to sustain their competitive advantage (Grant, 1996; Grant & Phene, 2021).

The 21st century saw the advent and surge of the digital economy, which has persuaded many organizations to undergo rapid digital transformations. Globally, the businesses are now hyperconnected with internet, mobile technology, smart devices, the Internet of Things (IoT) and digital platforms to name a few. This also has fueled technological advancements in the areas of big data, artificial intelligence, machine learning, robotics, block chains, etc. With all of these fast-paced developments, data is now being generated from different sources, and this is often dynamic, vast and multifaceted. All of these changes further put knowledge at the core of what organizations do. Analyzing and drawing insights from this data, managing the information derived from the same and maintaining the knowledge base for the organization are all activities that firms constantly engage with. In an international business context, the effective utilization of this knowledge also requires transmission to other organizational units, which in the case of multinational enterprises (MNEs) may be often geographically dispersed units with global value chains. Further, modern day MNEs often have a wider network of global partners, as part of their coopetition strategy, which may then necessitate knowledge exchange with their partner firms worldwide. These aspects mandate a greater focus on international or cross-border knowledge transfers in MNEs, which could subsequently steer organizational learning and innovation, which are all vital for sustaining a firm's competitive advantage (Argote & Ingram, 2000; Kogut & Zander, 1993; Lyles & Salk, 1996).

Literature on Cross Border Knowledge Transfer

Knowledge has been defined as a "fluid mix of framed experience, values, contextual information, and expert insight that provides a framework for evaluating and incorporating new experiences and information" (Davenport & Prusak, 1998, p. 5). This definition also leads us to the different dimensions of knowledge, which is normally categorized as tacit versus explicit (Polyani, 1966) or procedural versus declarative (Grant, 1996). While tacit knowledge is highly contextual and linked to personal experiences that make it difficult to communicate or codify, explicit knowledge, on the other hand, is easily codified and can be articulated better. These characteristics also make tacit knowledge more valuable and highly sought after, despite the difficulties in transmitting this knowledge (Kogut & Zander, 1992). On similar lines, procedural knowledge is linked to "knowing how" (mostly tacit) while declarative knowledge deals with "knowing what" (mostly explicit) (Brown & Duguid, 1998). Knowledge creation in organizations is based on the interaction between these tacit and explicit dimensions of knowledge via the SECI (Socialization, Externalization, Combination and Internalization) model (Nonaka, 1994).

Knowledge transfer can be defined as the "process through which one unit (e.g., group, department, or division) is affected by the experience of another" (Argote & Ingram, 2000, p. 151). The literature on knowledge transfer (KT) is mature and quite vast with diverse perspectives and, hence, is fragmented as well, which is also evident from the literature reviews and meta-analysis in this area (Michailova & Mustaffa, 2012; van Wijk et al., 2008; Zeng et al., 2018). In fact, knowledge creation and transfer figured as one of the prominent research streams (Kostova et al., 2016), based on a review of international management articles in *Journal of World Business* (starting from 1960). This could be due to the fact that MNE is a superior vehicle (and considered a social community) when compared with markets for the development and transfer of knowledge (Kogut & Zander, 1993).

KT was initially conceptualized as transmission of knowledge focusing on a sender, receiver and communication channel (Gupta & Govindarajan, 2000), which has its origins in communication theory (Shannon & Weaver, 1949). Gupta and Govindarajan (2000) examine the richness of communication channels, motivational dispositions of the sender and receiver and the absorptive capacity of the receiver. Following the seminal work of Gupta and Govindarajan (1991, 2000), studies exploring KT took off in a big way. Subsequent studies realized that the social context of the KT and the transformational nature of the process was largely being ignored (Becker-Ritterspach et al., 2010). So, there was a need to situate the transfer in the social context, which draws from the social learning perspective (Lave & Wenger, 1993). Thus, some studies (Lane et al., 2001; Dhanaraj et al., 2004) started treating KT as a proxy for organizational learning (Saka-Helmhout, 2010). Further, studies on KT have also been influenced by human capital theory (Becker, 1964)and agency theory (Eisenhardt, 1989) and they mostly adopted an HR angle. Such studies (Björkman et al., 2004, 2007; Fey & Furu, 2008; Minbaeva, 2008; Minbaeva et al., 2003; Mäkelä & Brewster, 2009; Simonin & Özsomer, 2009) seek to examine the effects of behavioral control mechanisms and incentive-based motivational mechanisms on KT.

The relationship between the sender and receiver units has also been examined by several KT scholars (Yamao et al., 2009; Li, 2005; Muthuswamy & White, 2005; Khan et al., 2015). Such studies employed the social capital perspective (Nahapiet & Ghoshal, 1998) and social exchange theory (Blau, 1964) to understand the effects of aspects such as trust, commitment, conflicts, shared vision, mutual respect and collaborations on KT. Country level effects (home versus host country) in terms of cultural distance, linguistic distance, geographical distance and institutional distance have also been found to hamper KT (Ambos & Ambos, 2009; Jensen & Szulanski, 2004; Evangelista & Hau, 2009). Relative economic development and competitiveness of home versus host country also influences the dynamics of KT (Ambos et al., 2006; Li et al., 2007). Studies on the role of language and culture in facilitating cross-border KT have also been gathering momentum (Peltokorpi & Yamao, 2017; Liu et al., 2015; Sarala et al., 2016; Welch & Welch, 2008).

In terms of the antecedents of KT, organizational mechanisms or unit level (sender or recipient) characteristics have been the most widely researched. The main unit level antecedents that have been examined include absorptive capacity (Cohen & Levinthal, 1990; Lane et. al., 2001; Nair et al., 2016; Peltokorpi, 2017), social and integrative mechanisms (Gupta & Govindarajan, 2000; Hakanson & Nobel, 2001; Björkman et al., 2004; Khan et al., 2015), communication frequency and intensity (Minbaeva et al., 2003; Bresman et al., 1999, 2009), autonomy and control (Noorderhaven & Harzing, 2009; Foss & Pederson, 2002) and strategic mandate and motives (Bartlett & Ghoshal, 1986; Roth & Morrison, 1992; Birkinshaw & Morrison, 1995). Characteristics of knowledge were another group of antecedents that captured scholarly attention. Causal ambiguity (Szulanski, 1996; Jensen & Szulanski, 2004; Szulanski et al., 2004), stickiness of knowledge (Szulanski, 1996), tacitness, complexity and asset specificity (Simonin, 1999a, 1999b, 2004; Dhanaraj et al., 2004) of knowledge have been found to hinder KT. Further, the attractiveness of knowledge in terms of its value, rareness, inimitability and non-substitutability (Pérez-Nordtvedt et al., 2008), as well as the relevance of knowledge (Schulz, 2001, 2003; Yang et al., 2008; Rui et al., 2016) prompt organizational units to engage with KT.

A vast majority of the extant literature focused on the KT from the parent unit to subsidiary units i.e. conventional KT (Ambos et al., 2006), going by the norm that in general subsidiaries depend on their parent units to develop their operational capabilities and enhance their knowledge base. However, as the business landscape evolved, several subsidiaries started developing superior capabilities, progressed to being centers of excellence, and became strategically important in the MNE network (Denrell et al., 2004). Such subsidiaries then became knowledge providers to the rest of the MNE network, thus triggering scholarly interest (Ambos et al., 2006; Rabbiosi, 2011; Rabbiosi & Santangelo, 2013; Mudambi et al., 2014; Nair et al., 2018) in lateral (between subsidiary units) and reverse KT (from subsidiary to parent). Similarly, prior research has also examined several dimensions of KT, namely the extent of KT (Gupta & Govindarajan, 2000; Harzing & Noorderhaven, 2006a, b), degree of KT (Minbaeva, 2008), frequency of KT (Monteiro et al., 2008). These studies make the implicit assumption that all knowledge flows are beneficial. However, it needs to be noted that not all KT proves to be beneficial for the recipient. This has prompted researchers to also examine other relevant dimensions of KT, such as the benefits of KT (Ambos et al., 2006), quality and quantity of KT (Tran et al., 2010), satisfaction from KT (Li & Hsieh, 2009) and the efficiency and effectiveness of KT (Ciabuschi et al., 2011).

Aims and Objectives of the Handbook

The primary aim of this handbook is to provide a systematic account of knowledge transfer in the international business context. To achieve this objective, we have assembled a range of interesting chapters that provide a useful insight into knowledge transfer and international business. The chapters included in this handbook offer important perspectives on knowledge transfer and international business.

Structure and Content of the Handbook

The collection of chapters is organized around the following themes.

Part I – strategic perspective of knowledge transfer
Driffield, Love and Menghinello look at technology and managerial flows between MNEs' parent units and their affiliates (located in Italy), in their chapter titled "Intra-firm trade,

embeddedness and international knowledge transfer in the MNE". The chapter highlights the dominant parent to affiliate knowledge flows and also reverse flows as part of two-way transfers, and is based on a quantitative analysis of a unique dataset by ISTAT (the Italian National Statistical Institute). Intra-firm trade is found to be strongly related to intra-firm knowledge flows. Thus, affiliates who are well embedded into their parent's supply chain are more likely to engage in knowledge flows. While knowledge capital investments of the affiliate positively influence the reverse flow of knowledge from the affiliate to the parent, a similar effect was not seen with respect to R&D investments. This indicates some degree of technology sourcing by these affiliates, which is then transmitted back to the parent. Export intensity was found to enhance the likelihood of affiliate–parent technology transfer while it diminished the likelihood of (one-way) parent–affiliate flows. This suggests that affiliates learn from their exporting operations and are able to develop technological capabilities, turning out to be knowledge providers for their parent units. Affiliates of Japanese MNEs were more likely (than European or American parents) to have traditional parent–affiliate technology transfer, and are very unlikely to engage in reverse transfer, indicating country specific effects. This chapter helps us understand the extent to which MNEs act as international conduits of KT.

In their chapter titled "Knowledge transfer and absorptive capacity in the context of a small multinational enterprise: A systematic study of the nexus of relationships", Øian, Kuivalainen and Vanninen examine the role of absorptive capacity in a rapidly internationalizing small MNE. This chapter is based on a single case study of a Norwegian software-as-a-service (SaaS) company founded in 2010. The study examines the four phases of absorptive capacity, namely acquisition, assimilation, transformation and exploitation and proposes antecedents that positively or negatively influence absorptive capacity. Widespread usage of ICT (informally) is found to help such small MNEs overcome resource constraints and facilitate knowledge acquisition. When it comes to assimilation, the experience of the firm is considered vital and the age of the firm and its path dependency act as mediators. Transformation is influenced by dominant logics, path dependencies, and internal harmonization of work structures within the company. Physical (stocks and other legal rights) and illusory (feeling of ownership due to a sense of purpose) ownership, which comes from having a growth-oriented culture, was found to contribute towards exploitation. Thus, this chapter delves into the development of absorptive capacity in a small MNE, which is relatively unexplored in the extant literature.

Ben Hamida examines reverse knowledge transfer in multinational companies by studying Swiss manufacturing industry. The author specifically investigates the factors that influence the extent to which knowledge transfer from foreign units to parent companies (RKT) enhances the productivity performance of the MNE at home. Based on interviews and regression analyses using detailed firm data from Swiss manufacturing, the study finds that good integration of foreign units in the whole company through close management cooperation with their parent companies contributes to enhancing the reverse knowledge transfer process, and the effect of reverse knowledge transfer is higher when MNEs' units at home have high technological capacities.

In the chapter titled "Intellectual property institutions and innovation of emerging multinational companies", Wu examines the effect of IP institutions (in host country) on the innovation in Chinese MNEs. The study examines the panel data on Chinese MNEs specifically with respect to their internationalization activities and product innovation from 2011 to 2013. It was seen that IP institutions (host country) have an inverted U-shaped relationship with Chinese

MNEs' innovation. Further, it was also found that absorptive capacity positively moderates this relationship.

Part II – Societal and human resource perspective of knowledge transfer

Saari, Kontkanen, Arslan and Hurmelinna-Laukkanen examine the role of social capital as a KT tool in their chapter titled "Social media as a knowledge transfer tool for intellectual capital accumulation during the international growth of small firms". The authors specifically use four case studies of Finnish software firms (small firms) and examine the intellectual capital accumulation (human capital, relational capital and structural capital) of these firms during their international growth. Human capital accumulation focuses on aspects such as recruitment, training and support sources, and gathering information about new technologies and international markets using various social media platforms such as LinkedIn, Facebook, Twitter, etc. These platforms help in honing employee skills, recruiting people with the required background and experience and more importantly gather the required information about potential international markets, which in turn may help them penetrate these markets. In terms of relational capital, social media enables these firms to achieve better customer inter-action and engagement, and maintain an active communication channel (also low-cost) with their partners. This in turn helps them build extensive international networks quickly, generate better international leads, sales growth and brand awareness. Social media also facilitates the maintenance and regular updating of the firm's processes, databases, and culture (which makes the structural capital). Social media thus enables firms to maintain better customer, country and market related databases; improve their marketing and sales processes; and promote a culture of learning and knowledge sharing. Thus, this chapter highlights the role of social media as an efficient KT tool (offering a low-cost option for quick, flexible KT) that facilitates international growth of SMEs.

In their chapter titled "Knowledge exchange within multi-stakeholder initiatives: Tackling the Sustainable Development Goals", Veeger and Westermann-Behaylo discuss the knowledge exchange between partners in Multi-Stakeholder Initiatives (MSIs), where MNEs, nongovernmental organizations (NGOs), and governments share information, resources, activities, and capabilities to address challenges. The cross-case analysis of four MSIs in Cape Town, South Africa, reveals that non-profit sector partners are the most actively engaged in knowledge exchange within the MSI, and the private sector is also engaged to some extent when compared with the public sector (government). The public sector is found to be least engaged, mainly because of lack of political will to engage, frequent staff reassignments, and less educated personnel. Knowledge exchanges based on joint learning, consultation, dialogue, mutuality, and trust (measures for collective stakeholder orientation) are found to be effective in MSIs. Further, the differences in absorptive capacity amongst the partners (knowledge gaps) adversely affect knowledge exchange and this can be reduced by adopting the above discussed measures of collective stakeholder orientation. Thus, an effective exchange of tacit and explicit knowledge between the MSI partners contributes to value creation and goal achievement of MSI and the private sector is increasingly embracing such collaborations to create a shared value.

In the following chapter, Tabata investigates regional talent mobility and knowledge diffusion issues in East Asia. This chapter is entitled, "Global talent mobility and knowledge diffusion: The role of staffing agencies in the growth of East Asian high-tech multinational corporations". The chapter demonstrates that labor market intermediaries such as staffing agencies become the trigger of talent mobility across borders, thus playing an important role in cross-national KT and regional development. The author gathered multiple-source secondary data and conducted in-depth interviews with staffing agencies of high-tech firms in Taiwan and Japan to analyze the various impacts of staffing agencies on the cross-national KT and learning, labor market institutions, and human resource development in the East Asian high-tech industry. In particular, the chapter explains that the rise and development of global staffing agencies in the East Asian region are related to the long-term recession, the restructuring of the Japanese labor market, the wage stagnation of the Taiwanese labor market and the booming economy of China. In this chapter, the author conclusively argues that East Asian capitalism has shifted from a "production-driven commodity chain", which emphasizes the internal labor market, to a "consumer-driven commodity chain", which focuses on cost reduction through the flexible arrangement of global value chain activities. From the global human resource mobility perspective, this chapter shows that staffing agencies accelerate the speed and flexibility of labor market adjustment, thereby making a crucial impact on knowledge diffusion across countries.

Part III – Subsidiary knowledge creation and development
Ho and Oh's chapter is entitled, "Technological overlap and cultural distance in MNCs' location choice of technological clusters in China". In the consideration of the fast rise of emerging economies and recently significant inward foreign direct investment to China (UNCTAD, 2021), the research setting of China (i.e., the largest foreign direct investment recipient in 2020) and multinational corporation (MNE) subsidiaries' R&D location choice in China are topical and relevant to MNEs' international knowledge management. In their chapter, the authors used 26,981 observations of 110 Fortune Global 500 corporations from 13 countries, which includes 352 R&D subsidiaries in 28 cities with New and High-Technology Industrial Development Zones in China between 1996 and 2007. The authors tested research hypotheses using a multi-level, mixed-effects, complementary log-log regression model. Their empirical results show that technological knowledge overlap between a focal MNE and the MNEs in a potential technological cluster has an inverted-U shape relationship with the likelihood that the focal MNE chooses to locate in the cluster, while cultural distance between the MNE's home and host countries positively moderates this relationship. Such interesting findings indicate that a focal MNE is unlikely to co-locate with other foreign MNEs that have distinct knowledge new to the focal MNE as the focal MNE will not be able to learn such knowledge from them. Nevertheless, when the knowledge of the two parties starts to become similar, the focal MNE becomes capable of relating, understanding, and valuing external knowledge. Thus, this chapter broadens existing knowledge on MNEs' KT and their geographical strategies in emerging economies.

In the next chapter, Lee, Park and Lew examine the relationship between MNE headquarters' control and their subsidiaries' capabilities. This chapter is entitled, "Building ambidextrous capabilities in foreign subsidiaries: Evidence from Korean multinationals", and investigates MNE subsidiaries' exploitative and explorative (thus ambidextrous) capabilities for knowledge development in the Korean MNE intrafirm context. In international business and management literature, it has been known that ambidextrous organizations aggressively and simultaneously pursue both exploitation and exploration of their existing and new knowledge and resources for international business activities, which leads to superior organizational performance and stability (Khan et al., 2020). However, little research has examined to what extent different use of control mechanisms exercised by MNE headquarters affects foreign subsidiaries' ambidextrous capabilities. As such, Lee and his colleagues develop a conceptual model based on organizational learning and ambidexterity literature and collected survey data from 398 overseas subsidiaries of 205 Korean MNEs, operating in 49 different countries. Empirical findings show that the use of outcome and social controls of MNE headquarters and double-loop organizational learning facilitate foreign subsidiaries' explorative capability. Thus, the chapter provides useful insights into subsidiary federalism and mandate as well as organizational learning and knowledge creation within an MNE.

In his chapter, Lee studies subsidiary-created knowledge utilization (SKU), conceptually drawing on organizational knowledge theory and the Socialization-Externalizatio n-Combination-Internalization (SECI) model (Nonaka, 1991; Nonaka & Takeuchi, 1995). This chapter is entitled, "Utilization of subsidiary knowledge in multinational enterprises: Revisiting the SECI model". The SECI model has been widely used to explain how new knowledge is created and shared throughout the firm in general. Nevertheless, little research on knowledge management in MNEs examines the effective SKU process within and across the MNE boundary. In this chapter, the author proposes that the utilization of subsidiary knowledge can be framed as a process of new knowledge amplification across MNE boundaries between headquarters and subsidiaries. In doing so, the chapter offers a conceptual foundation of knowledge management between headquarters and subsidiaries by examining the holistic process of SKU and the associated knowledge transformation, thus filling gaps in the subsidiary knowledge management literature.

In their chapter titled "Absorptive capacity, value creation and new service development in multinational enterprises: The role of knowledge flows between customers, subsidiaries and headquarters", Leposky, Arslan, Gölgeci and Callaghan examine absorptive capacity as manifested in the customer–subsidiary–headquarters interface, in the context of MNEs. The authors have developed a conceptual framework with some testable propositions that focus on the subsidiary's external relationship (with customers) and internal relationships (with the headquarters). The role of absorptive capacity in service development and value creation has been highlighted, and, more specifically, the initial contribution from the customers towards this process. The chapter further delves into the different phases of absorptive capacity (acquisition, assimilation, transformation and exploitation). Knowledge acquisition is largely dependent on the relational capabilities of the firm and the specificities of the external environment. Subsidiaries' power, motivation and position in the internal network and the prevalent social integration mechanisms in the organization influence the knowledge assimilation phase. Knowledge transformation is influenced by the social integration mechanisms and alignment of support functions with the business model while the knowledge exploitation is affected by the customer's perception of value and relationship-specific capabilities. Thus, the chapter throws light on the role of absorptive capacity when it comes to a firm's success in engaging in new service development efforts across borders.

As a collection, the chapters included in this volume provide important insights related to knowledge transfer and international business. Cross-border knowledge transfer is a complex phenomenon that requires the willingness, ability and absorptive capacity of the sender of knowledge as well as the recipient of knowledge. Effective knowledge transfer also requires common language between the sending unit and the receiving unit. Effective knowledge transfer in an international context can only take place when firms utilize diverse knowledge transfer modes and mechanisms. The timing of the knowledge transfer mechanisms is vitally important in order to effectively transfer knowledge across borders. We hope that this volume provides potential readers with important insights on this important topic, given the important role of firms in international business activities and the need for the transfer and integration of knowledge across firms' boundaries. The contributions included in this volume aim to address some of the key themes in the literature on knowledge transfer and international business. In addition, each chapter provides important and interesting directions for future research that scholars interested in this topic could pursue in greater depth.

References

Ambos, T. C. & Ambos, B. (2009). The impact of distance on knowledge transfer effectiveness in multinational corporations. *Journal of International Management*, 15, 1–14.

Ambos, T. C., Ambos, B. & Schlegelmilch, B. B. (2006). Learning from foreign subsidiaries: An empirical investigation of headquarters' benefits from reverse knowledge transfers. *International Business Review*, 15, 294–312.

Argote, L. & Ingram, P. (2000). Knowledge transfer: A basis for competitive advantage in firms. *Organizational Behavior and Human Decision Processes*, 82(1), 150–169.

Bartlett, C. A. & Ghoshal, S. (1986). Tap your subsidiaries for global reach. *Harvard Business Review*, 4(6), 87–94.

Becker-Ritterspach, F., Saka-Helmhout, H., & Hotho, J. J. (2010). Learning in multinational enterprises as the socially embedded translation of practices. *Critical Perspectives on International Business*, 6(1), 8–37.

Birkinshaw, J. & Morrison, A. (1995). Configurations of strategy and structure in subsidiaries of multinational corporations. *Journal of International Business Studies*, 26, 729–754.

Björkman, I., Barner-Rasmussen, W. & Li, L. (2004). Managing knowledge transfer in MNCs: The impact of headquarters control mechanisms. *Journal of International Business Studies*, 35(5), 443–455.

Björkman, I., Fey, C. F., & Park, H. J. (2007). Institutional theory and MNC subsidiary HRM practices: Evidence from a three-country study. *Journal of International Business Studies*, 38(3), 430–446.

Blau, P. M. (1964). *Exchange and power in social life*. New York: Wiley.

Bresman, H., Birkinshaw, J., & Nobel, R. (1999). Knowledge transfer in international acquisitions. *Journal of International Business Studies*, 30, 3, 439–462.

Bresman, H., Birkinshaw, J., & Nobel, R. (2010). Knowledge transfer in international acquisitions. *Journal of International Business Studies*, 41, 5–20.

Brown, J. S. & Duguid, P. (1998). Organizing knowledge. *California Management Review*, 40(1), 90–111.

Ciabuschi, F., Dellestrand, H., & Kappen, P. (2011). Exploring the effects of vertical and lateral mechanisms in international knowledge transfer projects. *Management International Review*, 51(2), 129–155.

Cohen, W. & Levinthal, D. (1990). Absorptive capacity: A new perspective on learning and innovation. *Administrative Science Quarterly*, 35, 128–152.

Davenport, T. & Prusak L. (1998). *Working knowledge: How organizations manage what they know*. Cambridge, MA: Harvard Business School.

Denrell, J., Arvidsson, N., & Zander, U. (2004). Managing knowledge in the dark: An empirical study of the reliability of capability evaluations. *Management Science*, 50(11), 1491–1503.

Dhanaraj, C., Lyles, M. A., Steensma, H. K., & Tihanyi, L. (2004). Managing tacit and explicit knowledge transfer in IJVs: The role of relational embeddedness and the impact on performance. *Journal of International Business Studies*, 35, 428–442.

Eisenhardt, K. (1989). Agency theory: An assessment and review. *Academy of Management Review*, 14(1), 57–74.

Evangelista, F. & Hau, L. N. (2009). Organizational context and knowledge acquisition in IJVs: An empirical study. *Journal of World Business*, 44, 63–73.

Fey, C. F. & Furu, P. (2008). Top management incentive compensation and knowledge sharing in multinational corporations. *Strategic Management Journal*, 29(12), 1301–1323.

Foss, N. J. & Pederson, T. (2004). Organizing knowledge processes in the multinational corporation: An introduction. *Journal of International Business Studies*, 35(5), 340–349.

Grant, R. M. (1996). Toward a knowledge-based theory of the firm. *Strategic Management Journal*, 17, 109–122.

Grant, R. & Phene, A. (2021). The knowledge based view and global strategy: Past impact and future potential. *Global Strategy Journal*, in press.

Gupta, A. K. & Govindarajan, V. (1991). Knowledge flows and the structure of control within multinational corporations. *Academy of Management Review*, (16), 768–792.

Gupta, A. K. & Govindarajan, V. (2000). Knowledge flows within multinational corporations. *Strategic Management Journal*, 21, 473–496.

Hakanson, L. & Nobel, R. (2000). Technology characteristics and reverse technology transfer. *Management International Review*, 40(1), 29–48.

Harzing, A.-W. & Noorderhaven, N. (2006a). Geographical distance and the role and management of subsidiaries: The case of subsidiaries down-under. *Asia Pacific Journal of Management*, 23(2), 167–185.

Harzing, A.-W. & Noorderhaven, N. (2006b). Knowledge flows in MNCs: An empirical test and extension of Gupta and Govindarajan's typology of subsidiary roles. *International Business Review*, 15, 195–214.

Jensen, R. & Szulanski, G. (2004). Stickiness and the adaptation of organizational practices in cross-border knowledge transfers. *Journal of International Business Studies*, 35(6), 508–523.

Khan, Z., Lew, Y. K., & Sinkovics, R. R. (2015). International joint ventures as boundary spanners: Technological knowledge transfer in an emerging economy. *Global Strategy Journal*, 5(1), 48–68.

Khan, Z., Shenkar, O., & Lew, Y. K. (2015). Knowledge transfer from international joint ventures to local suppliers in a developing economy. *Journal of International Business Studies*, 46(6), 656–675.

Khan, Z., Amankwah-Amoah, J., Lew, Y. K., Puthusserry, P., & Czinkota, M. (2020). Strategic ambidexterity and its performance implications for emerging economies multinationals. *International Business Review*, 101762.

Kogut, B. & Zander, U. (1992). Knowledge of the firm, combinative capabilities, and the replication of technology. *Organization Science*, 3, 383–397.

Kogut, B. & Zander, U. (1993). Knowledge of the firm and the evolutionary theory of the Multinational Corporation. *Journal of International Business Studies*, 24(4), 625–645.

Kostova, T., Marano, V., & Tallman, S. (2016). Headquarters–subsidiary relationships in MNCs: Fifty years of evolving research. *Journal of World Business*, 51(1), 176–184.

Lane, P. J., Salk, J. E., & Lyles, M. A. (2001). Absorptive capacity, learning, and performance in international joint ventures. *Strategic Management Journal*, 22, 1139–1161.

Lave, J. & Wenger, E. (1993). *Situated learning: Legitimate peripheral participation*. New York: Cambridge University Press.

Li, C.-Y. & Hsieh, C.-T. (2009). The impact of knowledge stickiness on knowledge transfer implementation, internalization, and satisfaction for multinational corporations. *International Journal of Information Management*, 29(6), 425–435.

Li, L. (2005). The effects of trust and shared vision on inward knowledge transfer in subsidiaries' intra- and inter-organizational relationships. *International Business Review*, 14(1), 77–95.

Li, L., Barner-Rasmussen, W., & Björkman, I. (2007). What difference does the location make?: A social capital perspective on transfer of knowledge from multinational corporation subsidiaries located in China and Finland. *Asia Pacific Business Review*, 13(2), 233–249.

Liu, X., Gao, L., Lu, J., & Wei, Y. (2015). The role of highly skilled migrants in the process of inter-firm knowledge transfer across borders. *Journal of World Business*, 50(1), 56–68.

Lyles, M. A. & Salk, J. E. (1996). Knowledge acquisition from foreign parents in international joint ventures: An empirical examination in the Hungarian context. *Journal of International Business Studies*, 27(5), 877–903.

Mäkelä, K. & Brewster, C. (2009). Interunit interaction contexts, interpersonal social capital, and the differing levels of knowledge sharing. *Human Resource Management*, 48(4), 591–613.

Michailova, S. & Mustaffa, Z. (2012). Subsidiary knowledge flows in multinational corporations: Research accomplishments, gaps, and opportunities. *Journal of World Business*, 47(3), 383–396.

Minbaeva, D. B. (2008). HRM practices affecting extrinsic and intrinsic motivation of knowledge receivers and their effect on intra-MNC knowledge transfer. *International Business Review*, 17, 703–713.

Minbaeva, D. B., Pedersen, T., Björkman, I., Fey, C. F., & Park, H. J. (2003). MNC knowledge transfer, subsidiary absorptive capacity, and HRM. *Journal of International Business Studies*, 34(6), 586–599.

Mudambi, R., Piscitello, L., & Rabbiosi, L. (2014). Reverse knowledge transfer in MNEs: Subsidiary innovativeness and entry modes. *Long Range Planning*, 47, 49–63.

Muthusamy, S. K. & White, M. A. (2005). Learning and knowledge transfer in strategic alliances: A social exchange view. *Organization Studies*, 26(3), 415–441.

Nahapiet, J. & Ghoshal, S. (1998). Social capital, intellectual capital, and the organizational advantage. *Academy of Management Review*, 23(2), 242–266.

Nair, S. R., Demirbag, M., & Mellahi, K. (2016). Reverse knowledge transfer in emerging market multinationals: The Indian context. *International Business Review*, 25(1), 152–164.

Nair, S. R., Demirbag, M., Mellahi, K., & Pillai, K. G. (2018). Do parent units benefit from reverse knowledge transfer? *British Journal of Management*, 29(3), 428–444.

Nonaka, I. (1991). The knowledge-creating company. *Harvard Business Review*, November-December, 96–104.

Nonaka, I. (1994). A dynamic theory of organizational knowledge creation. *Organization Science*, 5(1), 14–37.

Nonaka, I. & Takeuchi, H. (1995). *The knowledge-creating company: How Japanese companies create the dynamics of innovation*. Oxford: Oxford University Press.

Noorderhaven, N. G. & Harzing, A. W. K. (2009). Factors influencing knowledge flows within MNCs. *Journal of International Business Studies*, 40, 509–526.

Peltokorpi, V. (2017). Absorptive capacity in foreign subsidiaries: The effects of language-sensitive recruitment, language training, and interunit knowledge transfer. *International Business Review*, 26(1), 119–129.

Peltokorpi, V. & Yamao, S. (2017). Corporate language proficiency in reverse knowledge transfer: A moderated mediation model of shared vision and communication frequency. *Journal of World Business*, 52(3), 404–416.

Pérez-Nordtvedt, L., Kedia, B. L., Datta, D. K., & Rasheed, A. A. (2008). Effectiveness and efficiency of cross-border knowledge transfer: An empirical examination. *Journal of Management Studies*, 45(4), 714–744.

Polyani, M. (1966). *The tacit dimension*. London: Routledge.

Rabbiosi, L. (2011). Subsidiary roles and reverse knowledge transfer: An investigation of the effects of coordination mechanisms. *Journal of International Management*, 17, 97–113.

Rabbiosi, L. & Santangelo, G. D. (2013). Parent company benefits from reverse knowledge transfer: The role of the liability of newness in MNEs. *Journal of World Business*, 48, 60–170.

Roth, K. & Morrison, A. J. (1992). Implementing global strategy: Characteristics of global subsidiary mandates. *Journal of International Business Studies*, 23(4), 715–735.

Rui, H., Zhang, M., & Shipman, A. (2016). Relevant knowledge and recipient ownership: Chinese MNCs' knowledge transfer in Africa. *Journal of World Business*, 51(5), 713–728.

Saka-Helmhout, A. (2010). Organizational learning as a situated routine-based activity in international settings. *Journal of World Business*, 45(1), 41–48.

Sarala, R. M., Junni, P., Cooper, C. L., & Tarba, S. (2016). A sociocultural perspective on knowledge transfer in mergers and acquisitions. *Journal of Management*, 42(5), 1230–1249.

Schulz. M. (2001). The uncertain relevance of newness: Organizational learning and knowledge flows. *Academy of Management Journal*, 44(4), 661–681.

Schulz, M. (2003). Pathways of relevance: Exploring inflows of knowledge into subunits of multinational corporations. *Organization Science*, 14(4), 440–459.

Shannon, C. E. & Weaver, W. (1949). *The mathematical theory of communication*. Urbana: University of Illinois Press.

Simonin, B. L. (1999a). Ambiguity and the process of knowledge transfer in strategic alliances. *Strategic Management Journal*, 20(7), 595–623.

Simonin, B. L. (1999b). Transfer of marketing know-how in international strategic alliances: An empirical investigation of the role and antecedents of knowledge ambiguity. *Journal of International Business Studies*, 30(3), 463–490.

Simonin, B. L. (2004). An empirical investigation of the process of knowledge transfer in international strategic alliances. *Journal of International Business Studies*, 35, 407–427.

Simonin, B. L. & Özsomer, A. S. (2009). Knowledge processes and learning outcomes in MNCs: An empirical investigation of the role of HRM practices in foreign subsidiaries. *Human Resource Management*, 48(4), 505–530.

Szulanski, G. (1996). Exploring internal stickiness: Impediments to the transfer of best practice within the firm. *Strategic Management Journal*, 17(special issue), 27–43.

Szulanski, G., Cappetta, R., & Jensen, R. J. (2004). When and how trustworthiness matters: Knowledge transfer and the moderating effect of causal ambiguity. *Organization Science*, 15(5), 600–613.

UNCTAD. (2021). Global Investment Trend Monitor, 38(January), 1–11.

Van Wijk, R., Jansen, J. J. P., & Lyles, M. A. (2008). Inter- and intra- organizational knowledge transfer: A meta-analytic review and assessment of its antecedents and consequences. *Journal of Management Studies*, 45(4), 830–853.

Welch, D. E., & Welch, L. S. (2018). Developing multilingual capacity: A challenge for the multinational enterprise. *Journal of Management*, 44(3), 854–869.

Yamao, S., de Cieri, H., & Hutchings, K. (2009). Transferring subsidiary knowledge to global headquarters: Subsidiary senior executives' perceptions of the role of HR configurations in the development of knowledge stocks. *Human Resource Management*, 48(4), 531–554.

Yang, Q., Mudambi, R. & Meyer, K. E. (2008). Conventional and reverse knowledge flows in multinational corporations. *Journal of Management*, 34(5), 882–902.

Zeng, R., Grøgaard, B., & Steel, P. (2018). Complements or substitutes? A meta-analysis of the role of integration mechanisms for knowledge transfer in the MNE network. *Journal of World Business*, 53(4), 415–432.

PART I

STRATEGIC PERSPECTIVE OF KNOWLEDGE TRANSFER

1. Intra-firm trade, embeddedness and international knowledge transfer in the multinational enterprise

Nigel Driffield, James H. Love and Stefano Menghinello

INTRODUCTION

One of the key issues in the literature on innovation and international business is the extent to which the multinational enterprise (MNE) is an effective vehicle for international technology and knowledge transfer. This process is central to the dominant paradigm of the multinational enterprise (Dunning 1979; Buckley and Casson 1976). The paradigm essentially relies on the observation that the single most important determinant of a firm's decision to engage in foreign direct investment (FDI) is its ability to exploit its 'ownership advantages' or firm-specific assets in foreign environments where other options, such as licensing, are less attractive. The ability to transfer knowledge internally across international boundaries is therefore a central element of MNE theory.

Despite some important developments in this literature, relatively little in the empirical literature concerning international technology transfer has changed since Kotabe et al. (2007) noted that "… the study of international knowledge transfer processes within multinational firms is at a relatively early stage" (Kotabe et al. 2007: 259). Instead, much of the literature on international technology transfer has adopted a rather indirect approach to testing the hypothesis that knowledge is transferred within the MNE, and with very imperfect methods. Typically, the testing of this approach within a quantitative setting has sought to determine the relationship between foreign presence in a given location and productivity of host country firms. Where a positive association is found, this is taken as evidence not only of externalities or 'spillovers' from overseas affiliates to domestic firms, but implicitly of the transfer of knowledge from the MNE to its overseas affiliates (for reviews of this literature see Smeets 2008, and Meyer and Sinani 2009).

This emphasis on an indirect approach to assessing inter-firm knowledge transfer is understandable given the difficulties of gathering data on the internal operations of MNEs, but has led to some weaknesses in the literature. First, the emphasis on the spillovers literature tends to be on technology flows, and firm-specific assets have typically become characterised as technological capacity (see for example Cantwell 2009). However, this dismisses a wide range of other firm-specific assets, including managerial knowledge or competence. These are often ignored in the international technology transfer literature, despite these alternative measures of ownership advantage (and potential sources of international knowledge transfer) being discussed in detail in the conceptual analysis (e.g. Caves 1986). Second, the spillovers literature naturally tends to conflate two distinct processes, (international) knowledge transfer between parent and affiliate, and the extent to which this subsequently generates spillovers. At the same time, much of this literature presumes that the source of the 'spillover' is knowledge that is generated at the level of the parent, and fails to allow fully for the capacity of subsidiaries to self-generate knowledge even in the absence of intra-firm technology flows (Bell and Marin 2004; Driffield et al. 2010, 2016).

To some extent these problems have been alleviated by research on the 'embeddedness' of multinational affiliates. Conceptual analysis suggests that the nature of the knowledge flows between parent and affiliate depends on the strategic position of the subsidiary and its relative performance (Andersson et al. 2001, 2005, 2007). This literature highlights the importance of both the technological capacity and the success of the subsidiary in explaining subsidiary–parent technology transfer. Typically, however, the existing literature proxies embeddedness using only indirect measures such as the financial performance of the subsidiary We extend this by linking this conceptual literature to explicit measures of the importance of the subsidiary within the parent's supply chain. Specifically, we focus on intra-firm trade, and its relationship to knowledge and technology transfer.

Despite general agreement that it accounts for as much as 40% of total trade (see Bernard et al. 2010) intra-firm trade is rather under-researched. While the links between international trade and international knowledge flows have been examined (e.g. van Pottelsberghe de la Potterie and Lichtenberg 2001), there is very little consideration of the links between intra-firm trade and intra-firm knowledge transfer which is also international in scope. To the extent that this issue has been considered in the literature, it is invariably as a by-product of analyses of the roles of MNE subsidiaries rather than as a central issue in its own right (Kobrin 1991; Gupta and Govindarajan 1991, 1994; Harzing and Noorderhaven 2006). By contrast, we argue that intra-firm trade is strongly linked to intra-firm knowledge flows, and is an important indicator of how central to the activities of the MNE is a given subsidiary.

In this chapter we therefore put the emphasis back on the direct measurement of intra-firm knowledge flows across national boundaries. In doing so, we explicitly build on the analysis of Driffield et al. (2010). This earlier work focused on an empirical approach to the modelling of international technology transfer and its subsequent diffusion to the host economy that represents an advance on the rather indirect approaches that have been employed hitherto. We extend the existing literature in a number of ways. First, we provide direct evidence of knowledge transfer between MNE parents and affiliates, using a large-scale official survey designed for this purpose. Second, we are able to distinguish between technology and other forms of (managerial) knowledge flows, and so can shed further light on the 'black box' of intra-group and international knowledge transfer. Third, we examine how the characteristics of the MNE and its affiliates are linked to knowledge flows of different types, paying particular attention to the roles of R&D, knowledge capital, exporting and country of ownership in determining the nature and direction of knowledge flows. Finally, and centrally, we examine the nature of the relationship between intra-firm trade and intra-firm knowledge flows. As indicated above, this is another dimension of embeddedness of the affiliate, and we develop hypotheses relating intra-firm trade to intra-firm knowledge and technology transfer. To the best of our knowledge, this is the first analysis that addresses directly the links between international knowledge transfer and intra-firm trade, and formally tests the nature of the relationship between them.

The remainder of the chapter is structured as follows. The next section outlines the general conceptual model of the MNE as a vehicle for international knowledge transfer, and considers methodological issues relating to the measurement of knowledge flows. The third section develops specific hypotheses from the conceptual and empirical literature relating to intra-firm trade, embeddedness and knowledge transfer. The fourth section describes the dataset. The fifth section is concerned with the empirical testing of the hypotheses, and the sixth section concludes.

THE MNE AS A VEHICLE FOR INTERNATIONAL KNOWLEDGE TRANSFER

At a conceptual level there are (at least) two different perspectives that critically depend on the assumption of international intra-firm knowledge. First, intra-firm knowledge transfer is important per se within the framework of knowledge economics to corroborate the role of the hierarchy in general, and MNEs in particular, as a superior vehicle of knowledge transfer and diffusion with respect to arm's length market forces under uncertainty and other market failure conditions. Second, intra-firm knowledge transfer is important with the classical OLI approach to the theory of the MNE as indirect evidence of the superior competitive advantage of MNEs over domestic firms. Reverse knowledge flows (i.e. from affiliate to parent) are not in conflict with an enlarging view of the classical paradigm where MNEs do not necessarily hold a superior technological advantage, but where they do have a superior capability to coordinate knowledge flows internationally.

In extending our earlier work (Driffield et al. 2010), we offer a simple schematic of the traditional view of international knowledge transfer, as shown in Figure 1.1. At its simplest, the process first requires knowledge transfer from the MNE to its foreign affiliate (A1) followed by the potential for the generation of externalities (i.e. spillovers) from the foreign affiliates to domestic firms (A2). In practice, there is no guarantee that either condition A1 or A2 will be fulfilled. Not all affiliates automatically have access to the leading technology of their parent company, and, notwithstanding the possibility of inadvertent leakage, multinational enterprises frequently go to considerable lengths to internalise their knowledge and prevent or control its transfer to third parties. Therefore, even if intra-firm knowledge transfer occurs, there is no guarantee that the domestic economy in which the affiliate is located will benefit as a result. For example, in a study of MNE subsidiaries in Belgium, Veugelers and Cassiman (2004) find that, after controlling for their superior access to international technology, foreign subsidiaries are no more likely than local firms to transfer technology to the domestic economy. Going even further, Singh (2007) uses patent citation data to trace knowledge flows between MNEs and host country organisations in 30 countries, and concludes that there is a substantially higher likelihood of knowledge flows running from domestic entities to multinational subsidiaries than the reverse.

In recent years, a number of studies have questioned the conventional view of knowledge spillovers from parent MNEs to domestic host economies, channelled through foreign affiliates. Much of this has come from the recognition that the nature of the relationship between parent and affiliate, and between affiliate and the domestic economy, can be very flexible and mutually dependent. This frequently includes a substantial role for localised innovative activity at the affiliate level, and a substantial literature has developed on the internationalisation of R&D and its role in technology sourcing by MNEs.

For example, evidence suggests that corporations are increasingly moving their R&D facilities abroad, and that this is being done as part of a strategic move away from merely adapting 'core' technology to a foreign market towards a much more central role in product innovation and development. Companies that previously exerted rather tight control over their

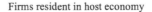

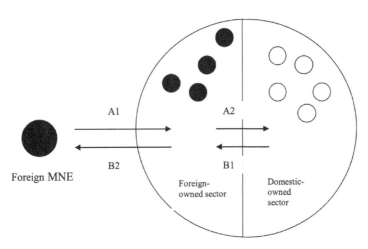

Figure 1.1   *Conceptual scheme of knowledge flows*

R&D sites are now granting more autonomy and empowerment to R&D laboratories situated abroad (Cantwell and Janne 1999). This literature suggests that in the 1970s and early 1980s organisations saw establishing R&D outlets abroad as little more than adapting products to local markets as hypothesised by the product life cycle hypothesis. However, during the 1990s, organisations began to take a more decentralised approach to R&D (Pearce 1999; Niosi 1999). In addition, the literature suggests that there is a growing willingness to locate such facilities close to leading centres of research and innovation, specifically with a view to absorbing learning spillovers from geographical proximity to such sites (Serapio and Dalton 1999; Ito and Wakasugi 2007). The possibility of this form of technology sourcing FDI depends on the existence of 'reverse spillovers' in which an externality effect runs from the domestic sector to MNE affiliates, support for which comes from Driffield and Love (2003). In terms of Figure 1.1, the reverse spillover effect is flow B1. To complete the process, knowledge transfer then occurs between the foreign affiliate and the parent company (B2).[1]

However, even the consideration of technology sourcing may underestimate the complexity of knowledge flows within MNEs and their associated spillover effects. Driffield et al. (2016), for example, highlight the contributions of Bell and Marin (2004), Marin and Bell (2006, 2010) and Mudambi and Navarra (2004). The former suggests that the role of affiliates in both knowledge creation and dissemination has been under-stated, while the latter highlight the nature of the potential agency problem this creates for the parent. As such, Driffield et al. (2016) develop a framework that considers knowledge transfer to be neither automatic nor a sufficient condition for generating increased performance at the level of the firm. We argue, therefore, that one needs to better understand the precise nature and drivers of knowledge transfer between parents and affiliates, and develop better models for capturing this. In turn, as Bell and Marin (2004) point out, this requires both better data and models more closely linked to theories of knowledge transfer and international business. They subsequently argue that even if there is statistical evidence of productivity increases among domestic firms where FDI is high, these need not stem from technology at the MNE's centre; they may result from technology developed directly by the affiliates, or from bi-directional spillovers between affiliates and the parent company. Indeed, the wider literature suggests that apparent host country productivity growth linked to FDI may be a result of other effects of FDI, such as competition, market structure or demand effects (Driffield et al. 2002). Bell and Marin (2004) develop an alternative to the standard 'centrally driven supply-side model', in which technology flows from MNE centre via subsidiaries to local firms via competition effects or through real or pecuniary spillovers. This alternative model allows for locally based and locally driven sources of spillovers in which affiliates play a crucial role in knowledge generation and development, so that knowledge either comes directly from the affiliates' innovation activity via spillovers to domestic firms, or they modify and enhance the knowledge coming from the centre in some way which improves the chances of knowledge-based productivity spillovers. Taken together therefore, we argue, and demonstrate here, that we need more direct indicators of knowledge transfer, as well as a better understanding of relationships between affiliates and parents (or between affiliates) at the level of the multinational.

This conceptual and empirical work suggests that the nature of the knowledge flows between parents and affiliates is crucial in determining both the affiliates' capacity for generating its own innovative activity, and the affiliates' ability to generate knowledge flows to local firms (see also Oh and Anchor 2017). In the Bell and Marin model, the externality effect of FDI (A2) is not necessarily dependent on knowledge flows from the parent (A1), and there is an enhanced role for two-way knowledge flows between the parent and affiliate (i.e. A1–B2). Importantly, this suggests that the existence or otherwise of intra-firm knowledge flows between an MNE and its affiliates cannot simply be inferred from the existence of spillover effects.

This in turn indicates the importance of obtaining more direct evidence on the nature and scale of the knowledge flows between affiliates and their parent companies. Semi-direct data on knowledge flows such as patent citations have helped our understanding of the process of technology transfer (Almeida 1996; Singh 2007; Phene and Almeida 2008). While this represents a significant step forward in this area, such analysis is still reliant on inferring intra-firm international technology transfer from links between knowledge stocks and patent citations, and ultimately employs a data source that is not gathered explicitly for the purpose to which it is being put. Veugelers and Cassiman (2004) seek to move towards a more direct approach towards prising open the 'black box' of knowledge transfer rather than relying wholly on inferring such flows from their indirect impact on local productivity. The empirical study below further helps to fill this gap by analysing knowledge flows involving foreign affiliates operating in Italy. Like Veugelers and Cassiman, this relies on direct survey evidence on knowledge flows, a crucial step in breaking the direct inferential link between spillover effects and the existence of the knowledge flows that are assumed to underlie them

KNOWLEDGE TRANSFER AND THE MNE SUBSIDIARY: THEORY AND HYPOTHESES

Foreign affiliates differ in the extent to which they play certain roles within the MNE, most importantly varying by strategic importance within the parent firm. Conceptual and empirical analysis suggests that the nature of the knowledge flows between parent and affiliate depends on the strategic position of the subsidiary and its relative performance (Andersson et al. 2001,

2005, 2007). This literature stresses that the more strategically important a subsidiary is to the parent, the more likely it is to be both a source and a recipient of technology and of other forms of knowledge. The existence of intra-firm knowledge flows therefore signals both the strategic importance and embeddedness of a foreign affiliate in the MNE's network.

However, empirical work in the area has largely lagged behind the conceptual analysis. In a review paper, Michailova and Mustaffa (2012) discuss many of the limitations in this literature, highlighting the fact that much of it focuses on the outcomes of knowledge flows, and typically, often due to data limitations, only in one direction, i.e. either from subsidiary to parent or from parent to subsidiary. This in turn suggests a disconnect between the conceptual embeddedness literature (e.g. Andersson et al. 2001) which focuses on the importance of multiple sources of embeddedness, and the empirical literature which, possibly due to a paucity of data, focuses on a limited number of sources. Michailova and Mustaffa (2012) highlight the need for research on flows both to and from subsidiaries, and the need for better theoretical underpinnings, linked to, for example, an explanation of how individual variables or constructs are linked to knowledge flows. A recent example of this is the work by McGuinness et al. (2013), who develop a more holistic multi-perspective model of knowledge transfer, but again are then limited to knowledge flows from subsidiary to parent. Equally, in common with the work by Rabiosi (2011), they are also limited by data availability in the extent to which they can control for differences in the nature of interactions between subsidiaries and their local environment.

The existing literature typically proxies embeddedness using only indirect measures such as the financial performance of the subsidiary. Ciabuschi et al. (2011) study how important internal networks, and associated embeddedness, are for innovation. They focus on the extent to which affiliate embeddedness into the parent determines how they create competitive advantage. They argue that embeddedness of subsidiaries drives competitive advantage through innovation at the level of the parent, arguing that one must view the network of subsidiaries, and their relation with the parent, through the lens of business network analysis. As they also go on to suggest, this requires further work and refinement in terms of understanding the nature of the relationships between parent and affiliate, and the form that this embeddedness takes. In a further interesting contribution, Rabiosi and Santangelo (2013) highlight the importance of organisational ecology in explaining variations in knowledge flows from subsidiary to parent. The focus of their subsequent analysis is the age of the subsidiary. We extend this by linking this conceptual literature to explicit measures of the importance of the subsidiary within the parent's supply chain. Specifically, we focus on intra-firm trade, and its relationship to knowledge and technology transfer.

In order to develop a more coherent analysis of international knowledge transfer, we build on Driffield et al. (2010) and seek to distinguish conceptually the different mechanisms by which international technology and knowledge transfer occur, and determine how such transfer may be identified empirically. Some existing typologies exist from the literature on subsidiary evolution and control. For example, Gupta and Govindarajan (1991, 1994) view the multinational enterprise as a network involving flows of knowledge, capital and goods. They argue that knowledge flows are the most important of these, and develop a typology of subsidiaries based around the nature (direction and extent) of internal knowledge flows within the MNE. Four categories of MNE subsidiary are identified: *global innovators* (high outflows of knowledge, low inflows); *integrated players* (high outflows, high inflows); *implementors* (low outflows, high inflows); *local innovators* (low outflows, low inflows).

Our concern is with the direct measurement and analysis of knowledge flows within the MNE, i.e. with flows A1 and B2 in Figure 1.1. Consistent with the analysis of Gupta and Govindarajan and the related literature (e.g. Kobrin 1991; Birkenshaw and Morrison 1995; Harzing and Noorderhaven 2006), four mutually–exclusive combinations of knowledge flows can be conceptualised.

Type 1: Two–way flows. Knowledge flows in both directions between the parent and/or other units and its foreign affiliate. This is a fully embedded affiliate within the MNE network, and is consistent with Gupta and Govindarajan's *integrated players.*

Type 2: Parent–affiliate flows. Knowledge flows only from parent to affiliate. This can be thought of as standard 'knowledge exploiting' behaviour within Dunning's OLI framework, in which an MNE exploits its superior knowledge in a host country by transferring the knowledge to its foreign affiliate. This is consistent with Gupta and Govindarajan's *implementors*, subsidiaries heavily dependent on knowledge inflows but which play relatively little role in knowledge creation.

Type 3: Affiliate–parent flows. Knowledge flows only from affiliate to parent and/or other organisational units. This may occur either because the affiliate is a research establishment set up for that purpose, or because it is a 'listening post' designed to source knowledge from the local economy. Each of these (non-mutually exclusive) cases can be thought of as a form of 'knowledge sourcing' activity. This is consistent with Gupta and Govindarajan's *global innovators*, which are "…a fountainhead of knowledge for other units" (Harzing and Noorderhaven 2006: 197).

Type 4: No knowledge flows. There are no knowledge flows between the parent and affiliate. This is consistent with Gupta and Govindarajan's *local innovators*; these are subsidiaries which are self-standing and which may be involved in knowledge creation, but from which there is no knowledge transfer to other organisational units. It may also occur where the affiliate forms no knowledge linkages with either the MNE of which it is part, or with other international actors. In a study of MNE affiliates in Argentina, Marin and Giuliani (2011) found this form of 'globally isolated' affiliate to be relatively common.

This typology of knowledge flows can be related to the extent to which the affiliate is embedded within the MNE network. Further, since the central strategic assets of MNEs are often managerial rather than technological, the conceptual analysis should allow for flows of managerial knowledge as well as technology within the MNE. The next stage is to link key characteristics of the MNE and its affiliate relationships to the four types of knowledge flows outlined above. We discuss in turn the roles of intra-firm trade, R&D and knowledge assets, and subsidiary exporting.

The Importance of Intra-firm Trade in International Technology Transfer

There are conceptual reasons for linking intra-firm trade to intra-firm knowledge transfer. Davidson and McFetridge (1985) show that the same firm-specific assets that facilitate FDI within the standard OLI paradigm of international business also facilitate intra-firm trade. They suggest that for reasons of transaction-cost minimisation and property rights protection, intra-firm trade will tend to be associated with the core technology of the firm, while more peripheral technologies, or the products that they embody, will be traded outside the firm. Cho (1990) advances this literature by examining the product-specific factors of intra-firm trade. In a study of US manufacturing multinationals, Cho shows that that knowledge intensity is indeed strongly associated with intra-firm trade at the product level, implicitly supporting the conceptual analysis of Davidson and McFetridge (1985).

This suggests that there is a link between intra-firm knowledge and trade flows, as there is between flows of trade and of knowledge internationally. Just as trade and investment are both seen as important vehicles for market-based technology and knowledge transfer between countries, intra-firm trade is an important indicator of links between a firm's subsidiaries, and of how central to the activities of the MNE is a given subsidiary. For example, Kobrin (1991) suggests that intra-firm trade is likely to be an indicator of knowledge flows within the firm, and thus of the extent to which the MNE is managed in a globally integrated manner. Feinberg and Gupta (2004) make the same inference in their analysis of the determinants of R&D location in foreign subsidiaries, arguing that since intra-firm trade is likely to involve intermediate and semi-finished products, it requires the existence of relatively well-developed communication and knowledge-exchange structures within the MNE. However, Feinberg and Gupta do not test this assumption, simply using it as the basis on which to develop the hypothesis that the likelihood of a subsidiary having an R&D function is positively related to the magnitude of intra-firm trade (which they find to be weakly supported in an analysis of R&D capacity among MNE affiliates in 11 OECD countries).[2]

In general, therefore, we expect a positive relationship between intra-firm trade and intra-firm knowledge flows: both are indicators of the strategic importance of the affiliate to the MNE, and are markers of the degree of embeddedness of the affiliate.

This analysis can be extended to the *nature* of knowledge flows and their relationship with intra-firm trade, allowing us to develop hypotheses linked to the four-way classification of affiliates outlined above. If Davidson and McFetridge (1985) are correct in their assertion that that intra-firm trade will tend to be associated with the core technology of the firm, then we would expect to see intra-firm trade closely associated with technology exploiting knowledge flows (where the parent transfers internally core technology and knowledge to the affiliate) and with two-way flows, because these indicate a high degree of embeddedness of the affiliate in the MNE network. By contrast, technology sourcing knowledge flows implies a situation where the affiliate is a research establishment or a 'listening post' designed to source knowledge from the local economy. Knowledge flows in this case are likely to comprise technology or other knowledge which is not yet core to the MNE activity, and is therefore unlikely to be associated with intra-firm trade. Consistent with this, in their empirical analysis of Gupta and Govindarajan's (1991) typology, Harzing and Noorderhaven (2006) hypothesise that integrated players and implementors (i.e. Types 1 and 2 above) will display relatively high levels of intra-firm product flows (i.e. intra-firm trade), a finding which is supported in their empirical analysis of 169 MNE subsidiaries.[3] Birkenshaw and Morrison (1995) also find a similar pattern of intra-firm imports among their equivalents of Types 1 and 2. This is consistent with the theoretical underpinnings of internalisation theory, building on Buckley and Casson (1976). This takes the firm as the unit of analysis, and seeks to explain how the firm determines its boundaries, and subsequently how it allocates activities, given the strategic and managerial resources that are available to it. Intra-firm trade is therefore an important indicator of the ability of the firm to manage and coordinate activities across countries. Further, it is an indicator of the nature of the internalisation that the firm has undertaken, with potential links to the drivers of location in the firm, and the embeddedness literature discussed above.

This leads to the following hypotheses:

H1: Intra-firm trade is positively associated with parent–affiliate and two-way knowledge flows, both technological and managerial.

H2: Intra-firm trade is unrelated to affiliate–parent technological or managerial knowledge flows.

R&D and Knowledge Assets

The availability of knowledge-based assets has long been central to the theory of the MNE. Our concern here is specifically with the knowledge assets available to MNE affiliates, and how these relate to the flows of knowledge and technology between the affiliate and its parent organisation.

R&D intensity of the affiliate is an indicator not only of subsidiary performance, but also of how the subsidiary is viewed strategically by the parent. Cohen and Levinthal (1989) stress that R&D capacity has two dimensions: it contributes directly to innovation and knowledge creation, and also forms the basis for absorptive capacity, permitting technology and knowledge to be absorbed from elsewhere. The absorptive capacity element of R&D provides the subsidiary with the capacity to absorb knowledge from the parent, and elsewhere within the MNE. However, this capacity can also be used to source and channel technology from host economies. The literature on the internationalisation of R&D suggests that there is a growing willingness to locate affiliate R&D facilities close to leading centres of research and innovation specifically with a view to absorbing learning spillovers from geographical proximity to such sites (Serapio and Dalton, 1999; Ito and Wakasugi 2007). Here, affiliate-level R&D provides the basis for technology sourcing from the host economy and subsequent transfer back to the parent. Thus, the absorptive capacity element of R&D provides the capacity for two-way flows of technology, both from parent to affiliate but also for transfers from affiliate to parent via technology sourcing from the host economy.

As described by Cohen and Levinthal (1989), R&D also has a strong direct effect on innovation and knowledge creation. In the context of the MNE, affiliate R&D and knowledge assets thus provide not only the capacity to absorb technology from the parent MNE and from the host economy, but also potentially the basis for affiliate's self-generated technology flows back to the parent even where technology flows from the parent are limited or absent (Type 3). Bell and Marin (2004) and Marin and Bell (2006) illustrate not only that such an effect may exist, but that it arises not merely from the R&D capacity of affiliates, but also from their investment in capital-embodied technology, mainly through intangible knowledge assets. However, there is less reason to expect this R&D effect to be present in managerial (rather than technological) knowledge flows, which are less likely to be based on the results of formal R&D activity. This discussion of the dual role of R&D and knowledge assets leads to the following hypotheses:

H3a: Affiliate investment in R&D and knowledge capital is positively associated with two-way technology flows and with affiliate–parent technology flows.

H3b: Affiliate investment in knowledge capital is positively associated with two-way and with affiliate–parent managerial knowledge flows.

While R&D is an important dimension of technology flows from affiliates to parents, by contrast, R&D-intensive and knowledge capital-intensive subsidiaries are relatively unlikely to be the recipients of one-way technology flows from parent companies (Type 2). An MNE is unlikely to invest heavily in the R&D capacity of an affiliate merely to channel technology from parent to affiliate. There may, of course, be some need for adaptation, but this does not normally require a high level of R&D intensity. This is especially true of relatively advanced host economies, in which there is typically relatively little need for technology adaptation before parental technology can be applied to the local market. As a result, the standard 'technology exploiting' transfers (Type 2 flows) are more likely to occur with respect to relatively less-R&D and knowledge-capital intensive subsidiaries. This leads to the next hypothesis:

H4: Affiliate investment in R&D and knowledge capital is negatively related to one-way parent–affiliate technology flows.

Exporting

As discussed in Driffield et al. (2010), the role of the affiliate with respect to exports is also important. There is strong evidence that firms entering export markets must first develop the capabilities required to compete in highly competitive international markets (Wagner 2007). In the case of MNE affiliates, even where an affiliate is initially a platform for exports built on technology derived from the parent, the affiliate may develop capabilities derived from exporting which can then serve as a possible source of knowledge flows back to the parent. This is consistent with the 'learning by exporting' hypothesis, in which exposure to the knowledge stocks of trading partners improves the firm's own knowledge and ultimately leads to performance improvement, especially in conjunction with R&D (Aw et al. 2008). Support for this hypothesis comes from Ito and Wakasugi (2007), who find that a high propensity to export is associated with a greater incidence of technology sourcing R&D among Japanese overseas subsidiaries. We therefore expect export intensity to be positively related to knowledge-sourcing behaviour: the exporting effect is hypothesised to be relevant to both technology and managerial knowledge flows.

H5: Export intensity is positively related to affiliate–parent knowledge flows, and negatively to one-way parent–affiliate knowledge flows.

Conditioning Variables

We also include a number of conditioning variables which may affect the nature of intra-MNE knowledge flows. We have no specific priors with respect to these variables, and regard them as conditioning variables. First, we allow for size of affiliate (by turnover) and its square. Second, we allow for affiliate performance in terms of profitability and productivity. As Andersson et al. (2001, 2005, 2007) point out, these aspects of performance are alternative indicators of the embeddedness of the affiliate, which may in turn be linked to knowledge flows. Failure to allow for performance variables could result in omitted variable bias and inaccurate coefficients on other key variables. Finally, we include dummy variables for the type of industry and parent country[4] of the MNE (see Tables 1.1 and 1.2).

Table 1.1   Sample distribution by industry classification

Industry code	Description of the industry	No.	Percent
HTI	High technology industries	85	11.18
MHTI	Medium–high technology industries	303	39.87
MLTI	Medium-low technology industries	167	21.97
LTI	Low technology industries	115	15.13
HTKIS	Knowledge intensive high technology services	90	11.84
Total		760	100.00

Note: Based on the OECD-EUROSTAT classification of high-technology industries and knowledge-intensive services

Table 1.2   Sample distribution by geographical area of foreign control

Country/Area code	Description of the geographical area	No.	Percent
US	United States	190	25.0
EU	European Union	439	57.8
JP	Japan	19	2.5
OC	Others	112	14.7
Total		760	100.0

DATA AND DESCRIPTIVE STATISTICS

The empirical part of this chapter exploits a unique dataset at the firm level produced by ISTAT (the Italian National Statistical Institute) for a large sample of foreign affiliates resident in Italy. This was part of an official survey of over 6500 foreign affiliates within the framework of an EU Regulation, which had a census nature for large and medium size companies (50+ employees) and a random nature (stratified by industry) for small businesses.[5] The questionnaire was addressed to top management positions (e.g. CEO, chief accounting officer) in the company; reply was mandatory under Italian law. The sample considered here focuses on manufacturing and high-technology services for a total of 760 companies.[6] Tables 1.1 and 1.2 show the distribution of firms in the sample by technological sector and country ownership.

The dataset combines standard quantitative data with unique information on Italian resident foreign affiliates. These are derived by linking the official survey on foreign affiliates with several other official surveys, including those based on company accounts, foreign trade in goods, and R&D. All variables originate from official surveys whose samples were drawn from the Italian business register set up and maintained by ISTAT, and are collected with respect to the same reference year and linked through the business register identification code. This guarantees the full consistency of the results. All variables, except those on knowledge transfer, are standard OECD measures as adopted by ISTAT.

Data on knowledge transfer within the MNE were collected by ISTAT in a special section of the questionnaire of the Italian survey on resident enterprises under foreign control. This was part of a study promoted by the OECD on the role played by foreign MNEs for the domestic economy. In particular, two questions were explicitly designed to focus on knowledge transfers between the foreign affiliates and their parent companies. These questions were formulated in a way that is consistent with the theoretical debate introduced in the previous sections, and are concerned with flows A1 and B2 of Figure 1.1. These discrete variables convey evaluations made by managers working in foreign affiliates. The first question refers to international technology transfer between the parent company and their Italian affiliates. This question considers both the nature and the direction of the *scientific or technical knowledge transfer*.[7] The second question relates to the nature and direction of the *transfer of managerial, commercial and other types of competencies*.[8] In both cases the direction of flow distinguishes between the flow from the Italian affiliate to the parent (affiliate–parent transfer), and the opposite (parent–affiliate transfer).

Table 1.3 shows the breakdown of intra-firm knowledge flows by category of affiliate as established earlier. Intra-group knowledge transfer is widespread in the sample, with 56.0% (61.2%) of affiliates experiencing some form of technology (managerial) transfer from their parent, roughly evenly split between two-way (Type 1) and parent–affiliate only (Type 2) flows. Perhaps more surprisingly, knowledge transfer from affiliates to parents is also relatively common, experienced by 31.2% of affiliates in terms of technology, and 31.6% in terms of other managerial knowledge. However, the vast majority of this takes place as part of a two-way process: one-way transfers from affiliate to parent (Type 3) are experienced by only 6% of affiliates. This does not necessarily imply that technology sourcing by affiliates is uncommon, simply that it generally occurs as part of a two-way process. Around one third of affiliates in the sample experience no knowledge flows with the parent.

Table 1.3   Pattern of knowledge transfer by category of affiliate

Type of flows	Intra-group technology transfer		Intra-group managerial transfer	
	No.	Percent	No.	Percent
1. Two-way flows	236	31.0	270	35.5
2. Parent–affiliate only	190	25.0	195	25.7
3. Affiliate–parent only	47	6.2	45	5.9
4. No knowledge flows	287	37.8	250	32.9
Total	760	100	760	100

Overall, therefore, the pattern is of extensive knowledge transfer between parents and affiliates, predominantly, but not overwhelmingly, running from parents to affiliates, with a substantial two-way element. This affords some contrast with the secondary patent citation analysis of Singh (2007), which suggests that the likelihood of knowledge flows between MNEs' home base and their foreign subsidiaries are very similar in both directions.

Table 1.4 shows the pattern of foreign trade, intra-firm trade and R&D activity broken down by industry grouping. Around one quarter of affiliates in the sample engage in R&D activity, with a predictable pattern with respect to technological intensity. By contrast, the vast majority of plants engage both in international trade and in intra-firm trade. Even affiliates involved in knowledge-intensive services are substantially involved in international and intra-firm trade, albeit to a markedly lesser extent than manufacturing affiliates in the sample.

Table 1.4   *Foreign affiliates in Italy engaged in trade and R&D activity by industry category (percent of the total)*

Industry code	Exports of goods and services		Imports of goods and services		R&D
	Total	Intra-firm	Total	Intra-firm	
High technology industries	92.94	88.24	95.29	85.88	31.76
Medium-high technology industries	93.40	79.21	87.79	70.96	36.96
Medium-low technology industries	92.81	76.65	93.41	77.25	14.97
Low technology industries	85.22	63.48	83.48	60.87	15.65
Knowledge intensive high technology services	58.89	44.44	68.89	56.67	11.11
Total	87.89	73.16	86.97	70.79	25.26

DETERMINANTS OF KNOWLEDGE FLOWS

Model and Estimation

A multinomial logit model (MNLM) is used to link different patterns of MNE behaviour in terms of knowledge transfer and diffusion to a set of explanatory variables. Within this analytical framework, each of the four types of MNE affiliate identified earlier identifies a specific category of a nominal outcome and it is compared, in terms of probability, to the other categories. These relative probabilities, called odds ratios, are then expressed as a non-linear function of the explanatory variables. Under the assumption that the non-linear function is exponential, the model can be written as the following system of four equations:

$$\ln \Omega_{m|b}(\mathbf{x}) = \ln \frac{\Pr(y = m \mid \mathbf{x})}{\Pr(y = b \mid \mathbf{x})} = \mathbf{x}\beta_{m|b} \qquad \text{for } m=1 \text{ to } 4 \qquad (1.1)$$

where $\mathbf{x}$ is the vector of explanatory variables, β the relative coefficient to be estimated and b the base category, which is also referred to as the comparison group. The system of four equations (1.1) can be solved to compute the predicted probabilities:

$$\Pr(y = m \mid \mathbf{x}) = \frac{\exp(\mathbf{x}\beta_{m|b})}{\sum_{J=1}^{4} \exp(\mathbf{x}\beta_{j|b})} \qquad (1.2)$$

In particular, errors in the logit model are assumed to follow the standard logistic distribution:

$$\lambda(\varepsilon) = \frac{e^z}{(1+e^z)^2} \qquad (1.3)$$

In addition, the MNLM makes the standard assumption known as the independence of irrelevant alternatives (IIA). Given the following equation:

$$\ln \Omega_{m|b}(\mathbf{x}) = \ln \frac{\Pr(y = m \mid \mathbf{x})}{\Pr(y = b \mid \mathbf{x})} = \mathbf{x}\beta_{m|b} \qquad (1.4)$$

This assumption requires that the odds do not depend on other outcomes that are available, in effect assuming that additional outcomes are irrelevant. The IIA assumptions can be tested either by the Hausman and McFadden (1984) test or by the McFadden et al. (1976) test, the latter being improved by Small and Hsiao (1985). Nevertheless, these tests often give inconsistent results and provide little guidance to violations of the IIA assumption. The parameters of the MNLM are usually estimated by a maximum-likelihood estimator. Robust error estimators are adopted to cope with heteroscedasticity.

The independent variables in the MNLM estimation comprise the sector and home country categories outlined earlier (Tables 1.1 and 1.2), and a series of quantitative variables derived from the survey. The variables selected are those which the conceptual and empirical literature suggests are most likely to distinguish between the different types of affiliate. In particular, we pay attention to intra-firm trade, R&D and other knowledge capital intensity, and exporting. Finally we allow for size of affiliate (by turnover) and its square, and for affiliate performance variables (profitability and productivity). As indicated earlier, we have no specific priors with respect to these variables, and regard them as conditioning variables along with the industry and parent-country dummies outlined earlier. Descriptive statistics for the affiliate-level independent variables are provided in Table 1.5a, and a correlation matrix in Table 1.5b.

Table 1.5a   Summary statistics on quantitative variables

Variable	Description (a)	Mean	Std. Dev.	Min	Max
SIZE	Turnover	10.07	1.88	3.04	16.28
SIZE2	Turnover squared	104.89	36.80	9.27	265.09
TFA	Tangible fixed assets	14.66	2.71	0.00	19.68
IFA	Intangible fixed assets	12.16	3.61	0.00	21.06
R&D	R&D expenditure	1.76	3.16	0.00	11.60
PROF	Profitability	0.10	0.12	−0.42	1.46
TFP	Total factor productivity	0.00	0.53	−2.22	2.72
TE	Total exports of goods and services	7.69	3.71	0.00	14.52
TI	Total imports of goods and services	7.23	3.64	0.00	13.74
IE	Intra-firm exports of goods and services	5.77	4.09	0.00	13.57
II	Intra-firm imports of goods and services	5.40	4.08	0.00	13.74

(a) variables in log, unless expressed as shares

Table 1.5b   Correlation matrix

	SIZE	SIZE2	TFA	IFA	R&D	TFP	PROF	TE	TI	IE	II
SIZE	1.0000										
SIZE2	0.9885	1.0000									
TFA	0.7452	0.7326	1.0000								
IFA	0.5553	0.5590	0.5142	1.0000							
R&D	0.4201	0.4417	0.3686	0.3342	1.0000						
TFP	0.2695	0.2417	−0.0000	−0.0000	−0.0184	1.0000					
PROF	−0.2716	−0.2400	−0.1313	−0.0983	−0.0795	0.3921	1.0000				
TE	0.7004	0.6837	0.6216	0.3719	0.3975	0.0689	−0.1865	1.0000			
TI	0.6953	0.6871	0.5502	0.3237	0.2868	0.1969	−0.2229	0.6346	1.0000		
IE	0.5559	0.5468	0.4898	0.2973	0.3307	0.0192	−0.1521	0.7432	0.5256	1.0000	
II	0.4983	0.4969	0.3728	0.1998	0.1678	0.0864	−0.2075	0.4318	0.7322	0.5826	1.0000

Results

Tables 1.6 and 1.7 show the results of the MNLM estimations for intra-group technology and managerial knowledge flows respectively, based on the four-way affiliate typology discussed above. In each case the coefficients of the model are expressed as log-odds ratios,[9] relative to the base category (Type 4 – no knowledge flows).

The coefficients on the intra-firm trade variables show a very clear pattern. Intra-firm trade, from parent to affiliate, is positively associated with parent–affiliate and with two-way technology (Table 1.6) and managerial (Table 1.7) knowledge flows. H1 is thus supported. Interestingly, intra-firm imports are more strongly associated with intra-firm technology transfer than are intra-firm exports,[10] a finding also noted by Harzing and Noorderhaven (2006). However, as with other studies in the area, Harzing and Noorderhaven do not distinguish between flows of technology and flows of other managerial knowledge. Our results indicate that, in the case of managerial knowledge flows, both intra-firm imports and exports are strongly linked to flows for Type 1 and Type 2 subsidiaries, whereas for flows of technology only intra-firm imports have a statistically significant effect. There is no evidence of any intra-firm trade relationship with either technology or managerial knowledge flows in the case of Type 3 (knowledge sourcing) affiliates. Intra-firm exports from subsidiaries are therefore not a crucial vehicle for international technology sourcing, consistent with H2.

As anticipated, therefore, flows of disembodied knowledge and flows of goods and services are closely linked within the MNE, but only where there is evidence of knowledge transfer from parent to subsidiary, either one-way (Type 2) or two-way (Type 1). This suggests that affiliates which are embedded into the parents' (physical) supply chain are more likely to receive and impart flows of new knowledge than those which are not: intra-firm trade is indeed an indicator of embeddedness.

By contrast, once allowance is made for the influence of intra-firm trade, the link between affiliates' R&D and knowledge flows is relatively modest. R&D intensity markedly lessens the likelihood of the affiliate simply being a vehicle for technology exploitation via one-way transfers from the parent (Table 1.6). This suggests, as hypothesised (H4), that standard 'technology exploiting' transfers (Type 2 flows) are more likely to occur with respect to relatively less-R&D-intensive subsidiaries. However, there is no evidence of any relationship between affiliate investment in R&D and technology or knowledge flows from affiliate to parent. Instead, the source of both technology and managerial knowledge flows in Type 3 (knowledge sourcing) subsidiaries is intangible fixed assets, which is the affiliates' investment in knowledge capital other than R&D. There is therefore only partial support for H3a and H3b: affiliate-level R&D does not increase the likelihood of technology flows from affiliate to parent, but other forms of intangible knowledge capital do have such an effect.

Table 1.6   *Multinomial logit estimates for intra-group transfer of technology*

Variables	Two-way transfer	Parent–affiliate only	Affiliate–parent only
Turnover	0.08	−0.19	1.04
	(0.52)	(0.47)	(0.96)
Turnover squared	−0.02	−0.00	−0.04
	(0.02)	(0.02)	(0.04)
Tangible fixed assets	0.15	0.09	−0.29
	(0.10)	(0.06)	(0.14)**
Intangible fixed assets	0.02	0.02	0.27
	(0.03)	(0.03)	(0.08)***
R&D expenditure	0.05	−0.15	−0.01
	(0.04)	(0.05)***	(0.06)
Total factor productivity	0.42	0.50	−0.87
	(0.34)	(0.31)*	(0.48)*
Profitability	−2.01	−1.22	4.48
	(1.39)	(1.48)	(1.49)***
Total exports	0.10	−0.11	0.29
	(0.05)*	(0.06)*	(0.12)**
Total imports	−0.01	0.05	−0.14
	(0.05)	(0.06)	(0.07)*
Intra-firm exports	0.02	0.08	0.03
	(0.04)	(0.05)	(0.06)
Intra-firm imports	0.13	0.17	0.10
	(0.04)***	(0.04)***	(0.07)
Industry-Country dummies			
HTI	0.83	0.95	1.71
	(0.40)**	(0.42)**	(0.83)**
MHTI	0.66	0.83	1.18
	(0.30)**	(0.32)***	(0.70)*
MLTI	0.45	0.68	1.99
	(0.32)	(0.34)**	(0.74)***
HTKIS	1.59	1.13	1.68
	(0.40)***	(0.42)***	(0.97)*
US	0.75	0.29	−0.29
	(0.34)**	(0.33)	(0.58)
EU	0.72	0.22	0.12
	(0.30)**	(0.28)	(0.48)
Japan	0.93	1.54	−34.41
	(0.89)	(0.80)**	(−2.46)***
Constant	−4.58	−1.40	−11.07
	(2.43)*	(2.19)	(4.65)**
Number of observations	760		
Obs in each quadrant	236	190	47
Log pseudo-likelihood	−825.83		
Wald $\chi^2(54)$	2827.00		
Prob > χ^2	0.00		
Pseudo R^2	0.13		

Notes: *, **, *** significant at the 10%, 5% and 1% level, respectively
Robust standard errors in brackets

Trade intensity also plays a role in explaining intra-firm technology and managerial knowledge transfer. Export intensity in general is associated with technology sourcing behaviour, suggesting that export-intensive plants are able to develop capabilities which in turn are able to develop into a source of technology flows back to the parent enterprise. This effect is restricted to technology flows, however. There is also a positive relationship between two-way knowledge flows (of both types) and exporting. There is therefore some support for H5. Because of the extensive evidence of endogeneity between exporting, productivity and R&D/innovation (Wagner 2007), one has to be cautious about inferring causality from correlation here: it is possible that exporting and technology flows are both determined by some other factor not accounted for in the model. However, the fact that export intensity is also *negatively* correlated with parent–affiliate knowledge exploiting flows (both technology and managerial) tends to suggest that export-intensive MNE affiliates in Italy are markedly more likely to be a source of technology or knowledge flows to their parent than to be the recipient of such flows, consistent with the learning-by-exporting hypothesis.

In terms of the conditioning variables, there is no effect of affiliate size in any of the estimations. It is interesting, however, to contrast the coefficients on the two measures of performance. In Table 1.6, for example, the productivity of the affiliate is only weakly related to technology flows, and indeed in the case of affiliate–parent flows, this is a negative relationship. However, the corresponding effect of profitability is positive and significant. This suggests that parents are more likely to source technology from profitable affiliates, rather than from productive ones.

There are also some marked differences in technology transfer behaviour among affiliates of different nationalities (Table 1.6). Specifically, Japanese affiliates are extremely unlikely to exhibit affiliate–parent technology sourcing behaviour compared with those from the US or EU, and more likely to exhibit technology exploiting behaviour. Affiliates from the latter two regions exhibit similar technology transfer patterns to each other, with two-way technology flows being significantly more likely among US and EU subsidiaries than among those from Japan. Intriguingly, these marked national differences are restricted to technology transfer; there is no evidence of any national variations in the patterns of managerial knowledge flows (Table 1.7).

Table 1.7   *Multinomial logit estimates for intra-group transfer of managerial and other competencies*

Variables	Two-way transfer	Parent–affiliate only	Affiliate–parent only
Turnover	−0.39	0.37	0.14
	(0.43)	(0.46)	(0.82)
Turnover squared	0.02	−0.02	0.00
	(0.02)	(0.02)	(0.04)
Tangible fixed assets	0.02	−0.01	−0.14
	(0.06)	(0.05)	(0.09)
Intangible fixed assets	0.01	−0.00	0.11
	(0.03)	(0.03)	(0.06)**
R&D expenditure	0.01	−0.02	−0.03
	(0.04)	(0.04)	(0.06)
Total factor productivity	0.54	−0.10	−0.35
	(0.28)**	(0.28)	(0.39)
Profitability	−2.31	1.84	2.02
	(1.41)*	(0.99)*	(1.27)
Total exports	0.09	−0.09	0.14
	(0.05)*	(0.05)*	(0.12)
Total imports	−0.01	0.01	−0.08
	(0.04)	(0.06)	(0.08)
Intra-firm exports	0.06	0.08	0.08
	(0.03)*	(0.05)*	(0.07)
Intra-firm imports	0.06	0.11	0.06
	(0.03)*	(0.04)**	(0.07)
Industry-Country dummies			
HTI	0.26	0.58	−0.86
	(0.38)	(0.41)	(0.83)
MHTI	0.43	0.60	0.36
	(0.29)	(0.32)*	(0.51)
MLTI	0.82	1.08	0.73
	(0.31)***	(0.34)***	(0.56)
HTKIS	0.71	0.50	−0.95
	(0.38)*	(0.40)	(1.22)
US	0.34	0.21	0.01
	(0.32)	(0.33)	(0.51)
EU	0.39	0.17	−0.61
	(0.27)	(0.28)	(0.48)
Japan	−0.32	0.25	0.33
	(0.72)	(0.68)	(0.89)
Constant	−0.28	−3.36	−4.36
	(2.05)	(2.17)	(3.82)
Number of observations	760		
Obs in each quadrant	270	195	45
Log pseudo-likelihood	−873.51		
Wald χ^2(54)	157.70		
Prob > χ^2	0.00		
Pseudo R^2	0.08		

Notes: *, **, *** significant at the 10%, 5% and 1% level, respectively
Robust standard errors in brackets

DISCUSSION AND CONCLUSIONS

The purpose of this chapter is to help open the 'black box 'of international knowledge transfer, and so contribute to the developing theoretical perspective of MNEs as a source of knowledge flows. The dominant paradigm is of the technologically superior MNE transferring knowledge to its foreign affiliates, with subsequent diffusion to the host economy. Although questions have been raised about this paradigm from a conceptual perspective, most empirical evidence questioning it comes from an indirect methodology, often inferring intra-firm technology flows from their effects on host country productivity and growth. This analysis has instead looked for direct evidence of intra-firm knowledge flows, and related these flows to intra-firm trade and other affiliate characteristics. The dataset is unique, first in being designed specifically for the purpose of identifying different types of knowledge flows within MNEs, and second in being based on an official survey carried out by a national statistical agency.

There are a number of key findings. First, there is clear evidence of very substantial knowledge flows between MNE parent companies and their Italian-based affiliates. Although knowledge flows from parent to affiliates are common, there is also evidence of extensive flows in the reverse direction, often as part of a two-way transfer. Unlike most studies, which concentrate on technology, we find that broadly similar patterns of flows exist for both technology and managerial knowledge.

Second, intra-firm trade and intra-firm knowledge flows are strongly related. Affiliates which are embedded into the parents' (physical) supply chain are more likely to receive and impart flows of new knowledge than those which are not. This suggests that the strong link identified between international flows of trade and knowledge noted in the economics literature (e.g. van Pottelsberghe de la Potterie and Lichtenberg 2001) is also a feature of knowledge and trade flows that take place *within* MNEs. This is consistent with the conceptual analysis of Davidson and McFetridge (1985) on the transfer of core technologies within the firm, especially since there is an absence of any relationship between technology-sourcing subsidiaries and intra-firm trade.

Third, affiliates' intangible capital intensity is strongly linked to 'reverse' knowledge flows from affiliates to parents. However, affiliate R&D capacity has no such effect after the intra-firm trade effect is allowed for. This appears to suggest that, at least for this sample of foreign affiliates in Italy, technology and managerial knowledge flows running from affiliates to their parents (and other units of the enterprise) are unlikely to flow directly from the technology developed within the affiliate by its R&D efforts, but indirectly from knowledge absorbed from elsewhere. This does imply a degree of technology sourcing by such subsidiaries.

Fourth, export intensity is associated both with a greater likelihood of affiliate–parent technology transfer *and* with a reduced likelihood of (one-way) parent–affiliate flows. This suggests that being exposed to external markets enhances the capabilities of the subsidiary, and makes it less (technologically) dependent on the parent organisation.

Finally, country of ownership matters in intra-firm technology transfer, but not in other forms of managerial knowledge flows. Specifically, Japanese affiliates are much more likely than those with European or American parents to have traditional parent–affiliate technology transfer, and are very unlikely to exhibit reverse transfer from affiliates to parents.

In terms of MNE theory, there is both comfort and a degree of concern in the findings. In aggregate, there is certainly support for the traditional model of the MNE as a vehicle for the international transfer of technology. Much of the overall flow of knowledge between MNEs and their affiliates runs from parents to affiliates. This is consistent with the role of the hierarchy in general, and MNEs in particular, as a superior vehicle of knowledge transfer and diffusion with respect to arm's length market forces under uncertainty and other market failures conditions. In addition, the fact that we find substantial evidence of the transfer of managerial competencies, while much of the FDI literature focuses exclusively on technology transfer and spillovers, is consistent with the standard theoretical framework of the superior ownership advantage held by MNEs. Nevertheless, the results detailed above clearly show that the model of the MNE as an international conduit of technology and knowledge does not hold everywhere and always. Around one third of surveyed affiliates received no form of technological or managerial knowledge flows from their parent. While these findings do not suggest that the theory of the MNE is fundamentally deficient, they do indicate the value of obtaining direct evidence on the nature and extent of knowledge flows to test the validity of established theory, and to determine the conditions under which theory does or does not hold. Here, our findings on the factors associated with different types of knowledge flows are relevant. In addition, the findings that affiliate–parent (especially two-way) knowledge transfer is commonplace supports the suggestion that knowledge sourcing is an important determinant of FDI, especially between advanced industrialised countries.

More generally, the evidence provided on the multidirectional and multifaceted nature of knowledge flows between parent companies and foreign affiliates might stimulate the development of a more articulated theoretical framework to examine MNE knowledge creation and transfer behaviour. This extended theoretical framework could usefully acknowledge that there is a great deal of complexity and heterogeneity in MNE knowledge transfer behaviour. Such an extended theory would also help in understanding the existence of cumulative processes spurred by virtuous circles of knowledge creation and transfers between the parent company, the foreign affiliate and domestic companies. In contrast, we should recognise that vicious circles can also occur, even in the presence of relevant 'static' one-way knowledge transfer, where subsequent diffusion to the domestic sector never occurs.

There are also managerial implications from this research. The first is that truly global integration involves consideration of both intra-firm physical (trade) as well as knowledge flows between MNE headquarters and subsidiaries. The fact that the link between intra-firm trade and knowledge flows is even stronger for managerial knowledge than for flows of technology also indicates support for the conceptual positions of Kobrin (1991) and Feinberg and Gupta (2004) on the nature of global integration within the MNE: intra-firm trade requires the existence of relatively well developed communication and knowledge-exchange structures within the MNE. Second, the results suggest that if MNEs want to engage in technology sourcing from subsidiary locations, building up the intangible capital of subsidiaries rather than their R&D capacity might be the way forward. This chimes with the analysis of Asmussen et al. (2013) who find not only that the internal and externally sourced knowledge of MNE subsidiaries interact, but that it takes balance between the extent of internal and external knowledge for effective knowledge transfer from and between subsidiaries to occur. Our research suggests that knowledge embedded in intangible assets as well as R&D stock may have a role to play in this interaction and balancing process. Finally, the fact that affiliate productivity is weakly linked to technology flows while affiliate profitability is strongly linked to such flows is intriguing from the MNE's perspective. This result supports the concepts of embeddedness and internalisation, in that affiliates which make a greater contribution to financial performance have better links to the parent. At the same time, financial performance of affiliates may result from any number of factors, such as transfer pricing, or the market structure in the host country, and may be independent of technological or managerial competence. In contrast, affiliates that are more productive (that is, make better use of internal resources) may also be good sources of technology for the parent, but the parent fails to capture this in terms of knowledge flows.

From the perspective of the future development of this stream of research, it is useful to point out the limitations of our work. First, the key questions on international technology and knowledge transfer are discrete in nature. We do not observe the strength or longevity of the knowledge flows, simply whether they occur. A future development would be to determine the importance of thresholds of the scale and scope of these transfers for facilitating knowledge development within the host or home country. Second, the data derive from affiliates of MNEs located in a single country, and we must acknowledge the possibility that there is some Italy-specific element to our findings. Third, in common with all cross-sectional datasets, even those backed by official sanction, we must be very cautious in imputing any degree of causation into the correlations between dependent and independent variables. Finally, the magnitude of any spillovers or productivity growth effects from these knowledge transfers are not measured. A key development in this area will be to couple direct survey evidence of this type to research on the motivation of FDI and its productivity effects. This would provide a powerful insight into the links between the motive for FDI, the capacity of firms to manage knowledge or technology flows, and the effects of MNEs on the host economy.

NOTES

1. Figure 1.1 does not purport to be a complete representation of potential knowledge flows involving MNEs and the domestic economy. Notably, it excludes knowledge flows and spillovers within the foreign-owned and domestic-owned sectors respectively. For an analysis of productivity spillovers within the foreign-owned sector of UK manufacturing see Driffield and Love (2005).
2. Note that Feinberg and Gupta (2004) posit this relationship between intra-firm trade and knowledge flows on the understanding that such a link indicates the ability of the MNE to absorb and utilise the R&D output and knowledge sourced by its subsidiary. Implicitly, therefore, they expect intra-firm trade to be linked positively to affiliate–parent technology sourcing knowledge flows, although such a link is not tested.
3. Harzing and Noorderhaven found stronger results for subsidiary intra-firm imports than for intra-firm exports.
4. Parent companies from the US, EU and Japan are separately identified, as these account for 85% of observations.
5. Micro-data used in this study refer to the Official Survey on foreign affiliates in Italy, carried out by the Italian National Statistical Institute (ISTAT) from 2005–2006. Qualitative questions on knowledge transfer were introduced following OECD recommendations to increase the stock of available information on MNE behaviour. Aggregated figures were disseminated by ISTAT in February 2007, while micro-data were made available for research purposes shortly after. The dataset used in this study can be accessed upon request at the ADELE laboratory located in the headquarters of ISTAT in Rome.
6. The reasons for concentrating this study on manufacturing and HTKIS companies are twofold. First, the focus of the research is on industries with a clear relevance of technology as a driver of the industry, this is clearly beyond the scope of most traditional service industries (dominated by, for example, retailing and wholesaling), where international intra-firm technological transfer is not a significant feature. Second, some firm level performance indicators, such as TFP and profitability,

could not be calculated with respect to most of the service industries, partly because of data constraints and also because TFP is not a particularly meaningful indicator for most traditional service sectors.

7. Scientific and technological knowledge can be embedded in material goods, formally incorporated in patents, licences or software, or stem from R&D, innovation or project activities. This is distinct from managerial competencies, including new managerial procedures or strategies. Note that the question allows for transfer to/from the Italian affiliate from/to any part of the MNE group, not merely headquarters.

8. Managerial, commercial and other types of competencies may include the adoption of new managerial procedures or strategies, in general or with respect to specific business functions: accounting, commercial, legal, and logistics.

9. Log-odds ratios are the standard manner of reporting the results of a MNLM, and refer to differences in the odds ratios between the considered modality and the baseline modality, or P(E)/(1–P(E)). They can also be interpreted as differences in probability. In this respect, log-odds ratios are particularly close to standard regression coefficients, since they assess the sign and magnitude of the covariate (marginal) effect on the 'relative' probability of the relevant event.

10. The coefficients on intra-firm exports for Types 1 and 2 in Table 1.6 are positive but insignificant.

REFERENCES

Almeida P (1996) 'Knowledge sourcing by foreign multinationals: Patent citation analysis in the US semiconductor industry', *Strategic Management Journal*, 17 (Special issue), 155–165.

Andersson U, Bjorkman I and Forsgren M (2005) 'Managing subsidiary knowledge creation: The effect of control mechanisms on subsidiary local embeddedness', *International Business Review* 14, 521–538.

Andersson U, Forsgren M, and Holm U (2001) 'Subsidiary embeddedness and competence development in MNCs – a multi-level analysis', *Organization Studies*, 22, 1013–1034.

Andersson U, Forsgren M and Holm U (2007) 'Balancing subsidiary influence in the federative MNC: a business network view', *Journal of International Business Studies*, 38, 802–818.

Asmussen C G, Foss N J and Pedersen T (2013) 'Knowledge transfer and accommodation effects in multinational corporations: Evidence from European subsidiaries', *Journal of Management*, 39, 1397–1429.

Aw B Y, Roberts M J and Xu D Y (2008) 'R&D investments, exporting, and the evolution of firm productivity', *American Economic Review*, 98, 451–456.

Bell M and Marin A (2004) 'Where do foreign direct investment-related technology spillovers come from in emerging economies? An exploration of Argentina in the 1990s', *European Journal of Development Research*, 16, 653–686.

Bernard A B, Jensen J B, Redding S J and Schott P K (2010) 'Intra-firm trade and product contractibility', NBER Working Paper No. 15881.

Birkinshaw J and Morrison A J (1995) 'Configurations of strategy and structure in subsidiaries of multinational corporations', *Journal of International Business Studies*, 26, 729–754.

Buckley P J and Casson M C (1976) *The Future of the Multinational Enterprise*, London: Macmillan.

Cantwell J (2009) 'Location and the multinational enterprise', *Journal of International Business Studies*, 40, 35–41.

Cantwell J and Janne O (1999) 'Technological globalisation and innovation centres: The role of technological leadership and location hierarchy', *Research Policy*, 28, 119–144.

Caves R E (1986) *Multinational Enterprise and Economic Analysis*, Cambridge: Cambridge University Press.

Cho K R (1990) 'The role of product-specific factors in intra-firm trade of US manufacturing multinational corporations', *Journal of International Business Studies*, 21, 319–330.

Ciabuschi F, Dellestrand H and Martin O M (2011) 'Internal embeddedness, headquarters involvement, and innovation importance in multinational enterprises', *Journal of Management Studies*, 48, 1612–1639.

Cohen W M and Levinthal D A (1989) 'Innovation and learning: The two faces of R&D', *Economic Journal*, 99(397), 569–596.

Davidson W H and McFetridge D G (1985) 'Key characteristics in the choice of international technology transfer mode', *Journal of International Business Studies*, Summer, 2, 5–21.

Driffield N and Love J H (2003) 'FDI, technology sourcing and reverse spillovers', *The Manchester School*, 71, 659–672.

Driffield N and Love J H (2005) 'Who gains from whom? Spillovers, competition and technology sourcing in the foreign-owned sector of UK manufacturing', *Scottish Journal of Political Economy*, 52, 663–686.

Driffield N, Love J H and Menghinello S (2010) 'The multinational enterprise as a source of international knowledge flows: Direct evidence from Italy', *Journal of International Business Studies*, 41, 350–359.

Driffield N, Love J H and Yang Y (2016) 'Reverse international knowledge transfer in the MNE: (Where) does affiliate performance boost parent performance?', *Research Policy*, 45, 491–506.

Driffield N, Munday M and Roberts A (2002) 'Foreign direct investment, transactions linkages, and the performance of the domestic sector', *International Journal of the Economics of Business*, 9, 335–351.

Dunning J H (1979) 'Explaining patterns of international production: In defence of the eclectic theory', *Oxford Bulletin of Economics and Statistics*, 41, 269–295.

Feinberg S E and Gupta A K (2004) 'Knowledge spillovers and the assignment of R&D responsibilities to foreign subsidiaries', *Strategic Management Journal*, 25, 823–845.

Gupta A K and Govindarajan V (1991) 'Knowledge flows and the structure of control within multinational corporations', *Academy of Management Review*, 13, 768–792.

Gupta A K and Govindarajan V (1994) 'Organizing for knowledge flows within MNCs', *International Business Review*, 43, 443–457.

Harzing A-W K and Noorderhaven N (2006) 'Knowledge flows in MNCs: An empirical test and extension of Gupta and Govindarajan's typology of subsidiary roles', *International Business Review*, 15, 195–214.

Hausman J and McFadden D (1984) 'Specification tests for the multinomial logit model', *Econometrica*, 52, 1219–1240.

Ito B and Wakasugi R (2007) 'What factors determine the mode of overseas R&D by multinationals? Empirical evidence', *Research Policy*, 36, 1275–1287.

Kobrin S J (1991) 'An empirical analysis of the determinants of global integration', *Strategic Management Journal*, Summer Special Issue 12, 17–32.

Kotabe M, Dunlap-Hinkler D, Parente R and Mishra H A (2007) 'Determinants of cross-national knowledge transfer and its effect on firm innovation', *Journal of International Business Studies*, 38, 259–282.

Marin A and Bell M (2006) 'Technology spillovers from foreign direct investment (FDI): The active role of MNC subsidiaries in Argentina in the 1990s', *Journal of Development Studies*, 42, 678–697.

Marin A and Bell M (2010) 'The local/global integration of MNC subsidiaries and their technological behaviour: Argentina in the late 1990s', *Research Policy*, 39, 919–931.

Marin A and Giuliani E (2011) 'MNC subsidiaries' position in global knowledge networks and local spillovers: Evidence from Argentina', *Innovation and Development*, 1, 91–114.

McFadden D K, Train K and Tye W B (1976), 'An application of diagnostic tests for the independence from irrelevant alternatives property of the multinomial logit model', *Transportation Research Record*, 637, 39–45.

McGuinness M, Demirbag M and Bandara S (2013) 'Towards a multi-perspective model of reverse knowledge transfer in multinational enterprises: A case study of Coats PLC', *European Management Journal*, 31, 179–195.

Meyer K and Sinani E (2009) 'When and where does foreign direct investment generate positive spillovers? A meta-analysis', *Journal of International Business Studies*, 40, 1075–1094.

Michailova S and Mustaffa Z (2012) 'Subsidiary knowledge flows in multinational corporations: Research accomplishments, gaps and opportunities', *Journal of World Business*, 47, 383–396.

Mudambi R and Navarra P (2004) 'Is knowledge power? Knowledge flows, subsidiary power and rent-seeking within MNCs', *Journal of International Business Studies*, 35, 385–406.

Niosi J (1999) 'The internationalization of industrial R&D: From technology transfer to the learning organization', *Research Policy*, 28, 107–117.

Oh K-S and Anchor J (2017) 'Factors affecting reverse knowledge transfer from subsidiaries to multinational companies: Focusing on the transference of local market information', *Canadian Journal of Administrative Sciences*, 34, 329–342.

Pearce R D (1999) 'Decentralised R&D and strategic competitiveness: Globalised approaches to generation and use of technology in multinational enterprises (MNEs)', *Research Policy*, 28, 157–178.

Phene A and Almeida P (2008) 'Innovation in multinational subsidiaries: The role of knowledge assimilation and subsidiary capabilities', *Journal of International Business Studies*, 39, 901–919.

Rabiosi L (2011) 'Subsidiary roles and reverse knowledge transfer: An investigation of the effects of coordination mechanisms', *Journal of International Management*, 17, 97–113.

Rabiosi L and Santangelo G D (2013) 'Parent company benefits from reverse knowledge transfer: The role of the liability of newness in MNEs', *Journal of World Business*, 48, 160–170.

Serapio M G and Dalton D H (1999) 'Globalization of industrial R&D: An examination of foreign direct investments in R&D in the United States', *Research Policy*, 28, 303–316.

Singh J (2007) 'Asymmetry of knowledge spillovers between MNCs and host country firms', *Journal of International Business Studies*, 38, 764–786.

Small K and C Hsiao (1985) 'Multinomial logit specification tests', *International Economic Review*, 26, 619–627.

Smeets R (2008) 'Collecting the pieces of the FDI knowledge spillovers puzzle', *World Bank Research Observer*, 23, 107–138.

van Pottelsberghe de la Potterie B and Lichtenberg F (2001) 'Does foreign direct investment transfer technology across borders?', *Review of Economics and Statistics*, 83, 490–497.

Veugelers R and Cassiman B (2004) 'Foreign subsidiaries as a channel of international technology diffusion: Some direct firm level evidence from Belgium', *European Economic Review*, 48, 455–476.

Wagner J (2007) 'Exports and productivity: a survey of the evidence from firm-level data', *The World Economy*, 30, 60–82.

2. Knowledge transfer and absorptive capacity in the context of a small multinational enterprise: a systematic study of the nexus of relationships

Jan-Tore Øian, Olli Kuivalainen and Heini Vanninen

INTRODUCTION

Of great importance to any firm is what is known as the absorptive capacity – its ability to acquire external resources and knowledge, and then assimilate and apply these (Cohen & Levinthal, 1990; Zahra & George, 2002). An especially interesting context for the study of absorptive capacity is among new ventures, as they typically lack resources (Nakos & Brouthers, 2002; Brouthers & Nakos, 2004), meaning that they have to look outside of the firm more often for new knowledge. A high degree of absorptive capacity is likely to significantly enhance the use of existing and often limited knowledge resources, thus contributing to building knowledge competency (Park & Rhee, 2012). If a new venture aims to establish operations in multiple countries and become a small multinational enterprise (small MNE), it needs to possess the skills and capabilities that enable the firm to implement this challenging internationalization strategy (Kuivalainen et al., 2007, 2012). Despite the significance of absorptive capacity in firms that operate internationally and the interest this has attracted over the years (Kogut & Zander, 1993; Subramaniam & Venkatraman, 2001), especially since 2005 (Apriliyanti & Alon, 2017), there is little research on the role of absorptive capacity in knowledge competency enhancement of rapidly internationalizing firms (Park & Rhee, 2012). Consequently, Cavusgil and Knight (2015, p. 11) suggest that the following questions should be studied: "What is the role of absorptive capacity in acquiring capabilities for early and successful internationalization? Does absorptive capacity differ in younger firms?"

Knowledge concerning absorptive capacity in the context of a large, multinational enterprise (MNE) cannot as such be transferred to the context of a small MNE (Shuman & Seeger, 1986) because smaller firms are different in terms of their structure and behaviour (Knight & Liesch, 2016). Small- and medium-sized firms (SMEs) typically have limited financial and personnel resources (Nakos & Brouthers, 2002; Brouthers & Nakos, 2004), and the smaller employee count may especially have an effect on the absorptive capacity. These firms also differ from large MNEs in terms of their ownership structure and management characteristics (Cheng, 2008; Pinho, 2007) as they are often managed by their original founder(s). SMEs are also characterized by flexibility and responsiveness to the constantly changing market conditions in countries where they are operating (Brouthers & Nakos, 2004, Lu & Beamish, 2001). As the rapidly internationalizing firms are often young, their employees usually have new roles that must be learned from scratch. New ventures have no former employees who can teach new skills as well as tacit know-how and organizational practices to new employees. It is also costly to create structure in the new organization. Further, new firms comprise people who are usually strangers and must learn to trust each other. Finally, new firms lack stable ties to those who use the firm's products or services – one of the main resources of old organizations (Stinchcombe, 1965).

Rapidly internationalizing firms have attracted a significant amount of research over the last decades (Zander et al., 2015). Much is known, for example, about the role of the external networks in the emergence and success of born globals (Coviello & Munro, 1997; Sullivan Mort & Weerawardena, 2006) but the internal side of the firm, such as how the absorptive capacity develops in this context, has not been studied much. There are even surprising findings such as those of Fernhaber et al. (2009) who found that top management teams with a low level of international knowledge benefited more from sources providing external knowledge. To address this gap, the focus of this study is on knowledge transfer and absorptive capacity in small MNEs, and our research question is: How does a small MNE transfer and absorb knowledge in its internal nexus of relationships?

The context of our study is a rapidly internationalized young and resource-constrained firm that has subsidiaries around the globe. We explore what being new and global actually means from the knowledge transfer perspective. Based on a single case study, we analyse the antecedents that increase and/or hinder absorptive capacity of the small MNE and discuss what kind of consequences being a small MNE has for this, including for the firm's capability to eventually develop in its quest for competitive advantage. We conceptualize absorptive capacity by using Zahra and George's (2002) conceptualization and focus on acquisition, assimilation, transformation, and exploitation of knowledge. The results indicate that a small MNE can overcome the resource constraints related to rapid and early internationalization and the problems this creates for knowledge transfer mechanisms by widely utilizing information and communication technology (ICT) within a firm as well as by encouraging informal communication. The young age of the firm also creates advantages, and the earlier expertise of the workers seems to be relevant. In addition, the "learning advantages of newness" (Autio et al., 2000) are an asset for this small MNE. Furthermore, both real ownership and the so-called illusionary ownership as special characteristics of the organizational culture enhance the absorptive capacity and especially exploitation of the possessed knowledge for the quest of competitive advantage.

THEORETICAL BACKGROUND

Coordination of operations in the context of large MNEs has been studied extensively but it remains unclear how the coordination of operations, such as knowledge transfer, evolve in the case of smaller MNEs. Even for large and resource-rich MNEs, it is extremely difficult to design and execute a global strategy and to manage operations across large geographical and psychic distances (Vahlne et al., 2011). If a small firm chooses to establish international subsidiaries instead of focusing on exporting, for instance, different organization structures and management practices have to be implemented (Lu & Beamish, 2006). When employees work from many geographical locations, the firm has to develop new ways of operating since traditional coordination and control mechanisms are less effective in this setting (Herbsleb & Mockus, 2003). The focal concepts in this chapter are knowledge transfer and absorptive capacity, the former being "the process through which one unit (e.g., group, department, or division) is affected by the experience of another" (Argote and Ingram, 2000, p. 151) and the latter being a concept which can be used to study the ability of the an organization to acquire, assimilate, transform and exploit knowledge (Zahra & George, 2002). Consequently, the concepts are intertwined.

Knowledge Transfer

The creation and replication of knowledge explains much of how firms grow and internationalize based on their possession of knowledge and their ability to transfer it to other markets (Kogut & Zander, 1993). Knowledge development is an integral part of the rapid international growth (Sullivan Mort & Weerawardena, 2006; Freeman et al., 2010), and foreign direct investment can allow a firm to gain superior knowledge from international markets (Hymer, 1976). MNEs, which transfer knowledge between different geographical locations, can transfer and exploit knowledge, resources, and competences more effectively inside the firm than through external market mechanisms. However, it is not easy to transfer information effectively and efficiently without significant effort (Gupta & Govindarajan, 2000; O'Donnell, 2000). Knowledge transfer's success is influenced by the characteristics of knowledge transferred, of the source and of the recipient, and of context (Szulanski, 1996). The maintenance of mutual knowledge tends to be problematic in a firm that operates from multiple locations (Cramton, 2001; Sidhu & Volberda, 2011). Distance between the employees and offices reduces the intensity of communications, and cultural differences, such as different languages, values, working and communication habits, as well as implicit assumptions that may cause misunderstandings and conflicts, cause challenges for the daily work (Kotlarsky & Oshri, 2005; Sidhu & Volberda, 2011). Time zone differences also reduce opportunities for real-time collaboration, as response time increases considerably when people work in different times in different locations (Kotlarsky & Oshri, 2005). Moreover, it is difficult to identify which distant colleagues have the necessary expertise and to communicate effectively with them (Herbsleb & Mockus, 2003).

One of the main challenges in a dispersed organization is to create rapport and connections between members of the dispersed teams (Kotlarsky & Oshri, 2005). Often, knowledge transfer is best facilitated through social control methods or "clan control" (Ouchi, 1979). The different parts of the global organization can create shared understanding by vertical integrating mechanisms, such as various types of contact and communication between the managers of foreign subsidiaries and the management in the headquarters (O'Donnell, 2000). Geographically dispersed firms may rotate key people between the head office and international subsidiaries (Manning et al., 2008). ICT also provides effective tools for supervision of subsidiaries (Yamin & Sinkovics, 2007). One way to accomplish the transfer of tacit knowledge is linking team members and leaders together by jointly set formal goals and through establishing and preserving routines to achieve these goals (Madhavan & Grover, 1998). Organizations have to articulate and amplify the new knowledge that individuals bring to the table for it to become profitable. The continuous dialogue of both tacit and explicit knowledge spirals creation and thereby enhances competitive advantage (Nonaka, 1994). Trust and interpersonal networking affect how the relationships are being built between subsidiaries and the headquarters. Further, inter-unit communication and a high frequency of contact – both formal and informal – raise the amount of knowledge transfer taking place (Ghoshal et al., 1994). All in all, we can note that characteristics of the knowledge transfer, i.e. what it transferred, how and when (e.g. frequency of the contact) are important in the process of gaining competitive advantage through absorptive capacity.

Absorptive Capacity

In order to harness knowledge and turn it into an innovative capability, it must be processed to a collective understanding (Subramaniam & Venkatraman, 2001). Collective understanding is not a static concept; it needs to be continuously adapted and improved (Barney, 1991). Communication by itself does not necessarily reflect learning and incorporation of new knowledge into daily operations. To begin with, it needs to be understood and absorbed. Absorptive capacity can be defined as "the ability of a firm to recognize the value of new external information, assimilate it and apply it to commercial ends" (Cohen & Levinthal, 1990, p. 128). In other words, it denotes how the organization acquires knowledge and exploits it to gain competitive advantage (Cohen & Levinthal, 1990). Absorptive capacity can also be specified as "a set of organizational routines and processes by which firms acquire, assimilate, transform and exploit knowledge to produce a dynamic organizational capability" (Zahra & George, 2002, p. 186). Absorptive capacity can be seen as having two components: potential absorptive capacity (knowledge acquisition and assimilation) and realized absorptive capacity (knowledge transformation and exploitation) (Zahra & George, 2002).

A firm's ability to learn is dependent on the similarities between units within the firm or between firms. Knowledge bases, dominant logics, organizational structures, and compensation policies are four factors suggested to measure this similarity level (Lane & Lubatkin, 1998). The complexity of the business environment creates a dynamic nature, and much because of the constraints of vision, and the wiring of human cognition, there might be unwillingness to acquire tacit procedural knowledge unless through interaction with other individuals (Kogut and Zander, 1993). Not only do organizational routines matter but so does the direction that works as a "principal means" by which knowledge can be transferred between specialists and a larger audience (Grant, 1996a). Organizational routines are a mechanism for coding tacit knowledge into explicit rules and instruction, and these can be categorized as formal means of knowledge transfer. Prior knowledge has been considered a key determinant for absorptive capacity (Cohen & Levinthal, 1990; Grant, 1996a, 1996b).

Organizational forms and combinative capabilities have also been shown as influential to a firms' absorptive capacity. Given the dynamic environment, both of these aspects might change over time because of path dependency, where previous choices affect the future ones (Teece et al., 1997). Grouping activities, the number of hierarchical levels, and the extent to which management is divided into various functional areas shape organizational forms and absorptive capacity (Van den Bosch et al., 1999). Combinative capabilities are the procedure of synthesizing and applying current knowledge, acquired by competitive consequentiality, to newfound knowledge (Kogut & Zander, 1992). The capability itself can be discerned by systems capabilities, formal and explicit rules changeable by management, coordination capabilities, knowledge enhancement through group relations, as well as socialization capabilities, collective interpretations of reality, and shared ideologies. A calibration of these factors needs to be done on the background of industry context and company history. It cannot be stated in general terms, but if managed successfully, all factors help to increase absorptive capacity (Van den Bosch et al., 1999). Small, rapidly internationalized firms might differ from large, established MNEs because the former do not have to unlearn many of their old, foundational premises before they can adopt new mindsets (Autio et al., 2000). Other reasons might be innovative thinking, entrepreneurial orientation, and resource constraints building on the premise of path dependency (Teece et al., 1997).

In summary, the skill of acquiring knowledge, recognizing its value, and the ability to assimilate and use it, i.e. absorptive capacity, can bring competitive advantage (Rodríguez-Serrano and Martín-Armario, 2019). It seems that there are two corporeal ways of absorbing knowledge: formally and informally. The former consists of rigid structures such as guidelines, directives, manuals, and rules made by management. The latter is more vulnerable to misunderstanding as it relies on group dynamics and socially embedded knowledge, such as shared visions and collective perceptions of actuality. A combination of both conducts should be applied to augment absorptive capacity, but it is likely that the age of the company, former knowledge, and path dependency all affect which method is favoured by the firm. Communication method, frequency of interaction and topics transferred also affect absorptive capacity – how can small rapidly internationalizing firms develop better processes for interaction (Rodríguez-Serrano and Martín-Armario, 2019).

METHODOLOGY

We have chosen a qualitative approach for this study due to the exploratory nature of the research question (Miles & Huberman, 1994; Berg, 2009; Ghauri & Grønhaug, 2010). The current study aims at understanding a largely unknown phenomenon, the role of knowledge transfer and absorption in a small MNE's nexus of relationships (Ghauri & Grønhaug, 2010). We chose this unique firm as the single case study as it fulfils both the criteria of a rapidly internationalizing firm (Knight & Cavusgil, 2004) and the criteria for an MNE (Hennart, 2009) as it has a global presence with its own offices and employees. This is an ideal representative setting to study knowledge transfer and absorptive capacity (Yin, 2009). The single case company of this study is Cxense, a Norwegian software-as-a-service (SaaS) company founded in 2010. Cxense was established by a group of former employees of a company called FAST. FAST was sold to Microsoft for USD 1.2 billion in 2008. Cxense's offering is a Data Management Platform (DMP) with Intelligent Personalization that gives companies insight about their individual customers and enables them to action this insight in real-time in all marketing and sales channels. In other words, Cxense enables publishers and marketers to transform raw data into a valuable resource for business use. Cxense has customers in EMEA, Japan, Latin America, North America, and Asia Pacific. During the time of data collection, Cxense technology was powering approximately 3000 web and mobile sites worldwide, with more than 160 million active unique users on a monthly basis. Cxense has software development offices in Oslo, Norway, and Melbourne, Australia. The Sales & Marketing and Operations & Implementation resources are located in Oslo, Melbourne, Tokyo, London, San Francisco, Boston and Miami. The Cxense group is headquartered in Oslo, Norway. The offices in Oslo, Melbourne, Tokyo, and the US all opened in 2010. At the time of data collection, the company employed 44 people and had employees from nine different nationalities. The group revenues amounted to USD 5.26 million.

The informants in this study (Table 2.1) cover management, sales, and R&D functions on a geographically dispersed level. Only two out of the seven informants had not worked at FAST, where most of the employees in Cxense had worked before Microsoft acquired FAST, and Cxense was established.

Table 2.1   Informants of the study

Title	FAST experience	Location
Chief Technology Officer	Yes	Oslo
General Manager: Japan	Yes	Tokyo
Business Development Manager: North America	No	Boston
Senior Vice President of Engineering	Yes	Melbourne
Technically Responsible for cX::Recs and cX::Search	Yes	San Francisco
Business Development Manager: Europe	Yes	London
Software Engineer: cX::Ad (Mainly)	No	Melbourne

Due to the geographical dispersion of the informants, the data was collected through semi-structured, in-depth interviews via Skype. The criteria used for selecting informants was the following:

1. Representatives from all the different offices.
2. Diversity in functions (sales, management, and R&D).
3. A reflected balance of former FAST, and non-former FAST employees.

Using these criteria for the selection of informants helped to ensure that the results of the study were credible. The process for the data collection started through a personal contact of one of the authors working in the firm who sent out an email to all the employees, asking if they were willing to participate. Based on the feedback received, the author suggested eight different people, which was the sample size needed to facilitate data saturation (Yin, 2009; Ghauri & Grønhaug, 2010). A sample size of eight was considered sufficient, being that the firm currently only has 44 employees. Eight represent an informant percentage coverage of 18%, close to one out of every five employees. One informant was lost due to conflicting schedules, hence, the final data consists of seven primary interviews.

The interviews started with a short introduction of the research and its objectives. In the first part, there were questions about informants' previous experience and current position. After these initial background questions, the interview guide was divided into sections inquiring about the knowledge transfer (what the interviewee considered to be critical knowledge in the firm and how the knowledge was shared inside the firm), absorptive capacity (how the firm managed to absorb knowledge and the challenges related to this) and competitive advantage (what the informants viewed as competitive advantage and if knowledge transfer and absorption of knowledge contributed to this in the informant's opinion). All of the interviews were recorded using computer software. The interviews lasted an average of 45 minutes. Each transcript is about 14–15 pages long (ca. 6000 words). After transcription, each of the informants received a copy via email, and they were asked to confirm that what they had said had been interpreted correctly. All of the seven informants confirmed positively without any request for changes to the transcripts. This also increased the validity of the findings.

Selective coding was utilized in data analysis for its emphasis on the core categories of knowledge transfer, absorptive capacity, and sustainable competitive advantage (SCA), as well as flexibility around associated themes (Ghauri & Grønhaug, 2010). Four formalized steps were used in the data analysis, following Sinkovics et al. (2008) example: organizing, coding (data reduction), searching, and modelling and interpretation. The selective coding method allowed us to prioritize the core categories and identify secondary and tertiary subjects of the data.

FINDINGS

Knowledge Transfer

Contact source and frequency

There is a significant amount of communication between the various locations of Cxense, and the different subsidiaries and the headquarters communicate with each other on a daily basis. Frequent communication inside the firm is needed because employees are spread around the globe, and the biggest office in Oslo hosts only 14 employees. The communication between the offices is rather informal, coinciding with the flat organizational structure. An important practice for efficient knowledge transfer inside the company is a weekly call where everyone in the company partakes in a web conference. The general agenda of these meetings is to keep everyone updated with company movements, product developments, prospects, and key accounts.

There are some differences in the communication frequency related to the position of the employee. Salespeople seem to communicate more frequently with other subsidiaries than, for example, software engineers, and to some extent that had caused a minor issue in the early months following the inception of the firm. It seemed that there was not a broad enough range of contact between the offices, and that much of the communication related to R&D had to go through gatekeepers, which slowed efficiency. However, it had improved recently, according to two of the informants who focused a lot on this issue, and it seemed that it was easier now for a software engineer in Melbourne, for example, to directly contact a software engineer in Oslo if they needed, rather than having to go through the gatekeeper. In this particular case, both parties encouraged a higher frequency of communication in order to avoid working based on assumptions. Assumptions that influenced the daily work in the early days of Cxense's operations may have been the result of cultural differences. Whereas Norwegians were considered egalitarian and self-dependent, employees from both the Australian and Japanese offices tended to ask for confirmation before addressing particular issues. For the Norwegians, this was considered a waste of time, and they believed it would benefit the company if other offices took more initiative. However, the offices that usually asked for confirmation thought it could prevent misunderstandings in the future. Actions needed to be implemented in order for this to happen:

> So, basically, just [make] sure that people are pushed to communicate and collaborate because they tend not to do that by themselves. (Informant of Cxense)

Knowledge type

The most common subjects for discussion between the offices were operational requirements and the needs of customers. Again, the role of the employee naturally influenced the preferred subject, but the creation of value was deemed paramount for all. Because Cxense is a technology and customer-oriented business, innovation came up frequently. Two different perspectives could be found, one being the way ideas were formed:

> It definitely comes from sales, you know, I can always write an email on my own time, telling them some feedback from a specific prospect or customer, or I can post something on the Wiki and start a discussion, then other people will join in and offer comments, and exchange ideas. People love doing that, and I feel it's a very open environment for everybody to have ideas and opinions and exchange them with other folks… (Informant of Cxense)

The second perspective, sourced from a person in a different role, was:

> So, there are two very distinct conversation types. There is operational type of things: who needs what, and when do they need it by, how many hour work is booked up this week, is he bound in any way that could interfere this week, [those] kind of things. And then there is sort of more kind of loose, research and things, thought processes where we are kind of kicking around ideas and things. Both of those things are done pretty regularly. (Informant of Cxense)

Product innovation was seen as equally important as operational requirements for Cxense. Strategically speaking, this focus of conversation might be one of the foremost mechanisms for enhancing and obtaining a sustainable competitive advantage.

Interaction Method

Face-to-face communication was the preferred and most-utilized interaction method inside each subsidiary. However, regarding inter-office communication at Cxense, four different ICT systems were frequently used: email, Skype, an internal Wiki, and Jira. The Wiki, as employees called it, is an internet relay chat (IRC) room where employees can create and contribute to companywide discussions. Jira, software created by a company called Atlassian, is a project tracker for product teams and can be used for planning, building, and launching software. The configurable web interface permits agile development planning, keeping track of projects, searching, and reporting. Jira was mainly used by the software engineers and the product development team to facilitate the ordering of new features, and to keep track of those developments.

> If [for] example, we need to communicate with R&D, we have that in Norway, and Australia currently, so we have the system, Jira, which [is] where we can share knowledge [on] technical issues and customer requirements. We always order a ticket on the website, [the] intranet site, which is easier, for we have time differences. We always get feedback in one day. (Informant of Cxense)

The Wiki was used for more general issues, and the informants all seemed content using it for various reasons. However, the many different forms of communication methods were seen as a bit complex.

> People make good use of the Wiki. People are very helpful and share information, and help people figure out, and prepare for different types of opportunities… It can get a little overwhelming. There are definitely multiple systems, and different ways that you are supposed to use them, and processes for each. You have to make sure you use it right, so that the other [party] can do their things right. Other people are relying on you, so you have to make a good effort to do it right, so yeah, it can get a little bit overwhelming. (Informant of Cxense)

Nonetheless, the company currently operates at a satisfactory level, even though some informants would have wanted more direct interaction.

> Yeah. I wish our video usage was more pervasive. A lot of the communication we have is text based … using web pages and things like the Wiki, or Jira tickets, chat, or IRC, especially with [the] Norwegians and Australians. (Informant of Cxense)

Not all can be explained through text, and to make sure that tacit knowledge is properly understood, Skype was the preferred form of interaction between offices.

> We use Skype a lot. I think we use the most modern ways of communicating, I mean, Skype is cheap, and it gives you also the opportunity to share things in real time, so I could share my screen, and things that I am actually working on. So, that seems to work really well… (Informant of Cxense)

This type of interaction was made easier by the fact that all employees attended an annual "All Hands" meeting where the informants found the most important goal was to get to know their co-workers.

> I don't think the most important learning outcome is technical or academic. I think that [it's] face-to-face time with everybody gathered at one place. (Informant of Cxense)

Time difference has a major impact on interaction method, as it also has on contact frequency. Time differences explain why much of the interaction between subsidiaries and headquarters takes place by means of ICT. The vast geographical spread makes it hard to communicate in real time, even though there are some certain work hours that overlap.

Formal coding

Employees who work on technological matters argued that they felt that knowledge was absorbed appropriately by formal coding since the key information they needed to do their jobs could be found in the codebook. However, on matters such as market conditions, sales, and general operational requirements, many felt it was not functioning optimally. In addition, salespeople tend not to be as technologically adept as the engineers, so they are not able to read the codebook without assistance with interpreting it. Proper management of knowledge could be seen as a potential problem in the future.

> Yeah. [Coding is used] in an OK manner, but … it works OK for now given our current size. If we had been 10 times the size we are, with a lot more people … 500 instead of 50 in the company, then a need for more formalized procedures would probably arise compared to today's methods. (Informant of Cxense)

Despite currently managing absorption, structural improvements in the way knowledge is absorbed are imminent. Many felt that it could save the company valuable time if employees could find the information they needed by themselves instead of having to rely on co-workers. Even though the Wiki functions as a form of documentation, it was not considered ideal, since many of the discussions were long and characterized as too conversational. Prioritization became central here as well; since not many of the business operations were in writing and kept where they could be easily located, mistakes had occurred. One example was the delay in delivery on a new feature to a customer, which caused a monetary penalty for Cxense. If proper documentation existed, the developers may have had a better chance of understanding that this was an urgent matter and could have prioritized it. Many of the informants were concerned that the tacit knowledge might be lost if there is no attempt at information being documented.

> So that we can make sure when we hear feature requests, … [there would be] "nice to haves" from customers, … these can be prioritized in a proper manner against our R&D. … [O]ur R&D has great ideas, but it may not be what our customers want right here and now. That is sometimes a problem, you know, R&D have the overall direction, but then the customer has requests which [R&D] may have not thought about, and these things, sometimes I would say, gets wrongly prioritized. (Informant of Cxense)

Informal coding

As mentioned earlier, informal coding seems to be the preferred way of absorbing knowledge. Most of the informants favoured talking to someone in person or through Skype rather than having to read messages or comb through documents. Some employees think that informal coding is the best way to do it, until they grow larger, since a more personalized learning environment seems to motivate the acquisition of a deeper understanding.

> I think that there should be more dedicated one-on-one time between technical people and non-technical people. [Also, it would be good to consider]… formal web conference training sessions, and things like that, because I think people learn exponentially better in one-on-one sessions where there is less pressure, and you can ask questions, go at your own pace, and things like that. (Informant of Cxense)

Many informants stated that software engineers tend not to willingly document their work and how they have created or solved problems on new or existing product features. Evidence also suggested that the same mentality could be found in salespeople. Rather than sharing successful stories and making sure that other sales employees learn from their successes, it seemed that they tend to prefer to move on to the next sale. This focus is clearly justifiable in the short term, but it is possible that a stronger emphasis on sharing sales pitches, prospects, and closing techniques might be more beneficial in the long term.

> Yeah, if you think of it as an engineer, and I ask you to paint a room, then you would have to. If you … break that process down, you have to measure the room, select colours, wash the walls, paint it, clean up, and put all the furniture back. You basically have to do the same thing over and over again, and from an engineer's perspective, [documentation is] kind of the same thing. … [If] I ask you to implement a software feature, then you have to think about what that feature needs, you have to design the feature, write it, and test it. By the time you get through that you really don't want to document it. Hehe. None are better than us. Most engineers kind of want to move on to the next thing, so it can be pretty hard to get them to communicate. (Informant of Cxense)

The lack of formal coding – and consequently preference for informal coding – may result in tacit knowledge remaining tacit instead of explicit. This is not necessarily a problem at the current lifecycle of the focal firm, but, in the future, if the company grows or key employees quit to work elsewhere, it could set back their good efforts, and slow down forthcoming progress.

Cross-comparison of dyadic relationships

A dyadic relationship is that between different units, and in this case, it is defined as that between a subsidiary and the headquarters. Knowledge and information flow may go either way in the relationship, and given Cxense's flat organizational structure, it is the case in this study.

The dyadic relationship between the offices in Japan and the headquarters in Oslo seem like the most culturally different, and it was made clear that in order to improve performance, the Japanese would need to understand the Norwegian culture better and vice versa. However, they were mostly happy in the way it worked, and the informant stated that folks at the headquarters were very helpful and willing to listen to their concerns. The Australian office felt that cultural differences led to misunderstandings, and more of the communication should be conducted using video as it would permit a better reading of emotion than text provides. Sometimes the Norwegians can be quite blunt in their way of communicating, and this could surprise the Australians. This led to misunderstandings that in turn would lower the absorptive capacity due to frustration, and sometimes even led to anger. Meanwhile, the folks at the Oslo headquarters sometimes felt that the office in Melbourne could try to take a bit more initiative and not seek approval as often as they have done in the past. However, these issues had already been addressed, and positive progress was being made. Both of the offices in the USA requested more one-on-one, personal time between software engineers and salespeople, perhaps due to the fact that there are no R&D offices in the USA and the salespeople may need to be more technologically aware regarding their products. This is a notion the team in Oslo was familiar with and recognized as important for their future success.

Absorptive Capacity

The All Hands meeting, organized frequently, seemed to contribute positively towards the company's absorptive capacity. When people are acquainted on a personal level rather than solely relying on digital communications, it is easier to understand different people, their culture, and the ways in which they communicate.

> We talked about a very good case study, ... how to sell to customers, [and] how to communicate with prospects. So, after the All Hands [meeting], we can change the sales talk to [focus on] the customer. [T]he big prospects ... liked our stories. (Informant of Cxense)

One notion that constantly came up was the issue of prioritization. It seems that there is not enough communication between the different departments – especially between sales and R&D – regarding what products needed to be updated, or new features that needed to be released, and at what times. Problems with prioritization are caused by a lack of understanding for what is crucial for operations, meaning there is room for improvement in absorptive capacity.

> ...[W]e did have a semi-collective understanding that we would hold demonstrations once every month. Nowadays, there is not so much of that anymore. Of course, it is always fun to see stuff like that, but now, purely as a transfer of knowledge, IRC and chat tools like that are used extensively. An advantage of such [tools] is that it's easy for everyone to see what we are doing, so people automatically pick up on topics they are interested in. By that consideration, I believe we are rather skilled, if people take responsibility and orient themselves on what others are doing. (Informant of Cxense)

Employees stated that they would rather have a system where someone monitored the situation and coordinated prioritization efforts according to operational needs and customer demand.

Employees preferred the informal coding rather than the more formal one, but also realized that as the company grows, more formalized procedures become a necessity to sustain their advantages.

Given that nearly 70% of the informants had previously worked together at FAST (a company sold to Microsoft), experiences from FAST might affect both positively and negatively the way employees comprehend, interpret, and learn.

> [It's] certainly been that people [have] changed things, [submitted] applications for others, or they haven't communicated that the application is coming. And [those applications have] been deployed to production and [have] broken the system. That hasn't happened as often in Cxense as it did in the previous company, so I think it's just that we know each other so well, and most people have known each other for a very long time at Cxense or worked together at FAST. We're pretty atypical for a [vastly] distributed team since we have worked together for a long time although Cxense is a new company. (Informant of Cxense)

> [W]e removed some of the bad things. We learned from the FAST days. One example could be, you know, that we don't want to become a big service organization as it has a lot of costs. So, we don't want to be on the consulting side of things, we just want to … [create] products and make customers successful. The product at FAST was very complicated, so many times we became consultants as opposed to software specialists. (Informant of Cxense)

The interviewees all indicated a positive evolution, where the mistakes had been found and fixed from the previous venture. The employees learn from previous experience but they still have areas in need of improvement. In addition, as pointed out earlier, informality seems to be a key factor:

> The biggest similarity which I like is that we work in a "Norwegian way" (egalitarian), where everybody [is] worth the same. We have people all over the world, and we have some formal roles to a certain extent. … We don't have [a] hierarchical regime like we [had] when [FAST was] acquired by Microsoft, where everything went up and down command lines, [and] you couldn't speak with anybody directly." (Informant of Cxense)

Another facet considered vital to assimilation in the focal case was that of an annual All Hands meeting. The All Hands meeting contributes positively towards the company's absorptive capacity as well, mainly by getting people acquainted on a personal level rather than solely relying on digital forums. This eases communication through ICT because employees are able to vividly imagine their communication partner and adhere differently to responses than they would have, had they not met in person:

> We talked about a very good case study, and how to sell to customers, how to communicate with prospects. So, after the "All Hands" we can change the sales talk to the customer. Currently, the big prospects, e.g. [company 1] and [company 2], very much liked our stories. (Informant of Cxense)

Each and every respondent indicated that being a shareholder lifted their work morale.

> What happens is that when people sign the contract they are offered to buy shares up to a certain price, and [so far] everybody has bought shares. Some have bought many, and some have bought [few]. Everybody has bought some. (Informant of Cxense)

Employees constantly seek to better themselves through teaching fellow colleagues/shareholders, and vice versa, to learn from colleagues/shareholders as it would benefit them all to exploit the knowledge acquired, assimilated, and transformed. However, much of the responsibility to learn for monetary gain lies with each employee – a notion that some did not appreciate. They would rather have a system where someone monitored the situation and coordinated prioritization efforts according to operational needs and customer demand. Such a task could easily be delegated to an employee. A formalized structure was requested:

> I don't think we [are] that particularly [good at utilizing our market strengths]. We don't have any formal programmes to sort of push that. So, ideally, I would like to see that. The kind of work that happens in Oslo is a lot more focused on computer science, theoretical things like algorithm design, and compression schemas, and things like that, whereas the work we do in Australia is probably more functional. You know, we build things like final edge extracts, and general ledger checks … I guess quite boring things like that. We have different kinds of skills, and different kinds of responsibilities, and we don't have any kind of formal programmes to push the other office to learn about these different areas. So, I don't think we do that kind of knowledge transfer from a training perspective particularly well. (Informant of Cxense)

Again, time and resource constraints show:

> I think, unfortunately, we are just too busy. Being a start-up where we are kind of focused on getting as many features built, and [as many] customers on board as possible. It's probably just being a small company with too much to do. (Informant of Cxense)

Lack of a solution and not having enough time should not be an excuse but it should rather be a motivator to improve and use creative thinking to solve the issues that arise.

Interconnectivity and Cross-dyadic Relationships

There are interlinkages between the antecedents and determinants and these increase intricacy in understanding how they affect each of the elements in absorptive capacity, i.e., acquisition, assimilation, transformation, and absorption. To understand this, one must first grasp the concept of a dyadic relationship. A dyadic relationship is that between units, and, in this case, it is defined as that between a subsidiary and the headquarters. Knowledge and information flow may go either way in the relationship, and so does the manner in which absorptive capacity facilitates the knowledge flows.

DEVELOPMENT OF THE FRAMEWORK

As an outcome of our study we put forward a framework of knowledge transfer and absorption. The model (Figure 2.1) illustrates how the findings of the current study contribute to the understanding of the knowledge transfer and absorptive capacity in the context of small MNEs. The framework has been formulated based on the earlier literature and complemented with the findings of the current study. Several elements have been added to the extant knowledge. The added elements are background/experience, perceived critical knowledge, annual meetings, and coordination role. These are critical for the proper utilization of knowledge transfer and increase of absorptive capacity to enhance sustainable competitive advantage.

Earlier international experience of many team members, which is crucial for born global firms (Knight and Cavusgil, 2004; Cavusgil and Knight, 2015) has helped the building process of the coordination and communication mechanisms and speeded up the development of young and small MNEs. Some aspects, such as personal relationships and cooperative interdependence, which lead to trust and development of tacit knowledge, and eventually the development of absorptive capacity, have also been mentioned in the extant literature (e.g. Freeman et al., 2010). However, our study covers, in detail, knowledge transfer mechanisms used in a fast-growing small multinational firm and how they help to increase absorptive capacity.

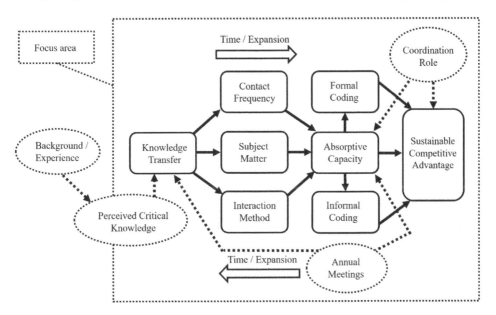

Figure 2.1   The model of knowledge acquisition, transfer and absorption in the context of small MNEs

Acquisition

Acquisition, or attainment of knowledge, can happen in many different forms and can be accomplished through various procedures and methods. Our case study implies that a widespread use and application of ICT, effectuated informally, may help firms to overcome resource constraints that are typical for many small firms. Modern ICT technologies are enablers of so-called born global firms (Knight and Cavusgil, 2004; Cavusgil and Knight, 2015). Without implying that the four core categories of absorptive capacity attribute to knowledge utilization step by step, these categories can intersect and be involved dynamically. As a result, acquisition does prove to be utterly crucial for proper absorptive capacity. The conducted interviews shed light on the importance of information and communication technology. Face-to-face communication was the preferred and most-utilized interaction method internally at each subsidiary. However, regarding inter-office communication at Cxense, four different ICT systems were frequently used. Reflecting on these issues leads to an understanding that the focal firm's ability to deliver sought-after products in today's market would not be possible without the constructive appliance of ICT systems, given the low barrier of exchanging feedback. These low barriers may be more typical for young and small international firms as they may be less locally embedded – whereas for traditional MNCs local embeddedness may create more knowledge deficits (cf. Yamin and Sinkovics, 2007). An informal communication sphere is important in order to facilitate knowledge acquisition.

Assimilation

Assimilation means understanding through interpretation, comprehension, and learning. It is like raw data before analysis, subject to a prior acquisition of knowledge. Dominant logic is often attributed to being decisive in the manner that an organization assimilates knowledge, where experience is considered as an antecedent, and the age of the firm and path dependency are the mediators of the assimilation process. The knowledge acquired from earlier endeavours can also benefit how an organization assimilates knowledge. By reflecting on the mistakes made in the past, it is easier to interpret how employees will react to various scenarios. Another facet considered vital to assimilation in the focal case was that of an annual All Hands meeting. The All Hands meeting contributes positively towards the company's absorptive capacity as well, mainly by getting people acquainted on a personal level rather than solely relying on digital forums, but also because when you know someone personally, it is easier to understand them, their culture, and the way in which they communicate. This meeting can also be a trust-building tool and helps employees in different locations see the other party as a trustworthy source, which is important for absorptive capacity (Szulanski, 1996; Freeman et al., 2010). This eases communication through ICT because employees are able to vividly imagine their communication partner and behave differently to responses than they would have, had they not met in person.

Transformation

A firm's capability to approach exploitation is related to its capability and willingness to develop and refine routines that facilitate using acquired and assimilated knowledge, in other words, its ability to transform. Much like assimilation, transformation is affected by dominant logics, path dependencies, and internal harmonization of work structures within the company. These three matters can be seen as interconnected as they allow the sharing of meaning and enable innovation and entrepreneurship. This includes development of established products and the creation of new ones. Again, the quote above related to sales pitches demonstrates that it incorporated all aspects of absorptive capacity up until exploitation; acquisition, assimilation, and the topic of this subchapter, transformation. Through the annual meeting, employees feel they can more easily transfer what they learn there into their daily routines, and they emphasized the ease of adjusting their tendencies in everyday work. Despite current ways of managing absorption, structural improvements in the way knowledge is absorbed are imminent. Many felt that it could save the company valuable time if employees could find the information they needed by themselves instead of having to rely on co-workers. For a growing firm, codifying of the knowledge may be a necessity in the future (Grant, 1996a).

Exploitation

The ability to utilize the market strengths and produce something consumers want, or businesses need to turn a profit, cannot be underestimated. It should be on the forefront at all times, as it is universally acknowledged as a crucial factor for success. Exploitation per our topic, absorptive capacity, is no exception. It relies on mediators such as physical and illusory ownership (as motivational factors to use the knowledge). Physical ownership refers to stocks and a legally valid sets of rights, and illusory ownership refers to a feeling of ownership by giving the individual meaning or purpose, for example. The antecedent for this element of absorptive capacity could be defined as organizational culture, and for a small multinational firm, more specifically a growth-oriented organization culture, where everyone can attribute simultaneously. The firm in this study has all employees as shareholders of the company. In many quantitative studies, exploitation has been measured with the number of patents but it can, for example, be measured on the basis of the knowledge component in products and services (Chauvet, 2014). However, all in all, an increase in absorptive capacity increases knowledge and can be seen leading to sustainable competitive advantage (e.g. Freeman et al., 2010).

DISCUSSION AND CONCLUSIONS

This chapter complements the extant knowledge transfer literature in the born global/international new venture domain, which has mostly focused on prior knowledge and knowledge acquisition (Fernhaber et al. 2009; Freeman et al. 2010; Fletcher & Harris, 2012), by focusing on absorptive capacity and knowledge transfer in small multinational firms (MNEs). Extant studies, with a few exceptions (e.g. Freeman et al., 2010) have not focused on absorptive capacity of small multinationals, which have both advantages and disadvantages in relation to knowledge transfer and development of absorptive capacity. After presenting the four factors of absorptive capacity as defined by Zahra & George (2002) in relation to our study and having incorporated antecedents and determinants of small multinational firms in relation to the research question, the visual map in Figure 2.2 illustrates how they may affect each other and contribute to absorptive capacity. Hence, we provide a contextualization – in the small multinational firm setting – of what the antecedents and other determinants of absorptive capacity can be like.

As portrayed, each of the antecedents has an effect on determinants in the middle, and each one of them is known to be common among rapidly internationalized firms (Oviatt & McDougall, 1994; Caves, 1998; Knight & Cavusgil, 2004; Hashai & Almor, 2004; Zahra et al., 2007). The determinants originate from the data and its analysis and show how they affect absorptive capacity. Each of the antecedents affects different types of determinants towards each of the four elements of absorptive capacity. Though, as noted, it is not always based solely on one singular element, e.g., informality can affect both acquisition and assimilation. The following propositions are made based on the findings:

1. Proper use of a widespread set of ICT systems, utilized and operated in an informal manner, increases absorptive capacity for resource-constrained firms.

2. The lack of manifested truths and foundational premises of young entrepreneurial firms combined with the benefits of positive path dependencies from earlier experiences increase absorptive capacity for small multinational firms.
3. Illusory and physical ownership in growth-oriented organizational cultures increase absorptive capacity in small multinational firms.

The empirical results answer the research question: How does a small MNE transfer and absorb knowledge in its internal nexus of relationships? The results confirm that the creation and replication of knowledge explains much of how Cxense has managed to grow so quickly, coinciding with Kogut and Zander (1993). It could be due to employee expertise and experience from a previous venture, FAST, where a large percentage of the staff came from (Preece et al., 1999; Kuivalainen et al., 2007; Gabrielsson et al., 2008). It is also clear that subsidiary isolation is feared for its negative effects on intra-firm knowledge transfer and corporate strategy, especially when employees discussed prospective growth (Monteiro et al., 2008). Consequently, Cxense, having realized that threat, has managed to establish an organizational culture inviting frequent communication between the different units. The different forms of communication help reduce uncertainty by easing the process of information exchange, both direct and reverse (Daft & Lengel, 1986; Yamin, 1999).

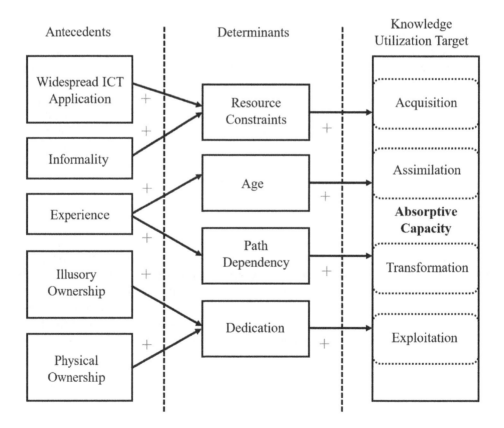

Figure 2.2   *Visual map*

Furthermore, the potential of these rich processing mechanisms constitutes a greater chance of new product development, and the promises such has on maintaining a sustainable competitive advantage (Subramaniam & Venkatraman, 2001). Continuous dialogue between the different subsidiaries and the headquarters, especially through the annual All Hands meeting and the weekly calls, has led to creation and great advances for Cxense (Nonaka, 1994; Ghoshal et al., 1994). Consequently, our findings support general knowledge management practices in many ways, as we can see aspects of positive, professional identity building and interunit knowledge flow provide opportunities for learning and for fostering innovation practices (Tagliaventi et al. 2010).

The young age and relatively small size of the company combined with its path dependency has led the focal firm to prefer informal coding (Teece et al., 1997; Autio et al., 2000). However, the idea of expansion and making all activities increasingly complicated due to a higher amount of replication and additional locations has made employees realize that a higher extent of formal coding will be necessary in the future (Grant, 1996a). It seems that the small multinational firm's focus on obtaining more business rather than documenting wins, and its emphasis on aspects that create value – such as innovation and sales – might be evidence of their tendency to grow fast. Perhaps the fact that all employees are stockholders has created a strong incentive to perform well and has led to a task-driven organizational culture (think "dedication"). This is emphasized by the notion that the employees do not communicate with teammates for fun.

We contribute to previous literature by highlighting entrepreneurial behaviour, global market orientation, mindset, and networking capability (Knight, 2001; Knight & Cavusgil, 2004; Gabrielsson et al., 2008; Freeman et al., 2010, Cavusgil and Knight, 2015). Additionally, the utilization of ICT has obviously improved the focal firm's absorptive capacity by easing access to offices around the world despite noting that the focal firm has areas that can be improved. This portrays the rather complexly intertwined web that is knowledge transfer and absorptive capacity in the context of a small, multinational firm's nexus of relationships. Small multinational firms seem to have less formal structures, an absence of bureaucracy, more openness, and looser social dynamics within the organization. Consequently, firms that have experience and are able to develop coordination and communication structures, whilst internationalizing early and rapidly, can benefit from flexibility (perhaps also from learning advantages of newness, see Autio et al., 2000), even though there are resource constraints.

Limitations and Future Research

A qualitative single-case study does not allow generalizing a broader populous or testing hypothesis, nor does it allow for confirming or disapproving suggested causalities (Berg, 2009; Ghauri & Grønhaug, 2010). The choice of utilizing an embedded single-case study as research design also affects this study. An embedded or holistic multiple-case study may have allowed a deeper insight into the phenomenon, but the uniqueness of the focal firm favoured the chosen approach. Multiple case studies could be utilized in the future studies of this topic. Another direction for future studies could be to explore the motivational aspects of the individual employees, as the data from this single-case study points to a direction that individuals' motivation to share knowledge might be an important factor in knowledge transfer. A process of building a culture of sharing in a small MNE can be tricky, however, especially if a person is alone in an office on the other side of the globe. Virtual mobility (which may be prevalent in small, global firms due to resource constraints) may also increase feelings of isolation (Daniel et al., 2018) – which is also an issue in smaller firms with small office head counts. Further, Rodríguez-Serrano and Martín-Armario (2019) found out that market orientation and entrepreneurial orientation, for example, led to a higher level of absorptive capacity in born global firms and this indicates that organization culture matters, and the study of motivations of individuals could provide more insights about the interplay between different levels of organization. Our idea about "illusory and physical ownership" could be studied in relation to these well-known strategic orientations in the future.

REFERENCES

Andersson, U. and Forsgren, M. (1996), 'Control and embeddedness in multinational corporations', *International Business Review*, **5** (5), 487–508.
Andersson, U., Forsgren, M., and Holm, U. (2001), 'Subsidiary embeddedness and competence development in MNCs – a multi-level analysis', *Organization Studies*, **22** (6), 1013–1035.
Apriliyanti, I. and Alon, I. (2017), 'Bibliometric analysis of absorptive capacity', *International Business Review*, **26** (5), 896–907.
Argote, L. and Ingram, P. (2000), 'Knowledge transfer: A basis for competitive advantage in firms', *Organizational Behavior and Human Decision Processes*, **82** (1), 150–169.
Autio, E., Sapienza, H., and Almeida, J. (2000), 'Effects of age at entry, knowledge intensity and imitability on international growth', *Academy of Management Journal,* **43** (5), 909–924.
Barney, J. (1991), 'Firm resources and sustained competitive advantage', *Journal of Management,* **17** (1), 99–120.
Berg, B. (2009), *Qualitative Research Methods: For the Social Sciences*, 7th ed. Boston: Pearson Education.
Birkinshaw, J. and Hood, N. (1998), 'Multinational subsidiary evolution: Capability and charter change in foreign-owned subsidiary companies', *Academy of Management Review*, **23** (4), 773–795.
Brouthers, K. and Nakos, G. (2004), 'SME entry mode choice and performance: A transaction cost perspective', *Entrepreneurship: Theory and Practice*, **28** (3), 229–247.
Caves, R. (1998), 'Industrial organization and new findings on the turnover and mobility of firms', *Journal of Economic Literature*, **36** (4), 1947–1982.
Cavusgil, S. T. and Knight, G. (2015), 'The born global firm: An entrepreneurial and capabilities perspective on early and rapid internationalization', *Journal of International Business Studies*, **46** (1), 3–16.
Chauvet, V. (2014), 'Absorptive capacity: Scale development and implications for future research', *Management International/International Management/Gestiòn Internacional*, **19** (1), 113–129.
Cheng, Y. (2008), 'Asset specificity, experience, capability, host government intervention, and ownership-based entry mode strategy for SMEs in international markets', *International Journal of Commerce and Management*, **18** (3), 207–233.
Cohen, W. and Levinthal, D. (1990), 'Absorptive capacity: A new perspective on learning and innovation', *Administrative Science Quarterly*, **35** (1), 128–152.
Coviello, N. and Munro, H. (1997), 'Network relationships and the internationalisation process of small software firms', *International Business Review*, **6** (4), 361–386.
Cramton, C. (2001), 'The mutual knowledge problem and its consequences for dispersed collaboration', *Organization Science*, **12** (3), 346–371.
Daft, R. and Lengel, R. (1986), 'Organizational information requirements, media richness and structural design', *Management Science*, **32** (5), 554–571.
Daniel, E., Di Domenico, M., and Nunan, D. (2018), 'Virtual mobility and the lonely cloud: Theorizing the mobility-isolation paradox for self-employed knowledge-workers in the online home-based business context', *Journal of Management Studies*, **55** (1), 174–203.

Fernhaber, S., McDougall-Covin, P., and Shepherd, D. (2009), 'International entrepreneurship: Leveraging internal and external knowledge sources', *Strategic Entrepreneurship Journal*, **3** (4), 297–320.

Fletcher, M. and Harris, S. (2012), 'Knowledge acquisition for the internationalization of the smaller firm: Content and sources', *International Business Review*, **21** (4), 631–647.

Freeman, S., Hutchings, K., Lazaris, M., and Zyngier, S. (2010), 'A model of rapid knowledge development: The smaller born global firm', *International Business Review*, **19** (1), 70–84.

Gabrielsson M., Kirpalani V., Dimitratos P., Solberg C., and Zucchella A. (2008), 'Born globals: Propositions to help advance the theory', *International Business Review*, **17** (4), 385–401.

Ghauri, P. and Grønhaug, K. (2010), *Research Methods in Business Studies*, 4th ed. Edinburgh: Prentice Hall.

Ghoshal, S., Korine, H., and Szulanski, G. (1994), 'Interunit communication in multinational corporations', *Management Science,* **40** (1), 96–110.

Grant, R. (1996a), 'Prospering in dynamically competitive environments: Organizational capability as knowledge integration', *Organization Science*, **7** (4), 375–387.

Grant, R. (1996b), 'Toward a knowledge-based theory of the firm', *Strategic Management Journal*, **17** (winter special issue), 109–122.

Gupta, A. and Govindarajan, V. (2000), 'Knowledge flows within multinational corporations', *Strategic Management Journal*, **21** (4), 473–496.

Hashai, N. and Almor, T. (2004), 'Gradually internationalizing born global firms: An oxymoron?', *International Business Review*, **13** (4), 465–483.

Hennart, J. (2009), *Theories of the Multinational Enterprise*. Oxford: Oxford University Press.

Herbsleb, J. and Mockus, A. (2003), 'An empirical study of speed and communication in globally-distributed software development', *IEEE Transactions on Software Engineering*, **29** (3), 1–14.

Hymer, S. (1976), *The International Operations of National Firms: A Study of Foreign Direct Investment*. Cambridge, MA: MIT Press.

Knight, G. (2001), 'Entrepreneurship and strategy in the international SME', *Journal of International Management*, **7** (3), 155–171.

Knight, G. and Cavusgil, T. (2004), 'Innovation, organizational capabilities, and the born-global firm', *Journal of International Business Studies*, **35** (2), 124–141.

Knight, G. and Liesch, P. (2016), 'Internationalization: From incremental to born global', *Journal of World Business*, **51** (1), 93–102.

Kogut, B. and Zander, U. (1992), 'Knowledge of the firm, combinative capabilities, and the replication of technology', *Organization Science*, **3** (3), 383–397.

Kogut, B. and Zander, U. (1993), 'Knowledge of the firm and the evolutionary theory of the multinational corporation', *Journal of International Business Studies*, **24** (4), 625–646.

Kotlarsky, J. and Oshri, I. (2005), 'Social ties, knowledge sharing and successful collaboration in globally distributed system development projects', *European Journal of Information Systems*, **14** (1), 37–48.

Kuivalainen, O., Saarenketo, S., and Puumalainen, K. (2012), 'Start-up patterns of internationalization: A framework and its application in the context of knowledge-intensive SMEs', *European Management Journal*, **30** (4), 372–385.

Kuivalainen, O., Sundqvist, S., and Servais, P. (2007), 'Firms' degree of born-globalness, international entrepreneurial orientation and export performance', *Journal of World Business*, **42** (3), 253–267.

Lane, P. and Lubatkin, M. (1998), 'Relative absorptive capacity and interorganizational learning', *Strategic Management Journal*, **19** (5), 461–477.

Lu, J. and Beamish, P. (2001), 'The internationalization and performance of SMEs', *Strategic Management Journal*, **22** (6–7), 565–586.

Lu, J. and Beamish, P. (2006), 'SME internationalization and performance: Growth vs. profitability', *Journal of International Entrepreneurship*, **4** (1), 27–48.

Madhavan, R. and Grover, R. (1998), 'From embedded knowledge to embodied knowledge: New product development as knowledge management', *Journal of Marketing*, **62** (4), 1–12.

Manning, S., Massini, S., and Lewin, A. (2008), 'A dynamic perspective on next-generation offshoring: The global sourcing of science and engineering talent', *Academy of Management Perspectives*, **22** (3), 35–54.

Miles, M. and Huberman, A. (1994), *An Expanded Sourcebook: Qualitative Data Analysis*, 2nd Ed. London: SAGE Publications.

Monteiro, L., Arvidsson, N., and Birkinshaw, J. (2008), 'Knowledge flows within multinational corporations: Explaining subsidiary isolation and its performance implications', *Organization Science,* **19** (1), 90–107.

Nakos, G. and Brouthers, K. (2002), 'Entry mode choice of SMEs in central and eastern Europe', *Entrepreneurship: Theory and Practice*, **27** (1), 47–63.

Nonaka, I. (1994), 'A dynamic theory of organizational knowledge creation', *Organization Science*, **5** (1), 14–37.

O'Donnell, S. (2000), 'Managing foreign subsidiaries: Agents of headquarters, or an interdependent network?', *Strategic Management Journal*, **21** (5), 525–548.

Ouchi, W. (1979), 'A conceptual framework for the design of organizational control of mechanisms', *Management Science*, **25**, 833–848.

Oviatt, B. and McDougall, P. (1994), 'Toward a theory of international new ventures', *Journal of International Business Studies*, **25** (1), 45–64.

Park, T. and Rhee, J. (2012), 'Antecedents of knowledge competency and performance in born globals: The moderating effects of absorptive capacity', *Management Decision*, **50** (8), 1361–1381.

Pinho, J. (2007), 'The impact of ownership: Location-specific advantages and managerial characteristics on SME foreign entry mode choices', *International Marketing Review*, **24** (6), 715–734.

Preece, S., Miles, G., and Baetz, M. (1999), 'Explaining the international intensity and global diversity of early-stage technology-based firms', *Journal of Business Venturing*, **14** (3), 259–281.

Rodríguez-Serrano, M. Á., and Martín-Armario, E. (2019), 'Born-global SMEs, performance, and dynamic absorptive capacity: Evidence from Spanish firms', *Journal of Small Business Management*, **57** (2), 298–326.

Shuman, J. and Seeger, J. (1986), 'The theory and practice of strategic management in smaller rapid growth firms', *American Journal of Small Business*, **11** (1), 7–19.

Sidhu, J. and Volberda, H. (2011), 'Coordination of globally distributed teams: A co-evolution perspective on offshoring', *International Business Review*, **20** (3), 278–290.

Sinkovics, R., Penz, E., and Ghauri, P. (2008), 'Enhancing the trustworthiness of qualitative research in international business', *Management International Review*, **48** (6), 689–713.

Stinchcombe, A. (1965), 'Social structure and organizations'. In J. March (Ed.), *Handbook of Organizations*, Chicago, IL: Rand McNally, 142–193.

Subramaniam, M. and Venkatraman, N. (2001), 'Determinants of transnational new product development capability: Testing the influence of transferring and deploying tacit overseas knowledge', *Strategic Management Journal*, **22** (4), 359–378.

Sullivan Mort, G. and Weerawardena, J. (2006), 'Networking capability and international entrepreneurship: How networks function in Australian born global firms', *International Marketing Review*, **23** (5), 549–572.

Szulanski, G. (1996), 'Exploring internal stickiness: Impediments to the transfer of best practice within the firm', *Strategic Management Journal*, **17** (S2), 27–43.

Tagliaventi, M., Bertolotti, F., and Macrì, D. (2010), 'A perspective on practice in interunit knowledge sharing', *European Management Journal*, **28** (5), 331–345.

Teece, D., Pisano, G., and Shuen, A. (1997), 'Dynamic capabilities and strategic management', *Strategic Management Journal*, **18** (7), 509–533.

Vahlne, J-E., Ivarsson, I., and Johanson J. (2011), 'The tortuous road to globalization for Volvo's heavy truck business: Extending the scope of the Uppsala model', *International Business Review*, **20** (1), 1–14.

Van den Bosch, F., Volberda, H., and de Boer, M. (1999), 'Coevolution of firm absorptive capacity and knowledge environment: Organizational forms and combinative capabilities', *Organization Science*, **10** (5), 551–568.

Yamin, M. (1999), 'An evolutionary analysis of subsidiary innovation and reverse transfer in multinational companies'. In: F. Burton, M. Chapman, and A. Cross (Eds), *International Business Organization: Subsidiary Management Entry Strategies and Emerging Markets*, London: Macmillan, 67–83.

Yamin, M. and Sinkovics, R. (2007), 'ICT and the MNE reorganization: The paradox of control', *Critical Perspectives on International Business*, **3** (4), 322–336.

Yin, R. (2009), *Case Study Research: Design and Methods*, 4th Ed. London: SAGE Publication.

Zahra, S. and George, G. (2002), 'Absorptive capacity: A review, reconceptualization and extension', *Academy of Management Review*, **27** (2), 185–203.

Zahra, S., Neubaum, D., and Naldi, L. (2007), 'The effects of ownership and governance on SME's international knowledge-based resources', *Small Business Economics*, **29** (3), 309–327.

Zander, I., McDougall-Covin, P., and Rose, E. (2015), 'Born globals and international business: Evolution of a field of research', *Journal of International Business Studies*, **46** (1), 27–35.

3. Reverse knowledge transfer in multinational companies: evidence from Swiss manufacturing industry

Lamia Ben Hamida

INTRODUCTION

Foreign expansion enables multinational companies (MNCs) not only to internalize existing ownership advantages in other markets (Buckley and Casson 1976), but also to build new capabilities (Kuemmerle 1999). By establishing R&D units abroad, MNCs access new knowledge, ideas, and technologies and develop a better understanding of local customers' needs. By transferring these intangible resources to the corporate headquarters and to other parts of the organization (a process known as reverse knowledge transfer, RKT), MNCs may in turn increase their productivity performance in the home country. It follows that RKT is a strategic mechanism that may explain inter-firm performance variations (Piscitello and Santangelo 2008; Ben Hamida and Piscitello 2009).

A good relationship between foreign R&D units and their parent companies contributes to improving the reverse knowledge transfer process. The technological characteristics of MNCs' units at home are important too for efficiently absorbing the knowledge transferred from foreign units abroad. Prior studies have offered valuable insights, suggesting that knowledge transfer depends on factors such as the age and the entry mode of the foreign affiliate, its integration within the multinational corporation (Håkanson and Nobel 2001), its embeddedness in host countries (Belderbos 2003; Blomkvist 2009), its willingness to share knowledge (Gupta and Govindarajan 2000; Simonin 2004; Giroud et al. 2009), and the extent to which the subsidiary's knowledge is related to the parent's knowledge base (Mudambi et al. 2007).

Despite their valuable contributions, prior studies analyzing the factors influencing the process of knowledge transfer have ignored the role of the relationship management between foreign affiliates and the parent MNC in enhancing the RKT process. In addition, little attention has been paid by scholars to examine the effect of RKT on innovation and productivity performance of the parent and home units of MNCs (Sanchez-Vidal et al. 2016). This chapter tends to fill in the gap and extend the RKT literature by:

a. Identifying the roles of collaboration and cooperation in the management between foreign R&D units and their parent MNCs in explaining the RKT process. It examines the contribution of MNC transmission and integration mechanisms to an effective knowledge transfer from foreign to home units (Hypotheses 1 and 2). "It is less trivial to expect that the level of reverse knowledge transfer will increase monotonically" (Mudambi et al., 2014, p. 51). RKT is a "complex process and as such should be analyzed in terms of all of its components and its broader context" (Kogut and De Mello, 2017, p. 14).

b. Testing the extent to which RKT enhances the productivity performance of the MNC at home (Hypothesis 3). We argue that only home units that have high technological capacity are able to absorb productively foreign knowledge transferred from their foreign affiliates.

To test our framework, we examine how Swiss MNCs succeed in increasing their performance by sourcing knowledge and technologies from their globally dispersed R&D subsidiaries. Switzerland is a particularly interesting case study. Swiss MNCs have been increasingly investing in R&D abroad since 1992, even more than in the home country (SFSO 2008) – their foreign R&D expenditures increased by 53% between 2000 and 2012 to reach 15 billion francs in 2012 (9.788 billion francs in 2000) (SFSO 2013).

The structure of the chapter is as follows. Following this introduction, the next section analyzes the theoretical framework underlying our hypotheses, together with a review of the relevant empirical studies. The third section presents our method. The fourth section analyzes the interviews we held with MNCs in Switzerland, and the fifth section reports the estimation results of RKT effects. The sixth section concludes and discusses limitations and future research.

THEORETICAL BACKGROUND

MNCs often conduct R&D in locations where they can further develop their innovation and productivity capabilities. They are increasingly decentralizing their units of R&D by investing abroad (Pearce and Papanastassiou 1999). This investment helps foreign units acquire the knowledge of the host country and learn from innovation made by host country's firms. This knowledge could be transferred back to investing MNCs' units in the home country by means of RKT. MNCs involved in the RKT process try to find technical diversity and capabilities that are complementary to those available in their home markets (Cantwell 1989; Ben Hamida and Piscitello 2010).

Prior RKT studies have analyzed the factors explaining the process of knowledge transfer from R&D units to the parent company and other units at home (namely, the entry mode of R&D units, their embeddedness in host countries, their investment motivations). By doing so, existing studies have observed the RKT phenomenon from the position of the foreign R&D firms alone. However, they have paid very little attention to examining the role of the relationship management between foreign and home units in RKT flows (Kumar, 2013). In addition, the resultant effect of RKT on productivity performance of the home units is still underexplored. "Despite the fact that many studies have investigated the RKT phenomenon, its effects on the receiving unit have usually been implicitly believed to be beneficial" (Rabbiosi and Santangelo, 2013, p. 168).

Concerning the RKT Process

Following RKT literature, MNCs make R&D investments that will either assist them in exploiting existing technological capabilities or in seeking new competences, sourcing knowledge and augmenting their assets. Knowledge-seeking investments are specifically designed to identify and internalize new knowledge from different markets, whereas knowledge-exploiting investments usually attempt to adapt the technology created by other subsidiaries to host countries' preferences (Kuemmerle 1997; Cantwell & Piscitello 2005). Knowledge-exploiting foreign units are therefore less interested in identifying and using knowledge and technologies from the location in which they operate. It is argued that MNCs use knowledge-seeking investment to source host countries' techniques and competences (Almeida 1996; Cantwell 1995; Dunning 1998; UNCTAD 2001, 2005) and then transfer them back to the parent company or other home units (Mudambi et al. 2008).

Knowledge developed abroad and transferred back to home country units depends on the embeddedness of foreign affiliates in the host country environment (Frost 2001; Piscitello and Rabbiosi 2004). Strong relationships between foreign affiliates and local businesses in the host country (e.g. suppliers, customers, competitors, R&D institutions and universities) enable rapid access to technological information (Andersson et al. 2005 and Giroud et al. 2009). When the environment of the R&D unit is familiar and better understood, knowledge-seeking activities are more efficient and the number of errors and unnecessary steps lower (Katila and Ahuja 2002). This would decrease the uncertainties of the parent company about the relevance of foreign new knowledge and enhance its interest and motivation in accessing external knowledge. In addition, compared with greenfield firms, acquiring R&D units in locations with rich resources (scientific talent and high quality infrastructure) reinforces the degree of the conviction of the parent company investing in knowledge-seeking activities.[1] The business network of acquired affiliates and the interactions between scientists and technicians engaged in R&D reinforce their embeddedness in host countries. This would be a valuable source of knowledge for foreign affiliates since it helps augment their competitive advantages and create new advantages by tapping into host countries' capabilities (Braconier et al. 2001), and then enlarging the knowledge base of the multinational group, and improving its performance.

Compared with traditional diffusion of knowledge from the parent to foreign affiliates, RKT depends heavily on the interest and commitment of the parent company in integrating foreign technological capabilities in its existing technological routines (Yang et al. 2008). Good relationships between foreign and home units facilitate the transfer and the integration of foreign knowledge. The direct contact between foreign and home units' employees is the most appropriate transmission channel for RKT,[2] since knowledge tends to be highly specific to the originating firm and tacit in nature, and then needs to be decoded. The richness of this channel depends heavily on the knowledge integration mechanisms employed by the parent company to successfully internalize new knowledge and therefore enhance the knowledge base of the MNC. We argue that appropriate knowledge integration mechanisms contribute to accelerating the RKT process. Parent companies need to set up an appropriate relationship management in the MNC group to manage the relationship between foreign and home units' employees in order to enhance their collaboration, communication, and interaction activities. Knowledge integration mechanisms lubricate this relationship and improve the RKT process (Ambos and Ambos 2009; Jeong et al. 2016).

According to Jeong et al. (2016), there exist informal and formal knowledge integration mechanisms. Formal mechanisms refer to key formal structural mechanisms for integrating multiple MNC's units, such as special committees and task force teams, whereas informal mechanisms consist of corporate socialization mechanisms that build interpersonal familiarity (Gupta and Govindarajan 2000). Both are important for sharing knowledge and facilitating RKT.

Many have studied the RKT process from the position of the foreign R&D firms alone (the entry mode of R&D units, their embeddedness in host countries, their investment motivations, and so on). Scholars have paid very little attention to analyzing the role of knowledge transmission and integration mechanisms on RKT. We argue that the parent company should have an appropriate relationship management within the MNC group. This is important for developing the direct contact between its home and foreign units' employees by means of formal and informal mechanisms. These management practices facilitate RKT activities and contribute to gaining the most benefit from foreign knowledge seeking investment.

Concerning the RKT Effect

The RKT process consists of seeking new knowledge from host economies, transferring it by means of RKT, decoding and integrating it productively in the knowledge base of parent MNCs, so raising their innovation performance, productivity and competitive advantage (Cantwell & Piscitello 1999; Griffith et al. 2004; and Piscitello & Rabbiosi 2006). The returns of reverse knowledge transfer depend therefore on the capacity of the parent MNC to absorb the knowledge transferred from their foreign R&D units. Jimenez-Jimenez et al. (2019) found that the absorptive capacity of the parent MNC facilitates RKT.

Absorptive capacity refers to the firm's ability to recognize valuable new knowledge, integrate it into the firm, and use it productively (Cohen and Levinthal 1990). Thereby, the firm's level of absorptive capacity depends upon its existing level of technological competence as well as its learning and investment efforts undertaken to be able to use foreign knowledge productively. "Absorption is not purely about imitation" (Narula and Marin 2003), in that technologies have a certain firm-specific aspect to them and then need to be decoded so as to be efficiently used by MNCs at home, raising their productivity. The richness of knowledge transfer and integration mechanisms contributes to the internalization of foreign technologies and enhances the knowledge base of the MNC at home. The use of unsuitable mechanisms, however, may cause loss of knowledge or high communication costs (Pedersen et al. 2003 and Piscitello and Rabbiosi 2004).

We argue that successful knowledge transfer requires from the receiving units at home a certain degree of technological capacity. Only units possessing sufficient technological capacity are likely to decode and efficiently exploit the knowledge that foreign R&D affiliates source from other countries around the world. Low technological capacity may thwart critical learning processes at the firm, which in turn would not benefit from new technologies (Cohen and Levinthal 1989; Piscitello and Rabbiosi 2004; Michel and Narula, 2009).

HYPOTHESES

Our discussion above points to the research model shown in Figure 3.1.

Hypothesis 1: The use of appropriate knowledge transmission mechanisms by parent MNCs facilitates and accelerates the transfer of knowledge from knowledge-seeking R&D affiliates to home units.
Hypothesis 2: The use of appropriate integration mechanisms by parent MNCs facilitates and accelerates the transfer of knowledge from knowledge-seeking R&D affiliates to home units.
Hypothesis 3: The effect of the reverse knowledge transfer is higher when receiving units at home possess higher technological capacity than when they have lower technological capacity.

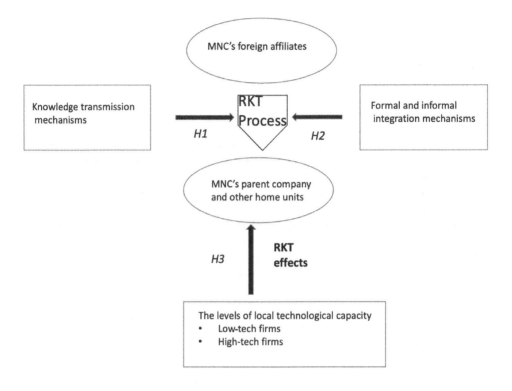

Figure 3.1   Research model

METHODS

To test our hypotheses, we employ both qualitative and quantitative methods. Mixed methods are regarded as "a good thing… they combine confirmatory and exploratory research at the same time…present greater diversity of views..." (Easterby-Smith et al. 2012, p. 63). We use interviews to examine the RKT process within MNCs and their relationship management strategy (Hypotheses 1 and 2), and we test the effects of RKT on home MNC performance using regression (Hypothesis 3). Appropriate transmission and integration mechanisms contribute to improving the RKT process by transferring the knowledge the MNCs' home units need. These units take advantage from RKT when they are able to decode and use foreign knowledge productively. This benefit depends on the technological capacity of home units. Our Hypotheses 1 and 2 concern the RKT process whereas Hypothesis 3 is devoted to test RKT effects.

Interview Methodology

We apply a qualitative method based on interviews to understand the RKT process within MNCs. We are interested in individual perceptions of parent MNCs regarding relationship management of their employees with those of their foreign R&D units. This method offers broad and rich insights of knowledge transmission and integration mechanisms employed by parent MNCs in order to facilitate and accelerate RKT from knowledge-seeking R&D investment.

Data collection was carried out by means of face-to-face interviews of different senior managers of private firms doing foreign R&D investment. Our interviews are conducted throughout the years 2012–2013 in the following industries: food, chemical/pharmaceuticals, non-metal mineral products, metalworking, machinery, banking, electronic equipment, watches, computer activities and consulting services. The interviews lasted on average 45 minutes per interview and were recorded. They address questions about:

1. The characteristics of MNCs' foreign affiliates and host country resources: What are the mandates assigned to foreign units? What are their principal activities? Are they acquired or greenfield units? What are the motives for doing foreign R&D investment? Do they collaborate with universities, suppliers, and/or other firms in the host market?
2. The relationship between the MNCs' parent company in Switzerland and their foreign affiliates: To what extent are foreign affiliates independent? To what extent are they integrated with the parent MNC? Do they work on technologies, products, and/or process that the parent MNC considers complementary to its existing knowledge? How does the parent company cooperate with their foreign affiliates? How does the parent company motivate employees of their foreign affiliates? How does it monitor innovations created externally? Does it have informal relations with the managers and the employees of their foreign affiliates? How do these interactions contribute in knowledge transfer between home and foreign firms?
3. The characteristics of the parent MNC: Does the parent company recognize the importance of the knowledge transferred by its foreign affiliates? Does it benefit from foreign specific knowledge, know-how and special skills? How does it succeed in absorbing and integrating the foreign knowledge in its existing technological routines? Does it give reward and recognition to individuals/units who integrate successfully foreign knowledge?

Regression Model

We model the effects of RKT from outward foreign investment in R&D for manufacturing using a production function,[3] in which the change in the natural log value added of the *i*th parent MNC at home is determined as follows:

$$\Delta LnY_{i,j} = \alpha_0 + \alpha_1 \Delta LnK_{i,j} + \alpha_2 \Delta LnL_{i,j} + \alpha_3 RKT_{i,j} + \alpha_4 Size_{i,j} + \alpha_5 Industry_j + \varepsilon_{i,j} \quad (1)$$

where the subscripts *i* and *j* denote firm and industry, Δ represents changes in the variables between 2003 and 2008, and α_0 to α_5 the parameters to be estimated. Table 3.1 describes the variables and their measurements.

Table 3.1   *Variable definitions*

Variables	Definitions
$\Delta LnY_{i,j}$	The log change in value added at firm level.
$\Delta LnK_{i,j}$	The log change in physical capital, measured by gross investment at firm level.
ΔLnL_{ij}	The log change in total number of employees at firm level.
$Size_{ij}$	The log total sales of the firm.
RT	A dummy variable equals 1 if there exists provision of services from the affiliates to the MNCs' units at home, 0 otherwise.
RKT	A dummy variable equals 1 if there exists provision of knowledge and know-how from the affiliates to the MNCs' units at home, 0 otherwise.
High–tech_industry	A dummy variable equals 1 if the firm fits in industries with high technological level, 0 otherwise.
Low–tech_industry	A dummy variable equals 1 if the firm fits in industries with low technological level, 0 otherwise.

Y denotes value added at firm level, *K* its physical capital measured by the gross investment, and L its employment measured by the number of employees. *Size*, defined by the sales of firm *i*, is expected to increase productivity as larger sized firms may be more efficient (Dimelis and Louri, 2002). The inclusion of industry dummies, Industry,[4] in equation (1) and the use of changes over the time control for the industry-specific productivity differences; they correct for the omission of unobservable variables that might undermine the relationship between reverse transfer variables and productivity growth of domestic firms at home (Aitken and Harrison 1999; Narula and Marin 2003).[5]

To assess the RKT effects on productivity performance of MNCs at home, we employ two variables (*RT* and *RKT*). First, *RT* is a dummy variable that denotes the provision of services (raw materials, intermediate products, patents, final products, software packages, and so on) from the affiliates to the parent company at home. Second, *RKT* is a dummy variable that denotes the provision of knowledge and know-how from the affiliates to the MNCs' units at home. Each variable is separately tested in order to assess the contribution of the knowledge transfer *RKT* regarding *RT*, and to demonstrate whether the effect of *RT* is to some extent the outcome of knowledge transfer controlled by *RKT*.

To test our Hypothesis 3, we divide our full sample of firms into two sub-samples characterized by the absorptive capacity levels of the MNCs' units at home and we proceed to make various tests using equation (1). We use the technological levels of Swiss industries (high-tech/low-tech) to determine the absorptive capacity levels of the MNCs' units at home. We argue that high technology firms capable of investing in the absorption of foreign knowledge should fit in industries with high technological level, and vice versa.[6]

The data we use to test our Hypotheses 3 is derived from the internationalization activity survey (2010) conducted at KOF institute.[7] The response rate was 42%. The survey was based on a stratified sample of firms according to the industry affiliation and the industry-specific firm size classes. Individual information covers the technological and international investment behaviors and productivity performance of firms located in Switzerland with at least five employees providing a full coverage of large firms. The data allows testing of the effects of international activities on innovation and productivity performance of firms in Switzerland.

All results refer to robust ordinary least squares (OLS) estimations of equation (1).

INTERVIEW RESULTS

The main focus during the interviews is to understand parent MNCs' views of RKT, relationship management strategy, and knowledge integration mechanisms. The interviews were transcribed and analyzed in order to identify some convergences of managers' perceptions of the reverse knowledge transfer process.

First, interviewed MNCs broadly invested in greenfields and acquisitions. Although they experienced some difficulties in integrating existing host firms' organization, the business network of acquired affiliates with host country firms was regarded as a valuable source of knowledge for their affiliates, in that it helped augment their competitive advantages and create new advantages by tapping into host countries' capabilities. R&D was carried out by R&D departments as well as by other firms' business units (such as marketing, sales, production, and so on.) In addition, foreign affiliates collaborated closely with suppliers and other companies at host markets.

Second, the interviewees qualified their affiliates as rather independent and fully integrated. Parent MNCs encourage too often labor mobility between MNCs' units. They also organized problem-solving sessions to better benefit from the synergies developed by the task force team. This stimulates knowledge transfer from foreign units and fosters local skill building.

Third, to monitor innovations created externally, all the know-how is registered in internal corporate programs in order to facilitate their findings afterwards. Most parent MNCs employed corporate socialization mechanisms based on informal interpersonal relationships with their foreign affiliates. They found these relationships very helpful for sharing knowledge and facilitating RKT. One manager from the interviewees said:

> At the very beginning, they (foreign units) had almost full autonomy. It was necessary to put up the business. But more mature business needs the reorganization. More closeness, more formalized, discussions should be closer, so we are in the process of becoming closer each to other. It is not only to control them better, but also to share the information better, because most of the time the affiliates have the same problems. And why not share these problems? So we put them together to exchange the information, their experiences, and their ideas so they could help each other. We are in the process to make them a little bit closer and to see other markets, to understand better each other: they understand better our strategy and we integrate them better and also understand each other better … The whole company is depending on the foreign affiliates' inputs, because, otherwise, the developing center in Switzerland will develop products that nobody needs.

Finally, most interviewees recognized that their firms benefit from the know-how, specific knowledge and special skills of their foreign affiliates. All participants confirmed the high importance of knowledge transferred by their affiliates.

REGRESSION RESULTS

How MNCs' units at home in Switzerland succeed in increasing their performance by sourcing knowledge and technologies from their globally dispersed R&D affiliates is the focus of our regression analysis.

Although most interviewees believed that the knowledge and special skills of their foreign affiliates are beneficial for their units in Switzerland, interviews analysis could not assess the effective benefit of RKT effect. In this context, regression analysis is the best tool allowing this kind of measurement. We regress the effects of RKT using a growth model and argue that this effect does not occur automatically; it depends rather on the technological characteristics of the receiving units at home.

The growth model presented earlier is estimated using the subsamples of MNCs' units in Switzerland according to different levels of their technological capacity. We employed ordinary least squares and conducted various robustness tests to address problems that could arise when estimating production functions using cross-sectional firm-level data. All standard errors are corrected for heteroscedasticity. The simultaneity problem that results from the fact that the firm may choose its output and input levels simultaneously, inducing high correlations between the parameters of the input variables and the error term, is minimized due to the fact that all production variables are measured in differences from their logarithmic levels (Dimelis, 2005).

In regressions 2.1–2.4 in Table 3.2, we tested the effect of *RT* and *RKT* on the productivity growth of Swiss MNCs and its relationship with the level of technological capacity of MNCs' units at home. The level of technological capacity is proxied by the technological level of its corresponding industry.[8] The value added of the MNCs in Switzerland increases with changes in their employment, their physical capital, and their size.[9] The estimated coefficients of *RT* are insignificantly positive for firms in high-tech industries and negative for firms in low-tech ones. This demonstrates that only firms with high technological capacities absorb and benefit from the provision of services from their foreign affiliates. This benefit is larger and significant for *RKT* (regression 2.2), indicating that this kind of firm succeeds in exploiting the reverse knowledge transfer by productively using foreign knowledge. The size of such benefits is 0.09, implying that the transfer of knowledge significantly leads to as much as 0.09 point increases in domestic productivity of these firms. Conversely, firms with low technological capacities appear to not benefit from new technologies as the estimated coefficient of *RKT* remains insignificant in regression 2.4. These findings corroborate Hypothesis 3, in which only receiving units at home possessing higher technological capacity are able to benefit from RKT.

Table 3.2   *Estimation results regarding the absorptive capacity of the knowledge receiver (parent MNC)*

Variables	High-tech industry		Low-tech industry	
	(2.1)	(2.2)	(2.3)	(2.4)
ΔLog_K_j	0.07***	0.07***	0.01	0.01
ΔLog_L	0.33***	0.35***	0.66***	0.65***
Size	0.03**	0.03*	0.01	0.01
RT	0.03	–	–0.01	–
RKT	–	0.09*	–	0.03
Industry	Yes	Yes	Yes	Yes
R^2	0.36	0.33	0.61	0.61
N	156	156	70	70

Note: All standard errors, in parentheses, are corrected for heteroscedasticity.
*, **, and *** denote significance at the 10%, 5%, and 1% levels, respectively.

CONCLUSION

This study examines how and when units in the home country increase their productivity performance by exploiting knowledge from foreign R&D units. We add to scholarly understanding of the value of foreign R&D investment by (a) examining the factors shaping the RKT process, especially, how parent MNCs manage their different relationships with their foreign affiliates, and (b) testing the resultant effect of RKT on productivity performance of MNCs' units at home.

Based on the analysis of 23 interviews conducted with top and middle managers of parent MNCs in Switzerland, we found that firms too often encourage labor mobility between MNCs' units (both foreign and home units). They manage sessions to solve problems and benefit from knowledge sharing between employees. They encourage formal and informal relationships by employing collaboration and integration mechanisms. This stimulates the RKT process.

Based on a sample of Swiss manufacturing MNCs, we show the importance of considering the technological behavior of the knowledge receiver when evaluating RKT effects generated from outward FDI in R&D. Our regression results show that only firms having a large technological capacity to absorb benefit from RKT effects. This indicates that MNCs' home units have to augment their technological capacities to be able to productively absorb knowledge and know-how from foreign R&D units.

The findings may help firms and countries to formulate policies to improve the transfer of knowledge from foreign to home units and maximize the effects of RKT. Since the technological behavior of a knowledge receiver appears to be a key determinant of the RKT process and effects, the Swiss government has to take into account that the heterogeneity of firms plays a crucial role in determining whether they benefit from foreign R&D investment in terms of RKT. Suggestions with respect to encouraging foreign R&D in Switzerland in light of such findings must consider that firms, according to their existing technological capacities, do not benefit from RKT effects in the same way. Parent MNCs' absorptive capacity should be improved in order to facilitate the RKT process (Jimenez-Jimenez et al., 2019).

Actions, in line with interview results, should also invite knowledge-seeking investors to mobilize their collaboration and integration mechanisms in order to facilitate formal and informal knowledge exchange between foreign and home employees and accelerate the process of reverse knowledge transfer.

Our study has some limitations, since it has not analyzed the behavior of the knowledge sender on the RKT process and effects (entry mode, FDI motivations, embeddedness levels in host countries, the host location, affiliate ages, etc.).[10] We have concentrated our research in this chapter on the behavior of the knowledge receiver in terms of their technological capacity to absorb foreign knowledge as well as their capacity to manage their relationship with foreign affiliates to receive the best knowledge they needed. The role of foreign affiliates in enhancing this relationship has not been investigated in this chapter.

The behavior of foreign affiliates in terms of the RKT process and home effects should be analyzed in future research. We believe that the RKT process and benefits tend to increase when foreign units are interested in transferring and sharing their knowledge with home units.

ACKNOWLEDGMENTS

I would like to acknowledge the RCSO program of the HES-SO for financing this research and Mrs. Valeriya Dominé for her help in qualitative analysis.

NOTES

1. The entry mode of the affiliate can also influence the knowledge transfer within MNCs (Kogut and Chang 1991; Kogut and Zander 1993; Bresman et al. 1999; Håkanson and Nobel 2000; Lane et al. 2001).
2. The literature recognizes a variety of transmission channels, such as personal movement, training, observation, patents, scientific publications and presentations (Argote and Ingram 2000).
3. The derivation of this model is explained in the appendix.
4. There are 18 industry dummies accounting for manufacturing.
5. The use of first differences between two time periods with a time lag of three years will control for fixed differences in productivity levels across industries (Narula and Marin 2003; Dimelis 2005).
6. Unfortunately, the data available does not allow us to precisely assess the existing technological capacity of the firm as well as its investment and learning investment in order to absorb foreign knowledge.
7. The questionnaire is downloadable from https://kof.ethz.ch/en/surveys/structural-surveys/other -surveys/internationalisation-2010.html
8. We use the industry classification of KOF institute.
9. The estimated coefficient of *Size* and physical capital are only significant in regressions 2.1 and 2.2 with a subsample of firms in high-tech industries.
10. Driffield et al. (2016) analyzed the affiliate performance of RKT effects. Rabbiosi and Santangelo (2013) analyzed the effect of affiliate age.

REFERENCES

Aitken, B.J. and Harrison, A.E. (1999), Do domestic firms benefit from direct foreign investment? Evidence from Venezuela. *American Economic Review*, 89, 605–618.

Almeida, P. (1996), Knowledge sourcing by foreign multinationals: Patent citation analysis in the US semiconductor industry. *Strategic Management Journal*, 17, 155–165.

Ambos, T.C. and Ambos, B. (2009), The impact of distance on knowledge transfer effectiveness in multinational corporations. *Journal of International Management*, 15(1), 1–14.

Andersson, U., Bjorkman, I. and Forsgren, M. (2005), Managing subsidiary knowledge creation: The effect of control mechanisms on subsidiary local embeddedness. *International Business Review*, 14, 521–538.

Argote, L. and Ingram, P. (2000), Knowledge transfer: A basis for competitive advantage in firms. *Organizational Behavior and Human Decision Processes*, 82(1), 150–169.

Belderbos, R. (2003), Entry mode, organizational learning, and R&D in foreign affiliates: Evidence from Japanese firms. *Strategic Management Journal*, 24, 235–259.

Ben Hamida, L. and Piscitello, L. (2009), Are foreign and domestic R&D activities complements? Evidence from Swiss manufacturing firms. In Proceedings of EIBA Conference, *Reshaping the Boundaries of the Firm in an Era of Global Interdependence*, December 13–15, Valencia.

Ben Hamida, L. and Piscitello, L. (2010), The impact of foreign R&D activities on the MNC's perfor-mance at home: Evidence from the case of Swiss manufacturing firm. *BJIR Conference and special issue on Outsourcing/Offshoring of Service Work*, November.

Blomkvist, K. (2009), Reverse technology diffusion: On the diffusion of technological capabilities from advanced foreign subsidiaries to headquarters of the MNC. In Proceedings of EIBA Conference,

Reshaping the Boundaries of the Firm in an Era of Global Interdependence, December 13–15, Valencia.

Braconier, H., Ekholm, K., and Midelfart-Knarvik, K.-H. (2001), Does FDI work as a channel for R&D spillovers? Evidence based on Swedish data. *Review of World Economics*, 137(4), 644–665.

Bresman, J., Birkinshaw, J., and Nobel, R. (1999), Knowledge transfer in international acquisitions. *Journal of International Business Studies*, 30, 439–462.

Buckley, P.J. and Casson, M.C. (1976), *The Future of the Multinational Enterprise*. London: Macmillan.

Cantwell, J. (1989), *Technological Innovation and Multinational Corporations*. Oxford: Basil Blackwell.

Cantwell, J. (1995), The globalisation of technology: What remains of the product cycle model? *Cambridge Journal of Economics*, 19, 155–174.

Cantwell, J.A. and Piscitello, L. (1999), The emergence of corporate international networks for the accumulation of dispersed technological competences. *Management International Review*, 39, 123–147.

Cantwell, J. and Piscitello, L. (2005), Recent location of foreign-owned research and development activities by large multinational corporations in the European regions: The role of spillovers and externalities. *Regional Studies*, 39, 1–16.

Cohen, W.M. and Levinthal, D.A. (1989), Innovation and learning: The two faces of R&D. *Economic Journal*, 99(3), 569–596.

Cohen, W. and Levinthal, D. (1990), Absorptive capability: A new perspective on learning and innovation. *Administrative Science Quarterly*, 35, 128–152.

Dimelis, S.P. (2005), Spillovers from foreign direct investment and firm growth: Technological, financial and market structure effects. *International Journal of the Economics of Business*, 12(1), 85–104.

Dimelis, S. and Louri, H. (2002), Foreign investment and efficiency benefits: A conditional quantile analysis. *Oxford Economic Papers*, 54, 449–469.

Driffield, N., Love, J.H., and Yang, Y. (2016), Reverse international knowledge transfer in the MNE: (Where) does affiliate performance boost parent performance? *Research Policy*, 45(2), 491–506.

Dunning, J.H. (1998), Location and the multinational enterprise: A neglected factor? *Journal of International Business Studies*, 29(1), 45–66.

Easterby-Smith, M., Thorpe, R., and Jackson, P.R. (2012), *Management Research*. Sage.

Frost, T.S. (2001), The geographic sources of foreign subsidiaries' innovation. *Strategic Management Journal*, 22, 101–123.

Giroud, A., Tavani, Z.N., and Sinkovics, R. (2009), Reverse knowledge transfer within MNCs: The case of knowledge-intensive services in the UK. In Proceedings of EIBA Conference, *Reshaping the Boundaries of the Firm in an Era of Global Interdependence*, December 13–15, Valencia.

Griffith, R., Harrison, R., and Van Reenen, J. (2004), How special is the special relationship? Using the impact of US R&D spillovers on UK firms as a test of technology sourcing. CEPR Discussion Paper, No. 4698.

Griliches, Z. (1998), *Practicing Econometrics: Essays in Methods and Applications*. Series: Economists of the Twentieth Century, Edward Elgar Publishing.

Gupta, A.K. and Govindarajan, V. (2000), Knowledge flows within multinational corporations. *Strategic Management Journal*, 21, 473–496.

Håkanson, L. and Nobel, R. (2000), Technology characteristics and reverse technology transfer. *Management International Review*, 40(special issue 1), 29–48.

Håkanson, L. and Nobel R. (2001), Organization characteristics and reverse technology transfer. *Management International Review*, Special Issue, 41, 392–420.

Jeong, G.-Y., Chae, M-S., and Park, BII. (2016), Reverse knowledge transfer from subsidiaries to multinational companies: Focusing on factors affecting market knowledge transfer. *Canadian Journal of Administrative Sciences*, http://onlinelibrary.wiley.com/doi/10.1002/cjas.1366/full

Jimenez-Jimenez, D., Martinez-Costa, M., and Sanz Valle, R. (2019), Reverse knowledge transfer and innovation in MNCs. *European Journal of Innovation Management*, https://doi.org/10.1108/EJIM-10-2018-0226

Katila, R. and Ahuja, G. (2002), Something old, something new: A longitudinal study of search behaviour and new product introduction. *Academy of Management Journal*, 45(6), 1183–1194.

Kogut, B. and Chang, S.J. (1991), Technological capabilities and Japanese foreign direct investment in the United States. *Review of Economics and Statistics*, 7, 401–413.

Kogut, C.S. and de Mello, R.C. (2017), Reverse knowledge transfer in multinational companies: A systematic literature review. *Brazilian Administration Review*, 14(1), 1–25.

Kogut, B. and Zander, U. (1993), Knowledge of the firm and the evolutionary theory of the multinational corporation. *Journal of International Business Studies*, 24(4), 625–646.

Kuemmerle, W. (1997), Building effective capabilities abroad. *Harvard Business Review*, March–April, 61–70.

Kuemmerle, W. (1999), The drivers of foreign direct investment into research and development: An empirical investigation. *Journal of International Business Studies*, 30, 1–24.

Kumar, N. (2013), Managing reverse knowledge flow in multinational corporations. *Journal of Knowledge Management*, 17(5), 695–708.

Lane, P.J., Salk, J.E., and Lyles, M.A. (2001), Absorptive capacity, learning, and performance in international joint venture. *Strategic Management Journal*, 22, 1139–1161.

Michel, J. and Narula, R. (2009), Reverse knowledge transfer and its implications for European policy. UNU-MERIT Working Paper Series 035, United Nations University, Maastricht Economic and Social Research and Training Centre on Innovation and Technology.

Mudambi, R., Mudambi, S.M., and Navarra, P. (2007), Global innovation in MNCs: The effects of subsidiary self-determination and teamwork. *The Journal of Product Innovation Management*, 24, 442–455.

Mudambi, R., Piscitello, L., and Rabbiosi L. (2008), Mandates and mechanisms: Reverse knowledge transfer in MNEs. Institute of Global Management Studies, Temple University, Fox School of Business, Discussion Paper 08-0129.

Mudambi, R., Piscitello, L., and Rabbiosi, L. (2014), Reverse knowledge transfer in MNEs: Subsidiary innovativeness and entry modes. *Long Range Planning*, 47(1–2), 49–63.

Narula, R. and Marin, A. (2003), FDI spillovers, absorptive capacities and human capital development: Evidence from Argentina. Working Paper, No. 2003-016, Maastricht Economic Research Institute on Innovation and Technology, The Netherlands.

Pearce, R. and Papanastassiou, M. (1999), Overseas R&D and the strategic evolution of MNEs. *Research Policy*, 28, 23–41.

Pedersen, T., Petersen, B., and Sharma, D.D. (2003), Knowledge transfer performance of multinational companies. *Management International Review*, 43(3), 69–90.

Piscitello, L. and Rabbiosi, L. (2004), More inward FDI? Medium-term effects of foreign acquisitions on target company productivity. *Applied Economics Quarterly*, 1(1), 21–40.

Piscitello, L. and Rabbiosi. L. (2006), How does knowledge transfer from foreign subsidiaries affect parent companies' innovative capacity. DRUID Working Papers, No. 06-22.

Piscitello, L. and Santangelo, G.D. (2008), The impact of international offshoring of R&D on the home country's knowledge creation. Preliminary evidence from OECD countries, Paper presented at the AIB Annual Conference, Milan, July.

Rabbiosi, L. and Santangelo, G.D. (2013), Parent company benefits from reverse knowledge transfer: The role of the liability of newness in MNEs. *Journal of World Business*, 48, 160–170

Sanchez-Vidal, M.E., Sanz-Valle, R. & Barba-Aragon, M.I. (2016), Repatriates and reverse knowledge transfer in MNCs. *The International Journal of Human Resource Management*, 29(10), 1767–1785.

SFSO (2008), Aspects internationaux de la recherche et développement suisse en 2008: De l'internationalisation des entreprises à la collaboration internationale publique SFSO publication. Neuchâtel.

SFSO (2013), Dépenses et personnel de recherche et développement des entreprises privées en Suisse 2012: Dépenses de recherche et développement toujours en augmentation, mais la conjoncture pèse. SFSO publication. Neuchâtel.

Simonin, B.L. (2004), An empirical investigation of the process of knowledge transfer in international strategic alliances. *Journal of International Business Studies*, 35, 407–427.

UNCTAD (2001), *World Investment Report 2001: Promoting Linkages*. United Nations publication, Sales No. E.01.II.D.12. Geneva and New York.

UNCTAD (2005), *Prospects for Foreign Direct Investment and the Strategies of Transnational Corporations, 2005–2008*. United Nations publication. Sales no. E.05.II.D.32. New York and Geneva.

Yang, Q., Mudambi, R., and Meyer, K.E. (2008), Conventional and reverse knowledge flows in multinational corporations. *Journal of Management*, 34, 882–902.

APPENDIX

The Model

Equation (1) is derived from a Cobb-Douglas production function with value-added Y, a function of two inputs, capital and labor

$$Y_{i,j,t} = A_{i,j,t} L_{i,j,t}^{\alpha 1} K_{i,j,t}^{\alpha 2} \quad (2)$$

The level of productivity is given by $A_{i,j,t}$, which is assumed to vary across firms within each sector j and across time t.

After taking logarithms of the variables to get equation (2) into a linear form and adding a stochastic disturbance term $U_{i,j,t}$ to account for variations in the productive capabilities of the ith firm, we can rewrite equation (2) for $t - 5 = 2003$ and $t = 2008$ as

$$LnY_{i,j,t} = a_{i,j,t} + \alpha_1 LnL_{i,j,t} + \alpha_2 LnK_{i,j,t} + u_{i,j,t}; \quad \left(a_{i,j,t} = LnA_{i,j,t} \right) \quad (3)$$

$$LnY_{i,j,t-5} = a_{i,j,t-5} + \alpha_1 LnL_{i,j,t-5} + \alpha_2 LnK_{i,j,t-5} + u_{i,j,t-5}; \quad \left(a_{i,j,t-5} = LnA_{i,j,t-5} \right) \quad (4)$$

Then, taking the difference (3)–(4) yields the change in value-added for domestic firms between 2008 and 2003. Δ denotes the $\Delta LnY_{i,j} = \Delta a_{i,j} + \alpha_1 \Delta LnL_{i,j} + \alpha_2 \Delta LnK_{i,j} + \varepsilon_{i,j}$ ariation between 2008 and 2003

$$\Delta LnY_{i,j} = \Delta a_{i,j} + \alpha_1 \Delta LnL_{i,j} + \alpha_2 \Delta LnK_{i,j} + \varepsilon_{i,j} \quad (5)$$

We test the hypothesis that the firm's productivity growth is affected by the reverse of knowledge transfer from its foreign affiliates, by modeling the change in a as

$$\Delta a_i = \alpha_3 RKT_{i,j,t} + \alpha_4 Size_{i,j,t} + \alpha_5 Industry_{i,j} \quad (6)$$

where, the change in a is also assumed to vary across sectors and the size of the investing firms (Griliches, 1998).

Finally, combining equations (5) and (6) yields equation (1).

4. Intellectual property institutions and innovation of emerging multinational companies

Jie Wu

INTRODUCTION

The globalization of innovation has evolved dynamically over the past two decades. This trend has further accelerated in recent years largely from the active participation of emerging economies in countries such as Brazil, India, and China (Cha et al., 2021; Kim et al., 2020). For example, the number of patents filed by Chinese companies in which at least one of the inventors was based in the US has increased dramatically from two in 2002 to 910 in 2014. In addition, the number of patents filed by Chinese companies in which at least one of the inventors was based in a foreign country (e.g., Japan or Germany) has also increased significantly (Wu et al., 2017). Despite the significant increase in offshore R&D by emerging multinational companies (EMNCs), such companies often face obstacles in exploiting these benefits because of institutional difficulties. As institutional environments in emerging economies are less developed than those in Western economies, many EMNCs expand to foreign markets to find discrepant institutional environments. Researchers have recently revisited the role of institutional environments in host countries, focusing on whether such environments may stimulate multinational companies' (MNCs') competitive advantage (Cuervo-Cazurra, 2008; Cuervo-Cazurra & Genc, 2008; Luo & Tung, 2007; Wu, Zhou, Park, Khan, & Meyer, 2021). However, the way that the institutional quality of host countries affects EMNCs' innovation has received less attention.

The institutional quality of host countries has become steadily more important for MNCs,[1] particularly with the advent of the knowledge-based economy and increasing globalization (Wu, Wood & Khan, 2021). The rise of interconnectedness between different business activities across markets results not only in more frequent global sourcing of various intermediate inputs (as well as production, marketing, and distribution activities), but also in more uncertainties than those faced by MNCs a few decades ago. MNCs respond to the more profound complexities embedded in the global marketplace by engaging in institutional hedging to reduce uncertainty in innovation activities (Almeida, 1996; Cantwell & Iammarino, 2000; Kim et al., 2020). According to the conventional international business view (Kostova, 1999; Kostova & Zaheer, 1999), which is mostly rooted in the Western context, as MNCs expand overseas to exploit advanced technologies and management practices, they unavoidably encounter distinct institutional environments in host countries. Such environments heighten the challenges for establishing and maintaining internal and external legitimacy, as well as the transnational transfer of strategic organizational practices within MNCs (Kostova, 1999). According to this view, it seems that EMNCs, depicted as having a lack of advanced technologies and management practices, are less likely to be affected by institutional environments in host countries as they develop innovation.

In reality, however, many EMNCs have expanded to host countries to boost their innovation (Wu & Park, 2017). Huawei and ZTE, two leaders in the telecommunication equipment manufacturing industry, for example, have aggressively expanded to Western economies, such as the US, to develop new technologies and products. This is partly due to the fact that, in accordance with a Sino-US investment treaty, the US offers preferential taxes for Chinese investors. US state governments have set up some offices, aiming to attract foreign investments from China and to help investors find potential local partners, lawyers, accounting firms, and so forth. In addition, the same officers are cautious in protecting their core technologies.

In this chapter, we theorize that better-developed intellectual property (IP) institutions of host countries could enable EMNCs to obtain advanced technologies for innovation, and that over-strict IP institutions decrease EMNCs' ability to transform new technologies into innovation output. Thus, the IP institutions of a host country may have an inverted U-shaped relationship with an EMNC's innovation such that moderate IP institutions would enable the EMNC to achieve the highest innovation output. Moreover, we examine important contingencies related to the role of IP institutions that may have differential effects on innovation across various firm-specific absorptive capacities (ACAPs) and knowledge transfer capabilities. We propose that a strong ACAP will increase the positive impact of IP institutions on innovation performance, and that strong knowledge transfer capability can help EMNCs to more efficiently transfer new technologies across markets and promote innovation.

THEORY AND HYPOTHESES

IP Institutions of Host Country and EMNC Innovation

With the growing interest in EMNC internationalization, business scholars have devoted sustained attention to such countries' expansion into foreign markets (e.g., Cuervo-Cazurra, 2008; Cuervo-Cazurra & Genc, 2008; Luo & Tung, 2007; Tsang & Yip, 2007; Wu, Zhou, Park, Khan, & Meyer, 2021). The institutional aspects of the business environment, which include regulatory systems, intellectual property regimes, tort laws, and antitrust laws, are widely deemed critically important for EMNCs' international activities (Wu & Vahlne, 2020), and such institutional environments vary significantly across regions and markets. These different institutional/policy settings, although not entirely firm specific, constitute a firm's institutional assets and shape its firm-level strategic posture (Teece et al., 1997).

In this study, "IP institutions" refers to a host country's institutional environment that enables cultivating new technologies, prevents piracy, and protects new inventions (Wu, Wood & Khan, 2021). Prior studies have argued that EMNCs face higher transaction costs in their home markets than in developed-country MNCs, which operate in environments with better governance and institutions (Prahalad & Hammond, 2002; Wu & Park, 2017). In their home markets, EMNCs face weak IP institutions accompanied by a lack of efficient market for cultivating new technologies, serious piracy, and ineffective invention protection, all of which make innovation costly (Chan et al., 2008). For example, EMNCs must protect their assets (especially the threat of expropriation of their intellectual property), prevent illegal dissemination, and defend against infringements of their property rights (Rodriguez et al., 2005). They must also commit substantial resources and managerial attention to dealing with local governments, which are powerful and capricious, and with hostility from non-governmental organizations (Wu, Zhou, Park, Khan, & Meyer, 2021). Moreover, searching for and gaining access to complementary technologies and assets, as well as market information, is costly because of EMNCs' underdeveloped and inefficient intermediary institutions (Khanna & Palepu, 1997). Obtaining information on such issues as customer demand, competitor moves, qualified suppliers, and effective intermediaries entails enormous search costs, which further strain firms' limited resources (North, 1990). These costs leave fewer resources and less attention to allocate to innovation, which stimulates firms to expand into countries with strong IP institutions where they could acquire advanced technologies, reduce innovation costs and protect new inventions (Wu & Ang, 2020).

In contrast, expanding into a foreign country with better-developed IP institutions enables EMNCs to overcome home-country IP institutional constraints. The knowledge spillover literature suggests that firms in markets with a good science base, a more skilled workforce, and a solid legislative systems of protecting IP rights are more likely to acquire advanced technologies and develop new technologies (Almeida, 1996; Cantwell & Iammarino, 2000; Jaffe et al., 1993). Viewed from this perspective, EMNCs expanding to a foreign country with better-developed IP institutions gain more exposure to advanced technologies that have been developed and concentrated. Exposure to advanced technologies stimulates EMNCs' interaction with local partners from which EMNCs can learn more sophisticated processes and product technology (Gong & Keller, 2003). Expanding to host countries with better-developed IP institutions also reduces transaction costs, which allows EMNCs to allocate more resources to reinforce their technological advantages and explore new available technologies (Wu et al., 2021). Reinforced technological capabilities help EMNCs to learn or adopt the most valuable technology and to find or develop the expertise needed to further enhance their technological capabilities, which can inspire EMNCs to introduce new products and increase their response to local markets (Wu, Zhou, Park, Khan, & Meyer, 2021). Therefore, as IP institutions of a host country increase from low to moderate levels, EMNCs are able to access technological resources in institutional environments to complement their own technological developments (Cantwell & Mudambi, 2005).

As IP institutions increase from moderate to high levels, however, the technological-access advantages increase rather incrementally, but the punishment for intellectual property right (IPR) infringements in these countries may be too costly for technological learning and acquisitions by EMNCs (Wu et al., 2017). At the low to moderate level of IP protection, EMNCs could acquire knowledge through adaptation, imitation, and reverse engineering and enjoy some learning-by-doing (Suthersanen, 2006). However, overly strong IPR institutions in host countries will increase the punishment cost to piracy prevention and infringements, which in turn inhibits effective learning and beneficial imitation by EMNCs (Wu et al., 2017). Using Korean firm-level data as a case study, Kim et al. (2012) found that IPR protection contributes to innovation and economic growth in developed economies, but not in emerging economies. Patent protection for industrial activities begins to matter only after countries have achieved a threshold level of indigenous innovative capacity along with an extensive science and technology infrastructure (Kim, 1997). More recently, Wu, Ma & Zhuo (2016) found that strong IPR protection in leading innovator countries has a negative impact on emerging innovator countries' national innovative capacity, because low to moderate IP protections can help EMNCs that are still in the early stages of building technological capabilities by permitting effective imitation and reverse engineering, and overly strict IP institutions stifle such learning

(Lall and Albaladejo, 2001). Thus, we predict that a moderate level of IP institutions is most beneficial to EMNC innovation.

Hypothesis 1. Host countries' IP institutions have an inverted U-shaped impact (first increasing and then decreasing) on EMNCs' innovation, such that moderate IP institutions of a host country generate the most innovation output.

Contingencies

While prior studies on the links among institutions, strategies, and performance suggest that the value of international strategies is correlated with the level of institutions in a foreign country (Kostova & Zaheer, 1999), an international network perception of MNCs has stressed the importance of dynamic capabilities in facilitating the extent to which MNCs acquire new knowledge and capture the opportunities provided by the institutional environment of a host country. Dynamic capabilities refer to a firm's "ability to integrate, build, and reconfigure internal and external competences to address rapidly changing environments" (Teece et al., 1997, p. 516). For example, gaining innovation benefits from the institutional environment of a host country not only requires that such institutional differences exist, but also that an MNC develops dynamic connectedness between local knowledge creation and exchange in each node of the network (Cantwell, 2009). ACAP and knowledge transfer capability are the two most important dynamic capabilities relevant for EMNCs' high-value creation and innovative activity.

Moderating effect of ACAP

Analysis of prior research reveals four major definitions of ACAP.[2] Cohen and Levinthal (1990) offer the most widely cited definition of ACAP, viewing it as a firm's ability to value, assimilate, and apply new knowledge. Mowery and Oxley (1995) offer a second definition of ACAP as a broad set of skills needed to deal with and modify the tacit component of transferred knowledge. Zahra and George (2002, p. 185) offer a third definition of ACAP as "a dynamic capability pertaining to knowledge creation and utilization that enhances a firm's ability to gain and sustain a competitive advantage." They further propose potential and realized ACAP. Potential ACAP enables firms to identify and acquire new external knowledge and assimilate knowledge obtained from external sources, while realized ACAP helps firms combine existing and newly acquired knowledge and incorporate transformed knowledge into operations. Tilton (1971) observes this phenomenon in the semiconductor industry and concludes that ACAP is important for keeping firms abreast of the latest technological developments and facilitating their assimilation. Lane et al. (2006) offer a fourth definition of ACAP as a firm's ability to sequentially recognize, assimilate, and apply externally held knowledge.

Consistent with previous studies (e.g., Lane et al., 2006; Zahra & George, 2002),[3] we conceptualize ACAP as a firm-specific capability that enables the firm to reconfigure its resource base to recognize, assimilate, and use external knowledge to create new knowledge and products that help it adapt to changing market conditions. In general, ACAP is developed through continuous funding of and engaging in research and development (R&D) over time (Cohen & Levinthal, 1990; Wu & Vahlne, 2020). High ACAP is achieved when firms accumulate internal learning at a point that they can value, assimilate, and apply external knowledge to specific product designs for product innovation (Carlile, 2004; Smith et al., 2005). Prior research has highlighted the critical role of ACAP in innovation activities. Cohen and Levinthal (1990) show that ACAP promotes organizational learning and innovative activities. Moorman and Slotegraaf (1999) find that ACAP not only fosters new product creativity, but also facilitates product development speed.

Although expanding into a host country with better-developed IP institutions can provide EMNCs access to advanced technologies, the extent to which they can effectively acquire and exploit those technologies is, however, highly dependent on firm-specific ACAP. Mere exposure to valuable external knowledge is not sufficient to ensure successful internalization (Jansen et al., 2005). EMNCs need to develop strong ACAP that enables them to effectively screen new technological trends, recognize new external knowledge, assimilate valuable external knowledge into the existing knowledge base, and apply assimilated external knowledge to emerging designs (Lane et al., 2006; Mowery, 1983).

When expanding into a host country with developed IP institutions, strong ACAP enables EMNCs to more effectively use new technology and available knowledge in a developed institutional environment (Wu & Vahlne, 2020). An EMNC with strong ACAP can analyze, process, interpret, and understand new external knowledge presented in an IP institutionally developed host country and identify the most valuable new technology and knowledge for its innovative activities (Kim, 1997; Szulanski, 1996). Strong ACAP also helps an EMNC more effectively assimilate valuable external knowledge and apply it to its own product innovation (Arora & Gambardella, 1994; Rothaermel & Alexandre, 2009; Wu & Ang, 2020), thus increasing product innovation performance.

Hypothesis 2. The positive effect of a host country's IP institutions on EMNC innovation is stronger when EMNCs develop strong ACAP.

Moderating effect of knowledge transfer capability
Knowledge is sticky, which results from the additional costs incurred during the adoption of complex technology and business processes, and involves conscious reconstruction, diffusion, and integration into new routines in an organization (Von Hippel, 1994; Wu et al., 2020). Such stickiness causes knowledge, particularly its tacit component, to lie inert in an organization, where it is not readily accessible or retrievable and therefore not deployable or convertible into value (Whitehead, 1929). As a result, "organizations may not necessarily know all that they know" (Szulanski, 2000, p. 10) and fall short of fully exploiting their know-how (Von Hippel, 1994). The source of competitive advantage thus resides in socially complex tacit knowledge diffused throughout the firm (Kogut & Zander, 1993). Although it is possible to convert some tacit knowledge into explicit knowledge (Nonaka & Takeuchi, 1995), most tacit knowledge is difficult, if not impossible, to codify and can never be made explicit (Berman et al., 2002; Wu et al., 2020). The two types of tacit knowledge are individual tacit knowledge (e.g., an individual's skills) and group- or team-based tacit knowledge (e.g., collective skills) (Berman et al., 2002). Although the stock of tacit knowledge accumulates over time as an individual learns a particular skill or as team members learn to interact (Berman et al., 2002), the transfer of tacit knowledge is confronted by various difficulties (Von Hippel, 1994). For example, the act of solving a problem rests on how the phenomena function; the formal expression of the solution is unlikely to fully capture this procedural knowledge leading to a solution. The ability to

transform tacit capabilities into a comprehensible code that is understood by large numbers of people resides in the collective experiences of firm members organized by maintained rules of coordination and cooperation (Zander & Kogut, 1995; Wu et al., 2020). Even in the area of problem identification and solving, the know-how of heuristic search precedes the formal knowledge of the solution (Kogut & Zander, 1993). The ability of accumulated experience to facilitate the communication and understanding of a new technology is a consistent finding in studies on the transfer of technology (Wu & Vahlne, 2020; Teece, 1977).

Knowledge transfer capability in this study refers to the ability to deal with the components of knowledge inside the firm by transferring tacit knowledge to subsidiaries across different markets, as well as the ability to modify a foreign-sourced technology for domestic applications (Mowery & Oxley, 1995). Knowledge transfer capability represents a key capability for EMNCs that transfer tacit knowledge contained in one subsidiary to other subsidiaries and markets (Wu & Ang, 2020).

Despite the fact that EMNCs expanding into a host country with strong IP institutions are likely to be exposed to advanced technologies, sufficient funding, and professional expertise, to what extent they diffuse new technology depends on knowledge transfer capability. While "objective" knowledge (e.g., product development) can be taught or acquired in international expansion, tacit knowledge is typically implicit and therefore can be secured only through experience – that is, learn by doing (Barkema & Vermeulen, 1998; Davidson, 1980). EMNCs with strong knowledge transfer capability can realize greater innovation benefits by transferring the tacit components of advanced technology and know-how obtained in a host market with strong IP institutions to other markets (Szulanski, 1996; Von Hippel, 1994).

When expanding simultaneously into a host country with IP institutions, strong knowledge transfer enables EMNCs to transfer advanced technology and tacit knowledge obtained in the former to subsidiaries in the latter (Birkinshaw & Hood, 1998; Cantwell & Mudambi, 2005). According to organizational learning theory (Levitt & March, 1988), institutionalization learning takes place through organizational codes, procedures, and routines in which inferences about past successes and failures are embedded (Luo & Tung, 2007; Wu & Ang, 2020). It requires EMNCs to develop knowledge transfer capability to secure tacit knowledge and transfer it back to the home market or other foreign markets, not just in terms of production and distribution, but also in other areas in which internationally competitive standards must be achieved (Child & Rodrigues, 2005; Simonin, 2004). Moreover, EMNCs with strong knowledge transfer capability can effectively transfer advanced knowledge, particularly tacit know-how, acquired in a host country with strong IP institutions back to the home country and combine it with home-country resources to offer new products at a competitive price (Wu, Wood & Khan, 2021). All of these factors contribute to better product innovation performance.

Hypothesis 3. The positive effect of a host country's IP institutions on EMNCs' innovation is stronger when EMNCs develop strong knowledge transfer capability.

DATA AND METHODS

Data and Sampling

We tested the hypotheses on a panel data about Chinese multinational companies (MNCs). The data collection administration quizzed the Chinese MNCs about their international expansion and product innovation during the period from 2011 to 2013. China is a particularly suitable setting for examining these research questions for two key reasons. First, China is the pre-eminent emerging market (Wu, Ma & Zhuo, 2016). Although substantial research exists on the Chinese context and companies, additional empirical research is likely to be of interest to scholars and practitioners alike, particularly if the research addresses a new question or adopts a novel perspective. Second, the empirical context of innovation strategies of Chinese MNCs offers us significant variation in the key aspects. A high degree of internationalization by active Chinese MNCs results in variations in IP institutions of a host country (Wu et al., 2017). Innovation outcomes are distinct among Chinese MNEs. The significant variation in the dependent variable and key independent variables will enhance our confidence in the estimates arising from the statistical analysis.

We implemented a random sampling method to identify 362 Chinese firms that had expanded internationally prior to the administration of the data collection. We contacted their top managers to explain the purpose of this study and to obtain their agreement for participation. In the first round of primary data collection, we hand-delivered the questionnaires to the top managers of companies that had agreed to participate, with an introduction letter explaining the purpose of the study. Follow-up telephone contact was made within two weeks to make appointments for onsite interviews. Our method ensured access to the appropriate respondents, that the terms used were correctly understood, and that a high response rate (65%) was provided. We compared the characteristics between 235 responses and 127 non-responses in terms of firm age, firm size, and respondents' age, gender, position, and so forth. We found no nonresponse bias. The data collection administrators (the authors of the paper) determined whether the respondents had provided the complete information in accordance with the instructions.

The first set of questionnaires sought information about firm characteristics and internationalization strategies. The questions included the year of establishment, the size of the firm in terms of number of total employees, the industry to which the firm belonged, and the competitive intensity in the product markets. We also asked the respondents to provide information about their firms' internationalization strategies, including into which foreign markets the firm expands (provide specific market names), the year, the amount of investment, the type of foreign entry mode (e.g., wholly owned or joint venture), and so forth. A year after we collected the first questionnaire set, we contacted the same companies and delivered the second questionnaire set to a different set of respondents who were knowledgeable about the innovation performance of their firm. The questionnaire included questions about the sales of the company and the percentage of sales derived from new products, among others. Our method of delivering two questionnaires to separate respondents within each firm and quizzing them about different aspects of our model (e.g., internationalization strategy to one set and innovation performance to the other set) was designed to reduce the common method variance, which often affects data gathered from questionnaire surveys (Eisenhardt & Tabrizi, 1995).

After excluding 38 responses with missing values from 235 responses, the sample consisted of 197 Chinese manufacturing companies. A majority (58%) of the respondents were male and had 11 years on average of working experience. To further check the issue of potential common method bias, we combined the two surveys and performed a Harman-factor test. The results of the Harman one-factor test clearly showed that the first factor explained less than 41% of the variance, indicating that common method bias was not a serious concern in this study.

Measures

We measured product innovation performance by the sales value of new products a firm had successfully introduced. The survey was conducted in two waves. The first wave was related to firm internationalization in 2013, while the second wave, one year later, related to innovation performance in 2014. The respondents provided information about innovation performance over the recent two years (2013 and 2014, respectively). In the analyses, the dependent variable, innovation performance in 2014, lagged one year behind independent variables in 2013 (e.g., internationalization strategy, ACAP, and knowledge transfer capability, etc.). We believe that revenue from new products is a better indicator of successful product innovation than alternative measures, such as the number of new products or patents granted, because it reflects the commercial significance of a firm's innovation activities related to a specific market (Katila, 2002). Prior studies have shown that introducing new products tends to increase market share and market value (Chaney & Devinney, 1992), improve firm performance (Roberts, 1999), and enhance a firm's survival likelihood (Banbury & Mitchell, 1995).

The rate of product innovation may depend on a firm's size and the industry segments in which it operates. To account for this, we adjusted this measure by the total number of a firm's R&D personnel to arrive at a firm-size-adjusted measure of innovation performance. Moreover, we included firm size and industry dummies in the analyses. In any case, without commercialization, even the most innovative development loses its value and meaning. To check the validity of this measure, we randomly selected five sampled firms and conducted in-depth interviews on the percentage of sales that new products have contributed, given that the respondents provided information on the percentage of sales contributed by new products. These interviews revealed that this measure of innovation performance correctly reflects the innovativeness outcome of these firms.

Following prior studies (Mansfield, 1994; Maskus, 2000), we measured IP institutions by a composite measure consisting of three indicators: (a) to what extent the host country pushes for technical and financial assistance, including an international fund (1 = little; 2 = less moderate; 3 = moderate; 4 = hard; 5 = very hard); (b) to what extent the host country reduces piracy and counterfeiting through awareness, fines, and penalties (1 = little; 2 = less moderate; 3 = moderate; 4 = strict; 5 = highly strict); and (c) to what extent the host country has a strong protection of intellectual property rights (1 = little; 2 = less moderate; 3 = moderate; 4 = rigorous; 5 = highly rigorous). The respondents answered the three questions with a mean value of 3.7, indicating that Chinese MNCs tend to expand to host countries with relatively developed IP institutions, rather than less-developed IP institutions. The values of these answers were aggregated at the country-level to arrive at the value of the IP institutions of a host country. We divided the values of each indicator by the highest value of the respective dimension to convert the original value to fall between zero and one. We then subjected these ratios to an exploratory principal factor analysis with varimax rotation; the results provide support for a single factor with an eigenvalue greater than 1 explaining 81.9% of the variance. The factor loadings of all three indicators were well above the accepted cutoff point of 0.70 (0.82, 0.85, and 0.88, respectively) and were highly significant ($p \leq 0.001$), indicating good construct validity. To account for different variances of the three IP institutional indicators, we transformed the ratios into standardized values with a mean of zero and a standard deviation of one. We then summed the standardized values of these indicators and averaged them to obtain one composite value that constitutes the index of IP institutions. We matched IP institution scores with the host country data with which the sampled Chinese MNCs were involved.

Building on prior studies (Cohen & Levinthal, 1989, 1990; Lane et al., 2006; Zahra & George, 2002), we developed the measure of a firm's ACAP based on responses to three questions: (a) does the firm have the ability to effectively screen new technological trends, recognize new external knowledge, assimilate valuable external knowledge into the existing knowledge base, and apply them? (Yes/No); (b) does the firm have the ability to combine its existing with newly acquired knowledge and incorporate transformed knowledge into operations? (Yes/No); and (c) does the firm have the ability to reconfigure its resource base to recognize, assimilate, and use external knowledge to create new knowledge and products? (Yes/No). Overall, the proportion of "Yes" answers across all questions was about 66%. The "Yes" answer for the first question was about 62%, the "Yes" answer for the second question was 63%, and the "Yes" answer for the last question was 71%. We used the average score of the sub-items to measure the intended construct.

Drawing on prior studies on knowledge transfer (Kogut & Zander, 1993; Mowery & Oxley, 1995), we measured knowledge transfer capability as a compound factor consisting of multiple responses provided by the respondents: (1) does the firm have the ability to transfer tacit knowledge from firm headquarters to subsidiaries across different markets? (Yes/No); (2) does the firm have the ability to transfer tacit knowledge from the subsidiaries back to the headquarters? (Yes/No); and (3) does the firm have the ability to transfer tacit knowledge from one subsidiary to other subsidiaries across different markets? (Yes/No). Overall, the proportion of "Yes" answers across all the questions was about 22%. The "Yes" answer for the first question was about 23%, the "Yes" answer for the second question was 21%, and the "Yes" answer for the last question was 20%. We used the average score of the sub-items to measure knowledge transfer capability.

We also checked the phrasing of questions by administering the data instrument to a group of ten individuals. The score from the first round test and the score from the second round test were highly correlated (e.g., $p = 0.95$ for ACAP; $p = 0.96$ for technology transfer capability), indicating a high stability of the measures over time. For internal consistency, we checked average inter-item correlation for each construct. The average of the correlation coefficients for ACAP was 0.95, while the average of the correlation coefficients for technological transfer capability was 0.94. These results indicated a high level of internal consistency. To check construct validity, we used a panel of experts[4] who are familiar with these constructs to assess each construct. The experts examined the items and determined what each specific item was intended to measure. Ninety-two percent of the panel agreed that the items adopted were actually assessing the intended construct, indicating high construct validity. By computing Raykov's reliability rho (ρ) (Raykov, 1998), the reliability of the multiple-item constructs was assessed. The results were greater than the recommended 0.70 ($\rho = 0.84$ for ACAP, $\rho = 0.85$ for technology transfer capability. search, $\rho = 0.81$ for market search), indicating high reliability for these measures.

We included several variables to take account of alternative explanations. First, prior studies have suggested that the host country's economic and cultural effects will affect product innovation (Wu, Pangarkar, & Wu, 2016; Shenkar et al., 2020). To control for the effect of the level of the host country's economic development, we created a variable, *level of economic development*, using the host country's gross domestic product per capita. We applied a natural logarithm transformation in the modeling (Tsang & Yip, 2007). We also controlled for *cultural distance* between China and each foreign country using Kogut and Singh's (1988) formula based on Hofstede's (2001) four cultural dimensions:

$$Cul\_dist_j = \sum_i^I \left[(I_{ij} - I_{ip})^2 / V_i \right] / I$$

where *Cul_dist*$_j$ is the cultural distance of foreign country *j* from China, I_{ij} refers to cultural dimension *i* in country *j*, *p* denotes China, V_i is the variance of cultural dimension *i*, and *I* is the sum of cultural dimensions, which is the average of all the pairs of cultural distance.

Second, geographic distance between the home and host countries is another factor that affects innovation performance (Stringfellow et al., 2008). We thus included *geographic distance* and measured it by the number of kilometers separating Beijing from a particular foreign country.[5] We used the logarithm of the averaged distance based on pairs in the analysis. Third, prior studies show that government ownership can have a negative effect on innovation performance (Piperopoulos et al., 2018), so *government ownership* was another control, which was measured by the percentage of a firm owned by the Chinese government. Fourth, as prior studies have provided different predictions of the effect of firm age on innovation performance (e.g., Sorensen & Stuart, 2000), we included firm age in the analyses, which was measured by the number of years since establishment. Fifth, larger firms may have more resources to devote to innovative activities (Eisenhardt & Tabrizi, 1995), so we controlled for *firm size*, which is measured by the logarithm of the number of employees. In addition, because the sample included firms from five manufacturing industries, we created four *industry dummy* variables. Finally, the study included four *location dummy* variables.

Statistical Modeling

Our primary objective was to examine the effect of host country IP institutions on firm innovation performance. Firms would self-select into a host country that provides a better match with their innovation capabilities to enhance innovation performance. In other words, firms choosing to enter host countries with more developed IP institutions may have particular capabilities that can enhance their innovation performance, whereas firms of countries with less-developed IP institutions may not have these capabilities. Specifically, innovativeness may prompt a firm to seek host countries with better-developed IP institutions that offer better innovation returns. Therefore, the IP institutions of a host country could be an endogenous variable. A popular econometric approach to deal with endogeneity is to obtain an exogenous proxy for the independent variable of interest (Larcker & Rusticus, 2010; Reeb et al., 2012). Thus, this study applied a two-stage least square (2SLS) with instrumental variables to deal with the endogeneity problem associated with the IP institutions of a host market.

The 2SLS approach centers on finding a variable or a set of variables (the preferred case), called an instrument or instruments, which influences the independent variable (the right-hand-side variable), but is unlikely to affect the dependent variable (the left-hand-side variable) except through its effect on the independent variable (Reeb et al., 2012). In other words, we needed to find some variable that correlates with the host country IP institutions, but not with the dependent variable. Research has proposed several approaches, such as industry averages and lagged endogenous regressors, to deal with the endogeneity problem. For example, Fisman and Svensson (2007) argue that if the endogeneity problem is specific to firms, but not to industries or locations, using industry-location level measures as instruments can net out this firm-specific component, thus yielding the industry-location measure that only depends on the underlying characteristics inherent to particular industries and/or locations. However, according to Larcker and Rusticus (2010, p. 196), "using industry aggregates as instrumental variables does not generally resolve direction of causality or correct for omitted variables... The endogenous aspect of the variable will not average out when aggregating to the industry level." In contrast, other scholars have proposed using lagged endogenous regressors as instruments in the analyses (e.g., Wang et al., 2012). The rationale behind the selection of lagged variables is that, because the events and decisions related to these variables occurred in the past, they are not correlated with the error term in the present (Gujarati & Porter, 2009; Wooldridge, 2009). Following this, we used the one-year lagged number of patents a firm received (i.e., 2012) as the instrumental variable for the IP institutions of a host country (2013). To assess the validity of the instrumental variable, we conducted Hansen's test of over-identifying restrictions and the Hausman test. The results consistently provide support for the validity of the instrumentation strategy.

The estimated function of 2SLS is expressed as follows. The first-stage model has the structure:

$$IP_{i,j,t-1} = a_0 + a_1 Patent_{i,j,t-2} + a_2 Age_{i,t-2} + a_3 Size_{i,t-2} + a_4 Foreign_{i,t-2} + \varepsilon ,$$

where represents the IP institutions of a host market j in year t_{-1}, is the number of patents firm i received in year t_{-2}, Age represents firm age, $Size$ represents firm size, $Foreign$ represents the percentage of foreign ownership, and is the normally distributed error term. The second model has the structure:

$$Product\ innovation_{i,t} = \beta_0 + \beta_1 IP_{i,j,t-1} + \beta_2 AC_{i,t-1} + \beta_3 KTC_{i,t-1} + \beta_4 IP_{i,j,t-1} \times AC_{i,t-1} +$$
$$\beta_5 IP_{i,j,t-1} \times KTC_{i,t-1} + \beta_6 Age_{i,t-1} + \beta_7 Size_{i,t-1} +$$
$$\beta_8 (R\&D\ intensity)_{i,t-1} + \beta_9 Government_{i,t-1} + \beta_{10} Foreign_{i,t-1} +$$
$$\beta_{11} (Economic\ distance)_{i,j,t-1} + \beta_{12} (Geographic\ distance)_{i,j} +$$
$$\beta_{13} (Culture\ distance)_{i,j} + \sum_{m=14}^{17} \beta_m industry_i + \sum_{n=18}^{21} \beta_n city_i + \omega$$

where *Product innovation*$_{i,t}$ refers to innovation performance of firm i in year t, $IP_{i,j,t-1}$ is the IP institutions of a host market j in year t_{-1}, Age represents firm age, $Size$ represents firm size, *R&D intensity* represents R&D intensity related to foreign market j, *Government* represents the percentage of government ownership, *Foreign* represents the percentage of foreign ownership, *Economic distance* represents the economic distance between the home and host markets, *Geographic distance* represents the geographic distance between the home and host markets, *Culture distance* represents the cultural distance between the home and host markets, *industry* represents the industry dummy, *city* represents the city dummy, and $\in$ is the normally distributed error term.

We evaluated the explanatory variables at t_{-1} and associated them with product innovation at t, accounting for a possible delay before the effects of firm-, institution-, and industry-level factors would be reflected in product innovation. We implemented the analyses in Stata 12 and assessed the "robust" correct standard errors for heteroscedasticity bias using the Huber–White sandwich estimator.

RESULTS

Table 4.1 reports descriptive statistics for the variables used in the analyses. A review of the correlations among the independent variables suggests that multicollinearity is not a major concern. This was confirmed by the analysis of the variance inflation factor (VIF). The VIF values ranged from 1.143 to 4.318, well below the cutoff threshold of 10, indicating no serious multicollinearity problems in the models (Hair et al., 1998).

Table 4.2 provides the estimation results testing Hypotheses 1, 2, and 3. Model 1 includes the controls; Model 2 adds the main effect of IP institutions of host country and its square term; Model 3 adds the main effect of ACAP and knowledge transfer capability (KTC); Model 4 adds a term representing the interaction between IP institutions and absorptive capability (IP Institutions × ACAP); Model 5 adds a term representing the interaction between IP institutions and knowledge transfer capability (IP Institutions × KTC); and Model 6 is the full model, including all the main effects and their interactions. To reduce the potential for multicollinearity, we mean-centered the predictor and moderator variables before creating the interaction terms (Aiken & West, 1991). The adjusted R-square values in Models 2 through 6 indicate significant explanatory power, and the changes in R-square in Models 3, 4, 5, and 6 indicate significant increases in explanatory power in those restricted models compared with Models 2, 3, 4, and 5, respectively. As such, we use Model 6 to discuss the results of hypotheses testing. Hypothesis 1 predicts the IP institutions of a host country have an inverted-U shaped impact on innovation performance. The coefficient of IP institutions in Model 6 is positive and significant ($\beta = 1.694$, $p = 0.002$), indicating that strong IP institutions of a host country promote innovation performance; whereas the coefficient of the squared term, IP institution,^{2} is negative and significant ($\beta = -1.531$, $p = 0.012$). Therefore IP institution has an inverted U-shaped relationship with innovation performance, with a turning point at 0.553. Thus, Hypothesis 1 receives support.

Hypothesis 2 predicts that the positive effect of a host country's IP institutions on innovation performance is stronger when EMNCs develop strong ACAP. The coefficient of the interaction term, IP Institutions × ACAP, is positive and significant ($\beta - 1.625$, $p - 0.034$), indicating that ACAP enhances the positive effect of strong IP institutions and innovation performance. To gain more insight into the interaction effect of Hypothesis 2, we plot the significant interaction effect in Figure 4.1 following Aiken and West's (1991) suggested procedure. The horizontal axis represents the quality of the host country's IP institutions, and the vertical axis represents the EMNC's innovation performance. We split the firms into two groups according to their ACAP: strong (one standard deviation above the mean) and weak (one standard deviation below the mean). The figure shows that the IP institutions of a host country have a nonlinear relationship with innovation performance in the way that innovation performance initially increases with the level of the host country's IP institutions and then decreases. Moreover, the upward slope is much steeper for firms with strong ACAP, as Hypothesis 2 predicts.

Hypothesis 3 suggests that the positive effect of IP institutions on innovation performance is stronger when EMNCs develop strong knowledge transfer capability. The coefficient of the interaction term, IP Institutions × KTC is positive and significant ($\beta = 2.342$, $p = 0.142$), indicating that strong knowledge transfer capability does not significantly enhance the observed positive effect of IP institutions on innovation performance. As such, Hypothesis 3 does not receive support.

Table 4.1   Means, standard deviations, and correlations

Variables	Mean	SD	1	2	3	4	5	6	7	8	9	10	11
1 Innovation performance	4.220	12.748	1.000										
2 IP institutions	0.713	0.175	0.112*	1.000									
3 Absorptive capacity Knowledge transfer	0.644	0.120	0.561*	0.020	1.000								
4 capability	0.270	0.640	0.181*	0.035	0.023	1.000							
5 Economic distance	9.089	1.489	0.127*	0.321*	0.029	−0.013	1.000						
6 Cultural distance	2.760	1.733	0.015	0.163*	0.020	−0.045	0.041	1.000					
7 Geographic distance	2.654	3.226	−0.005	−0.054	0.003	0.041	−0.224	0.317*	1.000				
8 Firm age	2.447	0.835	0.124*	−0.050	−0.146	0.180	0.066*	0.040	0.056	1.000			
9 Firm size	6.190	1.251	0.093	−0.184*	−0.095	0.250	−0.116	−0.031	0.080	0.303*	1.000		
10 State ownership	18.750	35.970	−0.092	−0.08*	−0.035	0.172*	−0.092*	−0.016	0.048	0.438*	0.184*	1.000	
11 Foreign ownership	28.560	35.630	0.140	0.120	0.060	0.22*	0.043	−0.016	−0.120	−0.120	−0.110	−0.292*	1.000

Note: * indicates significance at the 0.05 level of confidence.

Table 4.2 **Hypothesis testing**

Dependent variable Innovation performance	Model 1	Model 2	Model 3	Model 4	Model 5	Model 6
IP Institutions		1.651**	1.682**	1.648**	1.667**	1.694**
		(0.003)	(0.002)	(0.001)	(0.003)	(0.002)
IP institutions^2		−1.221*	−1.232*	−1.232*	−1.221*	−1.531*
		(0.011)	(0.013)	(0.012)	(0.013)	(0.012)
Absorptive capacity (ACAP)			16.813*	15.460*	16.159*	15.591*
			(0.012)	(0.013)	(0.011)	(0.012)
Knowledge transfer capability (KTC)			4.601*	4.009*	4.423*	4.864*
			(0.026)	(0.022)	(0.024)	(0.024)
IP institutions × ACAP				1.447*		1.625*
				(0.035)		(0.034)
IP institutions × KTC					2.155	2.342
					(0.146)	(0.142)
Firm age	0.852	0.811	0.824	0.843	0.890	0.872
	(0.113)	(0.171)	(0.179)	(0.176)	(0.178)	(0.177)
Firm size	0.625	0.652	0.660	0.744	0.716	0.663
	(0.312)	(0.314)	(0.323)	(0.313)	(0.332)	(0.316)
State ownership	−0.491	−0.470	−0.465	−0.479	−0.468	−0.484
	(0.137)	(0.139)	(0.140)	(0.138)	(0.141)	(0.148)
Foreign ownership	0.228	0.224	0.235	0.239	0.222	0.253
	(0.121)	(0.126)	(0.124)	(0.123)	(0.129)	(0.127)
Economic development	0.525*	0.518*	0.554*	0.560*	0.616*	0.652*
	(0.041)	(0.042)	(0.040)	(0.046)	(0.043)	(0.042)
Cultural distance	−0.127	−0.125	−0.174	−0.163	−0.154	−0.118
	(0.255)	(0.253)	(0.258)	(0.254)	(0.253)	(0.265)
Geographic distance	−0.032	−0.035	−0.043	−0.052	−0.047	−0.039
	(0.132)	(0.131)	(0.130)	(0.089)	(0.132)	(0.108)
Industry dummy	Yes	Yes	Yes	Yes	Yes	Yes
Location dummy	Yes	Yes	Yes	Yes	Yes	Yes
Adj. R^2	0.093	0.149	0.210	0.282	0.335	0.399
R^2 change		0.056*	0.061**	0.072**	0.053*	0.064**
F-test	0.000***	0.000***	0.000***	0.000***	0.000***	0.000***
Over-identifying test	36.812	39.516	39.322	41.127	43.245	44.192
Hausman test (F)	11.324	11.440	11.528	12.632	13.365	14.227
p-value	0.000	0.000	0.000	0.000	0.000	0.000

Note: ***statistically significant at 0.1%; **statistically significant at 1%; *statistically significant at 5%.
p-values are in parentheses. Intercept is not shown.

Additional Analyses

We conducted two tests to assess the appropriateness of the instrumental variable. First, we performed the standard Hausman test to assess the endogeneity of the instrumental variable. As Table 4.2 shows, the Hausman test strongly rejects the exogeneity of IP institutions (e.g., M6: $F = 14.447, p = 0.001$), indicating that the 2SLS estimate is preferable to the ordinary least squares (OLS) estimate. Second, we performed Hansen's test of over-identifying restrictions to assess whether the instrumental variable was uncorrelated with the error term. Lack of correlation is an essential condition for the validity of the instrumental variable. The results of the over-identifying restrictions test could not reject the null hypothesis that the instrument is valid in the model specifications. Together, the Hausman test and the over-identifying test suggest that the selected instrument is of good quality and thus likely to produce better estimates and inferences than the OLS (Larcker & Rusticus, 2010).

Moreover, we took several steps to test the robustness of these results. First, to reduce concerns that the sample contained observations without any new products, we re-estimated the models with a sub-sample of 175 firms, all of which had introduced at least one new product during the period studied. The results did not change in any substantial way. Second, in addition to 2SLS with instrumental variables, we estimated all models with a two-step generalized method of moments and LIMIL estimators. The results are consistent across estimation methods. In addition, one could argue that the pattern of overseas expansion in regulated industries (the transportation industry) may differ from that in unregulated industries, such as electronic equipment, because the Chinese government exerts more policy constraints on the former, creating more hurdles for transnational technology transfer. To eliminate this concern, we used the *Catalogue of Industries for Guiding Foreign Investment in 2010*, an official guideline issued jointly by China's Ministry of Commerce and National Development and Reform Commission, to exclude the vehicle sector from the sample analyses. The results remain consistent, providing additional evidence of their robustness.

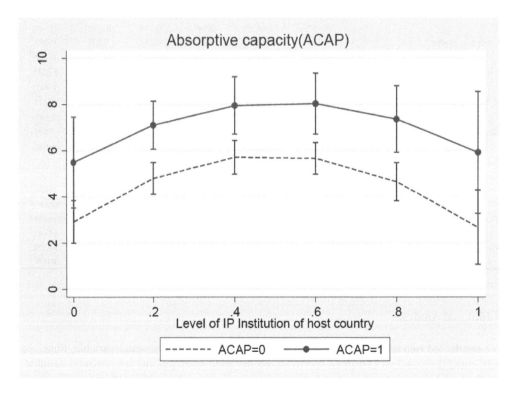

Figure 4.1   *IP Institutions of host country, absorptive capacity and innovation performance*

DISCUSSION AND CONCLUSION

Building on institutional theory and the resource-based view of capability, this study assesses the effect of a host country's IP institutions on EMNCs' innovation. Several questions were posed in the beginning of the article that are important to reconsider. The first question asked whether and how the host country's IP institutions affect EMNC innovation. The second question concerned its boundary conditions. The data of Chinese EMNCs' internationalization activities and innovation outcomes were collected to test the hypotheses. We found that the host country's IP institutions have an inverted U-shaped impact on EMNC innovation. Strong ACAP enhances the positive effect of IP institutions on EMNC innovation. These results contribute to the literature in several important ways.

Theoretical Implications

This study contributes to the institutional approach to international business by emphasizing the role of IP institutional environments. Prior studies have discussed institutional environments of host countries in a general way. While scholars in international business have examined how institutions constrain MNCs' strategies and structure, as well as their impact on the transnational transfer of organizational practices throughout MNCs (Kostova, 1999; Kostova & Zaheer, 1999), others have explored the impact of institutional environments on firm performance and competitive advantages (Cuervo-Cazurra, 2008; Wu, 2011). However, very limited efforts have been devoted to exploring the role of *IP institutions* of the host country that are most relevant for MNCs' cross-border innovation. We extend this stream of studies to examine a host country's IP institutions for EMNC innovation. We develop a new framework of IP institutions to explain its implications for innovation. By considering both the technology-access advantage and knowledge-integration disadvantage encountered by EMNCs when gaining benefits associated with host country IP institutions, our framework provides a more complete understanding of the role of IP institutions on EMNC innovation.

   This study also extends the resource-based view of capability by providing a more nuanced understanding of the roles of firm-specific capabilities for EMNC innovation performance. The theory highlights the importance of firm-specific ACAP in helping EMNCs utilize a host country's institutional advantages to improve the likelihood of innovation success. The results show that strong ACAP enhances the positive effect of expanding to a host country with a better-developed IP institutional environment. This is because ACAP enables a firm to identify and value new technology and integrate it with existing knowledge. These findings add insight to the recent studies on the international expansion of EMNCs by shifting the focus from how to transfer homegrown technology and capabilities to the host country, to how to acquire new knowledge and capabilities in a host country and integrate them with the existing knowledge base. This study thus advances the existing research by going beyond documenting the direct effect of firm-specific capabilities, to providing evidence that firm-specific ACAP interacts with the host country's IP institutional advantage to promote knowledge acquisition and innovation.

Practical Implications

The arguments and findings of this study offer some important implications for managers and policymakers. First, when making foreign-country expansion decisions, EMNCs should consider entering host countries with better-developed IP institutions that enable them to acquire advanced technological and critical resources for innovation. However, to what extent they could gain more innovation benefits from such international expansions depends on their own absorptive capacity. EMNCs should strive hard to build strong ACAP to identify valuable technologies in new markets and integrate them with their own technologies more effectively. Although we do not find the enhancing effect of knowledge transfer capability, the findings reveal that knowledge transfer capability has a positive and significant impact on EMNC innovation performance. This result draws managers' attention to tacit knowledge underlying cross-border knowledge transfer. Therefore, EMNCs need to develop strong knowledge transfer capability that will boost their innovation.

Second, the findings also have valuable implications for public policymakers. The governments of many emerging market countries (e.g., China, India) have developed preferential policies to encourage their indigenous firms to participate in global competition. The results of this study provide support for such policies by showing that expanding into host countries with developed IP institutions can significantly improve their MNCs' innovation performance. Equally important, the improvement of IP institutions in home countries will alleviate the difficulties of the home countries' MNCs who tend to encounter institutional disadvantages, as the home institutions are far behind the host institutions. Thus, policymakers should endeavor to strengthen IP institutions. In the long run, strong IP institutions along with the efficiency of important factor markets offering critical resources at home, and in conjunction with improved firm-level technological capabilities, may help EMNCs gain more innovation competiveness from participating in global competition.

Limitations and Further Research

Further research could improve and build on this study in several ways. First, our measurement of innovation performance relies on new product innovation. Although some forms of innovation are clearly related to process innovation, these were ignored in this research. Future studies could examine the role of IP institutions of the host country in such other forms of innovation performance. Research could also further develop our model to examine the impact of other types of institutions (e.g., inequality, incest taboo) on innovation outcomes. Second, this study attaches great importance to firm-specific ACAP and knowledge transfer capability. However, firms have other, equally important capabilities such as operation capability or marketing capability. Researchers might explore in greater depth the interplay of institutional environment and other types of firm-level capabilities and their impact on EMNC performance. Third, this study employed a sample of Chinese MNCs' internationalization activities and innovation. Although China is one of the largest emerging economies and the processes observed in China appear similar to those in other emerging market contexts, there may be some peculiarity of organizational structure, government action, or institutional setting associated with China or the period used. As such, the models could be extended by using data from firms in other emerging markets to establish their generalizability.

NOTES

1. In this study, we define MNCs as the sum total of all their value-creating activities over time (Cantwell et al., 2009).
2. Although Kim (1997) also defines ACAP as the capacity to learn and solve problems, we believe that learning capability and problem-solving skills reside in the domain of Cohen and Levinthal's (1990) stream of thought.
3. In this study, we regard Mowery and Oxley's (1995) view of ACAP as the ability to deal with the tacit component of transferred knowledge inside the organization as closer to a firm's knowledge transfer capability, and we further extend it to cross-market tacit knowledge transfer.
4. Experts consist of managers with rich international experiences and established scholars with decent publication records in the international business field.
5. Available at http://www.cepii.fr/anglaisgraph/bdd/distances.htm.

REFERENCES

Aiken, L. S., & West, S. G. (1991). *Multiple regression: Testing and interpreting interactions.* Thousand Oaks, CA: Sage Publications.

Almeida, P. (1996). Knowledge sourcing by foreign multinationals: Patent citation analysis in the US semiconductor industry. *Strategic Management Journal, 17*(Winter special issue): 155–165.

Arora, A., & Gambardella, A. (1994). Evaluating technological information and utilizing it. *Journal of Economic Behavior & Organization, 24*(1): 91–114.

Banbury, C. M., & Mitchell, W. (1995). The effect of introducing important incremental innovations on market share and business survival. *Strategic Management Journal, 16*(S1): 161–182.

Barkema, H. G., & Vermeulen, F. (1998). International expansion through start up or acquisition: A learning perspective. *Academy of Management Journal, 41*(1): 7–26.

Berman, S. L., Down, J., & Hill, C. W. (2002). Tacit knowledge as a source of competitive advantage in the national basketball association. *Academy of Management Journal, 45*(1): 13–31.

Birkinshaw, J., & Hood, N. (1998). Multinational subsidiary evolution: capability and charter change in foreign-owned subsidiary companies. *Academy of Management Review, 23*(4): 773–795.

Cantwell, J. (2009). Location and the multinational enterprise. *Journal of International Business Studies, 40*(1): 35–41.

Cantwell, J., & Iammarino, S. (2000). Multinational corporations and the location of technological innovation in the UK regions. *Regional Studies, 34*(4): 317–332.

Cantwell, J., & Mudambi, R. (2005). MNE competence-creating subsidiary mandates. *Strategic Management Journal, 26*(12): 1109–1128.

Cantwell, J., Dunning, J. H., & Lundan, S. M. (2009). An evolutionary approach to understanding international business activity: The co-evolution of MNEs and the institutional environment. *Journal of International Business Studies, 41*(4): 567–586.

Carlile, P. R. (2004). Transferring, translating, and transforming: An integrative framework for managing knowledge across boundaries. *Organization Science, 15*(5): 555–568.

Cha, H., Wu, J., & Kotabe, M. (2021). The vulnerability problem of business ecosystems under global decoupling. *Management and Organization Review.* In-press.

Chan, C. M., Isobe, T., & Makino, S. (2008). Which country matters? Institutional development and foreign affiliate performance. *Strategic Management Journal, 29*(11): 1179–1205.

Chaney, P. K., & Devinney, T. M. (1992). New product innovations and stock price performance. *Journal of Business Finance & Accounting, 19*(5): 677–695.

Child, J., & Rodrigues, S. B. (2005). The internationalization of Chinese firms: A case for theoretical extension? *Management and Organization Review, 1*(3): 381–410.

Cohen, W. M., & Levinthal, D. A. (1989). Innovation and learning: The two faces of R&D. *The Economic Journal, 99*(397): 569–596.

Cohen, W. M., & Levinthal, D. A. (1990). Absorptive capacity: A new perspective on learning and innovation. *Administrative Science Quarterly, 35*(1): 48–60.

Cuervo-Cazurra, A. (2008). The multinationalization of developing country MNEs: The case of multi-latinas. *Journal of International Management, 14*(2): 138–154.

Cuervo-Cazurra, A., & Genc, M. (2008). Transforming disadvantages into advantages: Developing-country MNEs in the least developed countries. *Journal of International Business Studies, 39*(6): 957–979.

Davidson, W. H. (1980). The location of foreign direct investment activity: Country characteristics and experience effects. *Journal of International Business Studies, 11*(2): 9–22.

Eisenhardt, K. M., & Tabrizi, B. N. (1995). Accelerating adaptive processes: Product innovation in the global computer industry. *Administrative Science Quarterly, 40*(1): 84–110.

Fisman, R., & Svensson, J. (2007). Are corruption and taxation really harmful to growth? Firm level evidence. *Journal of Development Economics, 83*(1): 63–75.

Gong, G., & Keller, W. (2003). Convergence and polarization in global income levels: A review of recent results on the role of international technology diffusion. *Research Policy, 32*(6): 1055–1079.

Gujarati, D. N., & Porter, D. (2009). *Basic econometrics* (5th ed.). New York: McGraw-Hill.

Hair, A., Anderson, R. E., Tatham, R. L., & Black, W. C. (1998). *Multivariate data analysis*. Upper Saddle River, NJ: Prentice Hall.

Hofstede, G. H. (2001). *Culture's consequences: Comparing values, behaviors, institutions, and organizations across nations*. Thousand Oaks CA: Sage Publications.

Jaffe, A. B., Trajtenberg, M., & Henderson, R. (1993). Geographic localization of knowledge spillovers as evidenced by patent citations. *Quarterly Journal of Economics, 108*(3): 577–598.

Jansen, J. J., Van Den Bosch, F. A., & Volberda, H. W. (2005). Managing potential and realized absorptive capacity: How do organizational antecedents matter? *Academy of Management Journal, 48*(6): 999–1015.

Katila, R. (2002). New product search over time: Past ideas in their prime? *Academy of Management Journal, 45*(5): 995–1010.

Khanna, T., & Palepu, K. (1997). Why focused strategies may be wrong for emerging markets. *Harvard Business Review, 75*(4): 41–54.

Kim, L. (1997). The dynamics of Samsung's technological learning in semiconductors. *California Management Review, 39*(3): 86–100.

Kim, Y.-K., Lee, K., Park, W.-G., & Choo, K. (2012). Appropriate intellectual property protection and economic growth in countries at different levels of development. *Research Policy, 41*: 358–375.

Kim, H., Wu, J., Schuler, D. & Hoskisson, R. (2020). Chinese multinationals' fast internationalization: Financial performance advantage in one region, disadvantage in another. *Journal of International Business Studies, 51*(7), 1076–1106.

Kogut, B., & Singh, H. (1988). The effect of national culture on the choice of entry mode. *Journal of International Business Studies, 19*(3): 411–432.

Kogut, B., & Zander, U. (1993). Knowledge of the firm and the evolutionary theory of the multinational corporation. *Journal of International Business Studies, 24*(4): 625–645.

Kostova, T. (1999). Transnational transfer of strategic organizational practices: A contextual perspective. *Academy of Management Review, 24*(2): 308–324.

Kostova, T., & Zaheer, S. (1999). Organizational legitimacy under conditions of complexity: The case of the multinational enterprise. *Academy of Management Review, 24*(1): 64–81.

Lall, S., & Albaladejo, M. (2001). *Indicator of the relative importance of IPRs in developing countries*. Geneva: UNCTAD.

Lane, P. J., Koka, B. R., & Pathak, S. (2006). The reification of absorptive capacity: A critical review and rejuvenation of the construct. *Academy of Management Review, 31*(4): 833–863.

Larcker, D. F., & Rusticus, T. O. (2010). On the use of instrumental variables in accounting research. *Journal of Accounting and Economics, 49*(3): 186–205.

Levitt, B., & March, J. G. (1988). Organizational learning. *Annual Review of Sociology, 14*: 319–340.

Luo, Y., & Tung, R. L. (2007). International expansion of emerging market enterprises: A springboard perspective. *Journal of International Business Studies, 38*(4): 481–498.

Mansfield, E. (1994). Intellectual property protection, foreign direct investment and technology transfer. Washington DC: International Finance Corporation, Discussion Paper number 19.

Maskus, K. (2000). *Intellectual property rights in the global economy*. Washington DC: Institute for International Economics. At http://www.iie.com/publications/publication.cfm?pub_id=99

Moorman, C., & Slotegraaf, R. J. (1999). The contingency value of complementary capabilities in product development. *Journal of Marketing Research*, 36(2): 239–257.

Mowery, D. C. (1983). The relationship between intrafirm and contractual forms of industrial research in American manufacturing, 1900–1940. *Explorations in Economic History*, 20(4): 351–374.

Mowery, D. C., & Oxley, J. E. (1995). Inward technology transfer and competitiveness: The role of national innovation systems. *Cambridge Journal of Economics*, 19(1): 67–93.

Nonaka, I., & Takeuchi, H. (1995). *The knowledge-creating company: How Japanese companies create the dynamics of innovation*. New York: Oxford University Press.

North, D. C. (1990). *Institutions, institutional change, and economic performance*. Cambridge, UK: Cambridge University Press.

Piperopoulos, P., Wu, J., & Wang, C. (2018). Outward FDI, home-country political ties and innovation performance of emerging market enterprises. *Research Policy*, 47(1): 232–240.

Prahalad, C. K., & Hamel, G. (1994). Competing for the future. *Harvard Business Review*, 72(4): 122–128.

Prahalad, C. K., & Hammond, A. (2002). Serving the world's poor, profitably. *Harvard Business Review*, 80(9): 48–59.

Raykov, T. (1998). Coefficient alpha and composite reliability with interrelated nonhomogeneous items. *Applied Psychological Measurement*, 22(4): 375–385.

Reeb, D., Sakakibara, M., & Mahmood, I. P. (2012). From the editors: Endogeneity in international business research. *Journal of International Business Studies*, 43(3): 211–218.

Roberts, P. W. (1999). Product innovation, product-market competition and persistent profitability in the US pharmaceutical industry. *Strategic Management Journal*, 20(7): 655–670.

Rodriguez, P., Uhlenbruck, K., & Eden, L. (2005). Government corruption and the entry strategies of multinationals. *Academy of Management Review*, 30(2): 383–396.

Rothaermel, F. T., & Alexandre, M. T. (2009). Ambidexterity in technology sourcing: The moderating role of absorptive capacity. *Organization Science*, 20(4): 759–780.

Shenkar, O., Tallman, S., Wang, H., & Wu, J. (2020). National culture and international business: A path forward. *Journal of International Business Studies*, https://doi.org/10.1057/s41267-020-00365-3

Simonin, B. L. (2004). An empirical investigation of the process of knowledge transfer in international strategic alliances. *Journal of International Business Studies*, 35(5): 407–427.

Smith, K. G., Collins, C. J., & Clark, K. D. (2005). Existing knowledge, knowledge creation capability, and the rate of new product introduction in high-technology firms. *Academy of Management Journal*, 48(2): 346–357.

Sorensen, J. B., & Stuart, T. E. (2000). Aging, obsolescence, and organizational innovation. *Administrative Science Quarterly*, 45(1): 81–112.

Stringfellow, A., Teagarden, M. B., & Nie, W. (2008). Invisible costs in offshoring services work. *Journal of Operations Management*, 26(2): 164–179.

Suthersanen, U. (2006). *Utility models and innovation in developing countries* (Vol. 13). International Centre for Trade and Sustainable Development (ICTSD).

Szulanski, G. (1996). Exploring internal stickiness: Impediments to the transfer of best practice within the firm. *Strategic Management Journal*, 17(Winter special issue): 27–43.

Szulanski, G. (2000). The process of knowledge transfer: A diachronic analysis of stickiness. *Organizational Behavior and Human Decision Processes*, 82(1): 9–27.

Teece, D. J. (1977). Technology transfer by multinational firms: The resource cost of transferring technological know-how. *The Economic Journal*, 87(346): 242–261.

Teece, D. J., Pisano, G., & Shuen, A. (1997). Dynamic capabilities and strategic management. *Strategic Management Journal*, 18(7): 509–533.

Tilton, J. E. (1971). *International diffusion of technology: The case of semiconductors*. Washington, DC: Brookings Institution.

Tsang, E. W. K., & Yip, P. S. L. (2007). Economic distance and the survival of foreign direct investments. *Academy of Management Journal*, 50(5): 1156–1168.

Von Hippel, E. (1994). "Sticky information" and the locus of problem solving: Implications for innovation. *Management Science*, 40(4): 429–439.

Wang, C., Hong, J., Kafouros, M., & Wright, M. (2012). Exploring the role of government involvement in outward FDI from emerging economies. *Journal of International Business Studies*, 43: 655–676.

Whitehead, A. N. (1929). *The aims of education and other essays*. New York: Macmillan.

Wooldridge, J. M. (2009). *Introductory econometrics: A modern approach*. Mason, OH: South-Western Publishing.

Wu, J. (2011). The asymmetric roles of business ties and political ties in product innovation. *Journal of Business Research, 64*(11): 1151–1156.

Wu, J. & Ang, S.-H. (2020). Network complementaries in the international expansion of emerging market firms. *Journal of World Business, 55*(2): 101045

Wu, J. S.-H., Ma, Z-Z., & Zhuo, S.-H. (2016). Enhancing national innovative capacity: The impact of high-tech international trade and inward foreign direct investment. *International Business Review*, http://dx.doi.org/10.1016/j.ibusrev.2016.11.001.

Wu, J., Pangarkar, N., & Wu, Z. (2016). The moderating effect of technology and marketing know-how in the regional-global diversification link: Evidence from emerging market multinationals. *International Business Review, 25*(6): 1273–1284.

Wu, J., Zhou, N., Park, S., Khan, Z., & Meyer, M. (2021). The role of FDI motives in the link between institutional distance and subsidiary ownership choice by emerging market multinational enterprises. *British Journal of Management*, in-press, 0: 1–24. (ABS 4).

Wu, J., & Vahlne, (2020). Dynamic capabilities of emerging market multinational enterprises and the Uppsala model. *Asian Business & Management*. doi: https://link.springer.com/article/10.1057/s41291-020-00111-5

Wu, J., & Park S. (2017). The role of institutional complexity on emerging multinationals' innovation outcomes. *Global Strategy Journal, 9*(2): 333–353.

Wu, J., Wood, G., & Khan, Z. (2021). Top management team's formal network and international expansion of Chinese firms: The moderating role of state ownership and political ties. *International Business Review*. In Press.

Wu, J., Zhang, X., Zhuo, S., Meyer, M., Li, B., & Yan, H. (2020). The imitation-innovation link, external knowledge search and China's innovation system. *Journal of Intellectual Capital, 21*(5): 727–752.

Wu, J., Zhuo, S., & Wu, Z. (2017). National innovation system, social entrepreneurship, and rural economic growth in China. *Technological Forecasting and Social Change, 121*: 238–250.

Zahra, S. A., & George, G. (2002). Absorptive capacity: A review, reconceptualization, and extension. *Academy of Management Review, 27*(2): 185–203.

Zander, U., & Kogut, B. (1995). Knowledge and the speed of the transfer and imitation of organizational capabilities: An empirical test. *Organization Science, 6*(1): 76–92.

PART II

SOCIETAL AND HUMAN RESOURCE PERSPECTIVE OF KNOWLEDGE TRANSFER

5. Social media as a knowledge transfer tool for intellectual capital accumulation during the international growth of small firms

Matti Saari, Minnie Kontkanen, Ahmad Arslan and Pia Hurmelinna-Laukkanen

INTRODUCTION

International growth of firms is an important topic in international business (IB) research. It has received particular interest from scholars in the last few years, as they have studied different aspects of it using a range of theoretical and methodological lenses (e.g., Yli-Renko et al., 2002; Ng and Hamilton, 2016; D'Angelo and Presutti, 2019; Felzenstein et al., 2019). As a result of this examination, it has become established that international growth patterns and choices of small firms tend to differ significantly from those of large firms (Nummela, 2010; Barber et al., 2016). A key reason for the different international growth patterns relates to lack of financial and human resources in the small firms (e.g. Barber et al., 2016). Findings in prior studies indicate that networks and relationships increase the possibility to get access to external resources, act as a channel for information and knowledge on foreign markets and enhance learning (see, for example, Ojala et al., 2018; Ryan et al., 2019) and thus are often linked to international growth (see, for example, Fernhaber and Li, 2013; Shneor et al., 2016). In general, in the case of small firms, intangible resources have been found to play a very important role in their international growth (Del Giudice et al., 2017). Therefore, it is important to analyse the role of different types of intangible resources in this context.

One such intangible resource is *intellectual capital* (IC). The systematic literature review on IC by Pedro et al. (2018: 2517) suggests that IC can be defined as "knowledge, intangible assets and resources that can be combined to create greater value added for stakeholders and to achieve a competitive advantage". IC is receiving increasing attention from scholars as a key determinant of small firms' performance (McDowell et al. 2018; Mansion and Bausch 2019). Therefore, it is highly relevant for such firms to understand how to accumulate and manage intellectual capital in different contexts. However, recent studies focusing on IC in the context of internationalization reveal that prior studies linking intellectual capital specifically to international growth of small firms are very limited (see Radulovich et al., 2018) even though some research exists in exploring the influence of intellectual capital on internationalization behaviour (e.g. Mansion and Bausch, 2019; Vătămănescu et al., 2019).

The limitations in the IB literature with regard to IC accumulation in small firms directs us to look at other discussions for advice. Prior research in the field of marketing indicates that social media plays an important role for small firms as it helps them overcome traditional barriers associated with business relationships development and access to networks and customers (e.g. Rialp-Criado and Rialp-Criado, 2018; Benitez et al., 2018; Hurmelinna-Laukkanen et al., 2020). A number of studies conducted during the last decade have stressed that social media is a very useful tool for knowledge transfer in all types of organizations (e.g. Hanna et al., 2011; Ngai et al., 2015) Recent studies have shown how social media's role in knowledge transfer is particularly relevant for small firms, as it helps them circumvent some of the resource barriers by offering access to open knowledge sources (e.g. de Zubielqui et al., 2019). These notions indicate that social media might provide valuable means of IC development.

Social media is also relevant regarding the aspect of internationalization. The role of social media for international growth of small and medium sized enterprises has been addressed in some recent studies (e.g., Rialp-Criado and Rialp-Criado, 2018; Dabić et al., 2019; Pergelova et al., 2019; Hurmelinna-Laukkanen et al., 2020; Moen et al., 2020). However, these studies have not considered the element of intellectual capital, and the role of social media as a knowledge transfer tool for IC accumulation during international growth of small firms is still poorly understood. There is a clear gap in the literature, which our chapter aims to fill.

These arguments form the starting point of our chapter, where we aim to analyse the role of social media as a knowledge transfer tool for IC accumulation by the small firms during their international growth. In our examination, we focus on the information technology (IT) sector in Finland and conduct case studies in four Finnish firms specializing in different software systems. The IT sector has been referred to as one of the most dynamic business sectors where social media has been found to play an increasingly important role in both operations and strategies (Akhtar et al., 2018; Band, 2019). The IT sector is a relevant context since the importance of knowledge transfer and IC accumulation is well established in extant literature for this specific business sector (e.g. Ramadan et al., 2017). Similarly, social media usage both in personal and organizational contexts is very high in the Nordic countries, including Finland (e.g. Ammirato et al., 2019; Koiranen et al., 2019), which makes our research setting a relevant empirical context.

The rest of the chapter is organized as follows. The next section introduces the relevant existing literature. The scrutiny of existing knowledge is followed by the discussion on research methodology and the case firms. Then study findings are then presented. The chapter concludes with the presentation of implications of the findings, and future research directions.

LITERATURE REVIEW

Intellectual Capital and International Growth of Firms

It has been argued that no universal definition for *intellectual capital* (IC) has been developed so far (Hormiga et al., 2011). Nevertheless, there are some common features in the relevant discussion. The definitions and categorizations of IC by Edvinsson and Sullivan (1996), Roos and Roos (1997), Bontis (1998) and Youndt et al. (2004) are among those most often referred to in IC studies (Pedro et al., 2018) offering somewhat different definitions, but still some similarity. As noted above, in this study we adopt the definition by Pedro et al. (2018: 2517) who describe IC as "knowledge, intangible assets and resources that can be combined to create greater value added for stakeholders and to achieve a competitive advantage". While at a broad level homogeneity exists in understanding the basic concept, there is more variety in terms of the components or dimensions forming IC. Although as many as 35 components have been identified in prior empirical studies (Pedro et al., 2018), a great majority of the studies have focused on one or more of the three main dimensions of IC which were identified by the pioneering scholars. Thus, human capital (HC), structural capital (SC) and relational capital (RC) represent the most common dimensions of IC (see, for example, Hormiga et al., 2011; Hsu and Wang, 2012).

HC comprises the knowledge, education, skills and characteristics of the members of the organization (see, for example, Edvinsson and Malone, 1997). It thus stands for the abilities of organizational actors to take skilful action and, thereby, produce value for the firm (Kianto et al., 2010). SC of the organization is defined as the knowledge that stays in the firm when members of staff leave (e.g. Roos et al., 1998). It includes both physical elements such as infrastructure and intangible elements such as a firm's culture and history (Edvinsson and Sullivan, 1996). RC refers to the ability of an organization to interact in a positive manner with the external stakeholders. It includes resources related to the firm's external relationships, such as its connections with its customers, suppliers, partners, and the local community, and the knowledge embedded in these relationships (Sveiby, 1997; Edvinsson and Malone, 1997; Bontis, 1998).

The link between IC as a whole and firm performance, specifically the financial performance, has been extensively studied and supported (see, for example, Bayraktaroglu et al., 2019; Xu and Li, 2019). In the IC literature, the general argument is that IC contributes to firm growth, but there is only a limited number of empirical studies that have explicitly explored this relationship (for a few exceptions see, for example, Kianto and Waajakoski, 2010). There also are some studies in which growth measures have been included as part of the performance scale (see, for example, Hussinki et al., 2017; McDowell et al., 2018), pointing to the same direction. The role of IC on performance in general is covered less in the international business context. Based on the reviews by Mansion and Bausch (2019) and Vătămănescu et al. (2019), the focus has mostly been on exploring the effect of IC on internationalization behaviour and, to a lesser extent, on performance implications. Likewise, a limitation is that in the international business context, most of the studies have not explicitly applied the specific IC dimension(s), but rather utilized concepts which are more applicable in the internationalization approaches such as in the Uppsala model, born-global view, and network theory (Vătămănescu et al., 2019). However, Vătămănescu et al. (2019) argue that most of the empirical papers have covered HC, focusing specifically on the managers' abilities, skills, education and international experience. RC has been the second most common type of IC. SC has received relatively little attention so far in IB literature. However, as knowledge and information, together with networks and relationships have been argued to be the most common drivers for international growth (see, for example, Autio et al., 2000; D'Angelo and Presutti, 2019; Yli-Renko et al., 2002; Fernhaber and Li, 2013; Shneor et al., 2016), the influence of IC and its dimensions is expected to have an important role for international growth.

The logic of this expectation can be grounded in existing studies. Although most of the empirical studies exploring the link between IC and performance have been based on large firms (see, for example, Bayraktaroglu et al., 2019; Sardo and Serrasqueiro, 2018; Komnenic and Pokrajcic, 2012; Molodchik et al., 2019), in the SME context the role of IC may be even more important because of their challenges to compete on scale or scope (McDowell et al., 2018). In fact, based on the review of empirical research on IC and firm performance, Inkinen (2015) found that the different dimensions of intellectual capital had an effect on performance either directly or through mediating models. Dynamic capabilities (see, for example, Hsu and Wang, 2012) and innovation capabilities (see, for example, Mathuraymatha, 2012) have been identified as potential mediating factors between intellectual capital and performance.

In addition, some contextual factors such as firm size (Corvino et al., 2019; Musteen et al., 2017), a firm's home country (Andreeva and Garanina, 2016) and industry (Molodchik et al., 2019) have been found to moderate the effect of IC on performance. What is interesting in the findings is that, depending on the context, different combinations of IC may improve performance and the relative importance of specific dimensions may vary (Andreeva and Garanina, 2016). The results also show that there are interaction effects between the dimensions of IC. However, how the dimensions of IC interact may vary (Agostini et al., 2017). Based on the findings by McDowell et al. (2018) on 460 small business owners in the US, both HC and SC were found to improve performance, while social capital, often used interchangeably with relational capital (Pedro et al., 2018) did not have any influence. Similar conclusions were made by Xu and Li (2019) for SMEs' performance in China. On the other hand, Agostini et al. (2017) found that, based on their sample of 150 Italian manufacturing SMEs, the firms with a combination of high HC and RC had higher innovation performance over the firms with a low combination of the same IC dimensions. In a similar way, Radulovich et al. (2018) found that HC and RC had positive influence on international performance for Indian professional service entrepreneurs.

These insights match with those few studies where IC dimensions have been addressed in the international business context. In those studies, HC has been seen as the critical component to create assets which are required in foreign markets (Vătămănescu et al., 2019). Elements of HC among others help in identifying business opportunities and exploiting them (Mansion and Baush, 2019; Ruzzier et al., 2007), thus forming the bases for international growth. Surprisingly, Vuorio et al. (2020) did not find HC to have any effect on mostly small ICT firms' internationalization. This can however be explained by the fact that they did not include international experience as part of the measurement of HC. Similarly, earlier findings indicate that RC seems to have an important role in all stages of internationalization (Jardon and Molodchik, 2017) and that RC has an effect on export propensity, intensity and scope (Mansion and Bausch, 2019). However, Laursen et al. (2012) found that home-region related social capital (RC), which was considered to be an important source for knowledge and thus supporting the globalization of the firm, could at a certain point start to exhibit negative influences because of the over-embeddedness in the local environment. In addition, the type of ties and bonding have been found to influence international growth (Totskaya, 2015). This indicates that depending on the source or type of RC, the performance outcome may be either positive or negative. The influence of RC stems from the access to networks and increased interactions with different partners which, in a similar way to HC, helps to identify opportunities, but also reduces the perceived uncertainty and risks linked to foreign markets (Mansion and Bausch, 2019; Fernhaber and Li, 2013) and thus may increase international growth. Finally, as mentioned above, SC has not been clearly covered in the international business context, which shows the need for empirical exploration.

The interaction effects of the IC dimensions may also play a role in the IB context. When it comes to interaction effects between the IC dimensions and their influence on performance, Inkinen (2015) concluded that although many studies have found that HC is considered as antecedent to SC and on RC – which then have an effect on performance – others have also emphasized that SC enables HC and RC to contribute to firm performance. In the international business context, Radulovich et al. (2018) found support for the indirect effect of HC through RC on performance. Agostini et al. (2017) further argue that the willingness to cooperate and share knowledge among employees is an important antecedent for developing employees' skills, thus also emphasizing the interaction effect between IC dimensions. Still, further studies are needed to increase the understanding of the interaction effects between the IC dimensions.

Intellectual Capital and Knowledge Transfer via Social Media

Intellectual capital is strongly linked to knowledge management (Seleim and Khalil, 2011) and studies have found similarities for supporting the development of intellectual capital and successful knowledge transfer. Combination and exchange have been suggested to be the two generic processes through which IC is created (Moran and Ghoshal, 1996) and they often form the bases for knowledge transfer too. In connection with these processes, the role of social capital has been emphasized. Nahapiet and Ghoshal (1998) argue that the dimensions of social capital have an influence on the conditions to exchange and combine existing intellectual capital, which are needed to create new intellectual capital. The structural dimension (e.g. network ties and configurations), cognitive dimension (e.g. shared codes and language) and relational dimension (e.g. trust, norms and obligations) have varying influences on offering the opportunity, motivation and capability for exchange and combination of intellectual capital as well as on the expectation for the activity to create value. Thus, social capital is argued to have an indirect effect on intellectual capital accumulation. In addition to creating supportive conditions for developing intellectual capital, social capital has been argued to influence positively on knowledge transfer (van Wijk et al., 2008). Maurer et al. (2011), for example, found that, in particular, the relational dimension of social capital measured by the strength of ties was found to increase knowledge transfer in the intra-organizational context.

Even though there are similarities in the supportive conditions for successful IC development and knowledge transfer, they are argued to serve different purposes (Zhou and Fink, 2003). Thus, intellectual capital can be seen as representing the knowledge stock at a certain point of time while knowledge management processes contribute to the accumulation of this knowledge base (Allameh, 2018; Hussi, 2004; Shih et al., 2010). Prior studies have explored the influence of knowledge management processes such as knowledge sharing and knowledge transfer on IC, but there is still limited understanding of the influence of the knowledge management process on the specific IC components. Allameh (2018) found knowledge sharing to contribute positively to HC, RC and SC while Seleim and Khalil (2011) found that knowledge transfer had a significant positive relationship with only relational capital. Knowledge sharing or knowledge transfer has mostly been treated in a general level and no clear implications of the specific type of knowledge transfer elements and their influence on IC components have been made. An exception to this is a study by Wang et al. (2014) who differentiated between explicit and tacit knowledge sharing. They found that explicit knowledge sharing had positive relationships with HC and SC while tacit knowledge sharing influenced positively in addition to RC. Similarly, the focus in knowledge transfer studies in the international context has mostly recognized only the explicit and tacit knowledge types, thus lacking the identification of more specific knowledge types (Zeng et al., 2018).

Knowledge transfer taking place across borders has been suggested to encounter several challenges because of the country level differences in institutions and culture as well as because of geographical distance and time (Gaur et al., 2019; Ho and Wang, 2015; Javidan et al., 2005). Knowledge transfer in the SME context brings additional challenges for knowledge transfer. Some of the challenges mentioned are a lack of formal and systematic approach towards knowledge transfer (Durst and Edvardsson, 2012) and the dependence on an owner-manager's ability to support knowledge transfer (Jones and Macpherson, 2006).

We argue that social media as a tool for knowledge transfer could offer possibilities for SMEs to tackle the challenges related to geographical distance and time. In addition, we see that what tools are employed in knowledge transfer has an effect on how knowledge transfer influences specific IC dimensions. In general, internet technologies offer firms the possibility to disseminate, acquire, and share information (Prashantham, 2005). Specifically, developments in social media have revolutionized how people share their knowledge, communicate, and collaborate with each other (Ahmed et al., 2019; Kaplan and Haenlein, 2010; Ngai et al., 2015; Hanna et al., 2011). Social media provides a channel through which organizations can create, share and maintain knowledge, communication and activities with their employees, peers, customers, partners and other stakeholders globally (Mangold and Faulds, 2009). A systematic literature review by Ahmed et al. (2019) found that knowledge-seeking, knowledge-contributing, and social interactivity are the three main activities used for knowledge sharing in social media at the individual level. However, organizational level studies are limited and there is a need to increase understanding of how firms utilize social media for knowledge transfer. Thus, social media can be seen as a valuable knowledge transfer tool for combining and exchanging relevant resources and thus creating and developing IC for SMEs.

So far, studies exploring the role of social media in the IC context have mostly focused on the effect of social media on disclosure of IC (Lardo et al., 2017; Sgrò et al., 2019) and the potential value implications on HC and RC. In addition, Wisniewski (2013) argued that different types of social media can have associations with HC, RC and/or SC. Even though Wisniewski (2013) focused on social media companies and their IC, similar associations between social media and IC dimensions may be present for other types of firms also through their knowledge transfer characteristics. Hence, social networking sites and virtual worlds may increase customer capital (relational capital) through virtual interconnectedness; blogs increase HC through communication of novel ideas, and content communities; and collaborative projects increase SC through disclosing and sharing information (Wisniewski, 2013). In addition, Archer-Brown and Kietzmann (2018) argued that different types of enterprise social media (ESM) may facilitate human and social capital by offering tools for co-creation of ideas, encouragement to share tacit knowledge, and a sense of community in collaborative work. Similarly, as social media platforms have different characteristics, it has been argued that, depending on the social media type, it can promote either knowledge sharing, knowledge creation, or keeping people connected (Bharati et al., 2015). Still, understanding of the linkages between social media as a knowledge transfer tool and IC dimensions is still in its infancy and requires further empirical studies.

RESEARCH METHODOLOGY

A multiple case-study method was selected for this study due to the explanatory nature of the research question. Eisenhardt (1989) suggests that multiple case studies enable studying patterns that are common to the cases and theory under investigation. In addition, the case-study method makes it possible to explain the significance and cause-and-effect relationships of the examined phenomena (Yin, 1994). In line with Eisenhardt's (1989) recommendation of four to ten cases, four case firms were included in this multiple case study.

Case Selection

The case firms were selected for this study on theoretical grounds, as advised in the study of Eisenhardt (1989). Thus, the selection criteria for the firms were as follows: first, the firms had to be Finnish and operate in the software sector and provide software as a service. Second, the firms had to meet the European Commission's definition of small and medium-sized enterprises: an SME is a firm that employs fewer than 250 employees with an annual turnover not exceeding €50 million. As an alternative for net sales, it is possible to determine the balance sheet, where sheet total may not exceed €43 million (European Commission, 2003). Third, the firms needed to be involved in exporting for at least two years. Fourth, they should be present on at least two social media platforms as well as have vivid international activities on these platforms. We focused on the Finnish software industry (especially software-as-a-service firms) since these firms are high technology firms and they are familiar with new digital tools and platforms such as social media (e.g. Ammirato et al., 2019). Moreover, the industry is an example of a highly internationalized industry signified by rapid change and growth. Finland was chosen as the country of origin owing to its small and open economy with a very limited domestic market. Owing to its small domestic market, international growth is generally a common growth strategy for Finnish software firms.

We selected the case firms from "The Finnish Software and E-business Association database", a database that lists and offers information about most Finnish software and e-business firms. The Finnish Software and E-business Association is a non-aligned association for professional and entrepreneurial software and e-business executives. The database includes 428 Finnish software and e-business firms of which 98 firms provide software as a service. The criteria of exporting experience and presence in two social media platforms limited the number of potential cases to 49. We started by contacting one potential case firm by telephone and then gradually continued to add firms in the same manner. All the firms that we subsequently contacted agreed to participate in the study. Data collection was stopped after four companies had been visited. Because the interviews conducted at the last two firms provided us with narratives similar to those we had previously heard, the data saturation point seemed to have been reached. New insights into the phenomenon were no longer gained, and the phenomenon, therefore, had been substantially explained (Eisenhardt, 1989). This may be due to the fact that case firms are small, they operate in a relatively narrow sector (software as a service) and they have similar activities and business functions.

Data Collection

The research uses three data collection methods, semi-structured interviews, observations and documents. Semi-structured interviews were chosen as the main data collection approach because they provide reliable and comparable qualitative data for the study. Interviews are a flexible data collection tool and involve direct linguistic interaction between the interviewer and the interviewee (Saunders et al., 2009: Yin, 1994). Interviews offer a possibility to guide and control data collection as well as offer possibilities to gain in-depth information and understand the motives behind the answers (Eriksson and Kovalainen, 2008). There were three requirements for the interviewees. The first requirement for an interviewee was that the person needed to be involved in the firms' international growth activities. The second requirement was that the person understands how and why the firm uses various social media platforms.

The third requirement was the interviewee's executive position in the firm. A person who is or has been a member of the management team was preferred. These requirements were set in order to maximize the gathering of the most reliable and meaningful data.

Interviews were conducted according to the theme interview framework. The first version of the framework was developed around three key themes: (1) intellectual capital (human, relational and structural capital), (2) international growth, and (3) social media. Then, the first version of the framework was tested with one pilot firm, which assisted in developing relevant and more specific questions related to the themes. All themes were developed by following the guidelines of Yin (1994), trying to make the questions as non-leading as possible. This allowed the interviewees to give genuine answers to the themes during the interviews. All interviews were conducted in Finnish since forcing the interviewees to give answers in anything other than their native language could affect the results in limiting the quality and the quantity of the output. The findings were translated back to English by a bilingual co-author who has experience in undertaking such qualitative analysis over many years. Interview details are summarized in Table 5.1.

Table 5.1   Interviews details

Firm/location	Interviewee	Date	Time	Duration	Language
Firm A/Finland	CEO	9 March 2020	14.30–15.25	55 min.	Finnish
Firm B/Finland	Co-Founder	11 March 2020	10.00–10.46	46 min.	Finnish
Firm C/Finland	CEO	13 March 2020	13.00–13.42	42 min.	Finnish
Firm D/Finland	Manager	14 April 2020	10.30–11.35	65 min.	Finnish

In addition, the collected data from interviews was compared with the observations of social media platforms that firms were using. We made observations on how firms use platforms, what kind of information they share and especially how firms use platforms as a knowledge transfer tool. Documents include the case firms' documents, webpages, public records and statistics. We collected basic information about the firms (e.g. year of foundation, products and services) on webpages and digital brochures (see Table 5.2). Key figures such as turnover and number of employees were collected on online service Fonecta Finder statistics (see Table 5.3).

Data Analysis

All research data were documented and appropriately stored in a case study database. The interviews were digitally recorded, carefully listened to, and transcribed verbatim. A second listening was arranged to ensure correspondence between the recorded and transcribed data. A qualitative data analysis tool, NVivo 12, was used to assist with the coding of the data into main themes and subcategories. The main themes were (1) Intellectual capital (human, relational and structural capital), (2) International growth, and (3) Social media. Each main theme included subcategories such as knowledge transfer and intellectual capital, international growth and intellectual capital, and social media and international growth according to which the answers were carefully coded. Then, the collected data from interviews was compared with the observations of social media platforms that firms were using. Data triangulation gave data that is more comprehensive and provided verification and validity while complementing similar information (Saunders et al., 2009).

The actual analysis was conducted in line with the recommendations of Yin (1994) and Miles et al. (1994) to identify similarities and differences in the cases. The data analysis included within-case and cross-case analysis (see Table 5.5) to find specific themes and patterns in the data (Miles et al., 1994). We used integrated comparative and within-case analysis (Welch et al., 2011). When identifying patterns, we discussed differences and similarities between the cases and the literature (Eisenhardt, 1989). Finally, the findings were reviewed and verified by the case firm to further increase the validity of the results.

FINDINGS

Description of the Case Firms

Firm A
Firm A provides a cloud-based inbound marketing service that enables companies to monitor and manage their online presence, monitor the position of their competitors, and show inbound marketing data from other web analytics tools. It offers solutions for inbound marketing and search engine optimization, including online marketing, product sales, and brand management. The firm has customers in Europe and the USA. Firm A was founded in 2011 and is based in Helsinki, Finland. Social media platforms have been agile and cost-effective tools for the firm when they have been gathering information about competitors, customers' needs and preferences, market trends and target markets. Through social media, they have been able to identify new opportunities abroad.

Firm B
Firm B is a Finnish software company, whose core competencies are cloud services and the sale of digital services online. The firm provides a digital platform that enables companies to automate the sale of digital products such as SaaS or cloud services online, including trial, sales, and payment phases, as well as ongoing maintenance after the sales transaction aimed at minimizing attrition. The company's customers include software as a service, cloud service and internet-of-things service providers in Europe. Firm B was founded in 2013 and is based in Helsinki, Finland. The firm uses social media platforms for various purposes. The competition in the international environment is fierce and social media provides tools to be competitive, especially in terms of visibility and market presence. Moreover, social media has been a powerful tool for networking with partners and customers.

Firm C
Firm C provides a cloud-based price monitoring service for retail and e-commerce firms. The solution collects accurate information on market pricing, which helps in analysis and margin optimization. Technologically advanced price monitoring enables combining internal data with online data collected into the solution. The firm has customers in Europe. Firm C was founded in 2015 and is based in Helsinki, Finland. The firm uses social media actively in marketing and communication activities to disseminate information about its products and services. With social media, the firm has been able to generate leads and build credibility

and awareness globally. Moreover, the firm has used social media as a partner and customer support channel (e.g. by providing video-instructions and manuals).

Firm D

Firm D provides a software solution for childcare centres, supporting all daily activities between educators, children and families. The solution has been designed by Finnish early childhood education professionals and is available in several languages. The firm has customers in Europe, South East Asia, Middle East, Africa and Latin America. Firm D was founded in 2014 and is based in Helsinki, Finland. Tables 5.2 and 5.3 offer an overview of key aspects of the case firms, including their target markets, products (services) as well as the number of employees, international growth, and social media usage. Social media platforms are the foundation of firm marketing and sales efforts. With social media, the firm can reach a larger target audience faster than traditional sales and marketing. Moreover, social media has been a cost-effective way of engaging and interacting with customers and partners.

Table 5.2   Case firms' overview

Firms	Founded	Internationalized	Target markets	Products/ services	Personnel	Social media usage in international environment
Firm A	2011	2013	Europe, USA	Inbound marketing software solutions	2 (+ external freelancers)	7 years
Firm B	2013	2014	Europe	Sales software platform, cloud services, digital services	10	6 years
Firm C	2015	2016	Europe, USA	Price monitoring service for retail and ecommerce firms	13	3 years
Firm D	2014	2015	Europe, South East Asia, Middle East, Africa and Latin America	Mobile solutions for child care centres	5 (platform development outsourced)	3 years

Human Capital Accumulation via Social Media

Since software firms provide high technology and knowledge-intensive products and services, human capital (HC) is essential for them. For example, the co-founder of Firm B emphasized that the knowledge and skills of their employees are key assets for them. Without skilled employees, they could not stay and compete in international markets. In line with this, the CEO of Firm A explained that they focus significantly on HC. For example, when they recruit new employees, they check very carefully the knowledge and skills of each candidate. The CEO emphasized that social media platforms such as LinkedIn and Facebook have been very useful in their recruitment processes. For example, on LinkedIn, it is very easy to check a person's complete work and education history. In addition, users may give extra information, such as a link to their portfolio or a video presentation.

Table 5.3   Key figures of the case firms (Fonecta Finder statistics, 2020)

	Year 2018	Year 2019	Annual growth
Firm A			
Number of countries	2	3	50 %
Number of customers (firms)	90	100	11.11 %
Number of employees	2 + external freelancers	2 + external freelancers	0 %
Turnover €	166,000	173,500	4.5 %
Exports €	16,600	26,025	56.78 %
Share of exports / total turnover	9.6%	15%	
Firm B			
Number of countries	3	5	66.67 %
Number of customers (firms)	15	20	33.33 %
Number of employees	8	10	25 %
Turnover €	330,000	480,000	45.45 %
Exports €	16,600	24,000	44.58 %
Share of exports/total turnover	5%	5%	
Firm C	Year 2018	Year 2019	Annual growth
Number of countries	3	7	133 %
Number of customers (firms)	33	36	9.09 %
Number of employees	7	13	85.71 %
Turnover €	264,000	450,000	70.45 %
Exports €	44,880	49,500	10.29 %
Share of exports/total turnover	17%	11%	
Firm D	Year 2018	Year 2019	Annual growth
Number of countries	3	14	366.67 %
Number of customers (firms)	25	50	100 %
Number of employees	5	5	0 %
Turnover €	120,000	260,000	116.67 %
Exports €	75,000	208,000	177.33 %
Share of exports/total turnover	62.5%	80%	

This may increase the reliability and credibility of the candidate. Similarly, the CEO of Firm C explained that they are active on Facebook, Instagram and LinkedIn and that this activity on social media has attracted educated and skilled people with international experience to contact them, which has led to recruitment and thus increased HC facilitated international growth:

> We are very active on social media and have found that skilled people apply for jobs after they have read about our firm on social media. (Firm C, CEO)

The CEO of Firm A further argued that learning is an essential skill in the software sector. Technology is evolving rapidly, and new tools and practices are appearing constantly. This means that in order to stay competitive, firms have to invest heavily in learning. The CEO explained that social media offers great platforms for knowledge development and learning. For example, discussion groups on Facebook and LinkedIn have been very useful for them. The advantage of these platforms is that they bring together a large number of (international) experts who are interested in the same issues. In addition, most of the users are willing to share their experience and knowledge online. The CEO of the firm A stated:

Discussion groups on Facebook and LinkedIn have been very useful for us. For example, if you have a problem, you can post the description of the problem to the group and get answers fast. There are thousands of users and a lot of knowledge in these groups.

In the same fashion, the co-founder of Firm B argued that social media provides useful and up-to-date training and support sources, which in turn increases employees' knowledge and adds HC in the firm. These resources are usually easy to reach and inexpensive. For example, they are using LinkedIn, YouTube, Facebook, Twitter and various discussion forums to increase HC. The co-founder of Firm B described these issues as follows:

> I believe that our employees have a willingness to develop their own skills. Since the software industry develops at a rapid pace, the latest information is often found on social media (or on the internet) For example, it can be difficult to choose the right technology when you are developing software. Social media provides good and up-to-date discussion forums on various software topics. These forums provide valuable information on technological developments and the experiences of the other developers all over the world.

Moreover, the CEO of Firm A stated that they use Blog, Facebook and Twitter to gain information about new technologies, potential customer groups and international markets. For example, they monitor competitors' webpages and social media activity to see how they interact and behave in the market. In addition, the firm monitors and analyses various online forums to understand in which direction markets are developing. The information gained via social media platforms has increased HC and enabled them to allocate the firm resources more efficiently, which has allowed them to focus on their core competences and international growth:

> For us, social media platforms such as Blog, Facebook and Twitter have been valuable tools for gaining information about foreign markets and competitors. (Firm C, CEO)

This is in line with the argument of the manager of Firm D, who stated that their main markets are in the emerging markets (i.e. South East Asia, Middle East, Africa and Latin America). They do not have any partners in these markets yet. However, they have been able to penetrate these markets by using internet and social media platforms. For example, they have used social media as a market research tool to find out where their potential customers are. The manager stated:

> At the moment, we are focusing our export efforts on emerging markets such as South East Asia, Middle East, Africa and Latin America. With the internet and social media, we have been able to penetrate into these markets and gain international growth. Without these online tools, it would have been impossible for us to grow so fast. (Firm D, Manager)

In sum, the case firms gain both tacit knowledge (embedded in the human mind through experience) and explicit knowledge (codified, e.g. documents, videos, manuals) on various social media platforms (see Ahmed et al., 2019; Kaplan and Haenlein, 2010; Ngai et al., 2015; Hanna et al., 2011, Mangold and Faulds, 2009). The most used solutions for gaining HC are Facebook, LinkedIn, Twitter, Blog, YouTube, Instagram, SlideShare and Twitter. These platforms enabled access to various knowledge sources domestically as well as abroad, which connects directly to increased knowledge sharing and accumulation of IC. Importantly, social media solutions facilitated learning and knowledge creation (see Bharati et al., 2015; D'Angelo and Presutti, 2019). This added HC in the firms, which in turn increased competitiveness, lead generation and international growth.

Relational Capital Accumulation via Social Media

The interviewees explained that relational capital (RC) is very important for their businesses. For example, the CEO of Firm A stated that the reliability and credibility of the company are essential from the relational capital perspective. The firm communicates actively with its partners and nurtures customers carefully. They often have partner meetings (both online and face-to-face) through which they are able to gain market- and customer-specific information. In addition, the company communicates and interacts with customers in various channels. It uses digital channels such as discussion forums, extranet and social media as well as traditional channels such as phones. The CEO of Firm A argued that social media is an important channel for them since it is low-cost, and it reaches a large number of people globally. In addition, social media enables better interaction and customer engagement, which enables the firm to build a sustainable business abroad. The combination of the social media channels varies according to the market. The firm uses Facebook, Blog, LinkedIn and YouTube in the European market and Twitter, Instagram and YouTube in the US market. This is because it has tested tools in various markets and based on that selected the most effective ones. Another explanation is that nowadays platforms enable the company to target markets better than before. As the CEO of the Firm A stated:

> Interaction, communication and knowledge sharing on social media is very important for us. The use of social media creates value not only for us, but also for our partners and customers. With social media, we are able to engage partners and customers better than before. This increases relational capital in our firm and facilitates growth. (Firm A, CEO)

This is in line with the arguments of the CEO of Firm C, who explained that social media is essential for their business. It allows them to reach, nurture, and engage partners and customers on a global scale. This in turn helps to generate international leads, sales, brand awareness, revenue, and growth. Moreover, the manager of Firm D stated that since they are a small company with limited resources, they are investing in online tools such as social media. This is because social media reaches partners and customers cost-effectively. For example, the company has customers in 14 countries, and it would be too expensive to arrange face-to-face meetings in every country. Social media platforms enable interaction with partners and increases trust and credibility, which in turn assists in improving the firm's foreign operations.

> We are a small company and thus have very limited resources. It would be impossible for us to arrange face-to-face meetings in various countries. Internet-based tools such as Skype, Facebook and LinkedIn have made it possible to communicate and interact with our customers and partners all over the world. (Firm D, Manager)

Social media enables the firm to build extensive international networks quickly, which can increase relational capital. However, building networks without a plan or strategy may be ineffective. The CEO of the Firm A argued that they have also tried to focus on the quality of networks, not only on the quantity. He noted that there are a large number of different networks on social media and if you do not have a strategy on how and with whom to network, it can be a waste of time. On the other hand, the manager of Firm D stated that they are trying to network on social media as much as possible and they do not have any specific plan for that. In fact, they have been able to identify growth opportunities by networking widely, without a plan, on social media.

> The more we have been able to network abroad, the more we have understood target markets and how customers behave. This has increased our company's international intellectual capital, which in turn has accelerated international growth. The growth of international intellectual capital has strengthened our competitiveness. (Firm D, CEO)

In sum, the case firms network actively with various stakeholders. The most used social media solutions for networking are Facebook, LinkedIn and Twitter. These platforms enabled firms to build large international networks easily and fast (see Wisniewski, 2013), which increased RC in the firms. This, in turn assisted firms to identify growth opportunities abroad more effectively (e.g. Hurmelinna-Laukkanen et al., 2020). Moreover, the firms communicated and interacted with their customers and partners on Facebook, Twitter, LinkedIn, Instagram, YouTube and Blog. The increased interaction – that is, increased knowledge transfer at multiple levels – on social media platforms led to better customer and partner engagement and RC accumulation, which enabled sustainable business and faster international growth.

Structural Capital Accumulation via Social Media

Structural capital (SC) exists in the case firms' processes, databases, and cultures (e.g. Bontis et al., 2005). According to the CEO of Firm A, structural capital exists mainly in the firm's processes. For example, the firm's marketing and sales processes are pre-defined and social media is an essential part of these efforts. In fact, social media is embedded into their processes. However, the impact of social media in the processes may vary. In certain cases, social media (e.g. Facebook) may be the only marketing or sales channel they are using, and thus these affect significantly their processes. On the other hand, social media can be used to support other marketing or sales efforts. For example, it can be used to speed up a customer's buying process by communicating online with him/her.

The co-founder of Firm B explained that since they are a small firm, staff changes can be fatal. For this reason, they have tried to increase structural capital (knowledge in processes and databases). For example, they have gathered customer-, country- and market-specific information into various databases. The basic idea is that information can be found in the databases if needed, and the employees can access the data widely. In particular, social media platforms such as Facebook and Twitter have been valuable tools when gathering the information into the databases. The data collected through social media has been combined with information drawn from other sources, which in turn has contributed to the accumulation of new knowledge assets.

> With social media, you can relatively easily collect information about competitors, market trends, target markets and customers. (Firm B, co-founder)

In line with this, the manager of Firm D explained that structural capital exists in the firm's processes and databases. For example, it has a customer register database that includes relevant information about its customers – including that gained via social media tools. Another example is a database that contains information about its products and services (e.g. support material for customers and partners, product version info). The databases are integrated into the firm's other IT systems, which enables various users in different locations to use the data:

> In our company structural capital exists mainly in processes and databases. We are using Customer Relationship Management system, which includes various databases and integrations to the other IT systems in the firm. (Firm D, Manager)

Structural capital exists also in the firms' cultures. The CEO of Firm C stated that the company is operating in a turbulent environment and faces market and technology changes at a rapid pace. For this reason, it has tried to build a flexible firm culture. This means that it has a culture that appreciates and values learning and knowledge sharing. A key element in the culture is communication and interaction between employees and the firm's partners/customers. Since social media reaches employees, customers and partners and enables knowledge sharing and learning, it has been an important tool. In fact, social media use has become integrated into the company's organizational culture. In line with this, the manager of Firm D explained that since the company culture embraces knowledge sharing and learning, platforms such as Facebook, LinkedIn and Twitter have been obvious choices.

> In our field, the change is normal. The market is changing, technologies are evolving, and new competitors are emerging constantly. In order to respond to these challenges, we have developed a flexible firm culture.(Firm C, CEO)

In sum, structural capital exists in the case firms' recruitment, marketing and sales processes, databases, and cultures – all of which necessitate knowledge transfer in order to function optimally. In marketing, sales and recruitment, social media was integrated into processes with an observable aim to secure and promote knowledge transfer (see Madia, 2011; Kwahk and Park, 2016). However, our findings indicate that the impact of social media on the processes and SC varies. For example, in certain cases social media was used to support other processes (e.g. sales or recruitment) and the impact of social media was lower, while in other cases social media was the only channel they were using (e.g. online-targeted marketing), then the impact of social media was higher. In addition, social media (mainly Twitter, Facebook and LinkedIn) enabled the gathering of customer-, country- and market-specific data into databases (see Hurmelinna-Laukkanen et al., 2020). The collected data increased SC and facilitated decision-making related to the internationalization and growth. Moreover, structural capital exists also in the firms' "flexible" cultures. The flexibility enabled information to flow throughout the organization and thereby facilitated knowledge transfer and learning. In addition, flexibility fostered innovations and allowed them to respond to problems fast, which in turn increased SC and competitiveness in the international market.

The findings of our study are summarized in Tables 5.4 and 5.5.

Table 5.4   *Cross-case analysis*

Intellectual capital dimension	Knowledge transfer function	Social media platforms and intellectual capital accumulation			
		Firm A	Firm B	Firm C	Firm D
Human capital	Recruitment, talent acquisition	*FB, LinkedIn* Potential employees' background check (skills, knowledge, education, history)	*LinkedIn and FB* Access to international "talent database"	*FB, LinkedIn* Activity on platforms attracts educated/skilled people	*LinkedIn* Access to international "talent database"
	Learning, knowledge creation, acquisition sharing/integration	*FB, LinkedIn, Twitter, YouTube, Blog* Data gathering about new technologies, customers and international markets → facilitate learning and knowledge sharing	*FB, LinkedIn, Twitter, YouTube, Blog, SlideShare, IG* Up-to-date trainings and support sources for the firm, facilitate learning	*FB, LinkedIn, Twitter, YouTube, Blog, SlideShare, IG* Enables to gain information about new markets → increases knowledge sharing/learning	*FB, LinkedIn, Twitter, YouTube, Blog, IG* Enables low-cost market research
Relational capital	Networking	*LinkedIn, Twitter, FB* Extensive and fast networking with partners/customers	*FB, Twitter, LinkedIn* Extensive and fast networking globally	*LinkedIn, Twitter, FB* Extensive and fast networking with partners/customers	*FB, LinkedIn* Extensive and fast networking globally
	Communication, collaboration, interaction and engagement	*FB, Twitter, LinkedIn, YouTube, Blog, IG* Enhanced interaction and customer/partner engagement → improved competitiveness abroad, sustainable business	*FB, Twitter, LinkedIn, YouTube, Blog, IG* Enhanced interaction and customer/partner engagement globally	*FB, Twitter, LinkedIn, YouTube, Blog* Enhanced interaction and customer/partner engagement → enables to identify growth opportunities abroad	*FB, Twitter, LinkedIn, YouTube, Blog, IG* Enhanced reach and partner/customer engagement → lead generation, increased sales, brand awareness, revenue, and growth
Structural capital	Marketing and sales processes	*FB, discussion forums* Social media is embedded into processes → enhances marketing and sales efforts	*FB, discussion forums* Support marketing/sales processes	*FB, discussion forums* Support marketing/sales processes	*FB, discussion forums, LinkedIn* Social media is the main marketing/sales channel
	Recruitment process	*FB and LinkedIn* Streamline the recruitment process	*LinkedIn and FB* Speed up and streamline the recruitment process	*LinkedIn* Streamline the recruitment process.	*LinkedIn* Streamline the recruitment process.

Intellectual capital dimension	Knowledge transfer function	Social media platforms and intellectual capital accumulation			
		Firm A	Firm B	Firm C	Firm D
	Databases	***Twitter, FB, discussion forums*** Enable to gather customer- country- and market-specific data into firm's databases	***Twitter, FB*** Enable to gather customer and partner data into firm's databases	***FB, Twitter, LinkedIn*** Enable to gather customer, partner and market data into firm's databases	***FB, Twitter, LinkedIn*** Enable to gather customer, partner and market data into firm's database
	Organizational culture	***FB, LinkedIn*** Enable information to flow throughout the organization → facilitate knowledge sharing	***FB, LinkedIn*** Knowledge sharing on platforms facilitate culture of learning	***Twitter, FB, LinkedIn*** Foster innovations and allows to respond to problems fast → increased competitiveness	***Twitter, FB, LinkedIn*** Knowledge sharing on platforms facilitates culture of learning

Table 5.5   *Intellectual capital accumulation through knowledge transfer using social media during international growth*

Intellectual capital (IC) dimension	Function	Social media platform	Social media impact on IC dimension	IC dimension impact on international growth
Human capital	recruitment, talent acquisition learning, knowledge creation, acquisition sharing and integration	LinkedIn, Facebook Facebook, LinkedIn, Twitter, YouTube, Blog, Instagram, SlideShare	enables to find skilled employees globally, facilitate recruitment enables access to various knowledge sources: tacit and explicit knowledge	increased international HC accelerate international growth increased HC and competitiveness accelerates lead generation and international growth
Relational capital (RC)	networking	LinkedIn, Facebook, Twitter	increases networking, enables agile and fast network building with partners/customers and other stakeholders globally	firms can identify growth opportunities abroad faster and more effectively
	communication, interaction, collaboration and engagement	Facebook, Twitter, LinkedIn, Instagram, YouTube, Blog	facilitates communication and collaboration between firm, partners and customers → better partner/customer interaction → increased partner and customer experience, improved engagement	increases interaction, collaboration and engagement between firm and its stakeholders increases trust and creditability → enables to build sustainable business abroad → competitive advantage
Structural capital (SC)	marketing and sales processes	Facebook, LinkedIn, discussion forums, Instagram	embedded into marketing and sales process, increases SC	a cost-effective way to target marketing and sales activities abroad, → enables agile marketing and sales efforts globally
	recruitment process	LinkedIn, Facebook	speeds up and simplifies the recruitment process (attracts skilled people, enables to reach potential candidates and check person's work and education history)	facilitates international growth
	databases	Twitter, Facebook, LinkedIn	enables to gather customer-, country- and market-specific data into databases → increases SC	the data/databases facilitates decision-making related to the internationalization
	organizational culture	Facebook, LinkedIn, Twitter	enables to share and manage tacit and explicit knowledge, enables to respond to problems more quickly/ online	flexible organizational culture increases competitiveness in international markets and facilitates growth

IMPLICATIONS AND LIMITATIONS

The findings of our chapter hold both theoretical and managerial implications. A key theoretical implication relates to the need of social media-specific theorization in management studies, and especially in IB management and IC-related discussion (see Dabić et al., 2019; Hurmelinna-Laukkanen et al., 2020; Rialp-Criado and Rialp-Criado, 2018; Vătămănescu et al., 2019). Despite the significant increase in social media focused research, there is a need to revisit existing theorization and evaluate whether the earlier discussions can be combined in meaningful ways to provide explanations to emerging phenomena.

We contribute to these endeavours by bridging IC and IB studies via social media. Identifying knowledge transfer as the common denominator for these literature streams, and a connecting factor for the dimensions of IC, we can see how social media has the potential to promote international growth especially of small firms by enhancing the accumulation of the different dimensions of IC.

We contribute to knowledge transfer literature by increasing the understanding of social media as a tool for knowledge transfer. Specifically, we extend prior studies on social media's use in knowledge sharing from individual level (see the review by Ahmed et al., 2019) to organizational level. The findings also support that at the organizational level the main activities for knowledge sharing are knowledge-seeking, knowledge-contributing and social interactivity. However, compared with prior studies our findings identify in more detail the various knowledge transfer elements. More precisely, the key knowledge transfer elements that emerge from our findings (see Table 5.4) such as talent acquisition, learning, networking, communication, interaction, engagement, among others add interesting elements compared with previously identified tacit and explicit knowledge elements both in the domestic (Wang et al., 2014) and international (Zeng et al., 2018) contexts. The findings indicate that social media offers SMEs an efficient knowledge transfer tool by offering a low-cost option for quick, flexible knowledge transfer, thus enabling firms to overcome the challenges of geographical distance and time in the international context mentioned in prior studies (Gaur et al., 2019; Ho and Wang, 2015; Javidan et al., 2005).

We contribute to IB literature by increasing understanding of the role of intellectual capital specifically on international growth, as the previous literature has mostly focused on exploring its role in internationalization behaviour in general (see, for example, Mansion and Bausch, 2019; Vătămănescu et al., 2019) or focused on limited intellectual capital dimensions. Our findings show that all the studied intellectual dimensions, HC, RC and SC, will influence international growth of small firms. Thus the results support the findings by Radulovich et al. (2018) in terms of the roles of HC and RC, but add by showing the potential of SC to contribute to international growth.

IC literature has acknowledged that context factors may act as moderators for the relationship between IC and performance (Andreeva and Garanina, 2016; Corvino et al., 2019; Molodchik et al., 2019; Musteen et al., 2017). Our findings show that the roles of HC, RC and SC in our case firms seem to have quite similar positive outcomes to international growth. This indicates that for small companies, operating in the software industry and originating from small and open economies with very limited domestic markets, the three studied IC dimensions are all important. Therefore, findings increase the understanding of the role of firm size, industry and home country as potential moderators for IC performance.

We believe that the key knowledge transfer elements and their link to different social media platforms offer a starting point for comprehending how social media connects to relevant IC dimensions and further to international growth. The findings of our study (and other prior studies focusing on social media usage in different management aspects) reveal rather distant elements (functions) associated with the utilization of social media platforms. We suggest that one possibility to advance theorization is to develop conceptual models or paradigms that highlight the functions and influences of specific platforms such as LinkedIn or Twitter for contemporary organizations. Specifically, the interconnectedness of the IC elements in the realm of social media, and their further connections to growth opportunities (and the limits of those; see Hurmelinna-Laukkanen et al. 2020), seem to provide the means to theorize along the functions.

For the managerial audience, the main takeaway from the current chapter is summarized in Table 5.5. Social media's importance is only expected to grow further in future especially for small firms. Therefore, we encourage managers to develop HC, RC and SC strategies in relation to social media usage in their firms. While we have not got to the details of possibly localizing or specializing social media contents for specific markets, these may become relevant issues especially for different functions (e.g., using social media for developing culture, recruitment purposes, or data collection) during international growth. Considering that the different IC dimensions have been found to have different influences on international growth of the firms, and that these dimensions are interconnected, alignment is needed in the social media use. Depending on the organizational needs as well as stage in the firm's international growth journey, managers can then, without disrupting other processes, focus on HC, RC or SC promotion in a way that strengthens the IC as a whole.

Our study has a number of limitations as well. The first limitation comes from conceptualization of IC in our study, where we focus on three commonly used dimensions, i.e. HC, RC and SC. Therefore, other dimensions of IC have not been conceptually and empirically analysed in our chapter. We also relied on interviews with CEOs in our data collection. Although this approach offered us first-hand insights into the complex relationships being analysed, it is likely that CEOs' or senior managers' perceptions on these topics are different from other employees'. Therefore, this perception-based data can also be considered a limitation. In addition, a limited number of interviews may limit the external validity of the findings. However, despite this, we believe that our chapter opens the door for further debate on these topics, and future studies can incorporate perceptions of more operational employees as well in the analysis to see if they match our findings or there are substantial differences. Although the findings from a qualitative study cannot be generalized widely, our findings are useful for managers of such firms, as software firms have been referred to as being quite universal in nature. Future research can also benefit from our study by taking it as a stepping-stone to build on, and specifically analyse the role of social media for IC accumulation via knowledge transfer in other contexts to see if the findings match ours or not. The hints of potentially relevant questions regarding the limits to the usefulness of social media also are relevant in pointing to future research. It might be particularly interesting to examine to what extent and under which conditions IC accumulation via knowledge transfer through social media is relevant for different organizational functions such as logistics, operations management, HR and marketing. We hope that the discussion in this chapter inspires new ideas for both scholars and managers.

REFERENCES

Agostini, L., Nosella, A., & Filippini, R. (2017). Does intellectual capital allow improving innovation performance? A quantitative analysis in the SME context. *Journal of Intellectual Capital*, 18(2), 400–418.

Ahmed, Y.A., Ahmad, M.N., Ahmad, N., & Zakaria, N.H. (2019). Social media for knowledge-sharing: A systematic literature review. *Telematics Inform*, 37, 72–112.

Akhtar, P., Khan, Z., Tarba, S., & Jayawickrama, U. (2018). The Internet of Things, dynamic data and information processing capabilities, and operational agility. *Technological Forecasting and Social Change*, 136, 307–316.

Allameh, S.M. (2018). Antecedents and consequences of intellectual capital: The role of social capital, knowledge sharing and innovation. *Journal of Intellectual Capital*, 19(5), 858–874. https://doi.org/10.1108/JIC-05-2017-0068

Ammirato, S., Felicetti, A.M., Della Gala, M., Aramo-Immonen, H., Jussila, J.J., & Kärkkäinen, H. (2019). The use of social media for knowledge acquisition and dissemination in B2B companies: An empirical study of Finnish technology industries. *Knowledge Management Research & Practice*, 17(1), 52–69.

Andreeva, T. & Garanina, T. (2016). Do all elements of intellectual capital matter for organizational performance? Evidence from Russian context. *Journal of Intellectual Capital*, 17(2), 397–412.

Archer-Brown, C. & Kietzmann, J. (2018). Strategic knowledge management and enterprise social media. *Journal of Knowledge Management*, 22(6), 1288–1309.

Autio, E., Sapienza, H.J., & Almeida, J.G. (2000). Effects of age at entry, knowledge intensity, and imitability on international growth. *Academy of Management Journal*, 43(5), 909–924.

Band, J. (2019). *Interfaces on trial: Intellectual property and interoperability in the global software industry*. Oxon: Routledge.

Barber, J., Metcalfe, S., & Porteous, M. (2016). *Barriers to growth in small firms*. Oxon: Routledge.

Bayraktaroglu, A., Calisir, F., & Baskak, M. (2019). Intellectual capital and firm performance: An extended VAIC model. *Journal of Intellectual Capital*, 20(3), 406–425.

Benitez, J., Castillo, A., Llorens, J., & Braojos, J. (2018). IT-enabled knowledge ambidexterity and innovation performance in small U.S. firms: The moderator role of social media capability. *Information & Management*, 55(1), 131–143.

Bharati, P., Zhang, W., & Chaudhury, A. (2015). Better knowledge with social media? Exploring the roles of social capital and organizational knowledge management. *Journal of Knowledge Management*, 19(3), 456–475.

Bontis, N. (1998). Intellectual capital: an exploratory study that develops measures and models. *Management Decision*, 36(2), 63–76.

Bontis, N., Wu, S., Chen, M.C., Cheng, S.J., & Hwang, Y. (2005). An empirical investigation of the relationship between intellectual capital and firms' market value and financial performance. *Journal of Intellectual Capital*, 6(2), 159–176.

Corvino, A., Caputo, F., Pironti, M., Doni, F., & Martini, S.B. (2019). The moderating effect of firm size on relational capital and firm performance. *Journal of Intellectual Capital*, 20(4), 510–532.

Dabić, M., Maley, J., Dana, L.P., Novak, I., Pellegrini, M.M., & Caputo, A. (2019). Pathways of SME internationalization: A bibliometric and systematic review. *Small Business Economics*, available online at https://link.springer.com/article/10.1007/s11187-019-00181-6

D'Angelo, A. & Presutti, M. (2019). SMEs international growth: The moderating role of experience on entrepreneurial and learning orientations. *International Business Review*, 28(3), 613–624.

Del Giudice, M., Arslan, A., Scuotto, V., & Caputo, F. (2017). Influences of cognitive dimensions on the collaborative entry mode choice of small- and medium-sized enterprises. *International Marketing Review*, 34(5), 652–673.

de Zubielqui, G.C., Lindsay, N., Lindsay, W., & Jones, J. (2019). Knowledge quality, innovation and firm performance: A study of knowledge transfer in SMEs. *Small Business Economics*, 53(1), 145–164.

Durst, S. & Edvardsson, I. (2012). Knowledge management in SMEs: A literature review. *Journal of Knowledge Management*, 16(6), 879–903.

Edvinsson, L. & Malone, M. (1997), *Intellectual capital: Realising your company's true value by finding its hidden brainpower*. New York, NY: Harper Collins.

Edvinsson, L. & Sullivan, P. (1996). Developing a model for managing intellectual capital. *European Management Journal*, 14(4), 356–364.

Eisenhardt, K.M. (1989). Building theories from case study research. *Academy of Management Review*, 14(4), 532–550.

Eriksson, P. & Kovalainen, A. (2008). *Qualitative methods in business research*. London: Sage.

European Commission (2003). Entrepreneurship and small and medium-sized enterprises (SMEs). SME definition. https://ec.europa.eu/growth/smes/sme-definition_en (accessed 1 September 2020).

Fernhaber, S.A. & Li, D. (2013). International exposure through network relationships: Implications for new venture internationalization. *Journal of Business Venturing*, 28(2), 316–334.

Felzenstein, C., Deans, K.R., & Dana, L.P. (2019). Small firms in regional clusters: Local networks and internationalization in the Southern Hemisphere. *Journal of Small Business Management*, 57(2), 496–516.

Fonecta Finder (2020). Key information about Finnish firms. Retrieved 3 April 2020.

Gaur, A.S., Ma, H., & Ge, B. (2019). MNC strategy, knowledge transfer context, and knowledge flow in MNEs. *Journal of Knowledge Management*, 23(9), 1885–1900.

Hanna, R., Rohm, A., & Crittenden, V.L. (2011). We're all connected: The power of the social media ecosystem. *Business Horizons*, 54(3), 265–273.

Ho, M.H. & Wang, F. (2015). Unpacking knowledge transfer and learning paradoxes in international strategic alliances: Contextual differences matter. *International Business Review*, 24(2), 287–297.

Hormiga, E., Batista-Canino, R.M., & Sánchez-Medina, A. (2011). The role of intellectual capital in the success of new ventures. *International Entrepreneurship and Management Journal*, 7(1), 71–92.

Hurmelinna-Laukkanen, P., Haapanen, L., & Holma, S. (2020). Social media and small entrepreneurial firms' internationalization. In: L. Schjoedt et al. (Eds), *Understanding social media and entrepreneurship*. Cham: Springer.

Hussi, T. (2004). Reconfiguring knowledge management-combining intellectual capital, intangible assets and knowledge creation. *Journal of Knowledge Management*, 8, 36–52.

Hussinki, H., Ritala, P., Vanhala, M., & Kianto, A. (2017). Intellectual capital, knowledge management practices and firm performance. *Journal of Intellectual Capital*, 18(4), 904–922.

Hsu, L.C. & Wang, C.H. (2012). Clarifying the effect of intellectual capital on performance: the mediating role of dynamic D2capability. *British Journal of Management*, 23(2), 179–205.

Inkinen, H. (2015). Review of empirical research on intellectual capital and firm performance. *Journal of Intellectual capital*, 16(3), 518–565

Jardon, C., & Molodchik, M. (2017). What types of intangible resources are important for emerging market firms when going international? *Journal of East European Management Studies*, 22(4), 579–595

Javidan, M., Stahl, G.K., Brodbeck, F., & Wilderom, C.P.M. (2005). Cross-border transfer of knowledge: Cultural lessons from project GLOBE. *The Academy of Management Executive*, 19(2), 59–76.

Jones, O. & Macpherson, A. (2006). Inter-organizational learning and strategic renewal in SMEs. Extending the 4I framework. *Long Range Planning*, 39(2), 155–175.

Kaplan A.M. & Haenlein M. (2010). Users of the world, unite! The challenges and opportunities of Social Media. *Business Horizons*, 53(1), 59–68.

Kianto, A., Hurmelinna-Laukkanen, P., & Ritala, P. (2010). Intellectual capital in service- and product-oriented companies. *Journal of Intellectual Capital*, 11(3), 305–325

Kianto, A. & Waajakoski, J. (2010). Linking social capital to organizational growth. *Knowledge Management Research and Practice*, 8(1) 4–14.

Koiranen, I., Keipi, T., Koivula, A., & Räsänen, P. (2019). Changing patterns of social media use? A population-level study of Finland. Universal Access in the Information Society, available online at https://link.springer.com/article/10.1007/s10209-019-00654-1

Komnenic, B. & Pokrajcic, D. (2012). Intellectual capital and corporate performance of MNCs in Serbia. *Journal of Intellectual Capital*, 13(1), 106–119.

Kwahk, K.Y., & Park, D.H. (2016). The effects of network sharing on knowledge-sharing activities and job performance in enterprise social media environments. *Computers in Human Behavior*, 55, 826–839.

Lardo, A., Dumay, J., Trequattrini, R., & Russo, G. (2017). Social media networks as drivers for intellectual capital disclosure: Evidence from professional football clubs. *Journal of Intellectual Capital*, 18(1), 63–80.

Laursen, K., Masciarelli, F., & Prencipe, A. (2012). Trapped or spurred by the home region? The effects of potential social capital on involvement in foreign markets for goods and technology. *Journal of International Business Studies*, 43(9), 783–807.

Madia, S.A. (2011). Best practices for using social media as a recruitment strategy. *Strategic HR Review*, 10(6), 19–24.

Mangold, W.G. & Faulds, D.J. (2009). Social media: The new hybrid element of the promotion mix. *Business Horizons*, 52(4), 357–365.

Mansion, S.E. & Bausch, A. (2019). Intangible assets and SMEs' export behavior: A meta-analytical perspective. *Small Business Economics*, Online first, available at https://doi.org/10.1007/s11187-019-00182-5.

Mathuramaytha, C. (2012). The impacts of intellectual capital on innovative capability: Building the sustain competitive advantage on a resource-based perspective of Thailand industrials. *International Business Management*, 6(4), 451–457.

Maurer, I., Bartsch, V., & Ebers, M. (2011). The value of intra-organizational social capital: How it fosters knowledge transfer, innovation performance, and growth. *Organization Studies*, 32(2), 157–185.

McDowell, W.C., Peake, W.O., Coder, L., & Harris, M.L. (2018). Building small firm performance through intellectual capital development: Exploring innovation as the "black box". *Journal of Business Research*, 88, 321–327.

Miles, M.B. & Huberman, A.M. (1994). *Qualitative data analysis: An expanded sourcebook*. Thousand Oaks, CA: Sage.

Moen, Ø., Rialp, A., & Rialp, J. (2020). Examining the importance of social media and other emerging ICTs in far distance internationalisation: The case of a western exporter entering China. In: M. Marinov, S. Marinova, J. Larimo & T. Leposky T. (eds), *International Business and Emerging Economy Firms*. Palgrave Studies of Internationalization in Emerging Markets. Cham: Palgrave Macmillan.

Molodchik, M., Jardon, C., & Bykova, A. (2019). The performance effect of intellectual capital in the Russian context: Industry vs company level. *Journal of Intellectual Capital*, 20(3), 335–354.

Moran, P., & Ghoshal, S. (1996). Value creation by firms. In *Academy of Management Proceedings* (No. 1, pp. 41–45). Briarcliff Manor, NY 10510: Academy of Management.

Moran, P. (2005). Structural vs. relational embeddedness: Social capital and managerial performance. *Strategic Management Journal*, 26(12), 1129–1151.

Musteen, M., Ahsan, M., & Park, T. (2017). SMEs, intellectual capital, and offshoring of service activities: An empirical investigation. *Management International Review*, 57(4), 603–630.

Nahapiet, J., & Ghoshal, S. (1998). Social capital, intellectual capital, and the organizational advantage. *Academy of Management Review*, 23(2), 242–266.

Ng, P.Y., & Hamilton, R.T. (2016). Experiences of high-growth technology firms in Malaysia and New Zealand. *Technology Analysis & Strategic Management*, 28(8), 901–915.

Ngai, E.W.T., Tao, S.S.C., & Moon, K.K.L. (2015). Social media research: Theories, constructs, and conceptual framework. *International Journal of Information Management*, 35, 33–44.

Nummela, N. (2010). *International growth of small and medium enterprises*. Oxon: Routledge.

Ojala, A., Evers, N., & Rialp, A. (2018). Extending the international new venture phenomenon to digital platform providers: A longitudinal case study. *Journal of World Business*, 53(5), 725–739.

Pedro, E., Leitão, J., & Alves, H. (2018). Back to the future of intellectual capital research: A systematic literature review. *Management Decision*, 56(11), 2502–2583.

Pergelova, A., Manolova, T., Simeonova-Ganeva, R., & Yordanova, D. (2019). Democratizing entrepreneurship? Digital technologies and the internationalization of female-led SMEs. *Journal of Small Business Management*, 57(1), 14–39.

Prashantham, S. (2005). Toward a knowledge-based conceptualization of internationalization. *Journal of International Entrepreneurship*, 3(1), 37–52.

Radulovich, L., Rajshekhar (Raj), G.J., & Scherer, R.F. (2018). Intangible resources influencing the international performance of professional service SMEs in an emerging market. *International Marketing Review*, 35(1), 113–135.

Ramadan, B.M., Dahiyat, S.E., Bontis, N., & Al-Dalahmeh, M.A. (2017). Intellectual capital, knowledge management and social capital within the ICT sector in Jordan. *Journal of Intellectual Capital*, 18(2), 437–462.

Rialp-Criado, A. & Rialp-Criado, J. (2018). Examining the impact of managerial involvement with social media on exporting firm performance. *International Business Review*, 27(2), 355–366.

Roos, G. & Roos, J. (1997). Measuring your company's intellectual performance. *Long Range Planning*, 30(3), 413–426.

Roos, J., Roos, G., Dragonetti, N., & Edvinsson, L. (1998). *Intellectual capital: Navigating in the new business landscape*. New York: New York University Press.

Ruzzier, M., Antoncic, B., Hisrich, R. D., & Konecnik, M. (2007). Human capital and SME internationalization: A structural equation modeling study. *Canadian Journal of Administrative Sciences/Revue Canadienne des Sciences de l'Administration*, 24(1), 15–29.

Ruzzier, M., Akbar, Y.H., Bortoluzzi, G., & Tracogna, A. (2017). The growth challenge of Western SMEs in emerging markets: An exploratory framework and policy implications. *Managing Global Transitions*, 15(3), 291–314.

Ryan, P., Evers, N., Smith, A., & Andersson, S. (2019). Local horizontal network membership for accelerated global market reach. *International Marketing Review*, 36(1), 6–30.

Sardo, F. & Serrasqueiro, Z. (2018). Intellectual capital, growth opportunities, and financial performance in European firms. *Journal of Intellectual Capital*, 19(4), 747–767.

Saunders, M., Lewis, P., & Thornhill, A. (2009). *Research methods for business students*. 5th ed. Essex: Pearson Education.

Seleim, A. & Khalil, O. (2011). Understanding the knowledge management-intellectual capital relationship: A two-way analysis. *Journal of Intellectual Capital*, 12(4), 286–614.

Shneor, R., Jenssen, J.I., Vissak, T., Torkkeli, L., Kuivalainen, O., Saarenketo, S., & Puumalainen, K. (2016). Network competence in Finnish SMEs: Implications for growth. *Baltic Journal of Management*, 11(2), 207–230.

Sgrò, F., Curina, I., Ciambotti, M., & Cioppi, M. (2019). *Social media influence on the intellectual capital growth of listed companies*. Kidmore End: Academic Conferences International Limited.

Shih, K., Chang, C., & Lin, B. (2010). Assessing knowledge creation and intellectual capital in banking industry. *Journal of Intellectual Capital*, 11(1), 74–89.

Sveiby, K.E. (1997). *The new organizational wealth: Managing and measuring knowledge-based assets*. New York, NY: Berrett-Koehlen.

Totskaya, N. (2015). Relational ties in emerging markets: What is their contribution to SME growth? *New England Journal of Entrepreneurship*, 18(2), 47–60.

van Wijk, R., Jansen, J.J., & Lyles, M.A. (2008). Inter- and intra-organizational knowledge transfer: A meta-analytic review and assessment of its antecedents and consequences. *Journal of Management Studies*, 45(4), 830–853.

Vătămănescu, E.-M., Gorgos, E.-A., Ghigiu, A.M., & Pătruț, M. (2019). Bridging intellectual capital and SMEs internationalization through the lens of sustainable competitive advantage: A systematic literature review. Sustainability, 11, 2510.

Vuorio, A., Torkkeli, L., & Sainio Liisa-Maija. (2020). Service innovation and internationalization in SMEs: Antecedents and profitability outcomes. *Journal of International Entrepreneurship*, 18(1), 93–123.

Wang, Z., Wang, N., & Liang, H. (2014). Knowledge sharing, intellectual capital and firm performance. *Management Decision*, 52(2), 230–258. doi:http://dx.doi.org.proxy.uwasa.fi/10.1108/MD-02-2013-0064

Welch, C., Piekkari, R., Plakoyiannaki, E. & Paavilainen-Mäntymäki, E. (2011). Theorizing from case studies: Towards a pluralist future for international business research. *Journal of International Business Studies*, 42, 740–762.

Wisniewski, P. (2013). *Intellectual capital (IC) in social media companies: Its positive and negative outcomes*. Kidmore End: Academic Conferences International Limited.

Xu, J. & Li, J. (2019). The impact of intellectual capital on SMEs' performance in China. *Journal of Intellectual Capital*, 20(4), 488–450.

Yin, R.K. (1994). *Case study research: Design and methods*. Newbury Park, CA: Sage

Yli-Renko, H., Autio, E., & Tontti, V. (2002). Social capital, knowledge, and the international growth of technology-based new firms. *International Business Review*, 11, 279–304.

Youndt, M.A., Subramaniam, M., & Snell, S.A. (2004). Intellectual capital profiles: An examination of investments and returns. *Journal of Management Studies*, 41(2), 335–361.

Zeng, R., Grøgaard, B., & Steel, P. (2018). Complements or substitutes? A meta-analysis of the role of integration mechanisms for knowledge transfer in the MNE network. *Journal of World Business: JWB*, 53(4), 415–432.

Zhou, A.Z. & Fink, D. (2003). Knowledge management and intellectual capital: An empirical examination of current practice in Australia. *Knowledge Management Research & Practice*, 1(2), 86–94.

6. Knowledge exchange within multi-stakeholder initiatives: tackling the Sustainable Development Goals

Jerra Veeger and Michelle Westermann-Behaylo

INTRODUCTION

"Globalization as we know it is undergoing a series of fundamental shifts" (Gereffi, 2013). Emerging economies are taking a more prominent place in international trade while various actors in developed economies are called to become more responsible. Within global value chains (GVCs), "the design, production and marketing of products involves a chain of activities divided between different enterprises often located in different places" (Humphrey & Schmitz, 2000; Gereffi & Fernandez-Stark, 2011). MNEs are increasingly embracing knowledge exchange collaborations within their GVCs in order to create value and competitive advantage (Almeida et al., 2002; Argote & Ingram, 2000; Bresman et al., 1999; Kogut & Zander, 1993; Pérez-Nordtvedt et al., 2008). But the legitimacy of MNEs has been critiqued as narrowly focusing on optimizing short-term financial performance. Therefore, Kramer and Porter (2011) call upon MNEs to "take the lead in bringing business and society back together" by creating economic value that, by addressing society's needs and challenges, creates value for society – the concept of shared value. MNEs are encouraged to set higher social and environmental standards for their suppliers and to take up extended responsibilities in their GVCs.

To create shared value and tackle these social and environmental challenges, MNEs must engage with stakeholders in their value chains to cooperate, contribute, and innovate (Warhurst, 2005; Yeoman & Mueller Santos, 2019). One approach seeking to create shared value is the Multi-Stakeholder Initiative (MSI): a collaborative approach that can be regarded as a "soft law" type of mechanism that regulates voluntary standards, practices, and policies within GVCs and their wider stakeholders (Abbott & Snidal, 2000; Gilbert & Rasche, 2008; Lee et al., 2020; Mena & Palazzo; Utting, 2002). MSIs have enormous potential to improve global value chains and achieve development goals when partners pool their resources and assets to solve problems (Kalibwani et al., 2018). MSIs are seen as a mechanism to encourage businesses of the future to "re-invent themselves as a force for positive good in society" (Warhurst, 2005). However, MSIs are not a 'magic bullet' as the requisite knowledge sharing is complicated when the stakes are high and multiple actors differ in their control over resources and diversity of interests (Dewulf & Elbers, 2018).

While overcoming differences within GVCs can be difficult, this is necessary to achieve the interconnectedness between MSI partners, which can result in the creation of shared value (Gereffi, 2013). One platform encouraging MSIs and other public–private partnerships to create shared value is the United Nations' Sustainable Development Goals (SDGs). This action plan focuses on "people, planet, and prosperity" in order to secure a sustainable future. Given the magnitude of the SDGs, the United Nations recognizes that truly sustainable development requires the joint efforts of multiple societal actors, and is best accomplished when the private sector is integrated into the policy process (Marx, 2019). This joint effort is encapsulated in the 17th SDG which calls for "partnership for the goals," to encourage effective MSIs to create shared value (Berrone et al., 2019).

The SDGs call for MSIs to "mobilize and share knowledge, expertise, technology and financial resources in all countries, in particular in developing countries" (Beisheim & Simon, 2018). Achieving the SDGs thus depends greatly on the quality of collaboration within MSIs (Haywood et al., 2018). To best create shared value and address social, economic, and environmental problems, MSI partnerships need to have a foundation of knowledge exchange (Austin & Seitanidi, 2012; Le Ber & Branzei, 2010; Kramer & Porter, 2011; Selsky & Parker, 2005). The success of MSIs depends not only on the independent knowledge of various partners but also on how this knowledge is exchanged among the partners (Okereke & Stacewicz, 2018). Weak communication between MSI partners can act as an obstruction, whereas strong communication is a vital element of successful MSIs. If MSI partners invest in knowledge exchange, they can align themselves to a common goal, leading to successful collaboration and shared value within the GVC (Biekart & Fowler, 2018)

The comprehensive literature review of De Bakker et al. (2019) stands at the forefront of literature on MSIs as it provides an overview of (i) "the input into creating and governing the MSIs, (ii) the institutionalization processes, (iii) and the impact of MSIs." Cross-disciplinary literature around MSIs greatly focuses on normative discourse (i.e., the case for why MSIs are morally good) (Soundararajan et al., 2019). The current study, therefore, builds upon this literature, as well as the theorizing of Soundararajan et al. (2019), who help to understand why MSIs may not have succeeded as promised and how their aspirations can be better realized. By recognizing the importance of MSIs together with the difficulty and significance of participation, it becomes clear that knowledge exchange and collaboration between MSI partners should be based upon a collective stakeholder orientation to realize their aspirations. Haywood et al. (2018) add that because of the various roles and responsibilities among partners within an MSI, development objectives cannot be achieved in isolation. There is a need for integration between the different partners in order to achieve the SDGs.

Collective stakeholder orientation is said to enable participants to seek and share value with each other, although the exact process by which this occurs in practice has not been established. Soundararajan et al.'s (2019) seminal work is foundational for understanding the conditions that enable a collective stakeholder orientation within MSIs, which is necessary for effective knowledge exchange. Scholars have called for research on knowledge exchange within MSIs focusing on the design of the exchange (Kolk et al., 2010; Sammarra & Biggiero, 2008; Seitanidi & Ryan, 2007). Knowledge exchange within MSIs is recognized as important to institutionalize MSIs, although the mechanisms by which this occurs deserve further attention (Klitsie et al., 2018). Thus, it is necessary to study how knowledge exchange between the private, nonprofit, and public partners in MSIs promotes the creation of shared value and collective stakeholder orientation (Villani et al., 2017). In order to develop propositions explaining MSI knowledge exchange in practice, this study asks: how does the exchange of tacit and explicit knowledge between partners within an MSI occur, and how is this exchange affected by partner-specific constructs (i.e., absorptive capacity and knowledge superiority)?

This study opens up the 'black box' of knowledge exchange between MSI partners to reveal the communicative skills required to construct value and achieve the objectives of the MSI, with particular regard to the role of the private sector. The SDGs cannot be achieved without the contribution of the private sector (van Zanten & van Tulder, 2018). As UN Secretary-General Ban Ki-moon states: "Governments must take the lead in living up to their pledges. At the same time, I am counting on the private sector to drive success" (UN News Centre, 2015). While previous scholars have emphasized the role of NGOs in creating shared value, the role of MNEs in exchanging knowledge within MSIs is due for further research (Yan et al., 2018).

This chapter fills these gaps and adds to the academic discussion by gaining first-hand insight into MSIs through a field study in South Africa. This multiple case study analyzes four MSIs within the global food and beverage supply chain, a setting where MSIs are increasingly being recognized as a means to better governance and improve social and environmental conditions (Clapp & Fuchs, 2009). The findings of this field study suggest how MSIs can enhance their knowledge management practices, providing propositions that emphasize how tacit and explicit knowledge is best exchanged while taking into account partner-specific constructs (i.e. absorptive capacity and knowledge superiority). These propositions demonstrate how MSIs can establish a collective stakeholder orientation that grants the partners the ability to seek and share value effectively, to reach their social and environmental goals.

THEORETICAL BACKGROUND

To understand how knowledge is exchanged between partners within MSIs, this study discusses the relevant theoretical literature. First, MSIs depend upon collaborative partnerships between multiple actors from various sectors. Within MSIs, knowledge exchange underlies the collaboration between partners given their differing knowledge expertise. Finally, the ease with which knowledge is exchanged is impacted by knowledge-specific (i.e., tacit and explicit) and partner-specific (i.e., absorptive capacity) constructs and is dependent on the dynamics of the relationship.

Multi-Stakeholder Initiatives

MSIs are cross-sectoral collaborations or partnerships that bring together representatives from different sectors to tackle the shared challenges and opportunities that arise from various political, economic, environmental, and social forces (Acosta et al., 2019; Austin, 2000a, 2000b; Selsky & Parker, 2005; Van Tulder et al., 2016). These challenges or opportunities include improving responsible business practices related to human rights, environmental degradation, agricultural and economic development, and sustainability (Bendell et al., 2010; Berger et al., 2004; Hermans et al., 2017; Moog et al., 2015). Concerns about these issues are shared by many actors at every level of society: MNEs, NGOs, the government, and individuals (e.g., scholars and academics). Within MSIs, such actors respond to the complexity of these challenges through collaboration, highlighting the interdisciplinary nature of MSIs (Austin, 2000a, 2000b; Bryson et al., 2006; Hermans et al., 2017; Shumate et al., 2018). Because of this collaboration "parties who see different aspects of a problem can constructively explore their differences and search for solutions that go beyond their own limited visions of what is possible" (Gray, 1989, p. 5). The focus on the collaborative nature of MSIs is necessary as incremental and unilateral efforts to overcome the problems typically produce less than satisfactory solutions (Bouwen & Taillieu, 2004).

According to Bryson et al. (2006), the inter-organizational nature of an MSI provides two or more partners from different sectors with the ability to link and share information, resources, activities, experiences, and capabilities. The gift in any MSI is the possibility to use these differences as an asset (Becker & Smith, 2018). To succeed, an MSI must combine the expertise of the different parties involved to overcome their distinctive constraints (Seitanidi & Crane, 2014; Warner & Sullivan, 2004). The various combinations of complementary core competencies created through MSIs are increasingly "at the forefront of creative organizational models" to propose innovative solutions to overcome social, political, environmental, and economic forces (Vurro et al., 2010, p. 39).

The success of MSIs is examined with respect to their ability to achieve organizational and societal goals while impacting those who are affected (Clarke & Crane, 2018). The MSI's ability to implement strategy is mostly understood in terms of the problem-solving capacity of the MSI to address the problem it set out to solve (Pattberg & Widerberg, 2016). While there is debate on how successful MSIs have been, they are often considered to be more capable of solving social and political problems than traditional state-centric arrangements (Okereke & Stacewicz, 2018).

Notwithstanding, MSIs cannot cure everything (Bryson et al., 2006). Cross-sector collaboration does not come easily, and outcomes are hardly assured (van Tulder & Keen, 2018). While early MSI research painted these collaborative approaches as a kind of magic bullet that could provide a solution to all sorts of problems, this optimistic view turned out to be underdeveloped (Powell et al., 2018; Rein & Stott, 2009). The main reason for MSI failure relates to power asymmetry between different partners within the MSI, which leads to exclusion (Soundararajan, 2017). Within MSIs, MNEs have been criticized for their lack of involvement, and governments and nonprofits need to find new ways to work with businesses in order to continually increase MSI success over time (United Nations, 2015; Bogie, 2016). Overall, designing and managing MSIs is not easy (Arora, 2017).

Another line of MSI research demonstrates that collaboration among the partners within an MSI should not solely be seen as an outcome; it should be viewed as a process (El Ansari et al., 2001). Success in any collaboration "rests on the quality of relationships that shape cooperation, trust, mutuality and joint learning" (Senge et al., 2007, p. 47). To make the collaboration among MSI partners more successful, recognizing differences between them is the first step. Ensuring open discussions and communications with all partners will help overcome the difficulties that differences bring with them (Houston, 2016). Dialogue within MSIs is important to collectively acquire and exchange the knowledge, values, and competencies needed to survive, adapt, and compete successfully within the increasingly complex environment (Spence & Bourlakis, 2009; Utting, 2002). The collaboration between partners is relational in nature, thus connections between the various partners must be created, and such connections must be nurtured and maintained over time (Hermans et al., 2017). According to Sammarra and Biggiero (2008), the collaborative nature of MSIs depends upon the exchange of knowledge among partners.

Knowledge Exchange

Over many years of scholarship, various types of knowledge (e.g. tacit vs explicit, divisible vs invisible) and knowledge categorizations (e.g. market, technological and managerial knowledge) have been identified (Sammarra & Biggiero, 2008). The concept of knowledge is defined as an "accumulated practical skill or expertise that allows one to do something smoothly and efficiently" (Kogut and Zander, 1992, p. 386). However, when integrating various streams of literature, knowledge exchange means different things for organizations within strategic alliances than for partners within an MSI.

From an organizational perspective, utilization of knowledge in an effective way can result in higher productivity, augmented performance, and improved capabilities to innovate (Cummings, 2004; Lin, 2007; Mesmer-Magnus & DeChurch, 2009). Many business scholars see it as a critical success factor and strategic resource (Asrar-ul-Haq & Anwar, 2016; Grant, 1996; Teece, 1998). The current and most recent focus of knowledge within organizations lies in the broader framework of the knowledge-based view of the organization (Grant, 1996). Within this view, Grant (1997) argues that knowledge is the prominent resource the firm contributes to add value when it is in a collaborative partnership.

The knowledge-based perspective of the firm also argues that creating and exchanging knowledge is of utmost importance for an organization to establish and sustain competitive advantage (Argote & Ingram, 2000; Dave & Koskela, 2009; Kanawattanachai & Yoo, 2007; Kogut & Zander; 1992; Nonaka & Takeuchi, 1995). In competitive markets, knowledge exchange and management have been identified as crucial elements for organizational survival allowing organizations to gain a competitive edge over others through innovative recombination of knowledge (Asrar-ul-Haq & Anwar, 2016). This, according to Bresman et al. (1999, p. 144), implies that "the winners in tomorrow's marketplace will be the masters of knowledge management."

While knowledge management and exchange are important for an organization to achieve a competitive advantage, these capabilities serve a different purpose within MSIs. MSIs create a connection between partners who have contending, sometimes even conflicting, sets of demands and priorities. Within MSIs, knowledge exchange serves as a learning platform wherein the partners can exchange experiences and knowledge, and learn from each other (Mena & Palazzo, 2012). Partners that interact and collaborate with each other on a regular basis are assumed to generate even more knowledge for the MSI, as the success of MSIs depends on more than just the independent knowledge of partners (Okereke & Stacewicz, 2018; Swan et al., 1999). This newly generated knowledge shared among MSI partners is believed to generate a long-term advantage for the MSI (Malhotra et al., 2005). Just as knowledge exchange within an organization allows it to gain competitive advantage, the focus of knowledge exchange between MSI partners contributes to a collaborative advantage to achieve the goals of the MSI (Lowndes & Skelcher, 1998). For knowledge exchange to occur, there is a need to establish dialogue between partners, requiring a communicative and norm-building component within an MSI (Moog et al., 2015).

As Fransen and Kolk (2007) discuss, knowledge exchange and communication as MSI components are especially important given that partners have different sorts of expertise. Because these partners are brought together, this can change the partners' behavior and can lead to synergies. Knowledge exchange within MSIs depends on the ability to bridge differences between MNEs, NGOs, and the government as they hold different kinds of knowledge that are, however, complementary, to strengthen the overall partnership (Inkpen, 2000). Therefore, MSI partners with different backgrounds can capitalize on the exchange of knowledge and expertise to be able to successfully reach their collective goals (Cheyns, 2011). However, this can be very challenging as MSI partners may have different underlying motivations (e.g. for-profit versus not-for-profit or public service) as well as different capabilities to exchange and communicate knowledge (e.g. absorptive capacity) (Dyer & Hatch, 2006; Szulanski, 1996).

A more thorough understanding of how knowledge is exchanged within MSIs is required, distinguishing between different types of knowledge, and the characteristics of the parties involved in the collaboration (Sammarra & Biggiero, 2008). Whereas the former relates to the nature and properties of the knowledge to be transferred (Kogut and Zander, 1993), the latter can be regarded as barriers between the source and the recipient of knowledge (Hsiao et al., 2003). Both factors are considered to impact the quality of knowledge exchange between MSI partners as well as the dynamics of relationships between partners.

Knowledge-Specific Constructs

There are many different perspectives on what knowledge is and how it is exchanged. This leads to confusion and misunderstanding concerning the attempt to create, exchange, and use different forms of knowledge (Bolisani & Scarso, 1999; Raymond et al., 2010). The basic contrast of knowledge is between tacit and explicit knowledge, which builds upon early works of Polanyi (1967).

Tacit knowledge, according to Boiral (2002), is most often seen as something that is almost inaccessible, hidden, and abstract as it resides in a person's mind, enhancing the need for and the importance of trust (Desouza, 2003; Mentzas et al., 2006, Roberts, 2000). Additionally, tacit knowledge is believed to cover knowledge that is unarticulated; tied to the senses, intuition, or implicit rules of thumb (Nonaka & von Krogh, 2009). Because of this, tacit knowledge is difficult to convey and requires more considerable effort to exchange. This difficulty leads to the implication that tacit knowledge can only be exchanged through hands-on experience, demonstration, or observation (Hamel, 1991). Hansen (2002) concludes that, when tacit knowledge is to be exchanged between partners within organizational networks, strong ties and trust facilitate its exchange.

While tacit knowledge represents the knowing how (i.e., the subjective knowledge), explicit knowledge represents the knowing about (i.e., the objective knowledge) and can be codified (Bolisani & Scarso, 1999). Wyatt (2001) adds that explicit knowledge relates to facts, rules, relationships, and policies and can therefore be articulated in, among others, manuals, computer programs, and training tools (Inkpen & Dinur, 1998). Because of the codifiability, Simonin (1999a, 1999b) argues that explicit knowledge can be transferred easier (Becerra et al., 2008). With relative ease, explicit knowledge can be combined, stored, retrieved, and transmitted with the use of various mechanisms (Ernst & Kim, 2002). However, within partnerships, organizations may be more hesitant to exchange explicit knowledge as it can be absorbed and utilized, potentially placing risk on partners (Becerra et al., 2008).

Becerra et al. (2008) notice that tacit and explicit knowledge can be challenging to disentangle. Inkpen and Dinur (1998) point out that the tacit-explicit knowledge distinction should not be regarded as a dichotomy. The types of knowledge should be seen as a spectrum in which tacit and explicit knowledge are the poles at either end (Tamer Cavusgil et al., 2003). However, their exchange takes place through different means and processes. Explicit knowledge can be transferred verbally or in writing, while tacit knowledge is primarily transferred through direct contact and observation. Knowledge is not solely context-driven or relational (Nonaka & Takeuchi, 1995). Knowledge is also embedded in the social practice of exchange, making it related to human (inter)action or the lack thereof. As knowledge is sticky, it must be given meaning with the use of active networking with partners that should be involved in negotiation and sense-making (Weick, 1990).

Partner-Specific Constructs

Partner-specific constructs relate to characteristics of partners that are engaged in collaboration (Sammarra & Biggiero, 2008). Knowledge exchange is dependent upon an individual's perspective or understanding of what knowledge is (Fazey et al., 2014). Organizational theorists have emphasized the need to understand knowledge exchange as embedded in social relations (Swan et al., 1999). Prior studies have indicated that knowledge exchange is dependent on the absorptive capacity of the partner (Cummings, 2003; Dhanaraj et al., 2004). However, theorizing is incomplete regarding the effect of partner-specific constructs on knowledge exchange between partners within an MSI.

Absorptive capacity

Absorptive capacity has become an essential construct in knowledge management (Lane et al., 2002). Cohen and Levinthal (1990, p. 128) define absorptive capacity as "the ability to recognize the value of new external information, assimilate it, and apply it to commercial ends." To expand the definition of Cohen and Levinthal (1990), Zahra and George (2002) add knowledge transformation (i.e., the organization's capability to combine the existing knowledge with newly gathered knowledge) as a capability that produces an organization's absorptive capacity.

The conceptualizations that Cohen and Levinthal (1990) and Zahra and George (2002) propose emphasize the path-dependent nature of absorptive capacity. This indicates that if an organization has already developed some absorptive capacity within a specific area, it could more readily accumulate additional, external knowledge. The organization's ability to evaluate new external information is dependent upon its prior related knowledge, influenced by past experience, and can be formed as it results from the cumulative effect of continuous learning (Cohen & Levinthal, 1990; Matthyssens et al., 2005; Ritala & Hurmelinna-Laukkanen, 2013).

An organization's absorptive capacity is considered to be of crucial importance for business success and has become a key driver of competitive advantage (Cockburn & Henderson, 1998; Cohen & Levinthal, 1990; Escribano et al., 2009; Roberts et al., 2012). Minbaeva et al. (2003), suggest this is because the absorptive capacity of the information recipient is the most significant determinant of knowledge exchange. The absorptive capacity of the recipient affects the way knowledge is seen, interpreted, and evaluated, and exchanged between parties (Cohen & Levinthal, 1990; Nooteboom, 2000). Absorptive capacity strongly affects the organization's ability to innovate, be competitive, and adapt to environmental changes. It should be regarded as an intangible asset (Jiménez-Barrionuevo et al., 2011; Muscio, 2007).

Organizations that have high levels of absorptive capacity have a better ability to identify, value, select, and assimilate knowledge from their external environment, applying it in their operations (Zahra, 2005). Moreover, these organizations have a greater chance of achieving competitive advantage because they are more able to understand new knowledge (Chen, 2004; Lin et al., 2012; Makhija & Ganesh, 1997; Tsai, 2001). When an organization's absorptive capacity is high, this increases the firm's speed and quality of learning (Zahra & George, 2002). Furthermore, it allows organizations to create new capabilities by absorbing the knowledge exchanged (Kogut & Zander, 1992). When an organization lacks absorptive capacity, it might decide not to exploit further information that could be of importance if the organization finds that it lacks the capabilities to eventually learn from this new information (Eriksson & Chetty, 2003).

Von Briel et al. (2019) focus on absorptive capacity in collaboration with external partners (i.e., inter-organizational knowledge exchange) and highlight the importance of social integration, referring to "the extent to which members of a group participate and collaborate" in recognizing, assimilating, applying and exploiting information. Within inter-organizational relationships, social integration is characterized by the linkages between members of a group and their joint effort to develop and pursue shared goals and values (Torres de Oliveira et al., 2019). Because of a difference between organizations, objectives are difficult to achieve if the collaboration happens in isolation, highlighting the importance of social integration (Haywood et al., 2018). However, limited research has gone into exploring the role of social integration on absorptive capacity in inter-organizational knowledge exchange, especially in MSI research.

In sum, while scholarship has extensively addressed knowledge exchange within organizations and in strategic partnerships, and guidelines can be applied to MSIs from the research on intra-/inter-organizational collaboration, the exact dynamics of knowledge exchange within MSIs could be further developed. Although the effect that knowledge exchange has on MSIs has been discussed in the literature, how knowledge exchange actually occurs between private, nonprofit, and public partners, and the impact of various knowledge- and partner-specific constructs remains underexplored. MSIs are often studied in isolation, neglecting how the dynamic social interactions among partners impact knowledge exchange. To provide more contextual information on how to design and improve knowledge exchange between partners within MSIs to promote sustainable development, it is necessary to study how MSIs can manage knowledge exchange in light of the above-described differences between partners. The current study contributes to academic research and managerial practice by developing propositions following an analysis of data collected through a field study in South Africa.

RESEARCH METHOD

In this study, a qualitative, inductive theory-building approach is used (Corbin & Strauss, 2014). This study is exploratory in nature in order to gain new, first-hand insight into the exchange of tacit and explicit knowledge within MSIs, and to better understand the challenges that partner-specific constructs bring to knowledge exchange between MNEs, NGOs, and the government within an MSI. Therefore, using an inductive approach, data on the phenomenon of knowledge exchange in MSIs is explored to identify and explain themes, patterns, and propositions.

Qualitative Multiple Case Study Design

A qualitative approach is a preferred design to analyze the emerging phenomenon of tacit and explicit knowledge exchange within MSIs (Saunders et al., 2015). In particular, case study research, according to Eisenhardt (1989), is particularly appropriate in new topic areas where the focus lies on understanding the dynamics present within single settings. A multiple case study design is especially appropriate for this study as the analysis is conducted both within and across cases, providing an overview from numerous angles (Yin, 2013).

Data Collection Methods, Case Selection and Research Context

The case selection relies on theoretical sampling; cases are selected because of their suitability for "illuminating and extending relationships and logic among constructs" (Eisenhardt & Graebner, 2007, p. 27). Because of this, the cases should not be seen as representing the population, but as experiments serving to contrast, replicate, and extend theory.

All data were collected through a field study conducted in Cape Town, South Africa, in October 2018 using semi-structured, in-depth interviews with representatives from selected MSIs, including interviewees from different functional areas in order to mitigate bias. Semi-structured interviews can be very helpful with studies that have an exploratory nature as they can provide valuable background or contextual materials necessary for the study (Saunders et al., 2015). The interviews were transcribed, and the analysis was completed using qualitative data analysis software (QDAS), specifically NVivo, to code and categorize the narrative text to ensure the findings, interpretations, and subsequent conclusions were grounded in the raw data (Ryan & Bernard, 2003).

To prevent excessive variation related to context, the study focuses on MSIs from South Africa, of which Table 6.1 summarizes their characteristics. The MSIs all aim to improve social and/or environmental impacts connected to the global food and agriculture supply chain. South Africa's participation in global production networks in the agri-food sector has been rising in the last decade (Balié et al., 2019), with more than US$10 million worth of agri-food products exported from South Africa in 2018 (UNCTAD STAT, 2020). Also, during the last decade, a "partnership boom" has occurred within South Africa, allowing for an enabling environment for MSIs that has been favored by government policies (Rein et al., 2005). Partnerships have been widely promoted in multiple sectors, including the three 'thematic areas': health, agriculture, and education (Rein & Stott, 2009). The favorable attitude towards partnerships is a combination of the international trend towards corporate social responsibility and the private sector taking its responsibility for the reconstruction of South Africa post-Apartheid.

South Africa, with an array of deep, historically rooted, and conflicting material challenges, is one of the world's most unequal societies due to the racial inequality before, during, and after Apartheid. MSIs within this post-Apartheid context are trying to pursue prosocial efforts in a context of deep inequality (Powell et al., 2018). These efforts, due to the persistence of hunger, malnutrition, as well as water shortages caused by droughts, are increasingly focusing on the food system and the challenges it faces. The goal is to ensure that a growing population has access to a healthy, affordable, and environmentally sustainable diet (Bitzer et al., 2015). Addressing these food insecurity issues in South Africa requires innovative responses as the challenges the food system faces cut across various sectors and scales (Drimie et al., 2018). Because of these issues, South Africa presents "a rich context for studying the possibilities and limitations of cross-sector partnerships trying to pursue prosocial efforts in a context of deep inequality" (Powell et al., 2018).

Table 6.1   Overview of MSIs – characteristics and selection criteria

	Pebbles Project	Southern Africa Food Lab	WWF-SASSI	Kingfisher II Programme
Year of establishment	2014	2009	2004	2013
Typology	Private–nonprofit	Tripartite	Tripartite	Public–nonprofit
Description of MSI	Pebbles enriches the lives of disadvantaged children and families in the Winelands farming communities in the Western Cape by providing support and intervention in five key areas: education, health, nutrition, community, and protection. Villiera Vineyard focuses on environmental awareness and social sustainability within the wine industry	SAFL creates an effective platform for authentic communication and innovation by bringing together diverse, influential stakeholders from the public, private and non-profit sector, to promote creative responses to the problem of hunger in South Africa	Initiative that engages South African key role players in the entire seafood supply chain intending to transform the landscape of the seafood industry in South Africa by informing and educating all participants. Improve fishing practices that are destructive to the ocean and encourage fishers to use more sustainable methods	VNG and Dutch Water Authorities focus on the creation of South African Catchment Management Agencies. These CMAs are supported in their water regulating role for improved water management and their further development as autonomous entities in order to contribute to sustainable development in South Africa
Partners	(Vineyard) farm owners in Stellenbosch, Wellington, Somerset West, Paarl, Citrusdal, and Hemel & Aarde. UK donor connection	Farming communities, civil society organizations, government, private sector organizations, academics. For example, Woolworths, Spar, TechnoServe, Oxfam, National Agricultural Marketing Council	Large retailers (Spar, Woolworths, Pick n Pay), restaurants, small supermarkets, fish shops, and all their suppliers	South African Catchment Management Agencies, Dutch Water Authorities, South African local government departments
SDGs related	Goal 3 and Goal 4	Goal 1 and Goal 2	Goal 12 and Goal 14	Goal 14

First, the Pebbles Project (hereafter referred to as Pebbles) is an MSI that has its main emphasis on education, health, nutrition, community, and protection for disadvantaged children and families in the Winelands farming community in Western Cape, South Africa. Pebbles focuses on the impoverished situation of the workers and their families in order to improve the global food and agriculture supply chain.

Second, the Southern Africa Food Lab (hereafter referred to as SAFL), promotes creative responses to the problem of hunger within the global food supply chain through multi-stakeholder dialogues within its MSI. This tripartite MSI consists of many partners such as South African governmental departments, international retailers (e.g. Spar and Woolworths), (smallholder) farmers, academics, and NGOs (e.g. WWF, Reos Partners, and Technoserve).

Third, WWF-SASSI is an MSI that consists of private, nonprofit, and public partners and has its focus on developing a seafood supply chain that is sustainable in every sense by creating awareness and inspiring consumers concerning various marine conservation issues. WWF-SASSI looks at marine resource issues with fisheries, MNEs (e.g. Spar), NGOs, and the government, having the goal to drive change across the entire seafood supply chain with the SASSI app.

Lastly, as over 60% of the freshwater in South Africa is taken up by agriculture, the Kingfisher II Programme is an MSI established by the South African Department of Water and Sanitation (DWS), The Dutch Association of Water Authorities (UVW), and the Association of Dutch Municipalities (VNG). On the national level, an agreement has been made between the Netherlands and South Africa, and local stakeholders were engaged as the South African government wanted to have more effective and efficient water management. The first Kingfisher Programme focused on the creation of nine Catchment Management Agencies (CMAs): water authorities in South Africa. The current MSI is focused on strengthening those CMAs on the technological side (performed by the UVW) and institutional capacity building (performed by VNG).

FINDINGS

This section presents and discusses the findings that resulted from the analysis of the data. The data were first analyzed in separate cases, providing a within-case analysis that allows for a thorough case-by-case analysis. The findings of the individual cases are discussed and compared in the following cross-case analysis with the aim to identify propositions for knowledge exchange between partners within an MSI. Through the detection of (dis)similar patterns across the cases and the connection of these findings to the literature, propositions are provided in the next section.

To analyze the individual cases and combine these findings for a cross-case analysis, three themes will be discussed in order to comprehend how tacit and explicit knowledge is exchanged between the partners within an MSI and how this exchange is impacted by the diversity of partners. These themes are made up of several sub-themes as displayed in Table 6.2.

The first theme that is discussed is the general knowledge exchange between partners within an MSI. There is a need to understand how often knowledge is exchanged (frequency), in which way this is done (formality), the engagement with which knowledge is exchanged (i.e., whether there is a sense of integration between the partners), and who experiences difficulty when exchanging knowledge. The second theme discusses the dynamics under which tacit and explicit knowledge is exchanged and the reasons behind this. Additionally, within this theme the collective stakeholder orientation is tested within each MSI, highlighting the importance of factors that are necessary to reach the ability to effectively seek and share knowledge exchange. The third theme highlights the partner-specific factors that affect the exchange of tacit and explicit knowledge. Throughout the cross-case analysis, various quotes will be provided that highlight the importance of a topic for specific cases.

The following cross-case analysis presents similarities and differences arising from the within-case analysis of four cases in order to seek patterns, of which Table 6.2 provides a short overview. These patterns result in propositions, about how MSIs can manage knowledge exchange between partners in light of differences between partners, given in the next section.

Table 6.2   *Short overview of cross-case analysis*

	Pebbles Project	Southern Africa Food Lab	WWF-SASSI	Kingfisher II Programme
Frequency	Once per month with the purpose of no fractured relationships	Based on necessity, not frequency	Based on others' needs – consistency is important	Based on others' needs
Engagement	Family-focused – low engagement leads to less collective stakeholder orientation	Collaborative approach leads to engagement	Success of MSI is dependent on proactiveness	Government is less integrated and engaged – less sense of collective stakeholder orientation
Formality	Informality	Informality		
Difficulty		Public sector due to frequent relocations	Public and private sector	Government cannot actively participate in knowledge exchange because of hostility – difficulty of knowledge exchange is attached to the severity attached to the problem
Tacit knowledge exchange	Dialogue via brainstorming sessions	Focus lies on dialogue and direct exchange	Face-to-face exchange	Focus on face-to-face meetings with extreme personal contact
Explicit knowledge exchange	Easier to convey	Can be put in writing, approachability	Always connected to tacit knowledge exchange	Complementary to tacit knowledge exchange
Collective stakeholder orientation	Learning (showing), listening, mutuality (feeling of being noticed), reciprocity, dialogue, trust is a driver	Consultation, trust, joint learning, two-way dialogues (listening not dictating), giving everyone a face, mutuality (human dignity), inclusion	Joint learning, trust Distrust impacts the partnership and effectiveness	Focus on a personal relationship, joint learning, and trust

Knowledge Exchange between Partners

Table 6.2 reveals that the four MSIs do not make use of strict or regular knowledge exchange protocols. It is observed that the overall focus regarding the frequency of knowledge exchange is based upon the needs of the partners. Partners strive towards frequent knowledge exchange to increase continuity of the partnership, which should result in less fractured relationships and better collaborations. However, as the case of WWF-SASSI shows, even if the knowledge exchange is not frequent, the process should be consistent.

What lies at the forefront of participation, according to all cases, is the degree of engagement of all partners. The interviews showed that it is important that the partners feel engaged within the MSI. To accomplish satisfactory knowledge exchange, it is important that partners are engaged, proactive, and, ultimately, have a collaborative approach that should result in a collaborative advantage.

> I think the reality with communicating about sustainability is that there are always particular organizations who want to be proactive in their communication. (...) And I say can, because we want to

make it work together. We try to by putting as much effort as possible in the partnerships. (…) And it's dependent upon who the key relationship managers are in each partnership and how much they are engaged in the partnership happening. And that you need to balance off the fact of how integrated the partnership actually is within the organization. (Justin Smith, WWF-SASSI)

This collective approach, as highlighted by many cases, leads to more successful MSIs and a possibility for every partner to learn. However, various MSI cases highlight that not every partner is as engaged as others.

> I think that within our partnerships there is more of a feeling of a family, which makes them more engaged. This makes the partners feel recognized and the farm owners seen. Some of the farm owners, it varies, are totally committed and invested. They are 100% on board. However, others think: "just do your thing, I don't have time for this." Sadly, however, it ranges from everywhere in between that range as well. When they are less receptive, you can see it ... Goals are not met. (Sophia Warner, Pebbles)

Often, the private sector is less engaged as companies belong to an MSI for goodwill, whereas the public sector is less engaged because of political instability in South Africa. Also, the difficulty one partner has with participating in knowledge exchange comes from the significance that the partner has attached to the problem. As the private sector is believed to participate in the MSI for goodwill reasons, indicating a low significance attached to the problem, it correlates with the difficulty the private sector experiences in exchanging knowledge. One notable practice comes from SAFL which includes various actors of the public, private and non-profit sector within its 'board of directors'; because of this, all partners are inclined to become more engaged and are therefore more receptive to knowledge exchange practices.

A last interesting fact regarding the knowledge exchange between partners that is observed refers to the relationship between the partners. Informality between partners seems to help to get knowledge across as there is more focus on the 'greater good' than the sole focus of one partner reaching a goal.

> We have a lot of informal discussions that involve all the key actors we work with, both in South Africa and within the EU. This has the objective, then, we hope that we can foster a debate, a dialogue that is open and constructive. Everyone can listen to each other, voice concerns, voice strengths. (Wessel Kremer, VNG)

VNG adds to this that, especially with the government, the focus should lie on an informal relationship to result in a dialogue that is both open and constructive.

Tacit and Explicit Knowledge Exchange

During this study, it became evident that there are quite a lot of challenges when it comes to the exchange of knowledge within MSIs. Specifically, the participants in MSIs perceive explicit knowledge to be easier to exchange than tacit knowledge.

Explicit knowledge is seen, by all, as numbers, updates, guidelines, and documents. When explicit knowledge is exchanged, MSIs take into consideration that it must be knowledge that is easy to read, understand, and implement. As this is mostly exchanged without face to face conversations, it is important that all partners within the MSI are able to understand the knowledge. However, because of the different partners in an MSI, and their differing capabilities, WWF-SASSI believes that, as documents do not lend themselves well for knowledge exchange, it should always be complemented with face-to-face conversations.

> Face-to-face meetings give rise to new ideas. It is a dialogue and people are likely to share. (…) With this dialogue, not only the people that ask the question gets more knowledge, but also the people within the meeting now know more. (Justin Smith, WWF-SASSI)

Tacit knowledge, on the other hand, is always exchanged through dialogue because of the fact that it is difficult to exchange, cannot be put into writing, and is not easily understood. The main focus with the exchange of tacit knowledge refers to capacity-building dialogues; by showing partners what needs to be done, rather than just telling them, it provides every partner with the same understanding. Having a dialogue to promote know-how appears to be extremely important, considering there is an opportunity to explain the reasons behind certain actions or decisions, and partners are shown what needs to be done. Additionally, because of these dialogues among the MSI partners, all partners are able to discuss ideas and understand the knowledge better. Most cases reveal that with the focus on face-to-face meetings, personal relationships can be built. VNG adds to this that creating personal relationships with partners is of extreme importance to South African partners. Additionally, within South Africa, face-to-face meetings provide the opportunity to follow up. These personal relationships can build momentum, having a positive relationship with the MSI as a whole. By focusing on face-to-face dialogue, the cross-case table reveals that the capacity of partners is heightened. This is especially important for tacit knowledge, as WWF-SASSI adds, that there is a need to spend time together in order for tacit knowledge to be understood. Additionally, these capacity-building dialogues provide an opportunity for partners to become more engaged, by actively participating in the MSI, providing the ability to achieve the MSI's goals.

> Events are for creating understanding. (...) Everyone is able to talk to each other in a capacity-building dialogue. Everyone is able to grasp what everyone is working on, struggling with, and interested in. I think that with these dialogues all the attendees are able to take in knowledge from across the supply chain, which is beneficial for the entire supply chain. (Carolyn Cramer, SAFL)

The partners, when seeking and sharing both explicit and tacit knowledge with each other, all focus on the goal of creating a collective stakeholder orientation in order for the knowledge to be most effectively exchanged. All cases highlight that collective stakeholder orientation comes from joint learning, mutuality, consultation, dialogue, and trust. It is essential that all partners learn from being in the MSI to collectively tackle problems. Additionally, the focus lies on mutuality: the notion of creating a feeling that every partner is noticed and equal. SAFL adds to this that mutuality is about human dignity.

> There is a value placed on human dignity, everyone feels that they matter, that they are taken seriously. It is the collectivistic tackling of the problems that make it so special, these events. (...) I think it's as simple as giving each person a voice and dignity. (...) Lessening the divides. And then again, creating a trustworthy relationship. (Carolyn Cramer, SAFL)

Lastly, trust is deemed necessary within all cases as it appears to create an open environment and a dialogue. Trust is even regarded as a driver of knowledge exchange, whereas distrust seems to lead to an ineffective knowledge exchange process. One contrary finding comes from WWF-SASSI, who believes that trust is not something that makes knowledge exchange effective, it is rather an end-goal for the overall MSI. Notable findings regarding the perceived effectiveness come from Pebbles, which believes in a partnership based on consultation coming from a two-way dialogue.

This form of collective stakeholder orientation that is achieved makes the process of knowledge exchange effective. The above-described factors allow for a collective, collaborative approach of knowledge exchange that is based on collective learning and growing, ultimately strengthening the MSIs' ability to reach their goals.

Partner-specific Effects on Knowledge Exchange between Partners

This study reveals that the exchange of tacit and explicit knowledge between partners within an MSI is affected by two partner-specific constructs: absorptive capacity and knowledge superiority. A different level of absorptive capacity between partners within an MSI makes it more difficult for knowledge to flow from one partner to another. Because of the lack of uniformity in a partner's ability to not only absorb but also implement, transform, and exploit knowledge, knowledge exchange is much more difficult.

Especially with the exchange of tacit knowledge, differences in absorptive capacity impact the knowledge exchange. The partners tend to focus more on simple information transfer channels. Face-to-face, personal channels aid the increase of the absorptive capacity of partners as it provides partners with an ability to let knowledge stick. When the knowledge is tacit it is challenging to bring across, especially when the partner has a lower level of absorptive capacity.

Related to the effect of absorptive capacity, another partner-specific construct that has been observed to affect the knowledge exchange between MSI partners is the knowledge gap that can be present between partners. Both WWF-SASSI and Pebbles believe that certain partners in their MSI hold knowledge that is superior to the other partners, which is in part connected to partners' absorptive capacity. Differences between the levels of experience and training that various partners hold appear to lead to difficulties with exchanging knowledge.

DISCUSSION

This section discusses the patterns found in the cross-case analysis and connects these findings to literature in order to develop propositions that, ultimately, provide an answer to the following research question: how does the exchange of tacit and explicit knowledge between partners within an MSI occur, and how is this exchange affected by partner-specific constructs (i.e., absorptive capacity and knowledge superiority)? These propositions show how MSIs can manage knowledge exchange in light of partner-specific constructs.

Within the literature of partnerships, internal knowledge management has been deemed vital as it determines the mere survival or the success of the partnership and can even result in gaining a competitive edge over others (Bresman et al., 1999; Dave & Koskela, 2009). The current study supports this claim of the importance of knowledge management within MSIs, as frequent knowledge exchange results in continuity of the MSI because of stronger collaborative relationships among the partners. This finding is in line with Okereke and Stacewicz (2018) and Swan et al. (1999) who argue that partners who interact with each other on a regular basis are assumed to generate even more knowledge. The observation of this study is additionally supported by Malhotra et al. (2005) who argue that the newly generated knowledge among the partners within an MSI is believed to generate long-term advantage. Given the positive effect of frequent opportunities for knowledge exchange between partners on knowledge exchange, the first proposition is formulated as:

Proposition 1: *Frequent knowledge exchange between partners within the MSI positively influences the MSI's goal achievement.*

Looking at the different typologies of MSIs (i.e., public–nonprofit, public–private, private–nonprofit, and tripartite), each MSI consists of a mix of partners that are represented by NGOs, the government, and MNEs who have very different objectives (Rivera-Santos et al., 2012). This study, interestingly, reveals that there is a difference in the engagement of the public and private partners within the MSI.

The findings show that the public sector appears to be less engaged in the process of knowledge exchange due to frequent personnel changes within government departments. Additionally, in South Africa, there seems to be a high variation in the degree of educational attainment within the government. Working with lower educated partners presents more challenges. These findings are consistent with prior literature, as government partners often appear to lack relationships as well as skills to tackle problems (Brinkerhoff, 2003). To add to this lack of engagement from the public sector, other scholars argue that developing country governments often appear to lack the capacity or political willingness to adequately address the problems (Hassan & Lund-Thomsen, 2018). Contrarily, other scholars argue that the government plays a significant role in the partnership through funding or initiating the network, leading to a steering role within the MSI (Head, 2008; Rivera-Santos et al., 2012). The latter could be referring to governments in more developed countries, as our findings are more in line with the prior arguments, as the South African government is mostly regarded as a liability within the MSIs in this study.

Additionally, this study observes that the private sector was regarded as participating in the MSI for instrumental reasons relating to implementing the MSI strategies. As already highlighted before, Kramer and Porter (2011) argued that MNEs focus on optimizing short-term financial performance. This finding adds to the argument of Roloff (2018) who depicts that international businesses choose to participate in an MSI to show their compliance and enhance their image and reputation. Furthermore, MNEs have been criticized for rushing to embark in MSIs as a means of capitalizing on the potential benefits while not investing a considerable amount of time into MSIs (Seitanidi et al., 2010; Austin, 2000a, 2000b). Connected to literature that critiques the role of the private sector in MSIs, this study illustrates that the private sector brings complementary and highly beneficial knowledge to the MSI, and therefore plays an important role in the MSI because of this knowledge. However, there are limits to the effort that MNEs will make to share this knowledge.

Besides the (lack of) engagement of the public and private sectors, this study shows that the nonprofit sector is more engaged and proactive when present within an MSI. Several scholars have verified this finding, as NGOs have the interest of local people on the ground in mind and are believed to engage in MSIs for altruistic reasons. NGOs appear to be the driver in facilitating large-scale social change and innovation (Brown et al., 2000; Yan et al., 2018; Roloff, 2008). Considering the characteristics of the partners and their motive for engaging in an MSI, the second proposition reads:

Proposition 2*: Within an MSI, the nonprofit and private sectors are more likely than the government to (actively) engage in knowledge exchange between partners in an MSI.*

Within MSIs that are formed by multiple actors, NGOs, governments, and MNEs bring different, but complementary, knowledge and capabilities to strengthen the overall partnership (Inkpen, 2000). Because of the different knowledge that these partners hold, this study shows that the partners have difficulty in conveying and absorbing that knowledge.

This study highlights that the public sector in developing countries such as South Africa has increased difficulty with participating in knowledge exchange because of the overall political turmoil, which leads to frequent reassignments of personnel among governmental departments. This finding is verified by Kolk et al. (2008), who argue that the government often lacks the ability to create an enabling environment, which negatively influences the knowledge exchange. Further, this study demonstrates that NGOs often take on consulting and coordinating roles as NGOs bridge the understanding of various political, economic, environmental, and social forces between partners, while simultaneously dealing with the various external stakeholder groups (Stephan et al., 2016). The NGOs, therefore, appear to have less difficulty with exchanging knowledge. This also seems to be the case for the private sector, who are interested in participating in MSIs by bringing in knowledge from outside, a fact also supported by Seitanidi and Crane (2014). Acknowledging these differences between partners leads to the third proposition:

Proposition 3*: Within an MSI, the public sector has increased difficulty with engaging in knowledge exchange, compared with the nonprofit and private sectors.*

The above-described differences between partners within MSIs affect the ability of partners to come together in seeking and sharing value across sectors. The results show that when a partner mainly participates in the MSI for instrumental reasons, this negatively affects the knowledge exchange between partners. Bosse and Philips (2016) even find that, under such circumstances, partners tend to avoid working with those who have a selfish orientation. This study highlights the need for a collective stakeholder orientation, which has been a starting point of Soundararajan et al.'s (2019) research. MSIs that consist of partners with differing orientations show that creating mutual benefits is difficult. The cases in this study, however, provide several factors that help to create a collective stakeholder orientation: the orientation that allows the partners to have complementary objectives while being integrated with each other. This study finds that a collective stakeholder orientation established between partners allows for more effective knowledge exchange between partners.

As already established, sufficient knowledge management impacts the survival and success of the MSI. Part of the knowledge management of MSIs regards the choice of how to exchange knowledge with other partners. The findings of this study highlight that the MSIs perceive explicit knowledge to be exchanged more easily than tacit knowledge. This study highlights that the success of an MSI and the exchange of tacit and explicit knowledge is dependent upon effective knowledge exchange between the partners, as weak communication hampers the ability of the partners to overcome differences and, ultimately, does not allow for the emergence of new ideas (Brouwer et al., 2016; Dave & Koskela, 2009). Rather, several factors allow for a collective stakeholder orientation, influencing the effectiveness of tacit and explicit knowledge exchange: joint learning, dialogue, mutuality, consultation, and trust.

Regarding the issue of joint learning, Greene (2001) argues that joint learning is about collective learning rather than individual learning. The perception of joint learning within MSIs is based on knowledge exchange as a dialogue where partners exchange opinions, interests, and expectations. This study's finding of dialogue to reach effectiveness is verified by Brouwer et al. (2016), who argue that knowledge exchange in dialogues positively impacts knowledge exchange and allows for transparency. Within dialogue, the focus should lie on collective learning rather than persuading and convincing others, as with a debate.

Connected to joint learning via dialogue, this study finds the interesting phenomenon of consultation. It appears that more knowledgeable partners within the MSI consult the partners who are less knowledgeable. This consultation is observed to create a collective stakeholder orientation, which impacts the perceived effectiveness of knowledge exchange as this form of intra-partner consulting results in the heightened performance of MSIs. This finding is verified by Ingram (2008), who argues that consultation aids knowledge exchange as partners are provided with the opportunity to understand the knowledge that is being exchanged.

This study additionally observes that MSI partners perceive knowledge exchange to be effective when there is a focus on mutuality. This phenomenon is connected to partners feeling valued, noticed, and listened to. This finding is in line with various scholars who argue that mutuality is a construct that lies at the basis of the partnership concept as it entails respective rights and responsibilities for each partner (Guest & Peccei, 2001; Brinkerhoff, 2002). Thus, the finding that mutuality increases the perceived effectiveness of the MSI is supported by scholars who argue that mutuality is an important aspect in sustaining and building partnerships (van Ewijk & Baud, 2009).

Lastly, this study contends that (building) trust is a criterion for creating a collective stakeholder orientation. Within MSIs, trust between the partners is essential as it results in a more open environment and stronger relationships, making the knowledge exchange more effective. Given this trust, this study shows that partners within an MSI are more inclined to exchange knowledge. This elaborates the finding by Becker and Smith (2018) that trust within partnerships concerns a set of expectations between partners considering each other's behavior and fulfillment of its perceived obligations. Additionally, a lack of trust will harm the knowledge exchange as it hinders the achievement of a shared culture, which creates barriers to an open environment (Becker & Smith, 2018; Goh, 2002; Zand, 1972).

Considering the previously described criteria that underline the perceived effectiveness of knowledge exchange between MSI partners, Proposition 4 reads:

Proposition 4: A collective stakeholder orientation within an MSI is achieved when the knowledge exchange is focused on (i) joint learning, (ii) consultation, (iii) dialogue, (iv) mutuality, and (v) trust, making knowledge exchange more effective.

As this study investigates MSIs in practice, some interesting findings become evident related to how knowledge exchange is affected by differences between partners in knowledge superiority and absorptive capacity.

Theorists have established that knowledge is dependent upon an individual's perspective or understanding of what knowledge is (Fazey et al., 2014). Cummings (2003) believed that the learning predisposition of the recipient and the broader environment in which the knowledge exchange occurs affects knowledge exchange. Organizational theorists emphasize the need to understand knowledge exchange as embedded in social relations and constructed from social interactions (Swan et al., 1999). Thus, knowledge exchange can be considered as a relational process (Wenger, 1998).

Within this study, it appears that knowledge exchange between partners within an MSI is affected by a knowledge gap that is present between various partners. Some refer to this gap as a partner having superior knowledge over others. Because there is a difference in the type of knowledge that a partner holds, there is a difficulty for one partner to convey it and the other partner to understand it. This finding is consistent with various scholars who argue that a knowledge gap between two partners negatively affects the perceived knowledgeability of another partner (Hau & Evangelista, 2007). This knowledge gap, in turn, affects the perceived effectiveness of the knowledge exchange as well as the willingness of partners to cooperate, as some believe that the less knowledgeable partners are solely participating for their own benefit (Hau & Evangelista, 2007; Simonin, 1999a, 1999b). Therefore, Proposition 5 reads:

Proposition 5*: A greater knowledge gap between partners within an MSI negatively influences the knowledge exchange.*

This study additionally observes that tacit and explicit knowledge exchange are impacted by differing levels of absorptive capacity between partners. It was observed that some partners within an MSI were less able to successfully absorb, implement, transform, and exploit the knowledge that was given to them. Within the literature, absorptive capacity is known to impact knowledge exchange. If partners within an MSI differ in their absorptive capacity, it is expected that knowledge exchange between partners is affected (Cohen & Levinthal, 1990). However, during this study, it was noted that the exchange of tacit knowledge is more affected by absorptive capacity, as this entails "knowing how." Nooteboom (2000) supports this finding as a lower level of absorptive capacity requires learning via interactions.

A complementarity effect was found between absorptive capacity and effectiveness. This study highlights that, even if a partner's absorptive capacity is inferior to others', making these partners less able to understand the tacit and explicit knowledge, effective methods of knowledge exchange partially reduce the negative effect of absorptive capacity. This means that knowledge exchange based on (i) joint learning, (ii) consultation, (iii) dialogue, (iv) mutuality, and (v) trust provides the MSI with a collaborative approach, thereby making partners more able to absorb knowledge. This is also highlighted by Vie et al. (2014) who argue that absorptive capacity can increase through participation in a collaborative setting. Additionally, Jansen et al. (2005) reveal that socialization capabilities (i.e., trust, joint learning, and dialogue) increase absorptive capacity. Because of this, Proposition 6 reads:

Proposition 6*: A greater difference in the level of absorptive capacity between partners within an MSI negatively influences knowledge exchange. However, when knowledge exchange is based on creating a collective stakeholder orientation by focusing on (i) joint learning, (ii) consultation, (iii) dialogue, (iv) mutuality, and (v) trust, the difference in absorptive capacity decreases.*

CONCLUSION

The Sustainable Development Goals (SDGs) present an original approach to global governance. The seventeenth SDG recognizes the importance of MSIs in addressing political, economic, environmental, and social forces by bringing together diverse actors from the public, private, and nonprofit sectors to reach a shared objective. The private sector, in particular, is increasingly embracing knowledge exchange collaborations in order to create a competitive advantage and to better create shared value within GVCs. Together with other partners, MNEs can link and share information, resources, activities, experiences, and capabilities. The gift within an MSI refers to its ability to use the differences between the various partners as an asset. There is an importance of knowledge exchange between MSI partners to collectively acquire and exchange the knowledge, values, and competencies needed to survive, adapt, and compete successfully within the increasingly complex environment.

Even though various scholars have argued that knowledge exchange between partners within an MSI is important, as it will result in a long-term advantage, there has been a dearth of research into the exact process of knowledge exchange between partners within an MSI (Klitsie et al., 2018; Kolk et al., 2010; Villani et al., 2017). As Soundararajan et al. (2019) assert, for the collaboration between the partners to be successful, the knowledge exchange should be based on collective stakeholder orientation to enable the partners to seek and share value with each other. However, further study can show the conditions that allow for a collective stakeholder orientation, thereby aiding this exchange (Sammarra & Biggiero, 2008; Seitanidi & Ryan, 2007). Therefore, this study investigated an important but under-researched dimension of MSIs by answering the following research question: ***how does the exchange of tacit and explicit knowledge between partners within an MSI occur and how is this exchange affected by partner-specific constructs (i.e., absorptive capacity and knowledge superiority)?***

This study was exploratory in nature as research was missing that investigated the process of knowledge exchange within MSIs. This study focused on literature from organizational collaborations and extended this to fit the partner collaboration within MSIs. With this inductive approach, data were collected through a field study in South Africa to explore that phenomenon first-hand by focusing on a qualitative multiple case study design of four South African MSIs in the food and agriculture supply chain.

The similarities and differences that arose from the within-case analysis of the four cases were presented in a cross-case analysis. The resulting propositions show how MSIs can manage knowledge exchange in light of differences between partners, aiming for collective stakeholder orientation. The propositions focus on the qualifications of the process of knowledge exchange between partners, how tacit and explicit knowledge is exchanged, and how partner-specific effects impact the knowledge exchange. These propositions provide MSIs with the ability to establish a collective stakeholder orientation that grants the partners the ability to seek and share value effectively, in order to realize the SDGs.

The findings of this study show that frequent knowledge exchange between partners is important as it increases continuity of the MSI and results in a long-term advantage. Second, within MSIs there is a difference in engagement from the various sectors. It was found that the nonprofit and private sectors are most likely to engage in the process of knowledge exchange, whereas the public sector in South Africa is less engaged because of a lack of political will to engage, frequent staff reassignments, and less educated personnel. Third, this study highlights that the public sector in South Africa has increased difficulty to engage in the process of knowledge exchange, whereas the private and nonprofit sectors actively exchange knowledge, though with different motivations. Fourth, tacit and explicit knowledge exchange is perceived as effective when it is based on a collective stakeholder orientation, resulting from (i) joint learning, (ii) dialogue, (iii) mutuality, (iv) consultation, and (v) trust. Lastly, this study showed that the knowledge exchange is negatively impacted by a knowledge gap between the partners (i.e., some partners having superior knowledge over other partners) and different levels of absorptive capacity between partners. When the aforementioned partner-specific constructs are affecting knowledge exchange between partners within an MSI, the study showed that the five measures of collective stakeholder orientation diminish the partner-specific effects.

In sum, this study researched knowledge exchange between MNEs, NGOs, and governmental departments in South African MSIs related to the agri-food industry. The findings of this study highlight the importance of collective stakeholder orientation for an effective process of knowledge exchange between partners within an MSI. The propositions developed through this study show how MSI partners can create shared value within GVCs extending to developed countries such as South Africa, and to continue tackling the SDGs together successfully.

Although this study provides insights into knowledge exchange between MSI partners, it is essential to recognize that the findings of this study are subject to several limitations. First, this study only involves MSIs based in South Africa. Therefore, this study has a relatively narrow focus. However, diversity within these MSIs was sought by focusing on different elements of the food and agricultural supply chain, which connect to global value chains. Second, this study has a small scale as only four MSIs were researched, which limits the generalizability of the study. Lastly, only a sample of the partners was available to participate in this study, although, across the four cases, multiple interviews were conducted with representatives of NGOs, MNEs, and government.

Because of the exploratory focus of this study, avenues for future research are threefold. By showing how knowledge exchange within MSIs occurs between various partners, an understanding of the dynamics of knowledge exchange within MSI collaborations is developed. Considering there is a necessity for design and management of knowledge exchange processes, while also there is little focus on collective stakeholder orientation, this study contributes to the under-researched area of partner interaction within MSIs (Bouwen & Taillieu, 2004; Clarke & Crane, 2018; Haywood et al., 2018). Nevertheless, considering the qualitative multiple case study design of this research, the propositions arrived at in the discussion should in the future be tested empirically with a quantitative approach, followed by a study with a bigger sample. Further, this study contributes to the knowledge exchange literature by adding an interdimensional discussion to MNE knowledge exchange literature with the addition of MSI partner knowledge exchange. Future research could investigate whether this process of knowledge exchange results in better GVC performance.

Finally, this study adds to the current focus on researching MSIs in practice, as highlighted by Vurro et al. (2010). By considering how partner-specific constructs impact knowledge exchange within MSIs, the process of interaction and communication is further elaborated, which helps explain the context of an MSI better, in response to points previously made in scholarship (Rein & Stott, 2009; Selsky & Parker, 2005; Sud et al., 2009). Future research should continue to explore MSIs in practice within different contexts, to evaluate the degree to which context matters for MSI knowledge exchange, and success of MSI goals.

Besides the theoretical contributions, this study contributes to managerial practices by providing MSIs with insights into knowledge exchange and propositions suggesting how differences between partners can impact MSI knowledge exchange. By taking into consideration partner-specific constructs (i.e., absorptive capacity and knowledge superiority) the complexity of inter-organizational collaboration is addressed. The patterns discussed in the propositions allow MSIs to anticipate and deal with difficulties in knowledge exchange and interaction between partners, in order to become more collectively orientated and achieve the SDGs.

REFERENCES

Acosta, M., Ampaire, E. L., Muchunguzi, P., Okiror, J. F., Rutting, L., Mwongera, C., Twyman, J., Shikuku, K. M., Winowiecki, L. A., Läderach, P., Mwungu, C. M., & Jassogne, L. (2019). The role of multi-stakeholder platforms for creating an enabling climate change policy environment in east Africa. In: T. Rosenstock, A. Nowak & E. Girvetz (Eds.), *The Climate-Smart Agriculture Papers*. Cham: Springer.

Abbott, K. W., & Snidal, D. (2000). Hard and soft law in international governance. *International Organization*, *54*(1), 4321–456.

Almeida, P., Song, J., & Grant, R. M. (2002). Are firms superior to alliances and markets? an empirical test of cross-border knowledge building. *Organization Science*, *13*(2), 147–161.

Argote, L., & Ingram, P. (2000). Knowledge transfer: A basis for competitive advantage in firms. *Organizational Behaviour and Human Decision Processes*, *82*(1), 150–169.

Arora, B. (2017). Multi-stakeholder initiatives: Journey and the future. *Annual Review of Social Partnerships*, *12*(1), 134–135.

Asrar-ul-Haq, M., & Anwar, S. (2016). A systematic review of knowledge management and knowledge sharing: Trends, issues, and challenges. *Cogent Business and Management*, *3*(1), 1–17.

Austin, J. E. (2000a). Strategic collaboration between nonprofits and business. *Nonprofit and Voluntary Sector Quarterly*, *29*(suppl. 1), 69–97.

Austin, J. E. (2000b). *The Collaboration Challenge: How Nonprofits and Businesses Succeed Through Strategic Alliances*. San Francisco: Jossey-Bass.

Austin, J. E., & Seitanidi, M. M. (2012). Collaborative value creation: A review of partnering between nonprofits and businesses: Part I. Value creation spectrum and collaboration stages. *Nonprofit and Voluntary Sector Quarterly*, *41*(5), 726–758.

Balié, J., Del Prete, D., Magrini, E., Montalbano, P., & Nenci, S. (2019). Food and agriculture global value chains: New evidence from Sub-Saharan Africa. In *Governance for Structural Transformation in Africa* (pp. 251–276). Cham: Palgrave Macmillan.

Becerra, M., Lunnan, R., & Huemer, L. (2008). Trustworthiness, risk, and the transfer of tacit and explicit knowledge between alliance partners. *Journal of Management Studies*, *45*(5), 691–713.

Becker, J., & Smith, D. B. (2018). The need for cross-sector collaboration. *Stanford Social Innovation Review*, Winter 2018, 1–3.

Beisheim, M., & Simon, N. (2018). Multistakeholder partnerships for the SDGs: Actors' views on UN metagovernance. *Global Governance*, *24*(1), 497–515.

Bendell, J., Collins, E., & Roper, J. (2010). Beyond partnerism: Toward a more expansive research agenda on multi-stakeholder collaboration for responsible business. *Business Strategy and the Environment*, *19*(6), 351–355.

Berger, I., Cunningham, P., & Drumwright, M. (2004). Social alliances: Company/nonprofit collaboration. *California Management Review*, *47*(1), 58–90.

Berrone, P., Ricart, J. E., Duch, A. I., Bernardo, V., Salvador, J., Piedra Peña, J., Rodríguez & Planas, M. (2019). EASIER: An evaluation model for public-private partnerships contributing to the sustainable development goals. *Sustainability*, *11*(8), 2339.

Biekart, K., & Fowler, A. (2018). Ownership dynamics in local multi-stakeholder initiatives. *Third World Quarterly*, pp. 1–19.

Bitzer, V., Hamann, R., Hall, M., & Griffin, E. W. (2015). *The Business of Social and Environmental Innovation: Frontier in Research and Practice in Africa*. Cape Town, South Africa: University of Cape Town Press; Berlin, Germany: Springer.

Bogie, G. M. (2016). *A Communicative Approach towards an Understanding of Multi-Stakeholder Cross-Sector Collaboration as an Issue Field: Perspectives from Sustainable Seafood Supply Chain Initiatives in an Emerging Market*. Stellenbosch University.

Boiral, O. (2002). Tacit knowledge and environmental management. *Long Range Planning*, *35*, 291–317.

Bolisani, E., & Scarso, E. (1999). Information technology management: A knowledge-based perspective. *Technovation*, *19*, 209–217.

Bosse, D. A., & Phillips, R. A. (2016). Agency theory and bounded self-interest. *Academy of Management Review*, *41*(1), 276–297.

Bouwen, R., & Taillieu, T. (2004). Multi-party collaboration as social learning for interdependence: Developing relational knowing for sustainable natural resource management. *Journal of Community & Applied Social Psychology*, *14*(1), 137–153.

Bresman, H., Birkinshaw, J., & Nobel, R. (1999). Knowledge transfer in international acquisitions. *Journal of International Business Studies*, *30*(3), 439–462.

Brinkerhoff, J. M. (2002). Assessing and improving partnership relationships and outcomes: A proposed framework. *Evaluation and Program Planning*, *25*(1), 215–231.

Brinkerhoff, R. (2003). *The Success Case Method: Find Out Quickly What's Working and What's Not.* Oakland: Berrett-Koehler Publishers.

Brouwer, H., Woodhill, J., Hemmati, M., Verhoosel, K., & van Vugt, S. (2016). *The MSP Guide: How to Design and Facilitate Multi-Stakeholder Partnerships.* Wageningen, NL: Wageningen University and Research, CDI, and Rugby, UK: Practical Action Publishing.

Brown, L. D., Khagram, S., Moore, M. H., & Frumkin, P. (2000). *Globalization, NGOs, and Multi-Sectoral Relations.* The Hauser Center for Nonprofit Organizations and The Kennedy School of Government. Harvard University. Working Paper No. 1.

Bryson, J. M., Crosby, B. C., & Stone, M. M. (2006). The design and implementation of cross-sector collaborations: Propositions from the literature. *Public Administration Review*, *66*(s1), 44–55.

Chen, C.-J. (2004). The effect of knowledge attribute, alliance characteristics, and absorptive capacity on knowledge transfer performance. *R&D Management*, *34*(3), 311–321.

Cheyns, E. (2011). Multi-stakeholder initiatives for sustainable agriculture: Limits of the 'inclusiveness' paradigm. In: S. Ponte, P. Gibbon, & E. Vestergaard (Eds.), *Governing Through Standards: Origins, Drivers, and Limitations.* Palgrave Macmillan.

Clapp, J., & Fuchs, D. (Eds.) (2009). *Corporate Power in Global Agrifood Governance.* Boston: MIT Press.

Clarke, A., & Crane, A. (2018). Cross-sector partnerships for systemic change: Systematized literature review and agenda for further research. *Journal of Business Ethics*, *6*(1), 1–11.

Cockburn, I., & Henderson, R. (1998). Absorptive capacity, coauthoring behaviour, and the organization of research in drug discovery. *The Journal of Industrial Economics*, *46*(2), 157–183.

Cohen, W. M., & Levinthal, D. A. (1990). Absorptive capacity: A new perspective on learning and innovation. *Administrative Science Quarterly*, *35*, 128–152.

Corbin, J., & Strauss, A. (2014). *Basics of Qualitative Research: Techniques and Procedures for Developing Grounded Theory.* SAGE Publications.

Cummings, J. N. (2003). *Knowledge Sharing: A Review of the Literature.* OED Working Series. World Bank, Washington, DC.

Cummings, J. N. (2004). Work groups, structural diversity, and knowledge sharing in a global organization. *Management Science*, *50*(1), 352–364.

Dave, B., & Koskela, L. (2009). Collaborative knowledge management – a construction case study. *Automation in Construction*, *18*, 894–902.

De Bakker, F. G. A., Rasche, A., & Ponte, S. (2019). Multi-stakeholder initiatives on sustainability: A cross-disciplinary review and research agenda for business ethics. *Business Ethics Quarterly*, *29*(3), 343–383.

Desouza, K. C. (2003). Facilitating tacit knowledge exchange. *Communications of the ACM*, *46*(6), 85–88.

Dewulf, A., & Elbers, W. (2018). Power in and over cross-sector partnerships: Actors strategies for shaping collective decisions. *Administrative Sciences*, *8*(43), 2–15.

Dhanaraj, C., Lyles, M. A., Steensma, H. K., & Tihanyi, L. (2004). Managing tacit and explicit knowledge transfer in IJVs: The role of relational embeddedness and the impact on performance. *Journal of International Business Studies*, *35*(1), 428–442.

Drimie, S., Hamann, R., Manderson, A. P., & Mlondobozi, N. (2018). Creating transformative spaces for dialogue and action: Reflecting on the experience of the Southern Africa Food Lab. *Ecology and Society*, *23*(3).

Dyer, J. H., & Hatch, N. W. (2006). Relations-specific capabilities and barriers to knowledge transfer: Creating advantage through network relationships. *Strategic Management Journal, 27*(1), 701–719

Eisenhardt, K. M. (1989). Building theories from case study research. *Academy of Management Review, 14*(4), 532–550.

Eisenhardt, K. M., & Graebner, M. E. (2007). Theory building from cases: Opportunities and challenges. *Academy of Management Journal, 50*(1), 25–32.

El Ansari, W., Phillips, C. J., & Hammick, M. (2001). Collaboration and partnerships: Developing the evidence base. *Health and Social Care in the Community, 9*(4), 215–227.

Eriksson, K., & Chetty, S. (2003). The effect of experience and absorptive capacity on foreign market knowledge. *International Business Review, 12*(1), 673–695.

Ernst, D., Kim, L. (2002). Global production networks, knowledge diffusion, and local capability formation. *Research Policy, 31*(8–9), 1417–1429.

Escribano, A., Fosfuri, A., & Tribó, J. A. (2009). Managing external knowledge flows: The moderating role of absorptive capacity. *Research Policy, 38*(1), 96–105.

Fazey, I., Bunse, L., Msika, J., Pinke, M., Preedy, K., Evely, A.C., Lambert, E., Hastings, E., Morris, S., & Reed, M.S. (2014). Evaluating knowledge exchange in interdisciplinary and multi-stakeholder research. *Global Environmental Change, 25*(1), 204–220.

Fransen, L. W., & Kolk, A. (2007). Global rule-setting for business: A critical analysis of multi-stakeholder standards. *Organization, 14*(1), 667–684.

Goh, S. C. (2002). Managing effective knowledge transfer: An integrative framework and some practice implications. *Journal of Knowledge Management, 6*(1), 23–30

Gereffi, G. (2013). Global value chains in a post-Washington consensus world. *Review of International Political Economy, 21*(1), 9–37.

Gereffi, G., & Fernandez-Stark, K. (2011). Global Value Chain Analysis: A Primer. Center on Globalization Governance & Competitiveness, (CGGC), Duke University, North Carolina, USA.

Gilbert, D. U., & Rasche, A. (2008). Opportunities and problems of standardized ethics initiatives – a stakeholder theory perspective. *Journal of Business Ethics, 82*(1), 755–773.

Grant, R. M. (1996). Toward a knowledge-based theory of the firm. *Strategic Management Journal, 17*(suppl. 2), 109–122.

Grant, R. M. (1997). The knowledge-based view of the firm: Implications for management practice. *Long Range Planning, 30*, 450–454.

Gray, B. (1989). *Collaborating: Finding Common Ground for Multiparty Problems.* San Francisco, CA: Jossey-Bass.

Greene, J. C. (2001). Dialogue in evaluation. A relational perspective. *Evaluation, 7*(2), 181–187.

Guest, D. E., & Peccei, R. (2001). Partnerships at work: Mutuality and the balance of advantage. *British Journal of Industrial Relations, 39*(2), 207–236.

Hamel, G. (1991). Competition for competence and inter-partner leaning within international strategic alliances. *Strategic Management Journal, 12*(1), 83–103.

Hansen, M. T. (2002). Knowledge networks: Explaining effective knowledge sharing in multiunit companies. *Organization Science, 13*(3), 232–248.

Hassan, A., & Lund-Thomsen, P. (2018). Multi-stakeholder initiatives and corporate social responsibility in global value chains: Towards an analytical framework and a methodology. *Corporate Social Responsibility: Concepts, Methodologies, Tools, and Applications.* IGI Global, 305–321.

Hau, L. N., & Evangelista, F. (2007). Acquiring tacit and explicit marketing knowledge from foreign partners in IJVs. *Journal of Business Research, 60*(1), 1152–1165.

Haywood, L. K., Funke, N., Audouin, M., Musvoto, C., & Nahman, A. (2018). The sustainable development goals in South Africa: Investigating the need for multi-stakeholder partnerships. *Development Southern Africa, 18*(1), 1–15.

Head, B. W. (2008). Assessing network-based collaborations. *Public Management Review, 10*(6), 733–749.

Hermans, F., Sartas, M., van Schagen, B., van Asten, P., & Schut, M. (2017). Social network analysis of multi-stakeholder platforms in agricultural research for development: Opportunities and constraints for innovation and scaling. *PLoS One, 12*(1), e0169634.

Houston, J. (2016). ClimateWise – An insurance industry partnership. *Annual Review of Social Partnerships, 11*(1), 107–108.

Hsiao, R., Tsai, S., & Lee, C. (2003). The problem of embeddedness: Knowledge transfer, situated practice, and the role of information systems. *Proceedings of the Twenty-Fourth International Conference on Information Systems*. Seattle, WA, 36–46.

Humphrey, J., & Schmitz, H. (2000). *Governance and Upgrading: Linking Industrial Cluster and Global Value Chain Research* (Vol. 120). Brighton: Institute of Development Studies.

Ingram, J. (2008). Agronomist-farmer knowledge encounters: An analysis of knowledge exchange in the context of best management practices in England. *Agriculture and Human Values*, *25*(3), 405–418.

Inkpen, A. C. (2000). Learning through joint ventures: A framework of knowledge acquisition. *Journal of Management Studies*, *37*(7), 1019–1044.

Inkpen, A. C., & Dinur, A. (1998). Knowledge management processes and international joint ventures. *Organization Science*, *9*(4), 454–468.

Jansen, J. J. P., van den Bosch, F. A. J., & Volberda, H. W. (2005). Managing potential and realized absorptive capacity: How do organizational antecedents matter? *Academy of Management Journal*, *49*(6), 999–1015

Jiménez-Barrionuevo, M. M., García-Morales, V. J., & Molina, L. M. (2011). Validation of an instrument to measure absorptive capacity. *Technovation*, *31*(1), 190–202

Kalibwani, R. M., Twebaze, J., Kamugisha, R., Kakuru, M., Sabiiti, M., Kugonza, I., Tenyqa, M., & Nyamwaro, S. (2018). Multi-stakeholder partnerships in value chain development: A case of the organic pineapple in Ntungamo District. Western Uganda, *Journal of Agribusiness in Developing and Emerging Economies*, *8*(1), 171–185.

Kanawattanachai, P., & Yoo, Y. (2007). The impact of knowledge coordination on virtual team performance over time. *Management Information Systems Quarterly*, *31*(4), 783–808.

Klitsie, E. J., Ansari, S., & Volberda, H. W. (2018). Maintenance of cross-sector partnerships: The roles of frames in sustained collaboration. *Journal of Business Ethics*, *150*(2), 401–423.

Kogut, B., & Zander, U. (1992). Knowledge of the firm, combinative capabilities, and the replication of technology. *Organization Science*, *3*(3), 383–397.

Kogut, B., & Zander, U. (1993). Knowledge of the firm and the evolutionary theory of the multinational corporation. *Journal of International Business Studies*, *24*(4), 625–645.

Kolk, A., Van Dolen, W., & Vock, M. (2010). Trickle effects of cross-sector social partnerships. *Journal of Business Ethics*, *94*(1), 123–137.

Kolk, A., Van Tulder, R., & Kostwinder, E. (2008). Business and partnerships for development. *European Management Journal*, *26*(4), 262–273.

Kramer, M. R., & Porter, M. (2011). Creating shared value. *Harvard Business Review*, *89*(1/2), 62–77.

Lane, P. J., Koka, B., & Pathak, S. (2002). A thematic analysis and critical assessment of absorptive capacity research. In: *Academy of Management Proceedings*, 2002(1), Briarcliff Manor, N 10510: Academy of Management, M1–M6.

Le Ber, M. J., & Branzei, O. (2010). (Re)forming strategic cross-sector partnerships: Relational processes of social innovation. *Business & Strategy*, *49*(1), 140–172.

Lee, S. H., Mellahi, K., Mol, M. J., & Pereira, V. (2020). No-size-fits-all: Collaborative governance as an alternative for addressing labour issues in Global Supply Chains. *Journal of Business Ethics*, *162*(1), 291–305.

Lin, C., Wu, Y-J., Chang, C., Wang, W., & Lee, C-Y. (2012). The alliance innovation performance of R&D alliances – the absorptive capacity perspective. *Technovation*, *32*(1), 282–292.

Lin, H. F. (2007). Knowledge sharing and firm innovation capability: An empirical study. *International Journal of Manpower*, *28*(3/4), 315–332.

Lowndes, V., & Skelcher, C. (1998). The dynamics of multi-organizational partnerships: An analysis of changing modes of governance. *Public Administration*, *71*(Summer), 313–333.

Makhija, M. V., & Ganesh, U. (1997). The relationship between control and partner learning-related joint ventures. *Organization Science*, *8*(5), 508–527.

Malhotra, A., Gosain, S., & El Sawy, O. A. (2005). Absorptive capacity configurations in supply chains: Gearing for partner-enabled market knowledge creation. *Management Information Systems Quarterly*, *29*(1), 145–187.

Marx, A. (2019). Public-private partnerships for sustainable development: Exploring their design and its impact on effectiveness. *Sustainability*, *11*(4), 1087.

Matthyssens, P., Pauwels, P., & Vandenbempt, K. (2005). Strategic flexibility, rigidity, and barriers to the development of absorptive capacity in business markets: Themes and research perspectives. *Industrial Marketing Management, 34*(6), 547–554.

Mena, S., & Palazzo, G. (2012). Input and output legitimacy of multi-stakeholder initiatives. *Business Ethics Quarterly, 22*(3), 527–556.

Mentzas, G., Apostolou, D., Kafentzis, K., & Georgolios, P. (2006). Inter-organizational networks for knowledge sharing and trading. *Information Technology and Management, 7*(4), 259–276.

Mesmer-Magnus, J. R., & DeChurch, L. A. (2009). Information sharing and team performance. A meta-analysis. *Journal of Applied Psychology, 94*(1), 478–496.

Minbaeva, D., Pederson, T., Björkman, I., Fey, C. F., Park, H. J. (2003). MNC knowledge transfer, subsidiary absorptive capacity, and HRM. *Journal of International Business Studies, 34*, 586–599.

Moog, S., Spicer, A., & Böhm, S. (2015). The politics of multi-stakeholder initiatives: The crisis of the Forest Stewardship Council. *Journal of Business Ethics, 128*(3), 469–493.

Muscio, A. (2007). The impact of absorptive capacity on SMEs' collaboration. *Economics of Innovation and New Technology, 16*(8), 653–668.

Nonaka, I., & Takeuchi, H. (1995). *The Knowledge-Creating Company.* Oxford: Oxford University Press.

Nonaka, I., & Von Krogh, G. (2009). Tacit knowledge and knowledge conversion: Controversy and advancement in organizational knowledge creation theory. *Organization Science, 20*(3), 635–652.

Nooteboom, B. (2000). Learning by interaction: Absorptive capacity, cognitive distance, and governance. *Journal of Management and Governance, 4*, 69–92.

Okereke, C., & Stacewicz, I. (2018). Stakeholder perceptions of the environmental effectiveness of multi-stakeholder initiatives: Evidence from the palm oil, soy, cotton, and timber programs. *Society & Natural Resources*, 1–17.

Pattberg, P., & Widerberg, O. (2016). Transnational multistakeholder partnerships for sustainable development: Conditions for success. *Ambio, 45*(1), 42–51.

Pebbles Project (2014). *Our Story.* Retrieved from: http://www.pebblesproject.co.za/pebbles-history/

Pérez-Nordtvedt, L., Kedia, B. L., Datta, D. K., & Rasheed, A. A. (2008). Effectiveness and efficiency of cross-border knowledge transfer: An empirical examination. *Journal of Management Studies, 45*(4), 714–744.

Polanyi, M. (1967). *The Tacit Dimension.* Garden City, NY: Doubleday Anchor.

Powell, E. E., Hamann, R., Bitzer, V., & Baker, T. (2018). Bringing the elephant into the room? Enacting conflict in collective prosocial organizing. *Journal of Business Venturing, 33*(1), 623–642.

Raymond, C., Fazey, I., Reed, M. S., Stringer, L. C., Robinson, G. M., & Evely, A. C. (2010). Integrating local and scientific knowledge for environmental management. *Journal of Environmental Management, 91*, 1766–1777.

Rein, M., & Stott, L. (2009). Working together: Critical perspectives on six cross-sector partnerships in Southern Africa. *Journal of Business Ethics, 90*(1), 79–89.

Rein, M., Stott, L., Yambayamba, K., Hardman, S., & Reid, S. (2005). *Working Together: A Critical Analysis of Cross-Sector Partnerships in Southern Africa.* Cambridge: University of Cambridge Programme for Industry.

Ritala, P., & Hurmelinna-Laukkanen, P. (2013). Incremental and radical innovation in coopetition – the role of absorptive capacity and appropriability. *Journal of Product Innovation Management, 30*(1), 154–169.

Rivera-Santos, M., Rufin, C., & Kolk, A. (2012). Bridging the institutional divide: Partnerships in subsistence markets. *Journal of Business Research, 65*(1), 1721–1727.

Roberts, J. (2000). From know-how to show-how? Questioning the role of information and communication technologies in knowledge transfer. *Technology Analysis & Strategic Management, 12*(4), 429–443.

Roberts, N., Galluch, P. S., Dinger, M., & Grover, V. (2012). Absorptive capacity and information systems research: Review, synthesis, and directions for future research. *Management Information Systems Research Quarterly, 36*(2), 625–648.

Roloff, J. (2008). A life-cycle model of multi-stakeholder networks. *Business Ethics: A European Review, 17*(3), 311–325.

Roloff, J. (2018). Learning from multi-stakeholder networks: Issue-focused stakeholder management. *Journal of Business Ethics*, *82*(1), 233–350.

Ryan, G. W., & Bernard, H. R. (2003). Techniques to identify themes. *Field Methods*, *15*(1), 85–109.

Sammarra, A., & Biggiero, L. (2008). Heterogeneity and specificity of inter-firm knowledge flows in innovation networks. *Journal of Management Studies*, *45*(4), 800–829.

Saunders, M., Lewis, P., & Thornhill, A. (2015). *Research Methods for Business Students* (5th Ed.). New York: Pearson.

Seitanidi, M. M., & Crane, A. (Eds.) (2014). *Social Partnerships and Responsible Business: A Research Handbook*. London: Routledge.

Seitanidi, M. M., Koufopoulos, D. N., & Palmer, P. (2010). Partnership formation for change: Indicators for transformative potential in cross-sector social partnerships. *Journal of Business Ethics*, *94*(1), 139–161.

Seitanidi, M. M., & Ryan, A. (2007). A critical review of forms of corporate community involvement: From philanthropy to partnerships. *International Journal of Nonprofit and Voluntary Sector Marketing*, *12*(3), 247–266.

Selsky, J. W., & Parker, B. (2005). Cross-sector partnerships to address social issues: Challenges to theory and practice. *Journal of Management*, *31*(6), 849–873.

Senge, P. M., Lichtenstein, B. B., Kaeufer, K., Bradbury, H., & Carroll, J. S. (2007). Collaborating for systemic change. *MIT Sloan Management Review*, *48*(2), 43–54.

Shumate, M., Fu, J. F., & Cooper, K. R. (2018). Does cross-sector collaboration lead to higher nonprofit capacity? *Journal of Business Ethics* (Thematic symposium on cross-sector partnerships for systemic change).

Simonin, B. (1999a). Transfer of marketing know-how in international strategic alliances: An empirical investigation of the role and antecedents of knowledge ambiguity. *Journal of International Business Studies*, *30*, 463–490.

Simonin, B. L. (1999b). Ambiguity and the process of knowledge transfer in strategic alliances. *Strategic Management Journal*, *30*(7), 595–623.

Soundararajan, V. (2017). Bringing the "multiple" bank into the multi-stakeholder initiatives. *Annual Review of Social Partnerships*, *12*(1), 121–123.

Soundararajan, V., Brown, J. A., & Wicks, A. C. (2019). Can multi-stakeholder initiatives improve global supply chains? Improving deliberative capacity with a stakeholder orientation. *Business Ethics Quarterly*, *29*(3), 385–412.

Spence, L., & Bourlakis, M. (2009). The evolution from corporate social responsibility to supply chain responsibility: The case of Waitrose. *Supply Chain Management: An International Journal*, *14*(4), 291–302.

Stephan, U., Patterson, M., Kelly, C., & Mair, J. (2016). Organizations driving positive social change: A review and an integrative framework of change processes. *Journal of Management*, *42*(5), 1250–1281.

Sud, M., Van Sandt, C., & Baugous, A. (2009). Social entrepreneurship: The role of institutions. *Journal of Business Ethics*, *1*(85), 201–216.

Swan, J., Newell, S., Scarbrough, H., & Hislop, D. (1999). Knowledge management and innovation: Networks and networking. *Journal of Knowledge Management*, *3*(4), 262–275.

Szulanski, G. (1996). Exploring internal stickiness: Impediments to the transfer of best practice within the firm. *Strategic Management Journal*, Winter Special Issue, *17*, 27–43.

Tamer Cavusgil, S., Calantone, R. J., & Zhao, Y. (2003). Tacit knowledge transfer and firm innovation capability. *Journal of Business and Industrial Marketing*, *18*(1), 6–21.

Teece, D. (1998). Capturing value from knowledge assets: The new economy, markets for know-how, and intangible assets. *California Management Review*, *40*(3), 55–79.

Torres de Oliveira, R. T., Sahasranamam, S., Figueira, S., & Paul, J. (2019). Upgrading without formal integration in M&A: The role of social integration. *Global Strategy Journal*, 2019.

Tsai, W. (2001). Knowledge transfer in intraorganizational networks: Effects of network position and absorptive capacity on business unit innovation and performance. *The Academy of Management Journal*, *44*(5), 996–1004.

UN News Centre. (2015). UN forum highlights "fundamental" role of private sector in advancing new global goals. [Online] Available: http://www.un.org/apps/news/story.asp?NewsID=51981# .Wf7X6FvWypo (accessed 21 January 2020).

UNCTAD STAT. (2020). Export diversification and employment. Available: https://unctad.org/system/ files/official-document/aldc2018d3_en.pdf (accessed 23 January 2020).

United Nations. (2015). The global goals for sustainable development: Goal 17 partnerships for the goals. [Online] Available: http://www.globalgoals.org/global-goals/partnerships-for-the-goals (accessed 22 January 2020).

Utting, P. (2002). *Regulating Business Via Multi-Stakeholders Initiatives: A Preliminary Assessment.* Geneva: United Nations Research Institute for Social Development.

Van Ewijk, E., & Baud, I. (2009). Partnerships between Dutch municipalities and municipalities in countries of migration to the Netherlands; knowledge exchange and mutuality. *Habitat International, 33*(1), 218–226.

Van Tulder, R., & Keen, N. (2018). Capturing collaborative challenges: Designing complexity-sensitive theories of change for cross-sector partnerships. *Journal of Business Ethics,* 1–18.

Van Tulder, R., Seitanidi, M. M., Crane, A., & Brammer, S. (2016). Enhancing the impact of cross-sector partnerships. *Journal of Business Ethics, 135*(1), 1–17.

van Zanten, J. A., & van Tulder, R. (2018). Multinational enterprises and the sustainable development goals: An institutional approach to corporate engagement. *Journal of International Business Policy, 2018*(1), 208–223.

Vie, O. E., Stensli, M., & Lauvas, T. A. (2014). Increasing companies' absorptive capacity through participation in collaborative research centers. *Energy Procedia, 58*(1), 36–42.

Villani, E., Greco, L., & Phillips, N. (2017). Understanding value creation in public-private partnerships: A comparative case study. *Journal of Management Studies, 54*(6), 876–905.

Von Briel, F., Schneider, C., & Lowry, P. B. (2019). Absorbing knowledge from and with external partners: The role of social integration mechanisms. *Decision Sciences, 50*(1), 7–45

Vurro, C., Dacin, M. T., & Perrini, F. (2010). Institutional antecedents of partnering for social change: How institutional logics shape cross-sector social partnerships. *Journal of Business Ethics, 94*(1), 39–53.

Warhurst, A. (2005). Future roles of business in society: The expanding boundaries of corporate responsibility and a compelling case of partnership. *Futures, 37*(2/3), 151–168.

Warner, M., & Sullivan, R. (2004). *Putting Partnerships to Work: Strategic Alliances for Development Between the Government, the Private Sector, and Civil Society.* Sheffield, UK: Greenleaf Publishing Limited.

Weick, K. E. (1990). Technology as equivoque: Sense-making in new technologics. In: P. S. Goodman, L. S. Sproull, & Associates (Eds.), *Technology and Organizations.* Oxford: Jossey-Bass.

Wenger, E. (1998). Communities of practice: Learning as a social system. *Systems Thinker, 6*(1).

Wyatt, J. C. (2001). Management of explicit and tacit knowledge. *Journal of the Royal Society of Medicine, 94,* 6–9.

Yan, X., Lin, H., & Clarke, A. (2018). Cross-sector social partnerships for social change: The roles of non-governmental organizations. *Sustainability, 20*(2), 558–575.

Yeoman, R., & Mueller Santos, M. (2019). Global value chains, reputation, and social cooperation. *Global Aspects of Reputation and Strategic Management, 18*(1), 69–91.

Yin, R. K. (2013). *Case Study Research: Design and Methods* (5th Ed.). Thousand Oaks, CA: SAGE.

Zahra, S. A. (2005). A theory of international new ventures: A decade of research. *Journal of International Business Studies, 36*(1), 20–28.

Zahra, S. A., & George, G. (2002). Absorptive capacity: A review, reconceptualization, and extension. *The Academy of Management Review, 27*(2), 185–203.

Zand, D. (1972). Trust and managerial problem solving. *Administrative Science Quarterly, 17*(1), 229–239.

7. Global talent mobility and knowledge diffusion: the role of staffing agencies in the growth of East Asian high-tech multinational corporations

Mayumi Tabata

INTRODUCTION

The geographical mobility of human resources, as well as the mobility of institutions, ideas, technical knowledge, and behavioral norms, has a great influence on the organizational knowledge cognition system (Jöns et al., 2017). Previous studies on global knowledge diffusion have pointed out that the mobility of human resources has played a crucial role in the flow of knowledge. These human resources have moved from one organization to the other across the globe through the channels of multinational corporations (MNCs), global inter-cluster brain circulation, and being hired as expatriates and technological experts (Almeida et al., 2002; Kawai and Chung, 2019; Richter, 2016; Song et al., 2003). In this dynamic global brain circulation, the channel of cross-national talent mobility – namely staffing agencies specializing in accessing and placing these human resources according to global demand – is growing very fast (Manning et al., 2008). However, little work has been done on staffing agencies as a channel of cross-national talent mobility in East Asian countries.

The staffing agencies industry became a formal enterprise after the end of the Second World War in the United States. It flourished after the 1970s and became a matchmaker between talent and employer in the development process of the "external labor market."[1] Most staffing agencies concurrently serve as manpower dispatching businesses. This study examined the impact of a headhunting company that introduces talent to high-tech companies on the knowledge transfer among companies and the impact of the human resource consulting company that dispatches, manages, and trains talent. Regardless of whether they are recruitment agencies or talent dispatching companies, they are playing a mediating role between job seekers and talent seekers in the external labor market. Due to the government's deregulation of the job market, staffing agencies have changed the salary adjustment mechanism, which was dominated by corporate organizations in the job market and has gradually begun to have a greater influence on the salary structure (Theodore and Peck, 2002: 463).

In the past 70 years, the staffing agency industry has transformed from a small intermediary enterprise in the mid-west of the United States to a large-scale talent resource industry and has launched a transnational business model. The large-scale staffing agency in the United States has begun to penetrate the employment market in Southeast Asia, South America, and Eastern Europe. These talent resource consulting companies not only provide more job opportunities to job seekers through the "external labor market", but also promote the cross-organizational flow of talent. The transnational development of staffing agencies is constantly creating flexible labor market-making activities (Ward, 2004).

Taiwan's wages have been sluggish for a long time, and the media often report the crisis of a brain drain. Various media in Taiwan have discussed the reasons for the brain drain. The analysis of the media is roughly divided into two opinions. One opinion is that Taiwan's economy has caused an industrial hollowing out due to the Taiwanese government's strict and closed economic policies on China, and the result of the deterioration of the investment environment has accelerated the brain drain (*China Times*, 2017). Another point of view is that the Taiwanese industrial world is not friendly to workers. Since 1995, Taiwan's average salary has barely risen. More than two-thirds of Taiwanese workers work in small and medium-sized enterprises. It is not until an employee submits a request for resignation that the employer reluctantly starts to think about raising salaries. Foreign companies generally believe that Taiwanese talent is "good quality and cheap" and employees are reluctant to participate in strikes (*Liberty Times*, 2015).

For nearly 40 years, Taiwan's technology industries, for example, the semiconductor and Liquid Crystal Display (LCD) panel industries, have played a very important role in the global and East Asian supply chain and have established a collaboration network of technology transfer and supply of components with Europe, the United States, and Japan. In the 1980s, the Taiwanese semiconductor industry introduced key technologies through Taiwanese executives and senior engineers who returned from the US (Hsu and Saxenian, 2000; Saxenian and Hsu, 2001). The network of technology communities between Hsinchu Science Park and Silicon Valley promoted and accelerated the exchange of technical talent and knowledge across the United States and Taiwan (Jou and Chen, 2000; Chen, 2008). From the late 1990s to the early 2000s, Taiwan's LCD panel industry quickly introduced and learned key technologies through the Japanese technological talent. In just five years, the Taiwanese LCD panel industry caught up with Japan's technological standards to establish a production base for the LCD panel industry in Taiwan (Tabata and Chuang, 2010; Tabata, 2012). These previous studies point out that Taiwan's technology industry introduced technological talent through a network of multinational technology communities to introduce tacit knowledge of key technologies. After the early 2000s, staffing agencies in Europe, America, and Japan started to open branches in Taiwan to provide channels for the domestic technology industry to hire foreign talent. Domestic talent also had the opportunity to seek job offers in foreign countries through human resource agencies. At present, the rise of the staffing agency industry has a great influence on the knowledge diffusion of the East Asian high-tech industry. For example, according to research by Xin (2006) and Ma (2005), Taiwan's high-tech MNCs have introduced foreign talent through staffing agencies, and Taiwan's technological talent also moved to the competing high-tech MNCs in China through staffing agencies.

This research was conducted using written material such as academic reports and media reports, and in-depth interviews with the heads and staff of staffing agencies and of the high-tech industry in Taiwan and Japan; namely, semiconductor and Thin Film Liquid Crystal Display (TFT-LCD) manufacturers and industry associations. Using the in-depth interviews, I attempted to understand the process of high-tech talent mobility through staffing agencies in East Asian countries and analyzed the various impacts of staffing agencies on the cross-national knowledge transfer and learning, labor market institutions, and human resource development in the East Asian high-tech industry.

FROM SOCIAL NETWORKS TO STAFFING AGENCIES: TRANSFORMATION OF HIGH-TECH TALENT JOB SEARCH CHANNELS

Due to the innovation of technology, fierce global competition, and the progress of corporate restructuring, the labor market has become increasingly complex and unpredictable. Affected by the unstable labor market and high frequency of job hopping, not only job seekers, but also increasingly employers need third-party intermediaries for job searching and counseling. With this trend, in the recent two decades, "temporary-help agencies" have penetrated the labor market in Europe and the United States (Benner, 2003: 621). Benner (2003) analyzed the role of "labor market intermediaries (LMIs)" in the relationship between high-tech companies in Silicon Valley and high-tech labor in the United States from a regional development perspective. Benner classifies LMIs into three types; namely, "intermediaries of the private sector," "member-based intermediaries," and "intermediaries of the public sector." "Intermediaries of the private sector" are the manpower dispatching companies, including temporary help firms, consultant brokerage firms, web-based job sites, and professional employer organizations. This sector evaluates core skills for high-tech firms. The second type of LMIs is "member-based intermediaries," which include professional associations, industry associations, and other unions. These provide job search information, as well as skills training and other services. "Intermediaries of the public sector" play the mediating role between job seekers and employers in the public sector (Benner, 2003: 623–625). Benner's classification shows that LMIs cover a diverse range of service models, and staffing agencies have facilitated rapid changes in job requirements, improved jobseekers' work ability, and accelerated job flexibility.

Previous studies on the social capital theory explored the various effects of social capital on individual social mobility, such as job search, wage raise, and promotion (Lin et al., 2010: 121). Granovetter (1973, 1974, 1995) and Lin (1990, 2001) explored the effects of social capital on job hunting from the perspective of weak ties. Their series of studies showed that not only strong ties such as blood relationship, friendship, and family ties, but also weak ties, enable job seekers to recognize people in different positions in various workplaces, and that it is easier for them to find diverse job opportunities. Bian (1997) conducted field research in Tianjin, China in 1988 and found that strong ties were a very important job search channel in the Chinese society. However, in 2009, Bian conducted another field research in eight cities in China and found different results. Job seekers usually find their first jobs through strong ties of their parents; however, when they change their jobs, they not only rely on strong ties but also utilize weak ties more often to get their second jobs (Bian and Huang 2015).

According to a study by an American anthropologist, Gershon (2017), "workplace ties," including inter-organizational and intra-organizational workplace networks, play a more important role in the job search process than social networks. She analyzed the job search strategy data of 380 highly educated white-collar professionals who worked in the San Francisco Bay Area from 2012 to 2013 and found that social networks still had a positive effect on job hunting. However, compared with the early 1970s, social networks had become less effective. In the early 1970s, 26% of job seekers found jobs through formal recruitment channels such as companies' job advertisements and newspapers, and about 74% of job seekers sought job opportunities through social networks. However, the results of Gershon's (2017) study showed that in early 2010, the percentage of job seekers finding jobs through social networks fell to 37.5%, and 35% of job seekers were recruited through recruiters or human resource agencies, and 26% of job seekers got employment opportunities through internet public recruitment information. In addition, 61% of job seekers commented that those who understood the job seeker's ability to work had a positive impact on the job-hunting activity. This type of "workplace ties" in the business or industrial professional communities is the most important trust mechanism for job seekers to apply for work. For example, people who met at the workplace (such as co-workers, former bosses, and former clients) in the same business community help job seekers to represent their competence for the task and to explain and assure employers of their ability to work. Gershon (2017) also points out that, in the early 1970s, job seekers and employers were only able to find jobs through formal channels such as company job advertisements and newspapers. However, recently, the internet has changed the business landscape of the traditional media. Online public recruitment information has replaced the role of weak ties. Job seekers can search for a variety of jobs from around the world and easily access their ideal work and workplace. Online recruitment information provides job seekers with diverse job opportunities and the chances of job hopping are increasing. With the frequent flow of talent across organizations, traditional social networks are gradually being replaced by online recruitment. "Workplace ties" are the inter-organizational and intra-organizational professional community network for working companions that plays a decisive role for candidates to get jobs (Gershon, 2017: 104–109).

The results of the above studies showed that in the past job market, traditional social networks, such as strong and weak ties, provided job seekers with various job opportunities. However, after the emergence of the internet, job seekers can access more diverse job opportunities through online recruitment. In the meantime, job seekers transmit their work abilities through "workplace ties" in the professional communities and companies obtain information about candidates from those social networks in the business or industrial professional communities.

Although "workplace ties" maintain their advantages in the local or domestic internet recruitment market, with the development of booming global internet recruitment it will become more difficult for companies to evaluate foreign job seekers' work ability through "workplace ties" in the professional communities. Drastic transformation has occurred in the global labor market during the last three decades. Former communist countries (China and Russia) have transformed from state employment into open labor markets, employers in the US and other developed countries have given up lifetime employment, and laying-off has become a normal labor management strategy. In earlier periods, large US firms filled 90% of vacancies internally. However, in recent years, employers in large companies in the US fill as many as two-thirds of all vacancies from the outside labor market (Bonet et al., 2013). Due to the rise of hiring from the external labor market, it has become inevitable for job seekers and companies to use staffing agencies and other LMIs to get good jobs or ideal candidates. For example, in early 2000, a quarter of questionnaire respondents had acquired jobs through staffing agencies during the past three years in Silicon Valley (Benner, 2003: 625). Why do so many job seekers in Silicon Valley acquire jobs in high-tech industries through staffing agencies? Benner (2003) points out that LMIs such as staffing agencies have played three roles in the labor market; namely, reducing transaction costs, establishing social networks with job seekers and talent seekers (customers), and risk control.

In the global labor market, job seekers and talent seekers need to find out each other's existence from the huge cross-national information and to negotiate salary levels. In the process of this negotiation, the two sides encounter many uncertain factors. For example, due to the increasing presence of LMIs in talent mobility and job hopping, the number and frequency of transactions in the labor market have become quite large. In particular, job seekers have high professional specificity in the high-tech industry. Due to this "asset specificity," it is not easy to get the ideal talent in the decentralized global labor market quickly and it is difficult to negotiate about wages. In the failure of free market mechanisms, LMIs mediate between job seekers and talent seekers to reduce transaction costs and allow them to negotiate smoothly.

With regard to the establishment of a social network with job seekers and talent seekers, temporary-help agencies have been integrated into the human resource management division in large companies and established long-term contractual relationships with customers to provide talent management and recruitment services for customers. In this long-term cooperation with customers, the experience and skills of talent management and relevant administrative work have accumulated in these staffing companies. Consultant recruitment agencies, professional associations, a variety of vocational training, and personnel placement programs also play a key role in the company's talent management and organizational innovation process. In addition, LMIs provide a wealth of job market information and talent to job seekers through the social network accumulated in the labor market. In terms of risk control, the technological innovation of the high-tech industry is very fast. It is now much easier to generate a high-risk labor market than it has been in the traditional industry, for example, in terms of layoffs, long-term unemployment, shrinking income, technology obsolescence, and financial turmoil. When a company experiences a recession, employers can adjust the hiring schedule of regular employees or they can cut off contracted employees through LMIs. In a severe economic downturn, the role of staffing agencies has indeed worsened unemployment. On the other hand, the unemployed can shorten their unemployment period through LMIs, and it is easy for them to find new job opportunities. The staffing agencies provide educational opportunities such as vocational training for the unemployed to help job seekers improve their employability and, consequently, job seekers can mitigate the damage of their unemployment (Benner, 2003: 625–628).

The results of Benner's (2003) study show that the staffing agency has become a very important mediation mechanism for adjusting the cross-national labor market in the development of the information and knowledge economy. More and more research and development businesses are carried out through cross-national inter-firm partnerships and job hopping has become a norm. In this flexible flow of technological knowledge and talent across organizations, it is not easy for enterprises to control the labor market and evaluate talent efficiency. The traditional job market based on the internal labor market and the long-term relationship between labor and employers has collapsed. LMIs have become the "market maker" that connects job seekers with employers. In the high-tech industry where technology innovation is very rapid, the staffing agency plays a central role in promoting talent trading on the global job market.

THE DEVELOPMENT OF STAFFING AGENCIES IN EAST ASIA: "CONSUMPTION-DRIVEN COMMODITY CHAIN" AND THE FLOW OF TECHNOLOGICAL TALENT

In the last 20 years, the development model of East Asian capitalism has changed from a "production-driven commodity chain" led by Japanese consumer electronics giants to a "consumption-driven commodity chain" led by Korean and Taiwanese electronics companies. This structural change of the commodity chain in East Asian high-tech industries has had a critical impact on the global job market and talent mobility. In the manufacturing sector, due to the drastic change of technology and market trend, it is not easy for professional and technological personnel to spend so much time doing research and development in a stable internal employment system. They need to adapt to the rapid changes in global market demand and frequently move and migrate across organizations and countries. Prior to the 1990s, Japanese electronics giants established an internal research team using the advantages of a lifetime employment system and an internal labor market to improve the quality of manufacturing goods. They developed a "production-driven commodity chain" in East Asia, integrating low-cost labor and a huge market to continuously improve the competitiveness of production technology and commodities with high price and best quality. However, after the mid-1990s, there were several large-scale global economic crises, such as the financial turmoil, and depressed personal consumption. Ordinary consumers in the global consumer electronics market started to buy relatively cheap mid-range products.

In Taiwan, since the mid-1990s, with the continuous growth of foreign direct investment of MNCs, domestic staffing agencies have begun to dispatch Taiwanese talent to foreign companies in Taiwan, such as American Express, Citibank, Hewlett-Packard, and Microsoft. In the early 2000s, small and medium-sized enterprises began to hire temporary staff to reduce personnel costs. Dispatching work includes cleaning, document typing, counter services, assistant's work, secretarial work, project management, and research and development. It also covers a wide range of business content from blue collar to white collar; from technological staff to research and development talent (Chiu, 2005: 38–69). Chiu (2005) also points out that although staffing agencies operated under the provisions of the Labor Standard Laws before the Employment Service Act was implemented, the competent authority of the employment agency was the Ministry of Economic Affairs. The Ministry of the Interior and the Council of Labor Affairs could not control the operation of an employment agency, as the chaotic state of management of this system caused communication problems among administrative agencies. The Taiwanese government is unable to supervise the illegal activities of employment agencies and staffing agencies (Chiu, 2005: 37). The Ministry of Labor in Taiwan has taken the situation of excessive abuse of dispatched labor by enterprises seriously and is promoting the legalization of the protection of dispatched labor. However, currently, the Dispatched Employment Act is still in the process of drafting, and the Ministry of Labor is trying to strengthen the protection of the rights of dispatched labor through administrative guidance and labor regulations education (ROC Ministry of Labor website, 2020).

In Japan, the Worker Dispatching Law was formally established in 1986 (Chiu, 2005: 119–160; "History of Human Resources Department, Temporary Staffing in Japan" webpage). At the beginning, the dispatch work was limited to professional white-collar business; namely, computer software development, secretarial, financial processing, translation, and interpretation. In 2003, the scope of the dispatch business expanded to information technology and finance-related work, as well as medical services covering care centers and nursing homes. However, after the bankruptcy of Lehman Brothers in 2007, serious illegal acts such as the termination of employment and layoffs for temporary dispatch workers occurred in Japan ('History of Human Resources Department, Temporary Staffing in Japan' webpage). Therefore, the Japanese government carried out several amendments to the Worker Dispatching Law. In 2015, the amendment of the Worker Dispatching Law was formally established and implemented. This Act stipulates that all staffing agencies need the government's business license to set the dispatch period for non-professional workers. When the time limit is exceeded, the staffing agencies must arrange new employment opportunities for dispatch workers and provide services such as dispatch workers' education and training to protect their labor rights, thus enabling them to plan long-term stable careers (Technological Outsourcing Industry and Meitec website).[2]

The development history of Taiwanese and Japanese staffing agencies and the worker dispatch business tells us that with the development of the global economy and the drastic changes in industrial structure, high-tech MNCs need to hire diversified talent that can respond to changes quickly on the global market. Staffing agencies help high-tech MNCs to find professionals as soon as possible and introduce more appropriate jobs to job seekers. In times of economic depression, employers can adjust the demand for talent through staffing agencies and can reduce redundant dispatch labor. Although the governments of Taiwan and Japan have tried to protect the rights of dispatch workers through the establishment or planning of dispatching labor laws, staffing agencies take the legalization as an opportunity to strengthen the legitimacy of the talent dispatch business model and have started to play a more central role in the East Asian labor market.

The technology industries in South Korea and Taiwan have long been outsourcing manufacturing business partnerships with Japanese electronics giants in the "production-driven commodity chain" and have learned the core technology of Japan in the process of cooperation. They then started to produce and offer high-quality goods at a lower price than that of Japanese goods and attracted consumers in the emerging market countries such as China, Latin America, Eastern Europe, South Africa, India, and Russia. Japanese electronics giants have increased their competitiveness through continuous improvement of technology and quality of manufacturing and production. However, South Korea and Taiwan's electronics industries started to compete fiercely with Japanese companies through the "consumer-driven commodity chain" in dynamic random access memory (DRAM), semiconductors, large-size LCD panels, and other semiconductor and home appliance markets at a lower price than that of their Japanese counterparts. They defeated Japanese electronics giants to capture the market share that Japanese companies originally dominated (Tabata, 2017). The Japanese general manager of a talent introduction business department of Japan's famous staffing agency told us that the process of the "production-driven commodity chain" in which Japan's electronics manufacturers played a central role had collapsed:

> Japan's GDP is about 5 trillion US dollars and the manufacturing industry accounts for about 1 trillion US dollars. This trend will not change in the future. However, the labor force in the manufacturing industry will be reduced by about 5% in 2020. Around 6.5 million to 7 million of the manufacturing workforces will disappear. The main reason is the large-scale layoffs of electronics companies such as SONY and other electronics manufacturers, as well as the introduction of automation and robots in the R&D departments. Also, the big change in the industrial structure... because now the competitive advantage of electronic appliances is how to improve cost performance. Consumers will not pursue high-priced electronic appliances with too high technical standards, for example, the price of 4K TV sets is about 10 thousand US dollars, but we won't buy such high price products. If there is a very cheap price for a 50-inch LCD TV, for example, if it is just only 500 US dollars per one, you will buy that one, won't you? Almost all the Japanese generally have a kind of philosophy to develop the best quality products through continuous innovation. However, the strategy of Korean and Taiwanese manufacturers is to produce mid-range products with high-cost performance. Because these products are relatively cheap, and their quality is also good, they can create a large market. South Korean and

Taiwanese manufacturers can sell good quality products at cheap prices, but Japanese manufacturers cannot produce such cheap mid-range electronic appliances. (HRJ-1)[3]

A Taiwanese senior manager at the Taipei branch of a Japanese staffing agency mentioned that Japanese technological skills have great advantages for research and development, but the sales skills for overseas markets are insufficient. Japanese professional and technological personnel cannot adapt to the business style in the "consumption-driven commodity chain":

> In the sales business of the technology industry in China, Japanese business persons have no fighting power, because Japanese are good at engineering, but not good in sales skills. The attitude of the Japanese is very different from that of the Chinese. Japanese are very careful, and they cannot open their big mouth. Japanese are always keeping a low profile. Chinese business people are totally different. They always open their big mouth; they're too ready to make promises. However, this style of communication fits the Chinese customers' needs. The Chinese customers' primary concern is not having the best quality, but cost performance. Japanese business people are not good at sales marketing, but very good at engineering, because the engineering skill is totally different from the sales marketing skill. Therefore, Japanese LCD panel manufacturers asked us to recruit local technological talent in China as sales staff and let them work at the China branch. (HRT-1)

Japanese technological professionals have great advantages for innovation in manufacturing technology; however, they are not good at sales and marketing strategy for overseas markets. As shown below, the key manufacturing technologies of the Japanese high-tech industry were transmitted to Taiwan through the mobility of Japanese talent, but the Japanese professionals encountered many difficulties in the marketing strategy of the international market. According to the international survey of the "World Talent Report 2016" published by the Institute for Management Development (IMD), Japanese talent ranked last among the 61 countries on the "international experience" indicator. They also ranked last on the "language competency" indicator. In other East Asian countries, Singapore ranked sixth and tenth on the "international experience" and "language ability" indicators, respectively, Hong Kong ranked second and 23rd, respectively, and South Korea ranked 52nd and 33rd, respectively. Taiwan ranked 42nd and 39th, respectively (IMD Business School, 2016). Japanese engineers spend a long time accumulating experience and technical capabilities in the company's internal R&D department. This "engineering technological capability" is the competitive advantage of Japanese electronics manufacturers.

However, in promoting overseas marketing, Japanese professionals lack international communication skills. It is therefore not easy for them to develop other East Asian markets and other emerging markets such as China. Consumers in emerging countries such as China need high-tech products with high-cost performance. The development of direction in the consumer electronics industry has shifted from the manufacturing technology-oriented "production-driven commodity chain" to the consumer market-oriented "consumer-driven commodity chain." This "consumer-driven commodity chain" has produced an extremely flexible production mechanism that focuses on "market-oriented capability" and keeps pace with the quickly changing demands of their customers in the emerging markets. From the late 1990s to the beginning of 2000, the growth of China's huge consumer market strengthened the flexible production mechanism of East Asian capitalism. It was a booming period of staffing agencies such as human resource dispatch companies in Taiwan and Japan. In the development process of LMIs in East Asian countries, the transnational talent flow in East Asian high-tech industries is becoming more and more common and active.

HEADHUNTING CAPITALISM: JOB MARKET AND STAFFING AGENCIES IN EAST ASIAN HIGH-TECH INDUSTRIES

After more than four years of negotiation between the world's largest Electronic Manufacture Service (EMS) manufacturer, Taiwan Foxconn Technology Group, and Japanese LCD panel manufacturer, Sharp Corporation, Foxconn Technology Group invested about 4 billion US dollars on March 30, 2016, acquired 66% share capital in Sharp, and successfully merged with Sharp. Sharp Corporation is a famous electronics manufacturer on the same scale as Sony and Panasonic in Japan. Such a large-scale Japanese electronics giant has accepted the acquisition and restructuring by foreign-invested enterprises for the first time, and the Japanese electronics industry, which has always disregarded the strength of other East Asian countries' high-tech industries, received a great shock (The Science & Technology Policy Research and Information Center 2016). Although Foxconn Technology Group merged with Sharp, there is no long-term mechanism for cultivating technological talent and core technology, such as an internal labor market, an internal promotion system, and a lifelong employment system similar to Japanese companies. Therefore, Foxconn Technology Group has always promoted the strategy of headhunting technological talent. In June 2013, in order to enhance the technology level of various LCD products (smartphones, tablets, notebooks, LED outdoor billboards, laptops, desktop computers, portable TVs, smart TVs, electronic whiteboards), Foxconn Technology Group established R&D centers in Yokohama and Osaka in Japan.

With regard to the introduction of Japanese technological talent, a Japanese expert on the TFT-LCD industry, Mr. Yano Kouzou, was hired as the general manager of the R&D center. Foxconn Technology Group also hired Japanese senior engineers who were laid off due to the poor management of Japanese electronics companies such as Sharp. In the rapidly changing high-tech product consumer market, high-tech companies no longer invest large amounts of money in the training of technological skills. In the development process of the "consumption-driven commodity chain," Foxconn Technology Group abandoned the extremely high-cost research and development activities and is promoting various strategies; namely, headhunting technological talent and purchasing core technologies in the global high-tech industry (*China Times*, 2013; Tabata, 2016: 18). The general manager of the talent introduction business department of a famous Japanese staffing agency explained the actual situation of Japanese senior technological talent mobility to other East Asian countries through headhunting by Taiwanese and other East Asian high-tech MNCs:

> Speaking of the brain drain of Japanese technological talent abroad, I remember that the first wave of brain drain occurred around the beginning of the 2000s. The main reason was the collapse of the bubble economy. Before 1995, there was no pressure of a serious economic downturn. However, in 1997, Yamaichi Securities was one of the four major security companies in Japan, but this company went bankrupt. We were all astonished beyond measure at the news. Because we all thought that such a large-scale security company would not go bankrupt. Then, large financial companies also faced a bankruptcy crisis. Before the beginning of 2000, one of the major consumer electronics giants in Japan, Panasonic, launched massive layoffs. Most Japanese companies began to cut personnel costs and entered the employment ice age—a hard time for job seekers. At that time, Samsung (South Korean multinational conglomerate), Chi Mei Optoelectronics Corporation (CMO) (a Taiwanese TFT-LCD manufacturer), and Taiwan Semiconductor Manufacturing Company Limited (TSMC) all had transactions with Japanese electronics manufacturers. They began to headhunt Japanese senior engineers and supervisors through their personal networks. About 40- to 50-year-old Japanese technological talent was the main target for South Korean and Taiwanese high-tech companies. These

companies offered excellent salaries and headhunted Japanese technological talent with double the pay of their annual income—about 70 to 80 thousand US dollars in Japanese equivalent. The first wave of brain drain of Japanese technological talent abroad occurred in 2000 and the second wave was in 2008. At that time, many Japanese professionals began to find relevant job opportunities through staffing agencies. We already established branches in Asia. The headhunters in Asian branches required Japanese talent and they asked us to evaluate the suitable talent in Japan. Since then, the demand for global talent has been increasing. (HRJ-1)

In the East Asian job market, after 2000, staffing agencies began to develop. Figures 7.1 and 7.2 show that the market for staffing agencies in Japan grew rapidly from 2000 to 2008. Affected by the financial turmoil in 2007, companies carried out large-scale layoffs. The Japanese government amended the Worker Dispatching Law to limit the operation of the staffing agency industry. The market scale was reduced in 2009. However, the overall development trend is gradually recovering. The market size of the Japanese staffing agency business on high-tech talent showed a similar development trend during the same period. In recent years, Japanese electronics giants have experienced the serious impact of financial crisis. One of the Japanese electronics giants, Toshiba, sold its memory chip business unit to Bain Capital's investment team, consisting of Apple, Dell, and SK Hynix in September 2017 (AFP, 2017). Well-known financial media in Japan, Nihon Keizai Shinbun, reported that the headhunters of staffing agencies contacted Toshiba's engineers to recruit senior technological talent:

> Are you worried about the future of your company [Toshiba: author's note]? You are an amazing talent, there are other better places where you will be more successful. … A senior engineer in his 40s, who currently works for Toshiba Memory Factory (Shikoku city in Mie Prefecture, Japan). After the spring of this year, he received two calls from the headhunters in staffing agencies. He declined these headhunting, and told reporters, "After this spring, several colleagues did not tell us where to go and resigned." Near Yokkaichi factory and Ofuna R&D center in Yokohama City, headhunters of staffing agencies talked to the engineers who came home from work and provided them with information on the recruitment. Headhunters evaluated and selected outstanding technological talent based on the introduction of the former employees in Toshiba and the research contents published by Toshiba's engineers in the academic seminars. (Nihon Keizai Shinbun News Online, 2017)

Figure 7.3 shows that at the end of 2006, the number of employees in the staffing agencies in Taiwan totaled 83,002, an increase of 69,719 in only five years, and the ratio of increase from the previous census was 524.87%.[4] On Taiwan's job market, more and more job seekers are looking for jobs through the staffing agency industry. Compared with the stable internal labor market, the scale of the external labor market has developed and the flexibility of the entire job market has made rapid progress in Taiwan. In recent years, domestic news media have reported that the average wages in Taiwan are extremely low compared with foreign countries, accelerating brain drain to the foreign job market. The average annual income of technological talent in Taiwan is lower than that of Singapore, Japan, South Korea, the United States, and other countries (see Figure 7.4). Although income tax in Taiwan is much lower than income tax in these countries (see Figure 7.5), the employment market in Taiwan has become quite flexible and the threshold for overseas mobility has become lower. It is easier for job seekers to search for various jobs abroad through the services of staffing agencies such as online employment agencies, LinkedIn (a business networking site), and human resource agencies. As shown in Figure 7.6, the score of "The Importance of Scientific Subjects in Schools" in Taiwan is ranked 16th in the world. The quality of scientific and technological talent is quite high, but the salary level is quite low. Therefore, it is easy for the technological talent in Taiwan to become an excellent target for foreign technology brand companies.

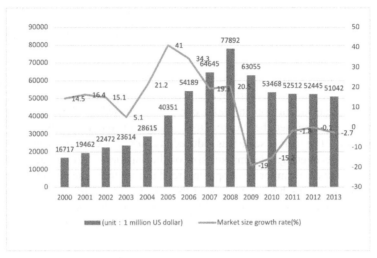

Source: According to information provided by Meitec Corporation in Japan.

Figure 7.1   Market size growth rate and sales amount of Japanese staffing agency industry

The phenomenon of the brain drain in Taiwan, as well as Korea, has also had a negative impact on the overall economic development of the country (see Figure 7.7). The development of the "consumption-driven commodity chain," which focuses on cost performance, planning and arranging global production bases to reduce production costs, is the core strategic consideration of the electronics industry. Therefore, the rise of the "red supply chain" threatens Taiwan's role in the global supply chain and puts considerable cost pressure on Taiwan's high-tech industry. The electronics industry in China has outgrown the labor-intensive business model, such as the final assembly of components, and has begun to supply high-end components for iPhone to Apple Inc. to put pressure on competitors in South Korea, Taiwan, and Japan (Taiwan Stock Exchange Research Project, 2016). Under these circumstances, the average salary of Taiwanese engineers in high-tech companies has become lower than previously. For example, in July 2017, the Hsinchu City Government supported the Hsinchu Science Park manufacturers' job fair. Thirty-four manufacturers carried out their recruiting activities, at least half of which were listed companies and opened 1178 jobs for engineers. However, the average monthly salary was only about 1300 US dollars (FTV News, 2017). In the meantime, high-tech companies in China offer salaries that are three to five times higher than their Taiwanese counterparts in order to headhunt Taiwanese engineers, and are even willing to pay the Taiwanese engineers' "confidentiality and non-competition agreement"[5] fee for the company hiring these engineers. There are also high-tech companies in China setting up offices in Taiwan; therefore, Taiwanese engineers do not need to move to China, as they can work at the Taiwan branch offices (Technews, 2015).

Currently, there are about eight foreign and local staffing agencies in Taiwan that are human resource management businesses dealing with white-collar workers (see Table 7.1). They started to operate in Taiwan from the 1990s to the middle of 2000. The staffing agencies mainly targeted middle and high-level supervisors. The headhunters in these staffing agencies support the clients in searching for suitable talent or helping the job seekers to search for employment opportunities. The headhunters look for specific candidates, by case. Therefore, there is also private talent evaluation that acts as a bridge to connect job seekers and employers. The profit of these staffing agencies is a certain percentage of the annual salary of the job seeker in the case of the transaction. Unlike staffing agencies, internet human resource banks provide various kinds of talent (from ordinary talent to top supervisors) and support employers in recruiting talent. They wait for job seekers to contact them through an internet platform. Internet human resource banks gain profit by collecting fees for posting job-related information from customers on the internet (Li, 2011; *Manager Today*, 2014).

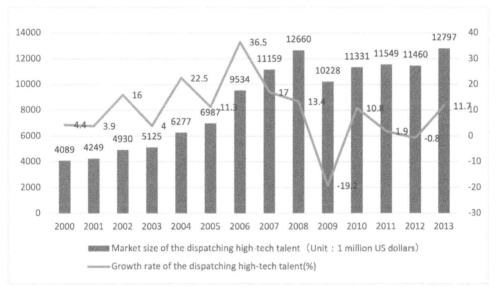

Source: According to information provided by Meitec Corporation in Japan.

Figure 7.2   *Market size and growth rate of dispatching Japanese high-tech talent in Japan*

What kind of channels do white-collar professionals in Taiwan use to access the overseas job market? Usually they do not only post their resumes onto the human resource banks' webpage on the internet but also upload their resumes to LinkedIn to attract the attention of headhunters and managers of the human resources divisions in MNCs. As shown in Table 7.2, the job search strategies change depending on the target country. Japanese companies have a culture of training those with little experience and mainly hire new graduates. Singapore companies evaluate and hire varieties of senior talent from all over the world, and the Singapore government collaborates with staffing agencies in East Asia to promote large-scale recruitment activities (CAREhER, 2015; Wang, 2008; FTV News, 2015).

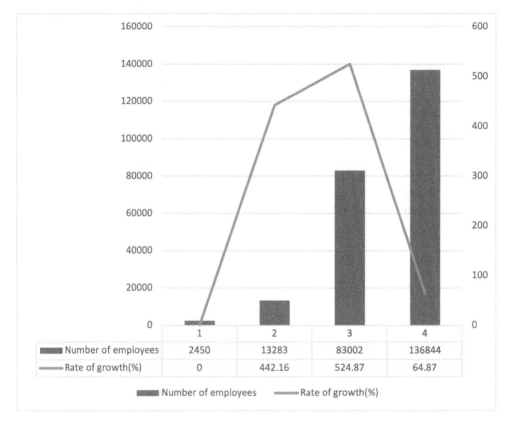

	1	2	3	4
▩ Number of employees	2450	13283	83002	136844
━━ Rate of growth(%)	0	442.16	524.87	64.87

▩ Number of employees ━━ Rate of growth(%)

Source: National Statistics Republic of China.

Figure 7.3   *Growth of the number of employees in Taiwan's staffing agencies (1996, 2001, 2006, 2011)*

My research shows that white-collar professionals in Taiwan not only change jobs on the domestic labor market but also seek employment opportunities abroad through staffing agencies and internet human resource banks. Considering the global employment market, staffing agencies established long-term cooperation and interpersonal networks between employers and job seekers, and began to provide a cross-national talent matching service, including career planning and talent training programs for enterprises, as well as evaluating talent (wage accounting in place of enterprises). A Taiwanese director of a staffing agency described the main functions of the staffing agencies in Taiwan:

> We will calculate salaries for employees on behalf of our customers. If the number of personnel of the customer's HR (human resource) division is insufficient, we will send consultants and directors from our company. The quality of our consultants and directors is the same as the head of the company's HR division. In addition, we also offer services such as talent development, training, and coaching. (HRT-2)

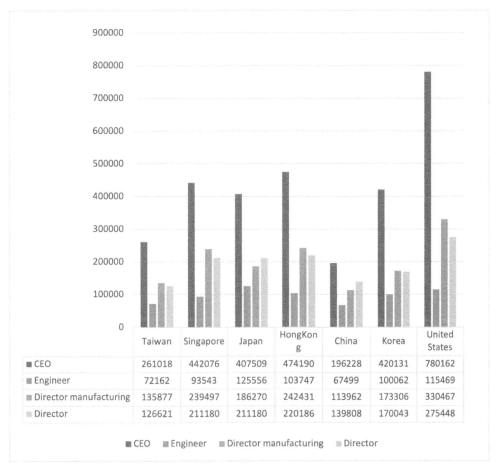

	Taiwan	Singapore	Japan	HongKong	China	Korea	United States
■ CEO	261018	442076	407509	474190	196228	420131	780162
■ Engineer	72162	93543	125556	103747	67499	100062	115469
■ Director manufacturing	135877	239497	186270	242431	113962	173306	330467
■ Director	126621	211180	211180	220186	139808	170043	275448

■ CEO   ■ Engineer   ■ Director manufacturing   ■ Director

Source: *IMD World Talent Report* (IMD Business School, 2016).

Figure 7.4   *International comparison of annual income of high-tech talents (total base salary plus bonuses and long-term incentives, unit: US dollar)*

In Japan, each university has an employment assistance department to help students and graduates with career guidance, but there are no similar departments and functions in Taiwan. As a result, staffing agencies in Taiwan provide guidance on career planning for new graduates (HRT-3). In the development of the "consumption-driven commodity chain," high-tech companies need to hire professionals with high-level foreign language communication skills to respond quickly to changes in the global consumer market, as well as professional knowledge of products and services technology. Staffing agencies can acquire significant information regarding senior technological talent with a high level of foreign language communication skills and expertise through their social network in the global high-tech industry. When Taiwanese companies set up offices and factories in China, they usually evaluate talent through staffing agencies. Staffing agencies also collaborate with a social network service (SNS) such as LinkedIn to build a multinational talent resource network.

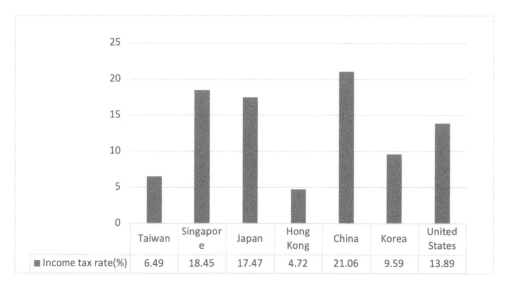

Source: *IMD World Talent Report* (IMD Business School, 2016).

Figure 7.5   International comparison of income tax rate (%)

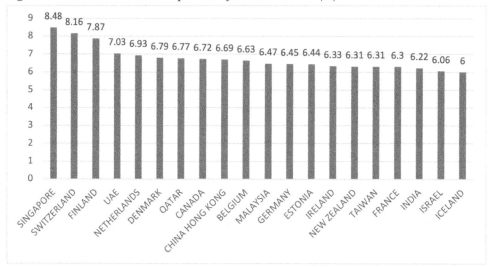

Source: *IMD World Talent Report* (IMD Business School, 2016).

Figure 7.6   The importance of scientific subjects in schools around the world

The Taiwanese director of a staffing agency pointed out that it is difficult for the human resources department (HR) in high-tech companies to find senior engineers with high-level English communication skills through their social network in their industrial communities. Therefore, they usually find suitable global talent through the support of staffing agencies

(HRT-1; HRT-2). English is rarely used in daily life and workplaces in Taiwan and Japan.

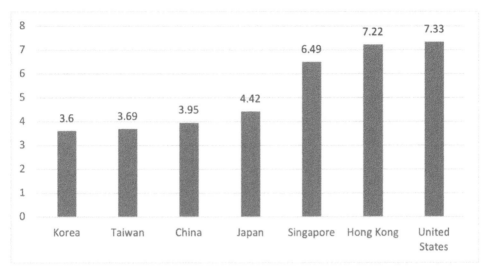

Note: The lower the degree, the more serious the impact of brain drain on economic development.
Source: *IMD World Talent Report* (IMD Business School, 2016).

Figure 7.7   *The extent to which economic development is affected by factors controlling
the impact of the brain drain*

It is not easy for high-tech companies to acquire senior engineers who have a satisfactory command of the English language. Therefore, the role of staffing agencies is becoming increasingly important in the process of transnational mobility of talent. Due to the drastic change of industrial structure, shrinking of the domestic labor market and sluggish wage growth, talent in Taiwan and Japan has flowed outside the country. Although senior Japanese technological professionals working for consumer electronics giants in Japan are the main target of headhunting in other East Asian countries (see Figure 7.8), they are usually hired for only three or four years by high-tech firms in South Korea, Taiwan, and China on a contractual basis. Japanese senior engineers instruct employees in other East Asian high-tech firms about Japan's core technology and experience through face-to-face guidance in the workplace. However, when the contract term ends, most of them will be dismissed and forced to leave the companies. These Japanese technological professionals are usually unable to return to their home countries after being dismissed from high-tech companies in Taiwan, Korea, and China. They continue to be employed or to wander in the East Asian countries and cannot be on the track of global "re-circulating" of talent. In this way, their technical knowledge and experience are forced to be continuously consumed (HRJ-1).

Table 7.1 *Business content of major staffing agencies in Taiwan*

Company name	Business content
1. Intelligent Manpower Corporation (IMC): Taiwanese firm http://www.jobnet.com.tw	Established in 1991. The major customers of IMC are well-known foreign, Japanese, and domestic companies. IMC provides job opportunities in a variety of industries and job types. The business area includes Taiwan and China.
2. Carewell: Taiwanese firm http://www.carewell.com.tw/html3/services02.asp	Carewell has a deep understanding of various industries and mainly focuses on electronics and consumer industries. The business area includes Taiwan and China.
3. Manpower: American firm www.manpower.com.tw	Manpower was established 70 years ago and has provided human resource development service for more than 400,000 customers in 80 countries and regions. Manpower also provides a total solution to discover, manage, and develop talent. In 1997, Manpower established a branch office in Taiwan.
4. Job178 (A subsidiary wholly owned by a Japanese firm) http://www.job178.com.tw/about	The job introduction and consultation service for new graduates and white collar. Job178 also introduces suitable Taiwanese talent to Japanese companies or branch offices of the Japanese company in Taiwan.
5. Pasona: Japanese firm http://www.pasona.com.tw/index.jsp	The branch office of Pasona in Taiwan was established in 1988. Pasona in Taiwan introduces Japanese talent to work in Taiwan and introduces Taiwanese talent to work in Japan.
6. Adecco Taiwan: Swiss firm https://www.adecco.com.tw/about-us-jobseeker	Adecco is the world's largest international HR service company with more than 7000 branches in 60 major countries and regions around the world. As the Taiwanese stock market boomed in 1989, Adecco was confident of the development of Taiwan's economy and in the same year established the Taiwan branch office.
7. Persol Taiwan (Intelligence Taiwan): Japanese firm https://www.persoltw.com	The Taiwan branch was established in 2007 and its main customers were Japanese companies in Taiwan. Prior customers were Japanese large companies such as semiconductor and LCD manufacturers and traders. However, in recent years, the Japanese service industries targeting pro-Japanese Taiwanese consumers expanded their business to Taiwan, and these Japanese service companies are increasing in Persol's customers.
8. Wanco Manpower: Singapore firm http://www.wanco-manpower.com	Wanco Manpower was established in 2000. Major customers are global large semiconductor manufacturers. Wanco Manpower introduces high-paid jobs abroad such as high-tech firms in Singapore to Taiwanese, Chinese, Malaysian, Korean, Indian, Filipino engineers.

Source: According to the webpages of various staffing agencies in Taiwan as shown in the table.

Table 7.2   *Global job search channels of Taiwanese talent*

	Taiwan's top college new graduates	Taiwanese senior engineers, middle management
Talent advantage	Highly educated	Job experience
Target country	Japan	China, Singapore
Motive	Recruitment of Japanese companies is mainly based on employment of new graduates. Japanese companies have a good training system and provide a good salary.	Good salary
Method of recruiting	Overseas recruitment, online recruitment, staffing agencies	Headhunting
Recruiting strategy	Job advertisement	Evaluate and headhunt the most qualified candidate for the position

Source: CAREhER (2015); Wang (2008); FTV News (2015).

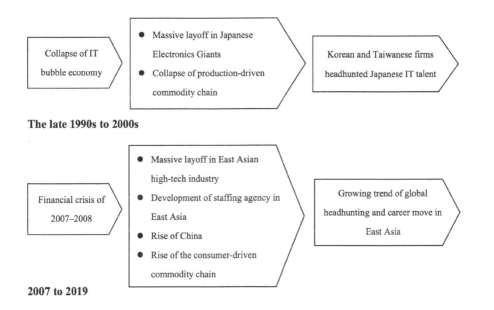

Figure 7.8   *Headhunting capitalism in East Asian high-tech industry*

CONCLUSION

As my analysis above shows, the development mechanism of East Asian capitalism has shifted from a "production-driven commodity chain" (which focuses on the internal labor market; that is, long-term talent training and in-house R&D activities and endlessly improving the quality of the product and service) to a "consumer-driven commodity chain" (which emphasizes cost reduction through the flexible arrangement of global production networks and logistics to produce high cost performance products). In accordance with the idea of market fundamentalism and neo-liberalism becoming stronger, governments in East Asian countries such as Taiwan and Japan promoted the deregulation of LMIs. High-tech firms in these countries started to seek and evaluate senior professionals through various LMIs, such as internet human resource banks, staffing agencies, and other channels, to quickly find experienced professionals who can respond to the trend in the mass consumer market in an emerging economy and provide goods and services with a high-cost performance ratio.

Staffing agencies collaborated with social networking sites such as LinkedIn and established a multinational talent resource network. The HR division of high-tech companies finds senior engineers with high English communication skills through the multinational talent resource network of staffing agencies. Under these circumstances, Foxconn from Taiwan and other East Asian high-tech MNCs started to promote the strategy of headhunting and acquire global technological talent. Headhunting has become an important driving force for the development of East Asian capitalism. The development of "headhunting capitalism" has both positive and negative effects. The positive effect is that employers can save money which they can invest in long-term technology development and cultivation of in-house technological talent, and can quickly find senior professionals in the external labor market through staffing agencies. However, it is easy for employers to regard high-tech professionals as consumables, resulting in the commodification and alienation of talent. Singapore, Hong Kong, and other countries and regions responded to the transformation of East Asian capitalism and integrated the resources of the government and private staffing agencies and the global social network of scientific and technological talent, quickly established the global technological talent pool, and started to promote "headhunting capitalism" by providing high paying jobs with benefits for global talent (HRT-4). Taiwanese and Japanese high-tech MNCs, high-tech professionals, and labor markets are presumed to be facing the risk of a large emigration of individuals with technological skills to foreign countries.[6] In future research, I aim to explore the impact of the rise of China on the growing trend of cross-national job change in East Asian technological talent communities. In addition, the effect of "headhunting capitalism" on personnel management systems in East Asian IT firms and staffing agencies remains an issue for further research.

NOTES

1. According to Lazear and Oyer (2004), the external labor market refers to the cross-organizational flow of labor. Salaries are usually determined by the principle of free market; the enterprise itself does not completely control the salary levels. In contrast, on the internal labor market, labor is promoted within the organization and rarely flows across the enterprise. Salaries are determined internally by the organization and are not easily influenced by the market.
2. Meitec Corporation is a Japanese staffing agency founded in 1974. It provides human resources and engineering services to domestic manufacturing companies. Unlike general staffing agencies, Meitec recruits design and development professionals in the high-tech industry as regular employees and then dispatches them to various manufacturing companies (Meitec Corporation official website, 2020).
3. Each quotation from an interviewee in this chapter was given a code to mark the source of information. The first letter of the code refers to the main product and service grouping to which the company interviewee belongs. The next letters stand for the country of the interviewee, and the Arabic number refers to the serial number of the interviewee.
4. Taiwan's staffing agencies include temporary staffing companies that dispatch foreign blue-collar workers to clients and human resource consultants who introduce or dispatch technology professionals and various industry-level white-collar workers to companies. Figure 7.3 shows the growth in the number of employees in the staffing agencies, including blue-collar and white-collar human resources.

5. The "non-competition agreement" is based on the "job competition reference manual" issued by the Ministry of Labor of the Executive Yuan in Taiwan. It is stated that the employees are required by the employers to protect the confidentiality of their companies. For example, an employee in company A is prohibited by his or her employer to be employed by other companies in the same trade or operate companies in the same trade by him or herself for a certain period after leaving company A. However, some employers abuse the "non-competition agreement" and restrict unjust employee job-changing. Therefore, on October 7, 2016, the Ministry of Labor added the implementation rules of the Labor Law, that employers must have a reasonable compensation for their workers. For example, the monthly compensation amount must not be less than 50% of the average monthly salary when the employee leaves the company. Foxconn Technology Group sued employees for switching to a competitor and violating the "non-competition agreement" clause and demanded payment of a penalty fee. However, the Taipei District Court judged that the requirement of Foxconn significantly damaged the labor rights of employees, and Foxconn lost the case. Although the "non-competition agreement," to some extent, prevents employees from changing jobs, if employers try to enforce this provision fully, employers must bear the corresponding compensation. In fact, it is not easy to restrict employees from switching to competitors (Hung, 2016; *China Times*, 2016; Huang, 2011).
6. As mentioned above, the status of foreign engineers from Taiwan and Japan is unstable. However, the development mechanism of the East Asian IT sector has shifted from the "production-driven commodity chain" to the "consumer-driven commodity chain." The global market share of Taiwanese and Japanese high-tech firms was prevented by Chinese and Korean firms. Taiwanese and Japanese engineers confronted the risk of losing their current job statuses and salary levels in their home countries. Therefore, they are taking a calculated risk and seeking job opportunities and high salaries in other East Asian countries.

REFERENCES

AFP (2017), *Toshiba's Annual Loss is Amazing. The President Apologized* (in Chinese), 24 October, accessed 21 January 2021 at https://tw.news.yahoo.com/東芝年度虧損驚人-社長鞠躬道歉-065002126--finance.html

Almeida, P., Song, J. and Grant, R. M. (2002), 'Are Firms Superior to Alliances and Markets?: An Empirical Test of Cross-Border Knowledge Building', *Organization Science*, **13**(2), 147–161.

Benner, Chris (2003), 'Labour Flexibility and Regional Development: The Role of Labour Market Intermediaries', *Regional Studies*, **37**(6&7), 621–633.

Bian, Yanjie (1997), 'Bringing Strong Ties Back in: Indirect Ties, Network Bridges, and Job Searches in China', *American Sociological Review*, **62**(3), 366–385.

Bian, Yanjie and Huang, Xianbi (2015). 'The Guanxi Influence on Occupational Attainment in Urban China', *Chinese Journal of Sociology*, **1**(3), 307–332.

Bonet, Rocio, Cappelli, Peter and Hamori, Monika (2013), 'Labor Market Intermediaries and the New Paradigm for Human Resources', *The Academy of Management Annals*, **7**(1), 341–392.

CAREhER (2015), *If You Want to Find a Job in Singapore, Global Head Hunters Will Advise You in This Way* (in Chinese), 24 December, accessed 21 January 2021 at https://careher.net/想找新加坡的工作%EF%BC%8C跨國獵人頭這麼建議%EF%BC%9A/

Chen, Dung-Sheng (2008), *Making It Integrated: Organizational Networks in Taiwan's Integrated Circuit Industry* (in Chinese). Taipei: Socio Publishing.

China Times (2013), (in Chinese) 1 December, accessed 21 January 2021 at https://www.chinatimes.com/newspapers/20130601000707-260110

China Times (2016), (in Chinese) 30 May, accessed 21 January 2021 at http://www.chinatimes.com/newspapers/20160530000309-260114

China Times (2017), (in Chinese) 2 April, accessed 21 January 2021 at http://opinion.chinatimes.com/20170402002949-262101

Chiu, Chi-hao (2005), *Research on Labor Dispatch Law System in Taiwan* (in Chinese). Taipei: J books.

FTV News (2015), *A New Type of Headhunting Firms in Japan Aim at University Students* (in Chinese), 24 November, accessed 21 January 2021 at https://tw.news.yahoo.com/日新型態獵人頭公司-專門鎖定在校生-091532826.html

FTV News (2017), *Salary Went Down: Engineers in Hsinchu Science Park Starting Salary 40k* (in Chinese), 25 July, accessed 21 January 2021 at https://www.youtube.com/watch?v=H-94NT6avEE

Gershon, Ilana (2017), *Down and Out in the New Economy: How People Find (or Don't Find) Work Today*. Chicago: The University of Chicago Press.

Granovetter, Mark (1973), 'The Strength of Weak Ties', *American Journal of Sociology*, **78**, 1360-1380.

Granovetter, Mark (1974), *Getting A Job: A Study of Contacts and Careers*. Cambridge, MA: Harvard University Press.

Granovetter, Mark (1995), 'Afterword 1994: Reconsiderations and A New Agenda' in Mark Granovetter (ed.), *Getting a Job*, Chicago: University of Chicago Press, pp. 139–182.

Hsu, Jinn-Yuh and Saxenian, AnnaLee (2000), 'The Limits of Guanxi Capitalism: Transnational Collaboration between Taiwan and the USA', *Environment and Planning A*, **32**, 1991–2005.

Huang, Yi-yun (2011), Is Job-hopping Illegal?: Five Requirements to Understand the Non-competition Agreement, *Common Wealth Magazine*, 28 April, accessed 21 January at http://www.cw.com.tw/article/article.action?id=5007375

Hung, Tsung-hui (2016), What is 'Non-competition Agreement'?: Is it Possible for Employers not to Compensate Employees? (In Chinese), CD Law Company Official Website, 21 October, accessed 21 January at http://www.cdlaw.com.tw/modules/news/article.php?storyid=160

IMD Business School (2016), *IMD World Talent Report*, accessed 21 January 2021 at https://www.imd.org/globalassets/wcc/docs/talent_2016_web.pdf

Jöns, Heike, Meusburger, Peter and Heernan, Michael (2017), 'Mobilities of Knowledge: An Introduction' in Jöns, Heike, Meusburger, Peter and Heernan, Michael (eds), *Mobilities of Knowledge*, Chicago: Springer Open, pp. 1–19.

Jou, Sue-Ching and Chen, Dung-Sheng (2000), 'Keeping the High-tech Region Open and Dynamics: the Organizational Networks of Taiwan's Integrated Circuit Industry', *GeoJournal*, **53**, 81–87.

Kawai, Norifumi and Chung, Chul (2019), 'Expatriate Utilization, Subsidiary Knowledge Creation and Performance: The Moderating Role of Subsidiary Strategic Context?', *Journal of World Business*, **54**, 24–36.

Lazear, Edward and Oyer, Paul (2004), 'Internal and External Labor Markets: A Personnel Economics Approach', *Labour Economics*, **11**(5), 527–554.

Li, Tsung-Yueh (2011), When the Head Hunter Finds You, *Cheers Magazine*, **13** (in Chinese), accessed 21 January 2021 at http://www.cheers.com.tw/article/article.action?id=5026215

Liberty Times (2015), (in Chinese) 30 March, accessed 21 January 2021 at http://news.ltn.com.tw/news/life/breakingnews/1272309

Lin, Nan (1990), 'Social Resources and Social Mobility: A Structural Theory of Status Attainment' in Ronald L. Breiger (eds), *Social Mobility and Social Structure*, New York: Cambridge University Press, pp. 247–271

Lin, Nan (2001), *Social Capital: A Theory of Social Structure and Action*. New York: Cambridge University Press.

Lin, Nan, Chen, Jay, Chih-Jou and Fu, Yang-Chih (2010), 'Patterns and Effects of Social Relations: A Comparison of Taiwan, the United States and China' (in Chinese), *Taiwanese Journal of Sociology*, **45**, 117–162.

Ma, Lan (2005), 'An Example of the Enterprise's Recruitment of Taiwanese Executives through the Staffing Agency Industry: The Case of High-tech Electronics Industry in Mainland China' (in Chinese), Master of Business Administration dissertation, School of Management, National Central University.

Manager Today (2014), *What the Head Hunter Didn't Tell You (Vol. 2)* (in Chinese), 4 May, accessed 21 January 2021 at https://www.managertoday.com.tw/columns/view/40712

Manning, Stephan, Massini, Silvia and Lewin, Y. Arie (2008), 'A Dynamic Perspective on Next-Generation Offshoring: The Global Sourcing of Science and Engineering Talent', *Academy of Management Perspectives*, **22**(3), 35–54.

Meitec Corporation official website (2020) (in Japanese), accessed 21 January 2021 at http://www.meitec.co.jp

Nihon Keizai Shinbun News Online (2017), *Toshiba, the Uncontrollable Talents Left, the Head Hunter Called Engineers in Toshiba to Provide Job Change Information* (in Chinese), 8 September, accessed 21 January 2021 at https://www.nikkei.com/article/DGXLASDZ08HPH_Y7A900C1EA6000

Richter, Cristiano (2016), 'The Interplay of Local Cluster Development and Global Inter-cluster Brain Circulation: A Governance Perspective in Emergent Economies', PhD dissertation, Federal University of Rio Grande do Sul.

ROC Ministry of Labor website (2020), (in Chinese), accessed 21 January 2021 at http://www.mol.gov.tw/topic/3072

Saxenian, AnnaLee and Hsu, Jinn-Yuh (2001), 'The Silicon Valley-Hsinchu Connection: Technical Communities and Industrial Upgrading,' *Industrial and Corporate Change*, **10**(4), 893–920.

Song, Jaeyong, Almeida, Paul and Wu, Geraldine (2003), 'Learning-by-Hiring: When Is Mobility More Likely to Facilitate Interfirm Knowledge Transfer?' *Management Science*, **49**(4), 351–365.

Tabata, Mayumi and Chih-Chia Chuang (2010), 'The Process of Technology Introduction and the Result of Development: A Comparative Study of Taiwanese and Japanese TFT-LCD Manufacturers,' (in Chinese), *Taiwanese Sociology*, **20**, 145–184.

Tabata, Mayumi (2012), 'The Absorption of Japanese Engineers into Taiwan's TFT-LCD Industry: Globalization and Transnational Talent Diffusion', *Asian Survey*, **52**(3), 571–594.

Tabata, Mayumi (2016), 'East Asian Capitalism and Cross-national Industrial Collaboration: The Impact of the Relationships with Japanese Firms on the Technology Strategy of Taiwanese Firms,' (in Chinese), *Asia-Pacific Research Forum*, **63**, 1–26.

Tabata, Mayumi (2017), 'Industrial Samurai: The Flow of Japanese Tech Workers to Taiwan', in Zong-rong Lee and Thung-hong Lin (eds), *Unfinished Miracle: Taiwan's Economy and Society in Transition*, Taipei: Institute of Sociology Academia Sinica, pp. 541–569 (in Chinese).

Taiwan Stock Exchange Research Project (2016), *Impact of Red Supply Chain on Taiwan's Industry* (in Chinese), accessed 21 January 2021 at http://www.tse.com.tw/ch/products/publication/download/0003000156.pdf

Technews (2015), *Brain Drain is Inevitable: Taiwan Industry Encounters Bottleneck* (in Chinese), 27 March, accessed 21 January 2021 at http://technews.tw/2015/03/27/taiwan-business-china

Theodore, Nik and Peck, Jamie (2002), 'The Temporary Staffing Industry: Growth Imperatives and Limits to Contingency,' *Economic Geography*, **78**(4), 463–493.

The Science & Technology Policy Research and Information Center (STPI) (2016), *Observation on Merger of Foxconn and Sharp* (in Chinese), 30 March, accessed 21 January 2021 at http://iknow.stpi.narl.org.tw/post/Read.aspx?PostID=12297

Wang, Chien-Ying (2008), More Than 10,000 Job Opportunities are Waiting for You: Where Do You Find a Well-paid Job in Asian Pacific Countries? *Business Weekly* (in Chinese), 17 January, accessed 21 January 2021 at http://www.gallop.com.tw/news_doc/story649.htm

Ward, Kevin (2004), 'Going Global? Internationalization and Diversification in the Temporary Staffing Industry', *Journal of Economic Geography*, **4**, 251–273.

Xin, Bin-Long (2006), 'Policy Analysis of Taiwan's Introduction of Technological Manpower' (in Chinese), Working Paper, Seminar on Government Reengineering and Constitutional Reform: Human Rights Protection and Talent Sharing under Globalization, Permanent Peace and Development Association, Department of Public Administration and Policy, National Taipei University, accessed 21 January 2021 at http://www.ntpu.edu.tw/~pa/news/94news/attachment/950221/2-1.pdf

PART III

SUBSIDIARY KNOWLEDGE CREATION AND DEVELOPMENT

8. Technological overlap and cultural distance in MNCs' location choice of technological clusters in China

Shuna Shu Ham Ho and Chang Hoon Oh

INTRODUCTION

Since 1988 (*China Daily*, 2018), China has been promoting the development of a technology structure by establishing technological clusters (Ning et al., 2016). To this end, it has designated hundreds of technological clusters called New and High-Technology Industrial Development Zones (NTZs) (Bloomberg, 2015) in which multinational corporations (MNCs), such as Microsoft and AMD from the USA, and Sony and Hitachi from Japan, have established research and development (R&D) centers (*China Daily*, 2011). In Chengdu's NTZ, more than 104 MNCs, including Intel, TI, Dell, Phillips, and Siemens, from various countries have chosen to co-locate with one another (PR Newswire, 2015).

A large body of international business literature has addressed how MNCs strategically choose to locate in different technological clusters to maximize the potential inward knowledge spillovers that result from clustering, while minimizing outward knowledge spillovers (Alcácer & Chung, 2007). The theory of the MNC (Dunning & Norman, 1983; Rugman, 1981) suggests that the existence of MNCs results from proprietary firm-specific advantages (Hennart, 1982; Hymer, 1976), such as superior technologies (Eapen, 2012), which can be non-location bound (Cano-Kollmann et al., 2016; Rugman & Verbeke, 1992). With the assumption that MNC subsidiaries, such as R&D centers, are the carriers of superior technology (Findlay, 1978), MNCs are reluctant to co-locate within a technological cluster because the risk of knowledge spillovers from MNCs to domestic firms is substantial (Lamin & Livanis, 2013), while the risk of reverse spillovers from domestic firms to MNCs is limited (Fu, 2012), especially within an emerging market (Eapen, 2012; Livanis & Lamin, 2016) unless the domestic firms possess unique technological knowledge (Eapen, 2012; Mariotti et al., 2010). In contrast, MNCs tend to cluster with other MNCs (Mariotti et al., 2010), depending on the superiority of their technological knowledge. Technologically leading MNCs (leaders) are less likely to cluster because the benefits they receive from inward knowledge spillovers are smaller than their losses from outward knowledge spillovers (Narula & Santangelo, 2009), while technologically lagging MNCs (laggards) are more motivated to cluster because the knowledge that they gain from technological leaders is larger than their knowledge contributions to the leaders (Shaver & Flyer, 2000).

Prior literature has suggested that co-location facilitates knowledge spillover not only through an informal form (Eapen, 2012), but also through formal relationships, such as alliances (Narula & Santangelo, 2009; Reuer & Lahiri, 2014) and acquisitions (Chakrabarti & Mitchell, 2013). However, some scholars have commented that prior literature has ignored some potentially important factors affecting knowledge spillover (Gilbert et al., 2008). For example, the literature on knowledge spillover has focused on firms' superiority of knowledge in terms of the sizes of their knowledge bases but has overlooked the heterogeneity among firms seeking valuable elements of knowledge that are non-duplicative to their own knowledge bases (Gupta & Govindarajan, 2000; Sammarra & Biggiero, 2008). Even when a firm has a large knowledge base, it will still have some technological opportunities to tap into external knowledge, if the external knowledge contains unique elements. This concept of non-overlapping technological domains among firms has already been identified as a key factor of knowledge transfer in the literature on the choices of alliances (Mowery et al., 1996, 1998) and acquisitions (Sears, 2017, 2018; Sears & Hoetker, 2014).

A potential research gap in the literature is examining the impact of technological overlap on location choice, as opposed to the choices of alliances and acquisitions, in addition to the impact of technological superiority. Another research gap is focusing on not only firm-specific heterogeneity in technology, but also country-specific cultural heterogeneity. The literature on knowledge spillover in international business has neglected the idiosyncratic nature of knowledge developed in a specific place (Grant, 1996; Hayek, 1945; Jensen & Meckling, 1995; Kogut & Zander, 1993), such as within a specific culture. The literature has assumed that MNCs have full access to one another's knowledge bases through knowledge spillovers regardless of in which host country they are co-locating. However, some research studies have already shown that cultural distance between where knowledge is created, such as the home country, and where knowledge is absorbed reduces the effectiveness of internal knowledge transfers within each MNC (Ambos & Ambos, 2009; Phene & Almeida, 2008). Hence, cultural distances among managers within a technological cluster potentially influence knowledge spillovers in the cluster.

This chapter aims to fill these gaps in the literature. To this end, it examines how technological overlap as a dimension of technology and cultural distance as a dimension of home country affect an MNC's location choice related to its R&D centers across different technological clusters. It is expected that an MNC's likelihood to locate its R&D center in a technological cluster increases with its technological overlap with the existing MNCs in the cluster to a certain extent, after which the likelihood declines. It is also expected that the inverted U-shaped relationship between technological overlap and co-location among MNCs is positively moderated by cultural distance. Empirically, we adopted a sample of R&D subsidiaries of Fortune Global 500 corporations that entered different NTZs in China between 1996 and 2007 and collected patent data for the sample of corporations to test our hypotheses. We contribute to the literature on knowledge-seeking subsidiaries in international business by revealing the characteristics of knowledge other than size and quantity that are significant in regard to explaining the location choices of these subsidiaries and, thus, the overall geographic organization of their MNCs.

The remainder of this paper is organized as follows. In the next section, the literature on technological overlap, co-location, and cultural distance is reviewed. Thereafter, the empirical model is specified, and the results of the analysis are provided. These sections are followed by a discussion of contributions, implications, and directions for future research. The study's conclusion is presented in the final section.

LITERATURE REVIEW

This section describes how heterogeneity in technological overlap and cultural distance affects the choice of MNCs related to locating their R&D centers in technological clusters. When MNCs choose to locate their R&D centers, which carry their firm-specific technologies from their home countries to their host countries (Cano-Kollmann et al., 2016; Eapen, 2012; Findlay, 1978), they evaluate in which of the technological clusters of a host country they will be able to maximize their net gains of knowledge (Alcácer & Chung, 2014; Mariotti et al., 2010; Shaver & Flyer, 2000). To value and absorb knowledge in a technological cluster (Mowery et al., 1996, 1998; Sears, 2017, 2018; Sears & Hoetker, 2014), a focal MNC needs to have some technological domains in common with the other MNCs in the cluster (Aharonson & Schilling, 2016; Cantner & Graf, 2006; Cohen & Levinthal, 1990; Mariotti et al., 2010). However, since the knowledge stocks are not only embedded in technological domains, but also in cultures (Barney, 1991; Fu, 2012), cultural differences influence knowledge transfers (Bhagat et al., 2002; Kedia & Bhagat, 1988; Sarala & Vaara, 2010). Thus, both technological overlap and cultural distance play important roles in an MNCs' location choice.

The Relationship between Technological Overlap and Co-location Choice

MNCs' subsidiaries, such as R&D centers, are carriers that bring MNCs' technologies from home countries to host countries (Findlay, 1978; Hymer, 1976). As knowledge has become important to the existence of MNCs (Kogut & Zander, 1993), their subsidiaries serve as agents of the MNCs in search of various elements of knowledge that support further developments of the MNCs' technological knowledge (Chung & Alcácer, 2002; Nachum & Zaheer, 2005). The need for specific knowledge varies by MNCs because the combinations of technological knowledge are unique across different MNCs (Sammarra & Biggiero, 2008). At the same time, since MNCs are geographically dispersed, knowledge is asymmetrically distributed at different locations (Lahiri, 2010). To seek valuable external knowledge that does not duplicate internal knowledge (Gupta & Govindarajan, 2000), an MNC must optimize the geographic distribution of its knowledge-seeking subsidiaries.

Co-location provides an opportunity for MNCs to gain knowledge from one another. First, co-location generally decreases the total search costs for novel knowledge (Catalini, 2017) because the number of subsidiaries needed for an MNC to access asymmetrically distributed external knowledge over geographic space is substantially lowered (Lahiri, 2010). Second, geographic proximity attributed to co-location facilitates social interactions that lower the cost for learning complex knowledge from the other MNCs at the location (Catalini, 2017; Nachum & Zaheer, 2005). However, new knowledge needs to be related to an MNC's prior knowledge. Merely interacting with the sources of new knowledge is not enough to learn from it (Cohen & Levinthal, 1990). The trade-off between the novelty of the external knowledge available and an MNC's ability to absorb such knowledge is where technological overlap comes into play in an MNC's location choice.

Technological overlap is the extent to which the unique elements of knowledge are common between multiple parties (Makri et al., 2010; Sears, 2017). A low level of technological overlap among parties implies that they are highly specialized in separate technological domains, while a high level implies that most parties hold duplicated technological elements that limit the possible recombination of elements (Kavusan et al., 2016; Mowery et al., 1998). Put differently, some degree of technological overlap provides a focal party with an existing knowledge base that helps it relate and absorb similar knowledge from the other parties (Cohen & Levinthal, 1990; Zahra & George, 2002), but a further increase in the overlap creates a path dependency that hampers novel development of technology (Makri et al., 2010).

When a focal MNC decides on whether it should locate its R&D center in a technological cluster and has minimum technological overlap with the other MNCs, the focal MNC faces difficulty in understanding the relevance and value of the technological knowledge possessed by the other MNCs (Makri et al., 2010), let alone its technological incapability of absorbing such knowledge (Cohen & Levinthal, 1990). With little knowledge to gain from this location, the focal MNC is better off locating its R&D center at another location to search for knowledge. At medium levels of technological overlap, a focal MNC is more able to understand the technological knowledge of the other MNCs in the same technological cluster, is more capable of identifying unique elements in contrast to its own knowledge, and can recognize the value of such knowledge more easily (Kavusan et al., 2016; Makri et al., 2010). Since the focal MNC is able to absorb non-redundant knowledge, it is likely to co-locate its R&D center with other MNCs in the same technological cluster at medium levels of technological overlap. If an MNC has an extreme overlap with the other MNCs across different domains of technological knowledge, then only a few elements exist that are possibly novel to the focal MNC (Kavusan et al., 2016; Mowery et al., 1998). Even if novel elements do exist, the focal MNC can choose to develop such elements internally (Mowery et al., 1998) using its existing resources incurring the costs related to establishing a new R&D center. In other words, the focal MNC will not co-locate its R&D centers with other MNCs at extremely high levels of technological overlap.

Overall, technological overlap among MNCs in a technological cluster presents both benefits and challenges. With increasing levels of overlap, enhanced ability to absorb knowledge outweighs the incomprehensible nature of new knowledge to a certain extent, beyond which the falling novelty of external knowledge overrides the ease of knowledge absorption. Taking both benefits and challenges into account, we expect that the technological overlap of a focal MNC with other MNCs in a technological cluster has a positive relationship with the focal MNC's choice to locate its R&D center in the cluster up to certain point, but a negative relationship past that point.

Hypothesis 1: The relationship between technological overlap and co-location choice is an inverted U-shape.

The Moderating Effect of Cultural Distance

Although R&D centers, as subsidiaries, are carriers of MNCs' knowledge (Findlay, 1978; Hymer, 1976), the proportion of knowledge they hold depends on their mutual understanding with their parent companies related to the knowledge. Since knowledge is formed within one's national culture (Barney, 1991; Fu, 2012), cultural compatibility between a parent and subsidiary is a necessary condition for knowledge to be communicated, transferred, and absorbed effectively in both directions (Ambos & Ambos, 2009; Lane et al., 2001; Phene & Almeida, 2008; Rugman & Verbeke, 1992; Sears, 2018). Hence, it is expected that R&D centers that are culturally distant from their parents not only possess a smaller share of knowledge stocks from their parents, but also contribute less to their parents' knowledge bases than their culturally proximate counterparts.

At the individual level, local employees of an MNC's R&D center in a host country may attempt to capture some knowledge of the MNC while working in the center (Sofka et al., 2014), but their differences in language with foreign managers (Buckley et al., 2005) have negative impacts on knowledge-sharing routines (Sears, 2018) that ultimately decrease their capacity for absorbing such knowledge (Zahra & George, 2002), especially when such knowledge is technologically unique to them. As such, even though local employees trigger outward knowledge spillovers through frequent face-to-face contact with other co-locating MNCs (Rosenthal & Strange, 2003) in community groups and industry events (Almeida & Kogut, 1999; Saxenian, 1990), the potential leakage of knowledge to the other MNCs will be trivial (Sofka et al., 2014). Especially in emerging markets, where managerial ties that fill institutional voids facilitate corporate absorption of new external knowledge in technological clusters (Gao et al., 2008), language barriers will hinder this facilitation. In the reverse direction, even when new employees bring what they have learned from other MNCs to the R&D center of a focal MNC (Livanis & Lamin, 2016) under high labor mobility within a technological cluster (Lee, 2018), the focal MNC will have a high cost-to-benefit ratio (Rugman & Verbeke, 2003; Teece, 1977) in understanding the vocabularies created by the other MNCs. If the R&D center of the focal MNC is unable to communicate with its new employees through the use of these new vocabularies, it will not be able to recognize the value of the incoming knowledge attached to these vocabularies, especially when the incoming knowledge is technologically novel.

Recall that the technological overlap of a focal MNC with other MNCs in a technological cluster has an inverted U-shape relationship with the focal MNC's choice to locate its R&D center in the cluster. As increased cultural distance between the focal MNC and its R&D center prevents outward spillovers of its unique knowledge to the other MNCs, while it absorbs novel knowledge from the other MNCs through inward spillovers, we expect that increasing cultural distance will make the positive slope of the relationship between technological overlap and co-location choice steeper. Meanwhile, since increased cultural distance heightens the costs for the focal MNC to recognize the value of external knowledge, while the novelty of such knowledge is falling, we expect that increasing cultural distance will flatten the negative slope of the relationship between technological overlap and co-location choice.

Hypothesis 2: Cultural distance makes the positive slope more positive and the negative slope less negative in the inverted U-shaped relationship between technological overlap and co-location choice.

EMPIRICAL ANALYSIS

We selected China as our empirical setting due to its large number of technological clusters (i.e., NTZs) where many MNCs possessing a range of technological domains from a diversity of home countries are located. We started with obtaining the whole series of *Report of Transnational Corporations in China*, which is published annually by the China Economic Publishing House. The report provides panel data of the city and year in which Fortune Global 500 corporations located their subsidiaries in China for such subsidiary functions as R&D, production, logistics, sales, and services. We filtered the data to focus only on R&D subsidiaries. To operationalize the sampled corporations' technological knowledge, we used the National Bureau of Economic Research's Patent Database (Hall et al., 2001). We then downloaded the measures of cultural, geographic, political, and economic distances from the Lauder Institute at the University of Pennsylvania (Berry et al., 2010). We gathered information about the Chinese cities and provinces from *China's Sustainable Development Strategy Reports*, compiled annually by the Chinese Academy of Sciences, as well as from *China Data Online*, managed by the University of Michigan. We collected financial information from Compustat, Bureau van Dijk and the annual reports of the sampled corporations. In our final sample, the number of observations with non-missing values was 26,981 and contained 110 Fortune Global 500 corporations from 13 home countries that had chosen to locate 352 R&D subsidiaries in 28 cities with NTZs between 1996 and 2007.

Variables

Our dependent variable is a binary variable set to 1 if a firm chose to locate an R&D subsidiary in an NTZ, and 0 otherwise. For the independent variable, we constructed technological overlap as the average pair-wise percentage of four-character patent classes (based on the International Patent Classification) that the patents of a focal firm have in common with the base of patents for each firm in the NTZ (Aharonson & Schilling, 2016). Following Sears's (2018) suggestion, we included all the patents for which the application date was within the seven years immediately prior to the year of location choice in the construction of the technological overlap measure. Our moderating variable is the cultural distance between China and the home country of the relevant Fortune Global 500 corporation.

   We controlled for location-, country-, and firm-specific characteristics. For location-specific characteristics, we included the percentage of technological leaders with larger knowledge bases in terms of patents than a focal corporation in the province as a control variable because, as shown in past research studies, corporations tend to co-locate with technological leaders (Narula & Santangelo, 2009; Shaver & Flyer, 2000). We also controlled for an index of technological resources in the province, provincial expenditure on innovation funds, and the strength of provincial socio-economic institutions because they attract R&D establishments in the sense that they are conducive to R&D performance (McCann & Folta, 2008). Following Zhou et al. (2002), we included a set of indicator variables to characterize four other types of policy designations in China, namely Special Economic Zone (SEZ), Opening Coastal City (OCC), Economic and/or Technology Development Zone (ETDZ), and Free Trade Zone (FTZ). For country-specific characteristics, we controlled for the log of geographic distance, political distance, and economic distance between the home country of the relevant focal corporation and China (Berry et al., 2010). For firm-specific characteristics, we controlled for the focal corporation's number of manufacturing subsidiaries and its number of sales subsidiaries in the city because sibling subsidiaries tend to co-locate (Dai et al., 2013; Salomon & Wu, 2012). We also controlled for the log of assets, R&D intensity, advertising intensity, and Tobin's Q (Oetzel & Oh, 2014). In addition, we included the fixed-effects for years and home countries.

Model

Our hypotheses were tested using a multi-level, mixed-effects, complementary log-log regression model. A complementary log-log regression model is preferable over other logistic regression models in our case because it is suitable for extremely asymmetric distribution of a binary dependent variable, while the positive responses of co-location choice are rare in the sample of observations. Our regression model consisted of two levels – specifically the company level (level 1) and the company-province level (level 2), where the random-effect of the company-city-year observations in level 1 was nested within level 2. Robust standard errors were clustered by companies. Following Perryman and Combs (2012), we standardized the continuous variables because logistic regression models are highly sensitive to scale differences (Bowen & Wiersema, 2004). The time-variant variables were lagged by one year to reduce reverse causality.

To show the explanatory power of each variable, we tested a series of models. In Model 1, we included only the control variables. In Model 2, we added technological overlap on top of Model 1. In Model 3, we added the square term of technological overlap on top of Model 2. In Model 4, we added the interaction of cultural distance with both the linear and square terms of technological overlap on top of Model 3.

RESULTS

Descriptive statistics, including mean and the standard deviation (SD) before the standardization of the variables, and the correlation matrix, are reported in Tables 8.1 and 8.2, respectively. Since the variance inflation factor (VIF) of our model was as low as 1.33, while the highest individual VIF was 1.87, the multicollinearity was trivial. The mean of the co-location choice, as small as 0.0130, justified the use of the complementary log-log regression model as the probability of a positive co-location choice was disproportionally smaller than the probability of a negative one.

The results of the multi-level, mixed-effects, complementary log-log regressions and the corresponding odd ratios are presented in Tables 8.3 and 8.4, respectively. For the control variables, we found that technological resources in the province (β=0.8564, p<0.001), provincial expenditures on innovation funds (β=0.0844, p<0.05), ETDZ (β=0.8199, p<0.001), a corporation's number of sibling subsidiaries with sales function (β=0.0852, p<0.001), and the log of assets (β=0.2526, p<0.05) significantly increased the likelihood of co-location choice. Opposite of our expectation, the percentage of technological leaders in the province marginally decreased the likelihood of co-location choice (β=–0.1105, p<0.1), implying that technological laggards may not co-locate with technological leaders for the size of the leaders' knowledge bases.

Hypothesis 1 predicted that the relationship between technological overlap and co-location choice would be an inverted U-shape. Following Lind and Mehlum's (2010) procedure (Haans et al., 2016), we first confirmed that the squared term of technological overlap was significantly negative (β=–0.2575, p<0.01). Then, using Fieller's (1954) method (Haans et al., 2016), we confirmed (as shown in Table 8.5) that the slope at the low end of the technological overlap was significantly positive (1.0077, p<0.001), while the slope at the high end was significantly negative (–0.7824, p<0.01). The graph of the relationship between the unstandardized values of technological overlap and co-location choice (see Figure 8.1) shows that the prediction of co-location choice increases with technological overlap until technological overlap reached about 45%, beyond which the prediction of co-location choice decreased with technological overlap. Overall, the results supported Hypothesis 1 that technological overlap has an inverted

U-shaped curvilinear effect on co-location choice ($p<0.001$). Based on a comparison of odds ratios, the economic significance of technological overlap was comparable with the log of assets and larger than the percentage of technological leaders in the province.

Hypothesis 2 predicted that, with increasing cultural distance, the impact of technological overlap on co-location choice will become more positive for the positive slope and less negative for the negative slope *in the inverted U-shaped relationship*. We confirmed that the interaction between cultural distance and the linear term of technological overlap was significantly positive ($\beta=0.3348$, $p<0.01$), while the interaction between cultural distance and the square term of technological overlap was negative with marginal significance ($\beta=-0.1312$, $p<0.1$). Since the two interaction terms were significant and their signs were consistent with the two independent variables, Hypothesis 2 was supported.

Table 8.1   *Descriptive statistics*

		Mean	SD
(1)	Co-Location Choice	0.0130	0.1135
(2)	Technological Overlap	36.9687	28.7745
(3)	Cultural Distance	16.2120	10.5370
(4)	Percentage of Technological Leaders in the Province	0.9194	0.1999
(5)	Technological Resources in the Province	101.9003	5.8804
(6)	Provincial Expenditure on Innovation Funds	28.4756	27.7155
(7)	Strength of Provincial Socio-Economic Institutions	99.8321	2.4191
(8)	SEZ	0.0804	0.2718
(9)	OCC	0.5227	0.4995
(10)	FTZ	0.1169	0.3213
(11)	ETDZ	0.5072	0.5000
(12)	Log of Geographic Distance	8.8235	0.5938
(13)	Political Distance	230.0553	79.2061
(14)	Economic Distance	10.0168	3.5793
(15)	Company's Number of Manufacturing Subsidiaries in the City	0.0178	0.1748
(16)	Company's Number of Sales Subsidiaries in the City	0.0122	0.1291
(17)	Log of Assets	10.6616	1.2453
(18)	R&D Intensity	0.0393	0.0495
(19)	Advertising Intensity	0.0100	0.0208
(20)	Tobin's Q	0.3810	0.3136

Note: Unstandardized coefficients.

DISCUSSION

In this chapter, we examined the impact of technological overlap and cultural distance on MNCs' location choices for their R&D centers in technological clusters using the NTZs in China as our empirical setting. We found that the technological overlap of a focal MNC with other MNCs in a technological cluster increased the focal MNC's likelihood to co-locate its R&D centers in that cluster up to certain point, beyond which technological overlap decreased the likelihood of co-location choice. This finding implied that a focal MNC is unlikely to co-locate with other MNCs that have distinct knowledge totally new to the focal MNC because the focal MNC will not be able to learn such knowledge from them.

Table 8.2   Correlation matrix

	(1)	(2)	(3)	(4)	(5)	(6)	(7)	(8)	(9)	(10)	(11)	(12)	(13)	(14)	(15)	(16)	(17)	(18)	(19)	(20)
(1)	1.000																			
(2)	-0.007	1.000																		
(3)	-0.014	0.036	1.000																	
(4)	-0.109	0.065	0.037	1.000																
(5)	0.116	-0.177	-0.042	-0.364	1.000															
(6)	0.108	-0.122	-0.038	-0.253	0.428	1.000														
(7)	0.026	-0.172	-0.101	-0.125	0.287	0.339	1.000													
(8)	-0.009	-0.132	0.001	-0.050	0.013	-0.062	0.190	1.000												
(9)	0.010	-0.169	-0.002	-0.086	0.231	0.338	0.485	0.282	1.000											
(10)	-0.017	0.026	0.003	0.083	-0.058	-0.115	-0.047	-0.108	-0.130	1.000										
(11)	0.060	0.023	-0.007	-0.192	0.134	0.020	-0.230	-0.004	-0.356	0.094	1.000									
(12)	-0.030	0.001	0.335	0.047	-0.017	-0.008	-0.019	0.001	0.001	0.001	-0.005	1.000								
(13)	0.010	0.022	0.262	-0.051	0.337	0.119	0.082	-0.017	-0.018	-0.009	0.103	0.358	1.000							
(14)	-0.023	0.046	0.321	0.049	-0.029	0.007	0.041	0.001	0.001	0.001	-0.012	0.588	0.477	1.000						
(15)	0.065	-0.006	-0.016	-0.105	0.168	0.142	0.036	0.001	-0.017	-0.017	0.064	-0.011	0.031	-0.019	1.000					
(16)	0.085	-0.035	-0.053	-0.074	0.094	0.154	0.039	-0.010	0.019	-0.001	0.054	-0.045	-0.024	-0.069	0.082	1.000				
(17)	0.026	0.077	-0.026	-0.144	0.097	0.042	0.036	-0.005	-0.005	-0.002	0.030	0.097	0.079	0.012	0.013	0.003	1.000			
(18)	0.007	0.021	0.100	0.025	0.024	0.004	-0.003	-0.001	-0.000	-0.001	0.007	0.116	0.139	0.152	0.080	-0.040	-0.212	1.000		
(19)	-0.005	-0.005	0.169	0.024	-0.027	-0.011	-0.006	0.001	0.000	0.001	-0.008	0.276	0.237	0.272	0.013	-0.035	-0.003	0.156	1.000	
(20)	-0.014	-0.034	0.080	0.022	0.036	0.016	0.017	-0.002	-0.002	-0.001	0.010	0.012	0.124	0.108	-0.014	0.009	-0.065	-0.079	0.112	1.000

Note: Following variables in Table 1.

Table 8.3   Results of multi-level mixed-effects complementary log-log regressions

Model	(1)	(2)	(3)	(4)
Technological overlap		0.2350**	0.3459**	0.3712**
		(0.0850)	(0.1163)	(0.1158)
Square of technological overlap			−0.2575**	−0.2913***
			(0.0817)	(0.0855)
Technological overlap				0.3348**
× cultural distance				(0.1102)
Square of technological overlap				−0.1312†
× cultural distance				(0.0724)
Cultural distance	−0.0277	−0.0313	−0.0385	−0.0886
	(0.0632)	(0.0647)	(0.0671)	(0.0993)
Percentage of technological leaders in the province	−0.1105†	−0.1157†	−0.1089†	−0.1132†
	(0.0605)	(0.0595)	(0.0588)	(0.0591)
Technological resources in the province	0.8564***	0.9140***	0.8561***	0.8489***
	(0.1329)	(0.1406)	(0.1337)	(0.1337)
Provincial expenditure on innovation funds	0.0844*	0.0853*	0.0924**	0.0924**
	(0.0344)	(0.0344)	(0.0348)	(0.0346)
Strength of provincial socio-economic institutions	0.0227	0.0418	0.0502	0.0489
	(0.0890)	(0.0890)	(0.0886)	(0.0880)
SEZ	−0.0576	0.0380	−0.0024	−0.0198
	(0.2265)	(0.2176)	(0.2140)	(0.2154)
OCC	0.3631†	0.3792†	0.2943	0.2819
	(0.2183)	(0.2178)	(0.2102)	(0.2111)
FTZ	−0.0773	−0.0618	−0.1586	−0.1665
	(0.1844)	(0.1838)	(0.1815)	(0.1809)
ETDZ	0.8199***	0.7857***	0.6641***	0.6640***
	(0.1732)	(0.1676)	(0.1640)	(0.1641)
Log of geographic distance	−0.2256	−0.2134	−0.1709	−0.0926
	(0.4367)	(0.4394)	(0.4348)	(0.4350)
Political distance	0.1227	0.1117	0.1089	0.0871
	(0.1924)	(0.1946)	(0.1943)	(0.1953)
Economic distance	−0.1343	−0.1430	−0.1612	−0.1840
	(0.3372)	(0.3393)	(0.3348)	(0.3347)
Company's number of manufacturing subsidiaries in the city	0.0201	0.0176	0.0166	0.0134
	(0.0180)	(0.0185)	(0.0190)	(0.0186)
Company's number of sales subsidiaries in the city	0.0852***	0.0857***	0.0875***	0.0830***
	(0.0179)	(0.0178)	(0.0176)	(0.0175)
Log of assets	0.2526*	0.2303*	0.2296*	0.2251*
	(0.1141)	(0.1117)	(0.1120)	(0.1121)
R&D intensity	0.1219	0.1137	0.0995	0.1038
	(0.1189)	(0.1130)	(0.1138)	(0.1105)
Advertising intensity	0.0199	0.0268	0.0247	0.0286
	(0.0837)	(0.0790)	(0.0783)	(0.0771)
Tobin's Q	−0.1876	−0.1639	−0.1777	−0.1779
	(0.1709)	(0.1477)	(0.1503)	(0.1475)
Year fixed dummy	Included	Included	Included	Included
Home country fixed dummy	Included	Included	Included	Included

Model	(1)	(2)	(3)	(4)
Log of random-effects parameter				
Company (Level 1)	0.3212**	0.3040**	0.2951*	0.2746*
	(0.1176)	(0.1152)	(0.1149)	(0.1124)
Company and province (Level 2)	−5.0962***	−5.1667***	−4.8413***	−4.8341***
	(0.4983)	(0.4967)	(0.4670)	(0.4610)
Log-likelihood	−1586.17	−1582.42	−1577.23	−1573.08
AIC	3246.34	3240.85	3232.45	3228.15
N	26,981	26,981	26,981	26,981

Note: † $p < 0.10$; * $p < 0.05$; ** $p < 0.01$; *** $p < 0.001$

Table 8.4   *Odd ratios*

Model	(1)	(2)	(3)	(4)
Technological overlap		1.26	1.41	1.45
Square of technological overlap			0.77	0.75
Technological overlap × cultural distance				1.40
Square of technological overlap × cultural distance				0.88
Cultural distance	0.97	0.97	0.96	0.92
Percentage of technological leaders in the province	0.90	0.89	0.90	0.89
Technological resources in the province	2.35	2.49	2.35	2.34
Provincial expenditure on innovation funds	1.09	1.09	1.10	1.10
Strength of provincial socio-economic institutions	1.02	1.04	1.05	1.05
SEZ	0.94	1.04	1.00	0.98
OCC	1.44	1.46	1.34	1.33
FTZ	0.93	0.94	0.85	0.85
ETDZ	2.27	2.19	1.94	1.94
Log of geographic distance	0.80	0.81	0.84	0.91
Political distance	1.13	1.12	1.12	1.09
Economic distance	0.87	0.87	0.85	0.83
Company's number of manufacturing subsidiaries in the city	1.02	1.02	1.02	1.01
Company's number of sales subsidiaries in the city	1.09	1.09	1.09	1.09
Log of assets	1.29	1.26	1.26	1.25
R&D intensity	1.13	1.12	1.10	1.11
Advertising intensity	1.02	1.03	1.02	1.03
Tobin's Q	0.83	0.85	0.84	0.84

Table 8.5   *Test of an inverted U-shaped relationship*

Estimated turning point	0.6716
95% confidence interval for turning point	[−1.2848, 2.1905]
Slope test – lower bound (Slope)	1.0077***
Slope test – upper bound (Slope)	−0.7824**
Overall test of presence of an inverted U-shape (*t*-value)	2.36**

Note: $p < 0.10$; * $p < 0.05$; ** $p < 0.01$; *** $p < 0.001$

However, when the knowledge of the two parties starts to become similar, the focal MNC becomes capable of relating, understanding, and valuing external knowledge. Thus, the focal MNC is likely to co-locate, until a point when the focal MNC recognizes external knowledge as too redundant and invaluable (i.e., not worth the cost of setting up a R&D subsidiary at the location).

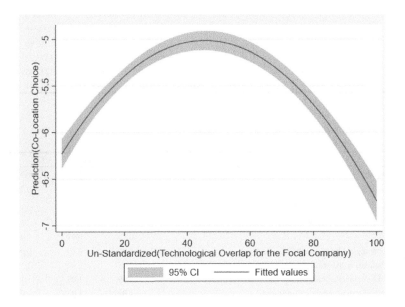

Figure 8.1   Inverted U-shape relationship between un-standardized technological overlap and co-location choice

Surprisingly, both the statistical and economic significance of technological overlap in a cluster were larger than the significance of the technological leaders at the location. Contrary to the findings of prior studies, which have suggested that technological laggards tend to co-locate with technological leaders (Mariotti et al., 2010; Narula & Santangelo, 2009; Shaver & Flyer, 2000), our results showed the opposite finding. We found that a focal MNC was unlikely to locate its R&D center in a technological cluster when a large proportion of MNCs in that cluster have a larger (versus smaller) knowledge base than its own. This finding implies that the focal MNC in this situation may lose its comparative advantage if it co-locates in the cluster. However, a focal MNC that has a comparatively small knowledge base compared with the other MNCs in a technological cluster may possess unique elements of technological knowledge that the other MNCs do not possess. In other words, the other MNCs that have a relatively larger knowledge base may be able to absorb unique knowledge from this MNC, if the MNC makes an unwise decision to locate its R&D centers within the same cluster.

Our results also showed that cultural distance makes the inverted U-shaped relationship between technological overlap and co-location choice more positive for the positive slope and less negative for the negative slope. Increased cultural distance between a focal MNC and its R&D center prevents outward knowledge spillovers, while allowing the MNC to enjoy inward knowledge spillovers through the social interactions of the center's employees with the employees of other MNCs. Hence, co-location seems more attractive to a certain extent in these situations. Yet, when cultural distance is too high, it is especially cost ineffective for the focal MNC to learn the highly overlapping knowledge brought by its employees from the other MNCs at the location, and so co-location seems less likely.

Theoretical Contributions

The significance of this study is multifaceted. First, it sheds light on important factors to be considered for MNCs' strategic location choices related to knowledge-seeking subsidiaries in international business. Prior literature on MNCs' location choice of R&D subsidiaries has stressed the importance of technological superiority in terms of the size of the MNCs' knowledge bases or R&D intensities (Alcácer & Chung, 2007; Eapen, 2012; Fu, 2012; Lamin & Livanis, 2013; Livanis & Lamin, 2016; Mariotti et al., 2010; Narula & Santangelo, 2009; Shaver & Flyer, 2000). However, even when a large amount or high intensity of knowledge is available, it does not mean that it is cost-effective for an MNC to seek this knowledge because it may be irrelevant to the MNC's circumstances, difficult for the MNC to learn, or not valuable from the MNC's perspective. As such, our study suggests that technological overlap plays a role in MNCs' strategic organization of R&D subsidiaries. By comparing the technological domains among MNCs before making location choices for the R&D subsidiaries, an MNC can project whether the knowledge-seeking mission of an R&D subsidiary can be fulfilled.

Second, we contribute to the literature on knowledge transfers in formal and informal relationships. Prior literature has discussed the impact of technological overlap on knowledge transfers in such formal relationships as alliances (Mowery et al., 1996, 1998) and acquisitions (Sears, 2017, 2018; Sears & Hoetker, 2014), the effect of co-location on knowledge spillovers as informal knowledge transfers among firms (Eapen, 2012), and the influence of co-location on the formation of alliances (Narula & Santangelo, 2009; Reuer & Lahiri, 2014) and acquisitions (Chakrabarti & Mitchell, 2013). This study fills this research gap by showing that technological overlap affects co-location choice. It thus reveals the triangulation among firms' technological overlap, co-location, and formal relationships, where technological overlap and co-location have a direct effect on formal relationships among firms, but co-location can also be a mediator between technological overlap and formal relationships.

Third, this study bridges two strands of literature, specifically the literature that focuses on knowledge transfers between an MNC and its subsidiaries within its internal network and the literature that examines knowledge spillovers between an MNC and its external parties. The former suggests that a subsidiary located in a host country distant from the home country is ineffective in receiving internal knowledge from and transferring external knowledge to its parent, while the latter assumes that any piece of knowledge that an MNC possesses can be spilled to external parties co-locating with any of its subsidiaries. This study unveiled that the latter assumption is flawed because the distance between home and host countries decreases the knowledge stock of an MNC's subsidiary, thereby reducing outward knowledge spillovers to the external parties at the subsidiary's location. Distance between home and host countries thus serves as a knowledge appropriation mechanism. Yet external knowledge gained from inward knowledge spillovers at a subsidiary may not fully be translated into an MNC's knowledge base due to the same reason. In a nutshell, this study connects the internal knowledge network (i.e. distance between parent company and R&D subsidiary) and the external knowledge network (i.e. co-location with external parties in technological clusters) of an MNC with the knowledge structure among MNCs (i.e. technological overlap among parties in technological clusters).

Fourth, this study adds cultural distance to the interaction between managerial ties and absorptive capacity in the literature on the technological clusters of such emerging markets as China. One of the prior studies that examined high-tech industrial zones in China suggested how managerial ties and absorptive capacity interact to support innovation within the institutional voids of emerging markets (Gao et al., 2008). In line with prior studies, this study considers that as a factor affecting absorptive capacity, managerial ties is part of the mechanism facilitating knowledge spillovers and technological overlap. This study showed additionally that cultural distance in these managerial ties had a moderating effect on the relationship between technological overlap and the absorption of knowledge through spillovers and, ultimately, co-location choice.

Managerial Implications

In terms of implications for managers, this study indicates that it is not wise to compare only the quantity or superiority of knowledge among MNCs without looking into the overlap or similarity of such knowledge before deciding on the geographic distribution or location choices for R&D subsidiaries of the MNCs. First, technologically leading MNCs with larger knowledge bases or higher R&D intensities may not necessarily lose comparative advantages by co-locating with technologically lagging MNCs if their knowledge is too specialized to be learned or too general to be valuable. Second, these types of technological leaders may consider co-locating with external firms that have balanced levels of specialized versus general knowledge to improve their capacities to further absorb knowledge or gain novelty in technological developments. Last, technologically lagging MNCs with smaller knowledge bases or lower R&D intensities will not have comparative advantages if their elements of knowledge fall in the middle of the knowledge structure of the existing MNCs. Since the knowledge of these MNCs is easily learned, while maintaining a certain level of novelty, their knowledge will be spilled out to external firms, especially when the number of external firms is large. These MNCs should counter-intuitively avoid co-location.

Limitations and Future Research

First, as our empirical findings are inconsistent with prior literature, which suggests that technological leaders are unlikely to co-locate with technological laggards, further research is necessary to vindicate this statement and uncover the potentially more complex mechanism underlying this statement. Second, while our study regards technological overlap as the similarity among firms that focuses on specific classes of knowledge, we have not explored the effect of technological complementarity, which is considered the extent to which firms overlap in the same subcategory, but with different classes of knowledge (Makri et al., 2010). As these two concepts are closely related, future research should examine how technological complementarity alone or along with technological overlap affects knowledge-seeking firms to co-locate. Third, future research should look into how co-location choices that are motivated by technological overlap among MNCs influence the MNCs' performances at the subsidiary level. If location choices of subsidiaries are made strategically to seek knowledge, then the subsidiaries are expected to produce a higher quantity or quality of technological output. Fourth, while prior literature found the impact of technological overlap on the choices of alliances or acquisitions as well as the impact of co-location on such choices, this study found the impact of technological overlap on co-location choice. Future research should confirm whether co-location is a mediator between technological overlap and alliance or acquisition choices, and whether co-location and the formation of alliances or acquisitions are substitutes. Fifth, while this study has looked into how distance affects knowledge spillovers at subsidiary locations, future research should look at how knowledge gained from spillovers at subsidiary locations affect MNCs' knowledge and productivity at the company level. Sixth, future research should explore how institutions other than cultural distance in managerial ties affect knowledge spillovers and co-location specifically in the technological clusters of emerging markets, such as the NTZs in China.

CONCLUSION

In conclusion, this chapter examined the extent to which technological overlap and cultural distance were significant in regard to explaining MNCs' location choices for their R&D subsidiaries in technological clusters. Our focus was the relevance and novelty of technological knowledge that brings value to MNCs rather than the quantity and superiority of technological knowledge in terms of the knowledge base and R&D intensity. By using a sample of MNCs that have R&D centers established in Chinese NTZs, our findings provided insight toward a better understanding of how MNCs geographically organize their knowledge-seeking subsidiaries in a host country.

REFERENCES

Aharonson, B. S., & Schilling, M. A. (2016). Mapping the technological landscape: Measuring technology distance, technological footprints, and technology evolution. *Research Policy*, *45*(1), 81–96.

Alcácer, J., & Chung, W. (2007). Location strategies and knowledge spillovers. *Management Science*, *53*(5), 760–776.

Alcácer, J., & Chung, W. (2014). Location strategies for agglomeration economies. *Strategic Management Journal*, *35*(12), 1749–1761.

Almeida, P., & Kogut, B. (1999). Localization of knowledge and the mobility of engineers in regional networks. *Management Science*, *45*(7), 905–917.

Ambos, T. C., & Ambos, B. (2009). The impact of distance on knowledge transfer effectiveness in multinational corporations. *Journal of International Management*, *15*(1), 1–14.

Barney, J. (1991). Firm resources and sustained competitive advantage. *Journal of Management*, *17*(1), 99–120.

Berry, H., Guillén, M. F., & Zhou, N. (2010). An institutional approach to cross-national distance. *Journal of International Business Studies*, *41*(9), 1460–1480.

Bhagat, R. S., Kedia, B. L., Harveston, P. D., & Triandis, H. C. (2002). Cultural variations in the cross-border transfer of organizational knowledge: An integrative framework. *Academy of Management Review*, *27*(2), 204–221.

Bloomberg. (2015). 'China wants Silicon Valleys everywhere.' http://www.bloomberg.com/news/articles/2015-07-23/china-wants-silicon-valleys-everywhere. July 23, 2015 (accessed 1 February 2019).

Bowen, H. P., & Wiersema, M. F. (2004). Modeling limited dependent variables: Methods and guidelines for researchers in strategic management. In *Research methodology in strategy and management* (pp. 87–134). Emerald Group Publishing.

Buckley, P. J., Carter, M. J., Clegg, J., & Tan, H. (2005). Language and social knowledge in foreign-knowledge transfer to China. *International Studies of Management & Organization, 35*(1), 47–65.

Cano-Kollmann, M., Cantwell, J., Hannigan, T. J., Mudambi, R., & Song, J. (2016). Knowledge connectivity: An agenda for innovation research in international business. *Journal of International Business Studies, 47*(3), 463–480.

Cantner, U., & Graf, H. (2006). The network of innovators in Jena: An application of social network analysis. *Research Policy, 35*(4), 463–480.

Catalini, C. (2017). Microgeography and the direction of inventive activity. *Management Science, 64*(9), 4348–4364.

Chakrabarti, A., & Mitchell, W. (2013). The persistent effect of geographic distance in acquisition target selection. *Organization Science, 24*(6), 1805–1826.

China Daily. (2011). Haidian Science Park – more than just a park. http://www.chinadaily.com.cn/cndy/2011-09/14/content_13680791.htm. September 14, 2011 (accessed 1 February 2019).

China Daily. (2018). High-tech zones are 'driving growth'. https://www.chinadaily.com.cn/a/201807/17/WS5b4d3ebda310796df4df6cf1.html. July 17, 2018 (accessed 20 November 2019).

Chung, W., & Alcácer, J. (2002). Knowledge seeking and location choice of foreign direct investment in the United States. *Management Science, 48*(12), 1534–1554.

Cohen, W. M., & Levinthal, D. A. (1990). Absorptive capacity: A new perspective on learning and innovation. *Administrative Science Quarterly, 35*(1), 128–152.

Dai, L., Eden, L., & Beamish, P. W. (2013). Place, space, and geographical exposure: Foreign subsidiary survival in conflict zones. *Journal of International Business Studies, 44*(6), 554–578.

Dunning, J. H., & Norman, G. (1983). The theory of the multinational enterprise: An application to multinational office location. *Environment and Planning A, 15*(5), 675–692.

Eapen, A. (2012). Social structure and technology spillovers from foreign to domestic firms. *Journal of International Business Studies, 43*(3), 244–263.

Fieller, E. C. (1954). Some problems in interval estimation. *Journal of the Royal Statistical Society: Series B (Methodological), 16*(2), 175–185.

Findlay, R. (1978). Relative backwardness, direct foreign investment, and the transfer of technology: a simple dynamic model. *The Quarterly Journal of Economics, 92*(1), 1–16.

Fu, X. (2012). Foreign direct investment and managerial knowledge spillovers through the diffusion of management practices. *Journal of Management Studies, 49*(5), 970–999.

Gao, S., Xu, K., & Yang, J. (2008). Managerial ties, absorptive capacity, and innovation. *Asia Pacific Journal of Management, 25*(3), 395–412.

Gilbert, B. A., McDougall, P. P., & Audretsch, D. B. (2008). Clusters, knowledge spillovers and new venture performance: An empirical examination. *Journal of Business Venturing, 23*(4), 405–422.

Grant, R. M. (1996). Toward a knowledge-based theory of the firm. *Strategic Management Journal, 17*(S2), 109–122.

Gupta, A. K., & Govindarajan, V. (2000). Knowledge flows within multinational corporations. *Strategic Management Journal, 21*(4), 473–496.

Haans, R. F., Pieters, C., & He, Z. L. (2016). Thinking about U: Theorizing and testing U- and inverted U-shaped relationships in strategy research. *Strategic Management Journal, 37*(7), 1177–1195.

Hall, B. H., Jaffe, A. B., & Trajtenberg, M. (2001). *The NBER patent citation data file: Lessons, insights and methodological tools* (No. w8498). National Bureau of Economic Research.

Hayek, F. A. (1945). The use of knowledge in society. *The American Economic Review, 35*(4), 519–530.

Hennart, J.-F. (1982). *A Theory of Multinational Enterprise*. Ann Arbor, MI: University of Michigan Press.

Hymer, S. (1976). *The International Operations of National Firms: A Study of Direct Foreign Investment*. Boston, MA: MIT Press.

Jensen, M. C., & Meckling, W. H. (1995). Specific and general knowledge, and organizational structure. *Journal of Applied Corporate Finance, 8*(2), 4–18.

Kavusan, K., Noorderhaven, N. G., & Duysters, G. M. (2016). Knowledge acquisition and complementary specialization in alliances: The impact of technological overlap and alliance experience. *Research Policy, 45*(10), 2153–2165.

Kedia, B. L., & Bhagat, R. S. (1988). Cultural constraints on transfer of technology across nations: Implications for research in international and comparative management. *Academy of Management Review, 13*(4), 559–571.

Kogut, B., & Zander, U. (1993). Knowledge of the firm and the evolutionary theory of the multinational corporation. *Journal of International Business Studies, 24*(4), 625–645.

Lahiri, N. (2010). Geographic distribution of R&D activity: How does it affect innovation quality? *Academy of Management Journal, 53*(5), 1194–1209.

Lamin, A., & Livanis, G. (2013). Agglomeration, catch-up and the liability of foreignness in emerging economies. *Journal of International Business Studies, 44*(6), 579–606.

Lane, P. J., Salk, J. E., & Lyles, M. A. (2001). Absorptive capacity, learning, and performance in international joint ventures. *Strategic Management Journal, 22*(12), 1139–1161.

Lee, C. Y. (2018). Geographical clustering and firm growth: Differential growth performance among clustered firms. *Research Policy, 47*(6), 1173–1184.

Lind, J. T., & Mehlum, H. (2010). With or without U? The appropriate test for a U-shaped relationship. *Oxford Bulletin of Economics and Statistics, 72*(1), 109–118.

Livanis, G., & Lamin, A. (2016). Knowledge, proximity and R&D exodus. *Research Policy, 45*(1), 8–26.

Makri, M., Hitt, M. A., & Lane, P. J. (2010). Complementary technologies, knowledge relatedness, and invention outcomes in high technology mergers and acquisitions. *Strategic Management Journal, 31*(6), 602–628.

Mariotti, S., Piscitello, L., & Elia, S. (2010). Spatial agglomeration of multinational enterprises: the role of information externalities and knowledge spillovers. *Journal of Economic Geography, 10*(4), 519–538.

McCann, B. T., & Folta, T. B. (2008). Location matters: Where we have been and where we might go in agglomeration research. *Journal of Management, 34*(3), 532–565.

Mowery, D. C., Oxley, J. E., & Silverman, B. S. (1996). Strategic alliances and interfirm knowledge transfer. *Strategic Management Journal, 17*(S2), 77–91.

Mowery, D. C., Oxley, J. E., & Silverman, B. S. (1998). Technological overlap and interfirm cooperation: Implications for the resource-based view of the firm. *Research Policy, 27*(5), 507–523.

Nachum, L., & Zaheer, S. (2005). The persistence of distance? The impact of technology on MNE motivations for foreign investment. *Strategic Management Journal, 26*(8), 747–767.

Narula, R., & Santangelo, G. D. (2009). Location, collocation and R&D alliances in the European ICT industry. *Research Policy, 38*(2), 393–403.

Ning, L., Wang, F., & Li, J. (2016). Urban innovation, regional externalities of foreign direct investment and industrial agglomeration: Evidence from Chinese cities. *Research Policy, 45*(4), 830–843.

Oetzel, J. M., & Oh, C. H. (2014). Learning to carry the cat by the tail: Firm experience, disasters, and multinational subsidiary entry and expansion. *Organization Science, 25*(3), 732–756.

Perryman, A. A., & Combs, J. G. (2012). Who should own it? An agency-based explanation for multi-outlet ownership and co-location in plural form franchising. *Strategic Management Journal, 33*(4), 368–386.

Phene, A., & Almeida, P. (2008). Innovation in multinational subsidiaries: The role of knowledge assimilation and subsidiary capabilities. *Journal of International Business Studies, 39*(5), 901–919.

PR Newswire. (2015). Chengdu Hi-tech Zone to build National Innovation Demonstration Zone in West China. http://www.prnewswire.com/news-releases/chengdu-hi-tech-zone-to-build-national -innovation-demonstration-zone-in-west-china-300138824.html. September 7, 2015 (accessed 1 February 2019).

Reuer, J. J., & Lahiri, N. (2014). Searching for alliance partners: Effects of geographic distance on the formation of R&D collaborations. *Organization Science, 25*(1), 283–298.

Rosenthal, S. S., & Strange, W. C. (2003). Geography, industrial organization, and agglomeration. *Review of Economics and Statistics, 85*(2), 377–393.

Rugman, A. M. (1981). *Inside the Multinationals: The Economics of Internal Markets.* New York, NY: Columbia University Press.

Rugman, A. M., & Verbeke, A. (1992). A note on the transnational solution and the transaction cost theory of multinational strategic management. *Journal of International Business Studies, 23*(4), 761–771.

Rugman, A. M., & Verbeke, A. (2003). Extending the theory of the multinational enterprise: Internalization and strategic management perspectives. *Journal of International Business Studies*, *34*(2), 125–137.

Salomon, R., & Wu, Z. (2012). Institutional distance and local isomorphism strategy. *Journal of International Business Studies*, *43*(4), 343–367.

Sammarra, A., & Biggiero, L. (2008). Heterogeneity and specificity of inter-firm knowledge flows in innovation networks. *Journal of Management Studies*, *45*(4), 800–829.

Sarala, R. M., & Vaara, E. (2010). Cultural differences, convergence, and crossvergence as explanations of knowledge transfer in international acquisitions. *Journal of International Business Studies*, *41*(8), 1365–1390.

Saxenian, A. (1990). Regional networks and the resurgence of Silicon Valley. *California Management Review*, *33*(1), 89–112.

Sears, J. B. (2017). When are acquired technological capabilities complements rather than substitutes? A study on value creation. *Journal of Business Research*, *78*, 33–42.

Sears, J. B. (2018). Post-acquisition integrative versus independent innovation: A story of dueling success factors. *Research Policy*, *47*(9), 1688–1699.

Sears, J., & Hoetker, G. (2014). Technological overlap, technological capabilities, and resource recombination in technological acquisitions. *Strategic Management Journal*, *35*(1), 48–67.

Shaver, J. M., & Flyer, F. (2000). Agglomeration economies, firm heterogeneity, and foreign direct investment in the United States. *Strategic Management Journal*, *21*(12), 1175–1193.

Sofka, W., Shehu, E., & de Faria, P. (2014). Multinational subsidiary knowledge protection: Do mandates and clusters matter? *Research Policy*, *43*(8), 1320–1333.

Teece, D. J. (1977). Technology transfer by multinational firms: The resource cost of transferring technological know-how. *The Economic Journal*, *87*(346), 242–261.

Zahra, S. A., & George, G. (2002). Absorptive capacity: A review, reconceptualization, and extension. *Academy of Management Review*, *27*(2), 185–203.

Zhou, C., Delios, A., & Yang, J. Y. (2002). Locational determinants of Japanese foreign direct investment in China. *Asia Pacific Journal of Management*, *19*(1), 63–86.

9. Building ambidextrous capabilities in foreign subsidiaries: evidence from Korean multinationals

Jae Eun Lee, Byung Il Park and Yong Kyu Lew

INTRODUCTION

In the international management of multinational corporations (MNCs), the possession of an overseas subsidiary with superior capability is an important source that determines the overall competitiveness and success of the MNCs (Birkinshaw and Hood, 1998; Park and Ghauri, 2011). Thus, it is critically important for the MNCs to manage headquarters (HQ)–subsidiaries relations so as to build up subsidiaries' capabilities and to cope with international business (IB) challenges to the MNCs (Nohria and Ghoshal, 1994). Thus, research into the overseas subsidiaries of MNCs has been regarded as a very significant element in the study of MNCs (Doz and Prahalad, 1981; Egelhoff, 1988; Ghoshal and Nohria, 1989; Ghoshal and Bartlett, 1990).

Overseas subsidiaries may build their capability by drawing upon their existing capability within the MNC boundary, or they may also establish entirely new capabilities absent in the MNC by means of the subsidiary's own innovative activities (Williams, 2007; Makino and Inkpen, 2003). The present research conceptually distinguishes the capabilities of the subsidiary into two categories, i.e., exploitative and explorative capabilities. In this chapter, the first, exploitative capability, is defined as the capability of the foreign subsidiary to modify or utilize the resources or technologies possessed by the MNC HQ to suit the local market conditions. The second, explorative capability, is defined as the capability of the foreign subsidiary to develop entirely new technologies or resources not owned by the headquarters within the local environments (March, 1991; Katila and Ahuja, 2002; Jansen et al., 2006). Taking these two notions of capabilities, it investigates the factors that influence them, with a focus on the control mechanism exercised by the HQs and the characteristics of the host country.

MNCs are composed of multiple overseas subsidiaries located in various countries (Roth and Nigh, 1992). Thus, research into how these foreign subsidiaries should be mediated and managed has been an important subject of discussion in the field of IB (Roth and Nigh, 1992; Werner, 2002, Birkinshaw and Hood, 1998). Previous studies often perceived the HQ and individual subsidiaries as being placed in a hierarchical relationship, regarding the strategies and activities of the individual subsidiaries as being conducted under the aegis of the global strategy of the HQ (Bartlett and Ghoshal, 2000). In other words, the main activity of the MNCs was conceived to be effectively transferring the specific knowledge developed by the headquarters to its overseas subsidiaries distributed across various countries, thus acquiring a competitive advantage. In this vein, subsidiary performance was evaluated in terms of how well the subsidiaries carried out the roles assigned by the HQ of which the main focus of attention was on the issue of how to manage their overseas subsidiaries.

However, recent studies that examine the relationship between the HQs and subsidiaries of MNCs place their focus on the unique functions exercised by the individual subsidiaries and the process by which the subsidiaries acquire leading agency within the MNCs network, going beyond the relationships associated with unilateral dependency and not merely limiting themselves to conducting business activities in the local country based upon the resources and capabilities already present in the HQ (Birkinshaw, 1997; Birkinshaw et al, 1998; Rugman and Verbeke, 2001).

The foreign subsidiary of an MNC conducts its business activities in a different environment, both as a member of the organization of MNCs and as an organization that carries out business activities in the local country (Rosenzweig and Singh, 1991). Owing to these unique characteristics, many scholars in the field of IB have recognized the importance of the role of foreign subsidiaries within MNCs and have proceeded to conduct research that examines these subsidiaries (Birkinshaw and Morrison, 1995; Gupta and Govindarajan, 1991, 2000; Bartlett and Ghoshal, 1989).

Due to the importance of this topic, preceding studies have emphasized that the capabilities of the subsidiaries are derived from the firm-specific advantages possessed by the HQ (Rugman and Verbeke, 2001; Vernon, 1966), or are acquired by learning through practical applications in the local country. Most have devoted their main attention to the factors that impact the differentiated capabilities of overseas subsidiaries (Birkinshaw and Hood, 1998; Chang and Rosenzweig, 2009). Nonetheless, there has not been an in-depth discussion of how the capabilities of the overseas subsidiaries – as members of MNCs as well as agents conducting business in the local country – develop into a distinct form due to the influence of the two differentiated environments. Furthermore, subsidiaries may need to develop different types of capabilities for utilizing their existing resources and knowledge within an MNC network, while developing their own capabilities for the development of new knowledge and innovation (see Luo and Rui, 2009; O'Reilly and Tushman, 2013). The development of such capabilities may require differing processes and resources within the MNC network (Holmqvist, 2004; He and Wong, 2004). However, most previous research has not paid attention to the factors that influence the development of different types of subsidiary capabilities at the HQ subsidiary level.

In order to overcome the above limitations of preceding studies, this study presents the following research question: how do the types of control by the HQ influence the exploitative and explorative capability of the subsidiary? An investigation from diverse theoretical perspectives will not only allow for an integrated inquiry into this research question, but also present the potential to achieve a strong understanding of the answers by means of empirical tests.

SUBSIDIARY EXPLOITATIVE AND EXPLORATIVE CAPABILITIES

The concepts of exploitation and exploration have expanded into a wide range of managerial contexts, including strategic management (e.g., He and Wong, 2004; Jansen et al., 2006; Uotila et al., 2009; Ghemawat and Ricart I Costa, 1993) and organizational studies (e.g., Siggelkow and Levinthal, 2003; Holmqvist, 2004). The seminal work of March (1991) describes exploitation as "refinement, choice, production, efficiency, selection, implementation, and execution," and exploration as "things captured by terms such as search, variation, risk taking, experimentation, play, flexibility, discovery, and innovation." Exploitation and exploration respectively require differing structures, processes and resources, and that their effects on outcome also exhibit significant differences (Ghemawat and Ricart I Costa, 1993; Holmqvist, 2004; He and Wong, 2004). However, there are a limited number of studies applied to IB (e.g., Luo, 2002; Makino et al., 2002).

Exploitation activities that reduce variety and increase efficiency while heightening adaptation to the current environment may have a positive impact on short-term performance. However, the diminished variety results in heightened dependency on the currently existing environment, which raises vulnerability to environmental changes. Companies that emphasize exploitation therefore fall short in their capacity to adapt to critical environmental changes; while these companies may have advantages for short-term success, their long-term survival and growth cannot be secured (March, 1991; Levinthal and March, 1993; Uotila et al., 2009).

In contrast, exploration activities stimulate the development of the capabilities required for a corporation to generate new knowledge and innovation. These exploration activities, however, have strong characteristics of uncertainty, and their influence on performance may become apparent only after a long period of time. In other words, exploitation using pre-existing resources or technologies allows for greater certitude in predicting the results of the input when compared with the case of exploration, which develops new resources or technologies. Moreover, the effects of the former are more identifiable. Therefore, in the short term it may be far more advantageous in terms of cost or effect to rely on exploitation utilizing pre-existing resources or technologies rather than on exploration, which seeks to develop new resources or technologies. However, without efforts devoted to exploratory activities, survival and growth may be threatened in the long term (March, 1991; Levinthal and March, 1993; Uotila et al., 2009; Lew et al., 2013). The following research applies these two concepts to examine the capabilities of overseas subsidiaries.

In general, an organization can utilize the capability it already possesses to secure survival, and it may also develop new capabilities (Makino and Inkpen, 2003; O'Reilly & Tushman, 2013). In the case of overseas subsidiaries as well, they may employ the unique capabilities or technologies already secured by the headquarters to obtain their competitive advantage (Wernerfelt, 1984; Luo, 2002; Tallman, 2001), or the subsidiaries may generate new alternatives such as the development of novel skills and know-how within the local country (Tallman, 1991; Luo, 2002). Traditional IB theories have identified one of the motivations behind foreign direct investment by MNCs to generate rents by means of transferring the technologies, resources, knowledge and management know-how owned by the HQ to the overseas subsidiary (Hymer, 1976; Dunning, 1988, Park and Choi, 2014; Rugman and Verbeke, 1992). In this study, we define the capability of the overseas subsidiaries to use the capabilities of the HQ, including its technologies or knowledge, for example, in their given state or in some cases by modifying and applying them to suit the host country as the concept pertaining to their exploitative capability. However, the overseas subsidiaries of MNCs conduct business activities not only as an organizational member of the entire MNCs network, but also as an organization conducting business within the host country, thus requiring them to perform these two ambidextrous roles. For the overseas subsidiaries to implement business activities successfully in the local country, they need to develop explorative capabilities absent in the HQ by means of an independent self-learning process. As such, subsidiary capability for self-developing technologies and knowledge are not in the possession of the HQ of the MNCs for the purpose of successful business management activities in the local country, i.e., explorative capability.

Once the capabilities of the overseas subsidiaries are distinguished as an exploitative capability and an explorative capability, the challenge of finding a balance between these two types becomes a critically important project in terms of both practical application and theorization. This is because the development of these two types of capabilities may be placed in mutual competition due to the scarcity of resources (March, 1991; Simsek, 2009). Therefore, finding the proper balance between the two becomes intimately related to the growth and survival of the organization.

Reliance on exploiting known alternatives may result in missing opportunities to explore new advantages, whereas reliance on exploring new alternatives may result in a short-term loss of efficiency (March, 1991). In consideration of the above characteristics, the organization must distribute its limited resources in a suitable balance between exploitation and exploration in order to achieve sustainable success. However, in many cases there is a tendency for firms to substitute investment in the lesser known area of exploration in favor of exploitation[1] (Levinthal and March, 1993; Uotila et al., 2009).

HYPOTHESES

Output Control and Subsidiary Capabilities

Compared with local business management, MNC management involves much more complex activities between HQ and subsidiaries within an MNC network (Bartlett and Ghoshal, 2000). In particular, the relationship between the HQ and a subsidiary can be viewed as a principal–agent relationship, in which the HQ (principal) tries to control the subsidiary (agent) to behave in accordance with the HQ's goal (Andersson et al., 2005). In the traditional literature, control refers to the process by which one entity influences the behavior and output of another entity (Geringer and Herbert, 1989) through the use of power, authority (Bachmann, 2001), and a wide range of bureaucratic, cultural and informal mechanisms (Baliga and Jaeger, 1984). These studies demonstrate the purpose of control is to minimize idiosyncratic behavior to hold individuals or groups to an enunciated policy, thus making performance predictable (Andersson and Forsgren, 1996; Aulakh and Gencturk, 2000; Tannenbaum, 1968).

Control has long been recognized as an important issue related to an organization's management scheme (Aulakh and Gencturk, 2000). Within the relationship between the HQ and the subsidiary, the HQ can commonly use two types of control: behavior control and output control (Egelhoff, 1984; Gupta and Govindarajan, 1991). Behavior control "is like the supervisor personally observing and checking the behavior of subordinates" in the relationship between the HQ and the subsidiary; it occurs "when an MNC assigns parent company managers to the key management positions of a foreign subsidiary." In contrast, output control involves "the extent to which data on sales, returns, exchanges, and so on were used to monitor operations." It can evaluate that "the performance reporting systems whereby foreign subsidiaries submit a variety of data to the parent are perhaps the most visible control systems in MNCs" (Egelhoff, 1984: 74).

Output control is largely exerted through performance reporting systems which evaluate the subsidiary's output (Chang and Taylor, 1999), implying that data such as sales figures, return or profit are considered suitable for monitoring operations. If the headquarters controls the output of the subsidiary by making the subsidiary report its financial situation and performance constantly, the subsidiary will have a relatively high degree of authority. HQs do not have a motive to be involved in the subsidiary's management as long as the subsidiary achieves its goal as set by the HQs. Also, in order to achieve the outcome set by the HQ, the subsidiary will attempt to develop its resources and capabilities; such activities will not acquire any additional constraints by the HQ. Therefore, if the headquarters implements output control on the subsidiary, it will have a positive effect on the explorative capability and a negative effect on the exploitative capability of the subsidiary.

H1a. The use of output control exercised by an HQ will have a negative impact on the exploitative capability of a foreign subsidiary.
H1b. The use of output control exercised by an HQ will have a positive impact on the explorative capability of a foreign subsidiary.

Behavior Control and Subsidiary Capabilities

Behavior control denotes control obtained by observing and monitoring the behavior of subordinates (Egelhoff, 1984; Lew and Sinkovics, 2013). However, personal surveillance requires a clear understanding of means–end relationships because only then are appropriate instructions possible. This form of control is considered to be the most direct. Taken to its logical extreme, behavior control would lead to behavior formalization. When the HQ uses behavior control as a control mechanism, the headquarters can formalize the behavior of a subsidiary. Because it is impossible to control a subsidiary's behavior directly due to the characteristics of an MNC, in which subsidiaries are dispersed geographically, it is necessary to create a specific behavior manual as an official behavior guide and create methods with which to respond to problems so that the subsidiary can have standards under which to act accordingly within the bounds of the policy of the headquarters. In a similar vein, the use of behavior control imposes strict guidelines on how activities should be performed. Subsequently, monitoring and correcting actions in an explicit manner is likely to reduce a subordinate's autonomy (John, 1984). On the other hand, the behavior controls by HQ can facilitate smooth communication between HQ and subsidiaries by allowing subsidiaries to act in accordance with guidelines of HQ. Therefore, use of behavior control will have a negative effect on a subsidiary's explorative capability but a positive effect on its exploitative capability.

H2a. The use of behavior control exercised by an HQ will have a positive impact on the exploitative capability of a foreign subsidiary.
H2b. The use of behavior control exercised by an HQ will have a negative impact on the explorative capability of a foreign subsidiary.

Social Control and Subsidiary Capabilities

HQs can use social control on their subsidiaries. This type of control varies in terms of the many terminologies it can entail, according to different scholars. For instance, social control is viewed as control by socialization (Edström and Galbraith, 1977), cultural control (Chang and Taylor, 1999), clan control (Ouchi, 1979), socialization (Nobel and Birkinshaw, 1998), shared values (Nohria and Ghoshal, 1994), social control (O'Donnell, 2000), among others. This type of control "involves the indoctrination of agents into principals' values and interest" (Chang and Taylor, 1999: 544). However, it is receiving relatively less attention than output and behavior control (Chang and Taylor, 1999). A central tenet of social control is to establish a shared set of values, objectives, and beliefs across MNC units (Nohria and Ghoshal, 1994; Björkman et al., 2004).

The corporate culture is considered to be a pattern of values, norms, beliefs and expectations shared by the organization's members (Schwartz and Davis, 1981). These patterns serve as adaptive and regulatory mechanisms and are an important guide to behavior and to explicit rules. In particular, social control can be effective when the use of behavior control or output control is difficult. For example, while it is impossible to monitor the behavior and output of a subsidiary effectively, the use of social control, which can align a subsidiary's activity in accordance with the HQ's intents by indoctrinating its value and norms, can be more effective in a case in which setting specific standards of behavior and output is difficult (Baliga and Jaeger, 1984). By looking at this dimension, this form of control is rather implicit, informal and coordinative compared with output and behavior control.

That is, implementing social control by dispatching an executive with home country nationality to a subsidiary and implanting shared values and norms can affect the capability building of the subsidiary. Such social control will promote informal communications between the headquarters and the subsidiary and enable intimate interactions. That is to say, social control influences the subsidiary through social interaction, which facilitates shared values and common understanding between the HQ and its subsidiary (Ouchi, 1979; Makhija and Ganesh, 1997). Social control requires a high amount of communication and interaction through organizational mechanisms, including various socialization methods such as rituals, ceremonies, and the creation of task forces (Makhija and Ganesh, 1997).

In other words, if headquarters utilizes social control against a foreign subsidiary, the communication between the headquarters and the subsidiary increases, instant interaction becomes possible, and ultimately it becomes convenient for headquarters to maintain an intimate relationship with the subsidiary (Ghoshal et al., 1994). An intimate relationship between the headquarters and the subsidiary provides an opportunity for members of headquarters and subsidiary to combine their own knowledge or develop new knowledge (Atuahene-Gima, 2003; McFadyen and Cannella, 2004). Moreover, it establishes legitimacy between the headquarters and the subsidiary and paves the way for the adoption of exploratory innovation (Subramaniam and Youndt, 2005). Therefore, if the headquarters imposes social control against its foreign subsidiary, it is expected to have a positive effect on the explorative capability of the foreign subsidiary.

First, an intimate relationship between the headquarters and the subsidiary helps to develop trust and cooperation among the employees of the headquarters and its subsidiary (Adler and Kwon, 2002; Walker et al., 1997). In addition, the implementation of social control not only increases knowledge of how to refine and improve the existing products, processes and markets by maintaining the intimate relationship between the headquarters and its subsidiary (Rowley et al., 2000), it also allows sharing of the experience of implementing the improvements to existing products, technology, and knowledge (Dyer and Nobeoka, 2000).

H3a. The use of social control exercised by an HQ will have a positive impact on the exploitative capability of a foreign subsidiary.

H3b. The use of social control as exercised by an HQ will have a positive impact on the explorative capability of a foreign subsidiary.

METHODS

Sample

The targeted subjects of this research are the subsidiaries of listed Korean MNCs that have penetrated into local foreign countries. The list of the sample firms was obtained through the Korchambiz website, operated by the Korea Chamber of Commerce and Industry and the Korea Exchange (KRX) homepage. Then, the information regarding the overseas legal entities of these listed companies was confirmed through the *2009/2010 Korean Overseas Business Directory* issued by Korea Trade-Investment Promotion Agency (KOTRA). This directory is a publication of the data obtained by direct investigations of Korean MNCS which have expanded abroad. It is compiled by the respective trade centers of KOTRA and lists information pertaining to the overseas subsidiaries of Korean MNCs that have set up subsidiaries in various countries across the globe (containing the name of Korean MNCs with overseas enterprises, addresses, phone numbers, fax numbers, dates of entry into the foreign country, mode of entry, number of employees, amount of investment, and other information). Through this process, a list of 2302 overseas subsidiaries of Korean listed companies that have made entry into 71 foreign countries was obtained, and these were targeted for the survey in the present research.

Data Collection

The data for this study were collected by means of surveys. The survey form was designed through the following procedure. First, the initial English version of the survey questionnaire was developed in order to check whether all questions on the questionnaire are valid, and then the initial draft was translated into Korean and then back translated into English by bilinguals. Through the process, we identified that the expression of all questions was designed properly. A pilot test was then conducted with five upper-level managers who had the status of a department manager or higher and who were employed in the Korean HQ of the company targeted for the survey. Their feedback was reflected in the modifications of the survey to finalize the survey form to be used in the investigation.

The survey was conducted in less than two months, from April 2010 to June 2010. The method of investigation included a variety of means, e-mails, fax, phone, and online survey systems. In order to increase the rate of response, phone calls were made to every company targeted for the examination to explain the purpose of the research and to request their response to the survey form. During this process, among the 2302 companies targeted for the survey, 56 companies – including those that had converted into independent companies rather than remaining as a foreign subsidiary of a Korean company due to changes in the shares of ownership and those which perform only as contact offices, deemed to be not in accordance with the purpose of the research – were excluded from the list of survey targets. Hence, the total number of surveyed companies was reduced to 2246. As a result of the implementation of the survey investigation, a total of 409 survey responses were collected up to June 2010 (a response rate of 18.21%). After excluding 11 cases of data unsuitable for inclusion in the analysis, the empirical analysis was conducted using the data from 398 subsidiaries. The regional distribution of the sample firms is indicated in Table 9.1. China was the source of 140 of the retrieved survey forms, constituting 34.2% of the total sample, and this was followed by the US and Vietnam. This indicates that the country distribution of the sample is similar to that of the initially selected population of the research, which consisted of 2302 research target groups.

Table 9.1   *Country distribution of sample firms*

Country	Population		Sample	
	Frequency	Percentage	Frequency	Percentage
China	708	30.8	140	34.2
US	286	12.4	58	14.2
Vietnam	122	5.3	27	6.6
Japan	119	5.2	18	4.4
Germany	64	2.8	13	3.2
Others	1003	43.5	153	37.4
Total	2302	100	409	100

MEASURES

The dependent variables in this research are the exploitative and explorative capability of the foreign subsidiaries of Korean MNCs. Drawing upon the study by He and Wong (2004) and Jansen et al. (2006), *exploitative capability* of the foreign subsidiaries was measured in terms of their capability of applying and adapting the Korean HQ's pre-existing (i) products and services, (ii) marketing and promotional methods, (iii) production methods, (iv) distribution and logistics methods, and (v) organizational management methods in a manner suited to the local conditions on a seven-point Likert-type scale. Based upon the study by He and Wong (2004) and Jansen et al. (2006), *explorative capability* was measured by a total of five questions covering the subsidiary's capability to develop (i) new products and services, (ii) new marketing techniques, (iii) new production methods, (iv) new distribution and logistics methods, and (v) new organizational management such as Human Resource Management methods which are different from those in the possession of the Korean HQ (e.g., those suited to the local conditions) on a seven-point Likert-type scale.

There are several independent variables used in this research. They are the types of control (i.e., output, behavior, and social control). The types of control in foreign subsidiaries were sub-categorized according to the method of Ouchi (1979) into output control, behavior control, and social control, and each type of control was measured on a scale of seven points, drawing upon the study by Aulakh and Gencturk (2000), Ramaswami (1996), Nobel and Birkinshaw (1998), and Chen et al. (2009). *Output control* was measured using a total of four items which posited the following cases: (i) HQs explicitly set managerial goals (e.g., sales, net profit, ROI) to be achieved in a quantitative manner, (ii) concrete managerial goals are established but the specific means by which they are achieved is delegated to the subsidiary, (iii) the degree of achievement of the managerial goals established by the HQ is directly related to the level of remuneration received by the employees of the subsidiary, and (iv) the subsidiary is evaluated by comparing the concrete goals established by the HQ against the performance outcome achieved by the subsidiary. *Behavior control* was measured by a total of four question items regarding the existence of (i) a presentation of concrete behavioral regulations, guidelines and procedures required to be followed by the subsidiary, (ii) continuous and attentive monitoring of the compliance of the subsidiary with the prescribed behavioral regulations, guidelines and procedures, (iii) demands for improvement in management methods to secure compliance with the prescribed behavioral regulations, guidelines and procedures in cases of a deficiency in compliance, and (iv) the perception of the degree of compliance with the prescribed behavioral regulations, guidelines and procedures as an important evaluative criterion. *Social control* was assessed with a total of four questions regarding whether (i) opportunities for meetings between the respective executive members of the HQ and the subsidiary were provided, (ii) training programs implemented at the level of the HQ were provided, (iii) the executive members of the subsidiary had previously had abundant work experience within the HQ, and also regarding (iv) the degree of comprehension regarding the culture or values of the HQ.

This study utilized the following control variables in its analysis to control the impact of other factors which potentially influence the dependent variables (i.e., explorative and exploitative capabilities) but are not directly associated with our research objective. *Subsidiary size* was measured according to the total number of employees in the foreign subsidiary. The value obtained through a natural logarithm was used. *Subsidiary age* was measured as the period of business operation by the foreign subsidiaries. It was calculated by summing the number of years from the year in which the company under examination initiated business operations locally up to the year 2010. The value acquired by a logarithm was utilized for the analysis. *HQ size* was measured according to the total number of employees in the HQ. In order to control for an industry effect on a foreign subsidiary, we controlled for *industry dummy*. A manufacturing dummy (MF dummy) was coded as '1' for manufacturing and '0' otherwise. *Ownership* of the HQ to the subsidiary was used as a control variable. The equity position of the HQ represents the committed resources from the HQ to the subsidiary. The higher the equity position, the greater the committed financial resources of the HQ to the subsidiary and the greater the control of the HQ to their subsidiary (Torbiörn, 1994).

Bias Testing

We conducted further analyses to check for potential non-response bias and common-method bias problems. First, the non-response bias was examined by means of an independent sample t-test comparing the two groups based upon the lengths of their period of business operation, numbers of their employees, and the amounts of investment. The results of the t-test revealed that the difference in average values for the length of the period of business operation, the scale of the company, and the amount of investment between the two groups were not statistically significant, demonstrating that the average between the respondents and non-respondents did not exhibit a large difference. Based upon the above analysis, the sample used in this research is judged to be properly representative of the population under examination in this study. Second, we tried to reduce the possibility of a common method bias problem by measuring each variable with a number of questions (Podsakoff and Organ, 1986). We also checked the common-method bias using Harman's one-factor test (Podsakoff and Organ, 1986), which loads all the perceptual items into an exploratory factor analysis. As a result of implementing this factor analysis in this study, not only was it possible to identify multiple factors having explanatory power, but it was also found that the factor with the greatest explanatory power constituted only 20.201% of the total variance. Hence it can be concluded that the problem posed by common method bias is not severe in this study (Podsakoff et al., 2003).

RESULTS

Descriptive Statistics and Quality of Measures

Prior to testing the hypothesis, the validity and reliability of the variables were analyzed first, and then the multiple regression analysis methodology was used to verify the hypothesis. We assess the construct validity of our measurements in several ways. First, exploratory factor analysis was performed to confirm the construct validity of independent variables that had been measured as multiple items. The factor analysis was derived by rotating the factors according to the varimax rotation method. The results obtained by rotating the factors following the varimax rotation method showed that there were five factors which had an eigenvalue of 1 or more, and that their cumulative variance was 71.542%. For the factor analysis, the Kaiser–Meyer–Olkin measure of sampling adequacy is 0.871, and Bartlett's test of sphericity is 8096.536 ($p<0.000$). Hence, the adequacy for this factor analysis shows a very high degree of adequacy.

We also checked for possible multicollinearity problems by inspecting variance inflation factors (VIF) and the Condition Index (CI). In particular, there was found to be a high correlation between each of the independent variables, including output control, behavior control, social control, HQs single support, and HQs double support, which indicated the possible presence of multicollinearity. In general, the possibility of multicollinearity can be ruled out as a concern if the values of the CI are lower than 30 and the VIF lower than 10 (Joseph et al., 1998). This research satisfies these criteria in all models, indicating that multicollinearity does not exist among the independent variables. Table 9.2 presents a descriptive statistics and correlation matrix.

Hypothesis Testing

Table 9.3 presents the result of the multiple regression analysis. The results from Model 1 to Model 4 show the regression analysis on the determinants of exploitative capability. In Model 1, which included only the control variables, it can be seen that the Subsidiary size ($p<0.05$), HQ size ($p<0.1$) and Industry Dummy (Electrics) have a positive effect on the exploitative capability of the subsidiary. Models 2, 3 and 4 were obtained by implementing regression analysis by sequentially including the independent variables (i.e., output control, behavior control and social control). All independent variables have significant positive effects on the building of exploitative capability ($p<0.001$). However, the result that output control has a positive effect on exploitative capability presented an opposite result, so H1a was not supported.

In the same manner, the results from Model 5 to Model 8 show the regression analysis on the determinants of explorative capability. Model 5 is the base model that examined the influence of control variables alone. Models 6, 7, and 8 were obtained by implementing regression analysis by sequentially including the independent variables.

Table 9.2   Descriptive statistics and correlation matrix

	(1)	(2)	(3)	(4)	(5)	(6)	(7)	(8)	(9)	(10)	(11)	(12)
(1) Explorative capability	1											
(2) Exploitative capability	0.480**	1										
(3) Subsidiary size	0.092	0.131**	1									
(4) Subsidiary age	0.098	0.109*	0.071	1								
(5) HQ size	0.101*	0.125*	0.211**	0.105*	1							
(6) Industry dummy (electronics)	−0.009	0.046	0.207**	0.104*	0.286**	1						
(7) Industry dummy (wholesales)	0.086	0.090	−0.113*	0.108*	−0.110*	−0.127*	1					
(8) Manufacturing dummy	−0.089	−0.005	0.258**	0.014	0.163**	0.275**	−0.463**	1				
(9) Ownership	0.010	−0.035	−0.038	0.034	−0.140**	0.050	−0.024	0.052	1			
(10) Output control	0.148**	0.248**	0.036	0.064	0.064	0.120*	0.069	−0.086	0.055	1		
(11) Behavior control	0.128*	0.279**	0.091	0.124*	0.139**	0.130**	0.120*	−0.084	0.008	0.607**	1	
(12) Social control	0.206**	0.248**	0.052	0.057	0.139**	0.109*	0.052	0.066	0.113*	0.452**	0.522**	1
MEAN	4.419	4.930	4.372	2.273	7.432	0.148	0.105	0.697	91.474	5.385	4.941	5.154
SD	1.166	1.000	1.824	0.740	1.740	0.355	0.307	0.460	18.237	1.252	1.384	1.125
MIN	1.000	1.000	2.302	0.693	2.890	0.000	0.000	0.000	0.000	1.000	1.000	1.000
MAX	7.000	7.000	9.105	7.606	11.352	1.000	1.000	1.000	100.0	7.000	7.000	7.000

Note. *p<0.05, **p<0.01.

In Model 5, which included only the control variables, it can be seen that the Subsidiary size ($p<0.05$) and HQ size ($p<0.05$) have a positive effect on the explorative capability of the subsidiary. On the other hand, Manufacturing dummy has a negative effect on the explorative capability of the subsidiary ($p<0.1$).

Models 6, 7 and 8 tested the effects of three types of control on the explorative capability of a subsidiary. Their outcomes confirmed that output control ($p<0.05$) and social control ($p<0.001$) have significantly positive influences on explorative capability, thus supporting *H1b* and *H3b*. However, behavior control was not found to have a significant influence on explorative capability. Therefore, *H2b* was not supported.

DISCUSSION AND CONCLUSION

Korean MNCs such as Samsung and LG have recently made notable achievements in the global market. Thus, it is worthy of investigating the factors behind their success from the HQ subsidiary capability building perspective. However, there has not yet been sufficient research into the internationalization of Korean MNCs which could offer an explanation in response to such inquiries. Although few studies have recently explored the impact of exploitative and explorative knowledge sharing within chaebol on the financial performance of Korean subsidiaries in China (e.g., Kang and Lee, 2017), we still do not know much about the link between the control and support types of Korean HQs and the distinctive capabilities of their overseas subsidiaries. An accurate understanding of the factors driving the recent success attained by Korean MNCs in global markets can provide a valuable reference for those MNCs from other newly industrialized economies. Furthermore, the results of this study help to design their control mechanisms within an MNC network, thus ensuring sustainable competitive advantage in the global market. As such, this research offers a deep insight into the development of the ambidextrous foreign subsidiary of Korean MNCs for sustainable growth and survival in overseas markets.

Analyzing 398 overseas subsidiaries of listed Korean MNCs located in 49 countries, this study examined factors that influence the development of both exploitative and explorative capabilities of the Korean MNCs' subsidiaries. The important role placed by the subsidiaries in successful internationalization has already received scholarly attention from IB researchers (Birkinshaw, 1997; Birkinshaw et al., 1998; Gupta and Govindarajan, 2000; Rugman and Verbeke, 2001; Frost et al., 2002). Such studies have emphasized the need for overseas subsidiaries to move beyond the limited function of selling the HQ products and services in the local area and to assume the role of centers of excellence to develop new core capabilities (Frost et al., 2002; Birkinshaw et al., 1998). In that vein, the results of this research serve as useful material for Korean MNCs when developing strategies for fostering outstanding overseas subsidiaries that can perform such roles. As shown in Table 9.3 (see Model 6, 7, and 8) the use of output and social control mechanisms facilitates explorative capability of the subsidiaries of Korean MNCs. This indicates that tight process control (i.e., behavioral control in the model) exercised by the HQ may not help in providing a subsidiary mandate for developing explorative capability. Thus, this study provides important insights into subsidiary federalism within an MNC network (Yamin and Forsgren, 2006; Andersson et al., 2015) and (break-through) innovation-creating subsidiary mandate literature (Cantwell and Mudambi, 2005; Dunlap-Hinkler et al., 2010).

Table 9.3   Determinants of explorative and exploitative capability

	Exploitative capability				Explorative capability			
Control variables	Model 1	Model 2	Model 3	Model 4	Model 5	Model 6	Model 7	Model 8
Subsidiary size	0.116*	0.108*	0.096†	0.114*	0.105*	0.100†	0.098†	0.103*
Subsidiary age	0.079	0.070	0.057	0.074	0.078	0.073	0.070	0.074
HQ size	0.102†	0.091†	0.074	0.071	0.108*	0.102†	0.098†	0.081
Industry dummy (electronics)	-2.92E-4	-0.031	-0.029	-0.013	-0.037	-0.054	-0.047	-0.047
Industry dummy (wholesales)	0.104†	0.095	0.081	0.079	0.050	0.045	0.041	0.029
Manufacturing dummy	-0.003	0.026	0.027	-0.019	-0.104†	-0.088	-0.093	-0.117*
Ownership	-0.016	-0.031	-0.021	-0.045	0.034	0.026	0.032	0.009
Independent variables								
Output control		0.234***				0.128*		
Behavior control			0.249***				0.090	
Social control				0.231***				0.196***
R^2	0.047	0.099	0.104	0.097	0.042	0.058	0.050	0.079
Adjusted R^2	0.029	0.081	0.086	0.079	0.025	0.039	0.030	0.060
ΔR^2		0.053***	0.058***	0.051***		0.016*	0.008†	0.037***
F	2.718**	5.362***	5.666***	5.239***	2.466*	2.999**	2.553**	4.152***
N	398	398	398	398	398	398	398	398

Note: Standardized regression coefficients are reported. † $p<0.1$, * $p<0.05$, ** $p<0.01$, *** $p<0.001$.

Taking the notion of Marchian capability, this study conceptually distinguishes the explorative capability from the exploitative capability at a subsidiary level. In so doing, it delves deeply into the development of capability building mechanisms of subsidiaries within an MNC network. Such a distinction applies the core perspective of organizational learning theory, which posits that a balance must be reached between the exploration and exploitation of knowledge to secure the growth and survival of a company (He and Wong, 2004; Jansen et al., 2006; Hsu et al., 2013; Kang and Lee, 2017). Although numerous previous studies on the development of subsidiary capability exist, preceding researchers defined the capabilities of subsidiaries only in very general and abstract terms, and the definitions of the capability of subsidiaries varied greatly depending on the researcher, leading to confusion. In contrast, this study has defined the capabilities of a subsidiary in accordance with the widely accepted principles of organizational learning theory, verifying these through practically applied research. This work is thereby expected to contribute to the development of a more universal and useful theory regarding the capabilities of subsidiaries.

Limitations and Future Research

The limitations of the current research can be identified as follows. First, although this study has distinguished the capabilities of the overseas subsidiary into exploitative capability and explorative capability and illuminated the factors that influence these two forms of capabilities according to the perspective of organizational learning theory, the targets of its analysis were restricted to the overseas subsidiaries of Korean listed companies, and hence there would be some difficulty in arguing that the results of this analysis are applicable to the overseas subsidiaries of companies from other countries. To overcome this constraint and to develop a more universal theory regarding the development of the capabilities of overseas subsidiaries, it will be necessary to apply the theoretical model presented by this research to the overseas subsidiaries belonging to other countries. Second, the current research relied upon only one individual respondent from each subsidiary when collecting its data, thus making it difficult to exclude the possibility that the subjective opinions of individuals may have distorted the analytical results. To address this problem, data should be collected from multiple respondents from each subsidiary. Lastly, this study used cross-sectional survey data that did not therefore take the dynamic aspects of the development of capabilities by overseas subsidiaries into consideration. Although it was established that the present research has demonstrated that the form of control exercised by the HQ and the environmental features of the local country do have significant effects on the explorative and exploitative capabilities of its overseas subsidiaries, this result may have a fragmented characteristic. The factors that impact the overseas subsidiaries' capabilities are more complex, and it is highly probable that they have a dynamic characteristic. Hence, for a more sophisticated analysis, longitudinal data should be accumulated and subject to additional analyses. Such attempts will lend clearer insight into the capabilities development of overseas subsidiaries.

NOTE

1. March (1991: 85) attested to this characteristic as follows:
   The essence of exploitation is the refinement and extension of existing competences, technologies, and paradigms. Its returns are positive, proximate, and predictable. The essence of exploration is

experimentation with new alternatives. Its returns are uncertain, distant, and often negative. Thus, the distance in time and space between the locus of learning and the locus for the realization of returns is generally greater in the case of exploration than in the case of exploitation, as is the uncertainty. Such features of the context of adaptation lead to a tendency to substitute exploitation of known alternatives for the exploration of unknown ones, to increase the reliability of performance rather more than its mean. This property of adaptive processes is potentially self-destructive.

REFERENCES

Adler, P. S. and Kwon, S. (2002). "Social Capital: Prospects for a New Concept," *Academy of Management Review*, 27(1): 17–40.

Andersson, U. and Forsgren, M. (1996). "Subsidiary Embeddedness and Control in the Multinational Corporation," *International Business Review*, 5(5): 487–508.

Andersson, U., Björkman, I. and Forsgren, M. (2005). "Managing Subsidiary Knowledge Creation: The Effect of Control Mechanisms on Subsidiary Local Embeddedness," *International Business Review*, 14(5): 521–538.

Andersson, U., Forsgren, M. and Holm, U. (2015). "Balancing Subsidiary Influence in the Federative MNC: A Business Network View." In: *Knowledge, Networks and Power*. London: Palgrave Macmillan: 393–420

Atuahene-Gima, K. (2003). "The Effects of Centrifugal and Centripetal Forces on Product Development Speed and Quality: How does Problem Solving Matter?" *Academy of Management Journal*, 46(3): 359–374.

Aulakh, P. S. and Gencturk, E. F. (2000). "International Principal-Agent Relationships: Control, Governance and Performance," *Industrial Marketing Management*, 29(6): 521–538.

Bachmann, R. (2001). "Trust, Power and Control in Trans-organizational Relations," *Organization Studies*, 22(2): 337–365.

Baliga, B. R. and Jaeger, A. M. (1984). "Multinational Corporations: Control Systems and Delegation Issues," *Journal of International Business Studies*, Fall: 25–40.

Bartlett, C. A. and Ghoshal, S. (1989). *Managing Across Borders: The Transnational Solution*. Boston. MA: Harvard Business School Press.

Bartlett, C. A. and Ghoshal, S. (2000). *Transnational Management: Text, Cases and Readings in Cross-Border Management* (3rd edition). Boston: Irwin/McGraw-Hill.

Birkinshaw, J. (1997). "Entrepreneurship in Multinational Corporations: The Characteristics of Subsidiary Initiatives," *Strategic Management Journal*, 18(3): 207–229.

Birkinshaw, J. and Hood, N. (1998). "Multinational Subsidiary Evolution: Capability and Charter Change in Foreign-Owned Subsidiary Companies," *Academy of Management Review*, 23(4): 773–795.

Birkinshaw, J., Hood, N. and Jonsson, S. (1998). "Building Firm-Specific Advantages in Multinational Corporations: The Role of Subsidiary Initiative," *Strategic Management Journal*, 19(3): 221–241.

Birkinshaw, J. and Morrison, A. J. (1995). "Configurations of Strategy and Structure in Subsidiary of Multinational Corporations," *Journal of International Business Studies*, 26(4): 729–753.

Björkman, I., Barner-Rasmussen, W. and Li, L. (2004). "Managing Knowledge Transfer in MNCs: The Impact of Headquarters Control Mechanisms," *Journal of International Business Studies*, 35(5): 443–455.

Cantwell, J. and Mudambi, R. (2005). "MNE Competence-creating Subsidiary Mandates," *Strategic Management Journal*, 26(12): 1109–1128.

Chang, E. and Taylor, M. S. (1999). "Control in Multinational Corporations (MNCs): The Case of Korean Manufacturing Subsidiaries," *Journal of Management*, 25(4): 541–565.

Chang, S. J. and Rosenzweig, P. M. (2009). "Subsidiary Capability Development in Multinational Enterprises: An Empirical Investigation". In Cheng, J. L and Hitt, M. (Eds.), *Managing Subsidiary Dynamics: Headquarters Role, Capability Development, and China Strategy*. JAI Press.

Chen, D., Park, S. H. and Newburry, W. (2009). "Parent Contribution and Organizational Control in International Joint Ventures," *Strategic Management Journal*, 30(11): 1133–1156.

Doz, Y. and Prahalad, C. K. (1981). "Headquarters Influence and Strategic Control in MNCs," *Sloan Management Review*, Fall 1981: 15–29.

Dunlap-Hinkler, D., Kotabe, M. and Mudambi, R. (2010). "A Story of Breakthrough versus Incremental Innovation: Corporate Entrepreneurship in the Global Pharmaceutical Industry," *Strategic Entrepreneurship Journal*, 4(2): 106–127.

Dunning, J. H. (1988). "The Eclectic Paradigm of International Production: A Restatement and Some Possible Extensions," *Journal of International Business Studies*, 19(1): 1–31.

Dyer, J. H. and Nobeoka, K. (2000). "Creating and Managing a High-Performance Knowledge-Sharing Network: The Toyota Case," *Strategic Management Journal*, 21(3): 345–367.

Edström, A. and Galbraith, J. R. (1977). "Transfer of Managers as a Coordination and Control Strategy in Multinational Organizations," *Administrative Science Quarterly*, 22(2): 248–263.

Egelhoff, W. G. (1984). "Patterns of Control in US, UK, and European Multinational Corporations," *Journal of International Business Studies*, 15(2): 73–83.

Egelhoff, W. G. (1988). *Organizing the Multinational Enterprise: An Information Processing Perspective.* Ballinger, MA: Cambridge.

Frost, T., Birkinshaw, J. and Ensign, P. (2002). "Centers of Excellence in Multinational Corporations," *Strategic Management Journal*, 23(11): 997–1018.

Geringer, J. M. and Hebert, L. (1989). "Control and Performance of International Joint Venture," *Journal of International Business Studies*, 20(2): 235–254.

Ghemawat, P. and Ricart I Costa, J. E. (1993). "The Organizational Tension between Static and Dynamic Efficiency," *Strategic Management Journal*, 14(S2): 59–73.

Ghoshal, S. and Bartlett, C. A. (1990). "The Multinational Corporation as an Interorganizational Network," *Academy of Management Review*, 15(4): 603–625.

Ghoshal, S., Korine, H. and Szulanski, G. (1994). "Interunit Communication in Multinational Corporations," *Management Science*, 40(1): 96–110.

Ghoshal, S. and Nohria, N. (1989). "Internal Differentiation within Multinational Corporations," *Strategic Management Journal*, 10(4): 323–337.

Gupta, A. K. and Govindarajan, V. (1991). "Knowledge Flows and the Structure of Control within Multinational Corporations," *Academy of Management Review*, 16(4): 768–792.

Gupta, A. and Govindarajan, V. (2000). "Knowledge Flows within Multinational Corporations," *Strategic Management Journal*, 21(4): 473–496.

He, Z. and Wong, P. (2004). "Exploration vs. Exploitation: An Empirical Test of the Ambidexterity Hypothesis," *Organization Science*, 15(4): 481–494.

Holmqvist, M. (2004). "Experiential Learning Processes of Exploration and Exploitation within and between Organizations: An Empirical Study of Product Development," *Organization Science*, 15(1): 70–81.

Hsu, C., Lien, Y. and Chen, H. (2013). "International Ambidexterity and Firm Performance in Small Emerging Economies," *Journal of World Business*, 48(1): 58–67.

Hymer, S. H. (1976). *The International Operations of National Firms: A Study of Direct Foreign Investment.* Cambridge, MA: The MIT Press.

Jansen, J. J. P., Van Den Bosch, F. A. J. and Volberda, H. W. (2006). "Exploratory Innovation, Exploitative Innovation, and Performance: Effects of organizational antecedents and environmental moderators," *Management Science*, 52(11): 1661–1674.

John, G. (1984). "An Empirical Investigation of Some Antecedents of Opportunism in a Marketing Channel," *Journal of Marketing Research*, 21(3): 278–289.

Joseph, F. H., Rolph, E. A., Ronald, L. T. and William, C. B. (1998). *Multivariate Data Analysis.* Prentice Hall.

Kang, J. and Lee, J. Y. (2017). "Performance Effects of Explorative and Exploitative Knowledge Sharing within Korean Chaebol MNEs in China," *International Journal of Technology Management*, 74(1–4): 70–95.

Katila, R. and Ahuja, G. (2002). "Something Old, Something New: A Longitudinal Study of Search Behavior and New Product Introduction," *Academy of Management Journal*, 45(6): 1183–1194.

Levinthal, D. A. and March, J. G. (1993). "The Myopia of Learning," *Strategic Management Journal*, 14(S2): 95–112.

Lew, Y. K. and Sinkovics, R. R. (2013). "Crossing Borders and Industry Sectors: Behavioral Governance in Strategic Alliances and Product Innovation for Competitive Advantage," *Long Range Planning*, 46(1–2), 13–38.

Lew, Y. K., Sinkovics, R. R. and Kuivalainen, O. (2013). "Upstream Internationalization Process: Roles of Social Capital in Creating Exploratory Capability and Market Performance," *International Business Review*, 22(6): 1101–1120.

Luo, Y. (2002). "Capability Exploitation and Building in a Foreign Market: Implications for Multinational Enterprises," *Organization Science*, 13(1): 48–63.

Luo, Y. and Rui, H. (2009). "An Ambidexterity Perspective Toward Multinational Enterprises from Emerging Economies," *The Academy of Management Perspectives*, 23(4), 49–70.

Makhija, M. and Ganesh, U. (1997). "The Relationship between Control and Partner Learning in Learning-related Joint Ventures," *Organization Science*, 8(5): 508–527.

Makino, S. and Inkpen, A. G. (2003). "Knowledge Seeking FDI and Learning across Borders." In Easterby-Smith, M. and Lyles, M. A. (Eds.), *The Blackwell Handbook of Organizational Learning and Knowledge Management*. MA: Blackwell Publishers: 233–252.

Makino, S., Lau, C. M. and Yeh, R. S. (2002). "Asset-exploitation Versus Asset-seeking: Implications for Location Choice of Foreign Direct Investment from Newly Industrialized Economies," *Journal of International Business Studies*, 33(3): 403–421.

March, J. G. (1991). "Exploration and Exploitation in Organizational Learning," *Organization Science*, 2(1): 71–87.

McFadyen, M. A. and Cannella, A. A. (2004). "Social Capital and Knowledge Creation: Diminishing Returns of the Number and Strength of Exchange Relationships," *Academy of Management Journal*, 47(5): 735–746.

Nobel, R. and Birkinshaw, J. (1998). "Innovation in Multinational Corporations: Control and Communication Patterns in International R&D Operations," *Strategic Management Journal*, 19(5): 479–496.

Nohria, N. and Ghoshal, S. (1994). "Differentiated Fit and Shared Values: Alternatives for Managing Headquarters-Subsidiary Relations," *Strategic Management Journal*, 15(6): 491–502.

O'Donnell, S. (2000). "Managing Foreign Subsidiaries: Agents of Headquarters, or an Interdependent Network?" *Strategic Management Journal*, 21(5): 525–548.

O'Reilly, C. A. and Tushman, M. L. (2013). "Organizational Ambidexterity: Past, Present and Future," *Academy of Management Perspectives*, 27(4): 324–338.

Ouchi, W. G. (1979). "A Conceptual Framework for the Design of Organizational Control Mechanisms," *Management Science*, 25(9): 833–848.

Park, B. I. and Ghauri, P. N. (2011). "Key factors affecting acquisition of technological capabilities from foreign acquiring firms in small and medium sized local firms," *Journal of World Business*, 46: 116–125.

Park, B. I. and Choi, J. (2014). "Foreign Direct Investment Motivations and Knowledge Acquisition from Multinational Enterprises in Overseas Subsidiaries," *Canadian Journal of Administrative Sciences*, 31: 104–115.

Podsakoff, P. M. and Organ, D. (1986). "Self-Reports in Organizational Research: Problems and Prospects," *Journal of Management*, 12(4): 531–544.

Podsakoff, P. M., MacKenzie, S. B., Lee, J. Y. and Podsakoff, N. P. (2003). "Common Method Biases in Behavioral Research: A Critical Review of the Literature and Recommended Remedies," *Journal of Applied Psychology*, 88(5): 879–903.

Ramaswami, S. N. (1996). "Marketing Controls and Dysfunctional Employee Behaviors: A Test of Traditional and Contingency Theory Postulates," *Journal of Marketing*, 60(2): 105–120.

Rosenzweig, P. M. and Singh, J. V. (1991). "Organizational Environments and the Multinational Enterprise," *Academy of Management Review*, 16(2): 340–361.

Roth, K. and Nigh, D. (1992). "The Effectiveness of Headquarters-Subsidiary Relationships: The Role of Coordination, Control, and Conflict," *Journal of Business Research*, 25(4): 277–301.

Rowley, T., Behrens, D. and Krackhardt, D. (2000). "Redundant Governance Structures: An Analysis of Structural and Relational Embeddedness in the Steel and Semiconductor Industries," *Strategic Management Journal*, 21(3): 369–386.

Rugman, A. M. and Verbeke, A. (1992). "A Note on the Transnational Solution and the Transaction Cost Theory on Multinational Strategic Management," *Journal of International Business Studies*, 23(4): 761–771.

Rugman, A. M. and Verbeke, A. (2001). "Subsidiary-specific Advantages in Multinational Enterprises," *Strategic Management Journal*, 22(3): 237–250.

Schwartz, H. and Davis, S. M. (1981). "Matching Corporate Culture and Business Strategy," *Organisational Dynamics*, summer: 30–48.

Siggelkow, N. and Levinthal, D. (2003). "Temporarily Divide to Conquer: Centralized, Decentralized, and Reintegrated Organizational Approaches to Exploration and Adaptation," *Organization Science*, 14(6): 650–669.

Simsek, Z. (2009). "Organizational Ambidexterity: Towards a Multilevel Understanding," *Journal of Management Studies*, 46(4): 597–624.

Subramaniam, M. and Youndt, M. A. (2005). "The Influence of Intellectual Capital on the Types of Innovative Capabilities," *Academy of Management Journal*, 48(3): 450–463.

Tallman, S. (1991). "Strategic Management Models and Resource-Based Strategies among MNEs in a Host Market," *Strategic Management Journal*, 12(4): 69–82.

Tallman, S. (2001). "Global Strategic Management." In Hitt, M. A., Freeman, R. E. and Harrison, J. S. (Eds.), *The Blackwell Handbook of Strategic Management*. MA: Blackwell Publishers: 464–490.

Tannenbaum, A. S. (1968). *Control in Organizations*. New York: McGraw-Hill.

Torbiörn, I. (1994). "Dynamics of Cross-Cultural Adaptation." In Althen, G. (Ed.). *Learning Across Cultures*. Washington, DC: NAFSA Publications.

Uotila, J., Maula, M. Keil, T. and Zahra, S. A. (2009). "Exploration, Exploitation, and Financial Performance: Analysis of S&P 500 Corporations," *Strategic Management Journal*, 30(2): 221–231.

Vernon, R. (1966). "International Investments and International Trade in the Product Cycle," *Quarterly Journal of Economics*, 80(2), 190–207.

Walker, G., Kogut, B. and Shan, W. (1997). "Social Capital, Structural Holes, and the Formation of Industry Network," *Organization Science*, 8(2): 109–125.

Werner, S. (2002). "Recent Developments in International Management Research: A Review of 20 Top Management Journals," *Journal of Management*, 28(3): 277–305.

Wernerfelt, B. (1984). "A Resource Based View of the Firm," *Strategic Management Journal*, 5(2): 171–180.

Williams, C. (2007). "Transfer in Context: Replication and Adaptation in Knowledge Transfer Relationships," *Strategic Management Journal*, 28(9): 867–889.

Yamin, M. and Forsgren, M. (2006). "Hymer's Analysis of the Multinational Organization: Power Retention and the Demise of the Federative MNE," *International Business Review*, 15(2): 166–179.

10. Utilization of subsidiary knowledge in multinational enterprises: revisiting the SECI model

Jong Min Lee

INTRODUCTION

Over the past decades, multinational enterprises (MNEs) have become knowledge-driven, and the global leveraging of knowledge has been flagged as a crucial source of competitive advantage of MNEs (Meyer et al., 2011; Narula & Lee, 2020). New competences are increasingly developed at the subsidiary level (Birkinshaw & Hood, 1998; Rugman & Verbeke, 2001). MNEs have become "meta-integrators" (Narula, 2014) or "orchestrators" (Pitelis & Teece, 2018) that seek to combine and leverage the knowledge assets of a variety of subsidiaries together. The ability of headquarters to manage and utilize subsidiary-created knowledge[1] in multiple locations has become an important competitive advantage of modern MNEs (Lee et al., 2021; Verbeke, 2009).

Studies have examined how MNEs leverage and utilize subsidiary-created knowledge across the MNE network. In particular, researchers have drawn attention to the "unconventional" knowledge flows from a subsidiary to its parent firm (Yang et al., 2008), facilitated or impeded by a variety of factors, such as willingness and capabilities of sending and receiving units (Minbaeva et al., 2003; Rabbiosi & Santangelo, 2013), knowledge attributes (Schulz, 2001), and organizational practices (Liu & Meyer, 2020; Rabbiosi, 2011). The literature has also addressed some important issues associated with subsidiary-created knowledge utilization (SKU), such as the role of headquarters' attention (Bouquet & Birkinshaw, 2008; Plourde et al., 2014) and knowledge search (Monteiro & Birkinshaw, 2017; Monteiro et al., 2008), changes in the mandate of the subsidiary (Rugman et al., 2011), and the degree of internal and external embeddedness of the subsidiary (Ciabuschi et al., 2014; Narula, 2014; Yamin & Andersson, 2011).

Although these studies have provided important insights into the knowledge management in MNEs, little research has been directed to the overall process of SKU. The literature has suggested that the utilization of subsidiary knowledge across the MNE network requires at least four sequential processes: (i) identifying subsidiary knowledge that is relevant to MNE activities and potentially beneficial to MNEs (Ambos et al., 2006); (ii) transferring identified knowledge back to headquarters (i.e., reverse knowledge transfer) (Yang et al., 2008); (iii) modifying reverse-transferred knowledge or integrating it with existing assets to be utilizable in the wider context (Narula, 2014; Verbeke, 2009); and (iv) diffusing and exploiting new integrated knowledge assets across foreign markets. Although these four processes conclude one complete cycle of SKU across the MNE network, the literature has typically examined these processes separately rather than jointly. The entire process of SKU has rarely been addressed in the literature. Moreover, much of the literature has revealed that transferring and utilizing knowledge across different locations involves a variety of transformations of knowledge (Hedlund & Nonaka, 1993), including adaption, decontextualization, recontextualization, and internalization by the recipient unit (Jensen & Szulanski, 2004; Kostova, 1999). Yet, to date, few studies have considered how knowledge created by the subsidiary is transformed during its utilization.

This chapter aims to fill these gaps by examining the holistic process of SKU and the associated knowledge transformation. Drawing on organizational knowledge creation theory and the SECI (Socialization-Externalization-Combination-Internalization) model that explain how new knowledge is created and shared throughout the organization (Nonaka, 1991; Nonaka & Takeuchi, 1995), this chapter argues that SKU can be framed as a process of new knowledge amplification across organizational boundaries between headquarters and subsidiaries. The study also addresses knowledge management strategies (i.e., personalization strategy and codification strategy) used by headquarters and subsidiaries during the process of SKU (Hansen et al., 1999). The relations between headquarters and subsidiaries become more complex, and so do their goals, capabilities, and functions in the course of SKU (Mudambi & Navarra, 2004; Nohria & Ghoshal, 1994). It is crucial to understand the interdependence between headquarters and subsidiaries because they must work together to utilize subsidiary knowledge across the MNE network.

This chapter makes several contributions. First, it provides a comprehensive explanation of SKU in MNEs by pointing to a series of activities conducted by both headquarters and subsidiaries. Second, it extends the SECI model to MNEs by exploring how subsidiary-created knowledge is shared and utilized across organizational boundaries between headquarters and subsidiaries. Finally, it provides an in-depth look at MNE knowledge management by addressing various strategies employed by headquarters and subsidiaries.

This chapter begins with a discussion of the SECI model in organizational knowledge creation theory. Next, it describes two types of organizational knowledge management strategies used by headquarters and subsidiaries. It then builds on the SECI model to explain the holistic process of SKU, suggesting that headquarters and subsidiaries play different roles and engage in different processes in the SECI model. Finally, it discusses the implications of these insights and provides future research directions.

ORGANIZATIONAL KNOWLEDGE CREATION THEORY: THE SECI MODEL

The prime argument of organizational knowledge creation theory (Nonaka & Takeuchi, 1995; Nonaka & von Krogh, 2009) is that the subject that creates new knowledge in an organization is not an organization itself, but a group of employees who belong to it. Individuals are invariably affected by the surrounding environment and social structure, and they consistently recreate their environments through social interactions (Giddens, 1984). Nonaka and colleagues have argued that organizational knowledge is created through "continuous and dynamic interactions between tacit and explicit knowledge" possessed by organization members who consistently interact with their environments. They explained that such interactions take place in four different forms of knowledge conversion, namely, socialization, externalization, combination, and internalization (SECI), which have different attributes of input and output knowledge (Nonaka, 1991; Nonaka & Takeuchi, 1995; Nonaka & Toyama, 2003; Nonaka et al., 2006).

The SECI model references two forms of knowledge. Tacit or procedural knowledge refers to the knowledge embedded in human actions, procedures, skills, and routines such as know-how (Anderson, 1996; Polanyi, 1966). Often, people cannot explain their know-how and skills or reduce them to mere words although they obviously know how to do something (Nickols, 2000); therefore, tacit knowledge is often difficult to articulate or codify explicitly, which makes the transfer of tacit knowledge to other people costly and difficult (Nonaka & Takeuchi, 1995). By contrast, explicit or declarative knowledge refers to the knowledge that is articulable or codifiable as text, for example, product specifications (Anderson, 1996). Explicit knowledge is, therefore, relatively easy to transfer to other people as it typically comprises descriptions of facts, information, and methods.

Based on the difference between tacit and explicit knowledge, organizational knowledge creation theory argues that new knowledge creation begins with "socialization" that refers to the process of acquiring new tacit knowledge by individuals in an organization through shared experiences in daily social interactions. For example, one can learn and share the tacit knowledge of customers, suppliers, and even competitors by empathizing with them through shared experience. Organizational routines are part of tacit knowledge because they are developed in close interaction between organization members over time. Tacit knowledge is then translated into explicit knowledge through the process of "externalization." Some tacit knowledge can be made explicit through dialogue and reflection by organization members. This knowledge is then shared with other members to become the basis of new knowledge such as concepts, images, and written documents. Explicit knowledge is collected from inside and outside the organization, then combined, edited, or processed to form more sophisticated and systematic explicit knowledge through the "combination" process. The new explicit knowledge is then disseminated to organization members through communication networks. The shared new explicit knowledge is then converted into tacit knowledge by the users, when it is applied and used in practical situations. This process is referred to as "internalization." Specifically, explicit knowledge, such as product concepts or manufacturing procedures, must be actualized through action, practice, and reflection of individuals. Through the internalization process, organization members can embody explicit knowledge as their tacit knowledge. The four modes of knowledge conversion constitute a knowledge spiral in which knowledge is amplified and expanded horizontally and vertically, even beyond the organizational boundaries (see Nonaka & Toyama, 2003, for a detailed review).

Previous studies typically adopted a bipolar classification of tacit and explicit knowledge (Kogut & Zander, 1992). Although this distinction is useful, it often fails to reflect the true complexity of knowledge, because knowledge often contains both tacit and explicit components (Howells, 2000). Moreover, the literature identifies tacit knowledge with an inability to articulate and communicate it. Some scholars, however, regard tacit knowledge as "not yet explicated" knowledge, implying that knowledge exists on a continuum ranging from tacit to explicit, rather than as a dichotomy (Nonaka & von Krogh, 2009; Spender, 1996). It has also been argued that what is regarded as tacit knowledge is, in practice, "unarticulated" knowledge whose codebook and contents are implicit but have been thoroughly and exclusively internalized by the group of knowers (Cowan et al., 2000). Therefore, organization members who share the same codebook can articulate the knowledge that is seen as tacit only to outside observers (Håkanson, 2007). This chapter postulates that the SECI model is more suitably aligned with this perception of knowledge attributes than with the dichotomous division into tacit and explicit knowledge, so that in the process of conversion, knowledge moves along the tacit–explicit continuum rather than being transformed into its counterparts.

ORGANIZATIONAL KNOWLEDGE MANAGEMENT STRATEGY

Organizations can utilize two types of knowledge management strategies: personalization and codification (Hansen et al., 1999). Personalization strategy refers to a mechanism of storing knowledge in individuals or organization members who developed it. In this case, knowledge is closely tied to the individuals and embedded in their skills and problem-solving abilities. This knowledge is tacit and not easily transferable to others. It tends to be working knowledge that is relevant to the members' current work and that involves a high level of customization (Haesli & Boxall, 2005; Kumar & Ganesh, 2011). Organizations adopting a personalization strategy endeavor to promote direct interaction between organization members to facilitate knowledge exchange within the organization. For example, they typically use corporate databases and department specifications to provide information about who has what expertise. Organizing communities of practice (Brown & Duguid, 1991; Lave & Wenger, 1991) and providing shared physical and virtual spaces for organization members (Nonaka & Konno, 1998) are also common practices of the personalization strategy (Kumar & Ganesh, 2011).

By contrast, codification strategy refers to a mechanism of storing knowledge in organizational repositories. This strategy allows organization members to search and retrieve knowledge without having to contact the individuals who originally developed it. A codification strategy makes it possible to scale knowledge reuse. Organizations collect knowledge from individuals that is potentially usable in other contexts. They codify the selected knowledge and store it in their repositories. During the codification process, the concrete contexts of the knowledge tend to be discarded to make it applicable in wider contexts (Schulz, 2001). This enables organization members to retrieve necessary knowledge with fewer of the constraints ensuing from direct interaction with knowledge sources (Hansen et al., 1999).

By adopting a personalization mechanism, organizations can effectively retain original (tacit) knowledge to help them achieve rich information sharing and effective problem-solving. A personalization strategy, however, incurs high costs for knowledge sharing in time and accessibility because it requires direct interaction between knowledge sources and recipients. Moreover, organizations are at high risk of losing valuable knowledge with the loss of members (e.g., retirement, separation) (Chai et al., 2003; Droege & Hoobler, 2003). Alternatively, a codification strategy enables organizations to retain knowledge despite the loss of employees, but it may cause a problem of information overload, that is, the accretion of unused knowledge (Schulz & Jobe, 2001). It also requires substantial investment in establishing and maintaining corporate knowledge repositories (Earl, 2001). Because a codification mechanism deals with explicit or codified knowledge that is highly mobile and imitable, it involves relatively higher risks of knowledge leakage to competitors (Jasimuddin et al., 2005) and of knowledge loss during the process of codification (Mudambi, 2002). Last, with a codification strategy, knowledge users may obtain necessary knowledge quickly and relatively easily, but they often need to modify and adapt the retrieved knowledge to fit the circumstances of use (Hansen et al., 1999).

KNOWLEDGE MANAGEMENT STRATEGIES AT MNES: DUAL MECHANISM

Although firms may employ both personalization and codification strategies at the same time, they generally use one knowledge management strategy predominantly, based on their strategic orientation, and use the other in a supportive manner (Gammelgaard & Ritter, 2005; Haesli & Boxall, 2005; Hansen et al., 1999; Kim et al., 2014). Some firms resort to a mixed knowledge management strategy to align with a variety of contingencies, such as the attributes of knowledge (Jasimuddin et al., 2005; Mukherji, 2005), external environment changes (Kim et al., 2014), and organizational changes (Imran et al., 2016). Firms can also follow a dynamic approach. They begin by employing one knowledge management strategy predominantly, gradually expanding the other strategy over time (Kumar & Ganesh, 2011; Scheepers et al., 2004).

This chapter argues that in the case of MNEs, headquarters and subsidiaries adopt different knowledge management strategies, as they have different roles and capabilities (Nohria & Ghoshal, 1994). Although headquarters and subsidiaries may, to some extent, use both personalization and codification strategies simultaneously, headquarters predominantly prefer codification over personalization, whereas subsidiaries are more likely to rely on personalization.

Subsidiaries are embedded in the host country environment. Subsidiary employees acquire and create new knowledge through direct experience in the local environment and direct interaction with various local actors, including customers, institutions, suppliers, distributors, and even competitors (Andersson et al., 2002; Birkinshaw, 1997). By nature, this knowledge is tacit, as it is embodied in individuals who developed it or embedded in their routines, mostly in uncodified form. Subsidiary employees can exchange or share this knowledge relatively easily through face-to-face interaction, as they reside in the same location and work in the same environment where the knowledge is developed. Therefore, it is less required of subsidiary members to convert tacit knowledge into explicit forms and store it in a repository system to share the knowledge with other members. Instead, repository systems can be used to help individuals link with each other and exchange information about the source of knowledge. Moreover, codifying tacit into explicit knowledge and maintaining knowledge-storing repositories are generally costly and require extensive resources (Chai & Nebus, 2012). Given that many subsidiaries typically possess fewer resources than those available at headquarters, the costs of adopting a codification strategy may exceed its benefits. Therefore, MNE subsidiaries are more likely to adopt a personalization rather than a codification strategy to manage their knowledge.

Headquarters, however, tend to predominantly use a codification strategy over a personalization one. MNEs expand abroad to exploit their proprietary knowledge (i.e., ownership advantages or firm-specific advantages) in foreign markets (Buckley & Casson, 1976; Dunning, 1980). Such firm-specific knowledge is initially created by the direct interaction and experiences of headquarters employees in the home country environment. This knowledge is naturally embedded in individuals who created it at headquarters. In the early period, firms are likely to rely on a personalization strategy to manage their knowledge. But when they expand abroad to exploit their knowledge in foreign markets, they often need to adapt or recontextualize their knowledge to fit local environments (Bartlett & Ghoshal, 1989; Szulanski & Jensen, 2006). Firms can still manage their knowledge across borders using a personalization strategy if they have a small number of subsidiaries. Transferring managers or expatriates to foreign subsidiaries has long been considered an effective way to manage firm-specific knowledge across borders (Chang et al., 2012; Hocking et al., 2007; Kawai & Chung, 2019; Lee, 2019). Yet a personalization strategy may not be able to provide a sustainable option when firms expand into many different markets. MNE headquarters that simultaneously manage a large number of subsidiaries face an incentive to codify their knowledge and store it in a corporate repository for quick access and wide use in many locations, and for the potential use of knowledge in a new location (Chai & Nebus, 2012). Given that a codification strategy enables firms to share knowledge across borders without direct contacts with knowledge sources (i.e., between headquarters and subsidiaries), codification becomes a more reasonable knowledge management strategy for MNE headquarters that simultaneously deal with various business activities dispersed in many different locations and time zones. Therefore, together with the growth and expansion of the MNE, headquarters tend to rely more on a codification strategy rather than on a personalization strategy to manage their knowledge assets. The above discussion suggests Proposition 1 as follows:

Proposition 1: Headquarters tend to predominantly resort to a codification strategy for knowledge management over a personalization strategy, whereas subsidiaries predominantly use a personalization strategy over a codification strategy.

SUBSIDIARY KNOWLEDGE UTILIZATION: BRINGING THE SECI MODEL INTO THE MNE CONTEXT

This chapter applies the SECI model of organizational knowledge creation theory to the MNE context to advance the holistic process model of SKU. As illustrated in Figure 10.1, the model addresses the entire process or cycle of SKU, which begins with subsidiary knowledge creation and proceeds to subsequent processes, such as reverse transfer of subsidiary-created knowledge, integration of the reverse-transferred knowledge, and diffusion and utilization of the integrated knowledge at other subsidiaries. The proposed model illustrates the four modes of knowledge conversion that take place across organizational boundaries, i.e., between headquarters and subsidiaries, at the aggregate MNE level. Organizational knowledge creation theory suggests that both headquarters and subsidiaries can have their own SECI cycle within their organizational boundaries. This chapter aims to extend this view by proposing that the SECI cycle executing at each MNE subunit can amplify across organizational boundaries and interact with the proposed SECI cycle that spans the aggregate MNE level.

Knowledge creation at MNEs occurs in all functional areas, but to keep the discussion within manageable bounds, this chapter focuses more narrowly on downstream knowledge that typically derives from subsidiary employees' local experience and interaction with local actors. Much of the literature on subsidiary evolution and reverse knowledge transfer has focused on upstream knowledge (e.g., research and development (R&D) and technological assets), which is often the result of the headquarters' specific mandates and carefully designed investment (Cantwell & Mudambi, 2005; Criscuolo & Narula, 2007; Papanastassiou et al., 2019). Relatively little attention has been paid to downstream knowledge, but because of the increasing importance and benefits of downstream knowledge to MNEs (Ambos et al., 2006; Rugman et al., 2011), this chapter focuses on it to provide complementary insights into SKU by MNEs.

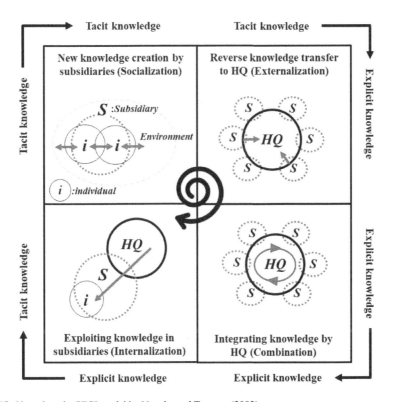

Note: Modified based on the SECI model by Nonaka and Toyama (2003)

Figure 10.1   The holistic process model of subsidiary knowledge utilization in the MNE

First, SKU at MNEs starts with subsidiary knowledge creation. Subsidiaries accumulate local resources and experience over time, and some subsidiaries develop new knowledge (products and services) for regional or global markets, either spontaneously or following the mandates of headquarters, by bundling internal and external resources[2] (Birkinshaw & Hood, 1998; Cantwell & Mudambi, 2005; Hennart, 2009). New knowledge created by these subsidiaries is often tacit and location-specific, because subsidiaries produce new knowledge through the "socialization" process (Nonaka & Toyama, 2003). Tacit knowledge developed and possessed by subsidiary employees converts into new tacit knowledge through shared experience in day-to-day social interactions with local customers, suppliers, and institutions (Andersson et al., 2005; Nell et al., 2010). This knowledge is likely to be embedded in the individuals and routines of the subsidiary (Andersson et al., 2002; Gulati, 1999).

Second, some new knowledge created by subsidiary employees – for example, successful marketing practice, new product development idea, and managerial know-how of dealing with consumer groups – can be utilized in other locations (Rugman et al., 2011). Leveraging such knowledge across geographic boundaries is beneficial to the MNE. Headquarters seek to collect such knowledge from their subsidiaries (Ambos et al., 2006; Narula, 2014; Yang et al., 2008). When transferring subsidiary-created knowledge to headquarters, tacit knowledge embedded in subsidiary employees or routines is likely to convert into explicit forms, such as reports or written documents that are easier and faster to transfer (Nonaka & Takeuchi, 1995; Szulanski, 1996). Not all subsidiary knowledge is codifiable, and some knowledge can be simply missed during the codification and transfer process (Roberts, 2000). To ensure the effective reverse transfer of tacit knowledge from subsidiaries, headquarters may use direct interaction such as face-to-face communications, expatriation, and repatriation (Harzing et al., 2015; Rice, 1993). However, maintaining direct communication with many overseas subsidiaries is costly for both headquarters and subsidiaries. Moreover, given that headquarters have limited managerial resources, it is hardly possible to use direct and rich communication as a regular mechanism for interacting with multiple subsidiaries and collecting knowledge from them (Hutzschenreuter et al., 2011; Penrose, 1959). Therefore, headquarters are likely to formalize their communication mechanism with subsidiaries using indirect forms of communication, such as written documents and reports. When collecting knowledge from subsidiaries, headquarters tend to use explicit forms of knowledge, accepting the associated risks of knowledge loss. While such a formalized, indirect mechanism functions as a default, regular option, headquarters may also use direct and rich communication methods as an ad hoc option when required, for example, to transfer highly tacit but necessary knowledge from subsidiaries.

This suggests that reverse knowledge transfer from subsidiary to headquarters involves the process of "externalization", in which tacit knowledge created by subsidiaries is converted into explicit knowledge through codification (Nonaka & Toyama, 2003). This process enables headquarters to collect knowledge effectively from multiple subsidiaries. Externalization may also involve the transformation of location-bound into non-location-bound knowledge by decontextualizing location-specific attributes from subsidiary knowledge (Rugman & Verbeke, 2001; Schulz & Jobe, 2001).

Third, some subsidiary knowledge can be used at headquarters and other locations with minor adaptation, but in most cases, it needs to be recombined with other complementary knowledge to be applicable in different or wider contexts. Therefore, headquarters seek to combine explicit knowledge sourced from subsidiaries with existing knowledge to create new firm-specific knowledge assets (Kogut & Zander, 1992). This "combination" process of bundling diverse explicit knowledge to form "more complex and systematic explicit knowledge" (Nonaka & Toyama, 2003, p. 5) coincides with the recent view of MNE headquarters as a meta-integrator that blends a variety of complementary knowledge dispersed across the MNE network to create new competences (Narula, 2014; Verbeke, 2009).

Finally, newly recombined knowledge by headquarters is diffused to subsidiaries for local use. This knowledge, like other conventional firm-specific knowledge, is barely usable as it is, and requires adaptation to the local environment (Bartlett & Ghoshal, 1989; Szulanski & Jensen, 2006). Some knowledge can be used with simple transplanting or replication in the local contexts (Mudambi, 2002), but often it needs to be grafted onto local markets or adapted to them (Huber, 1991). This is done through the process of "internalization" by individuals at the subsidiary, who apply explicit knowledge to practical situations, embody it through concrete practices, and make it their own through application (Nonaka & von Krogh, 2009). During this process, subsidiary employees convert the transferred explicit knowledge into tacit knowledge by incorporating it into their own experience and by embodying it in their routines. It is through this internalization process that subsidiary employees can utilize the transferred knowledge and add value to the MNE. Therefore, the internalization process accomplishes the utilization of subsidiary-created knowledge across the MNE network, while starting a new cycle of subsidiary knowledge creation in the local context. Once individuals in the subsidiary internalize the transferred knowledge, they can use it to create new knowledge in local contexts through the socialization process. Therefore, following the mechanism of the knowledge spiral explained in the original SECI model, the holistic process model of SKU involves an evolutionary expansion, transcending individual and organizational boundaries. The above discussion suggests Proposition 2, as follows:

Proposition 2: The process of subsidiary knowledge utilization involves four sequential and complementary processes of socialization, externalization, combination, and internalization at the aggregate MNE level.

THE ROLES OF HEADQUARTERS AND SUBSIDIARIES IN THE PROPOSED SECI MODEL

The proposed model of SKU extends the original SECI model by suggesting that, in the MNE context, four modes of knowledge conversion do not necessarily take place in the same organization or the same location, but they can take place across organizational and national boundaries. The uniqueness of the MNE as an organizational form is that its different constituent units, i.e., subsidiaries, are embedded in different national environments and have different resources, abilities, and functions (Bartlett & Ghoshal, 1989). This chapter argues that the four modes of knowledge conversion in the proposed SECI model take place across intra-organizational boundaries (between headquarters and subsidiaries) within an MNE, while headquarters and subsidiaries play different roles.

Initially, the subsidiary (or its employees) creates tacit knowledge in the host country through socialization, that is, through direct experience and interaction with local environments. Therefore, socialization takes place in the subsidiary. Some knowledge potentially usable at other locations is then transferred or externalized to headquarters. Thus, externalization takes place between headquarters and subsidiaries. However, during the process, headquarters tend to play key roles. Although subsidiaries have some incentive to transfer their knowledge to headquarters and other subsidiaries, for instance, to increase their power and enhance their strategic positions within the MNE (Mudambi & Navarra, 2004), they often have limited resources and capabilities to conduct reverse knowledge transfer by themselves without the support of headquarters (Forsgren & Pedersen, 2000; Holm & Pedersen, 1999). Moreover, reverse knowledge transfer is usually the process of a problemistic search initiated by headquarters (Monteiro et al., 2008), and the attention, willingness, and involvement of headquarters significantly increase the performance of reverse knowledge transfer (Ciabuschi et al., 2011; Mudambi et al., 2013). Therefore, headquarters often lead reverse knowledge transfer through externalization by converting the tacit knowledge of the subsidiary into explicit knowledge. Headquarters also play a leading role when creating new firm-specific knowledge by combining subsidiary knowledge with existing knowledge assets. Therefore, the combination process usually takes place at headquarters. Finally, the newly combined knowledge is diffused to subsidiaries for utilization in practice. This knowledge often requires adaptation to the local environment (Foss & Pedersen, 2002; Szulanski & Jensen, 2006), which is conducted by subsidiary employees through internalization, and it embodies the explicit knowledge transferred from headquarters to be used in their action, practice, and routines. The internalization process enables subsidiary employees to understand and utilize explicit knowledge from other locations through a learning-by-doing process that is "an effective method to test, modify and embody explicit knowledge as one's own tacit knowledge" (Nonaka & Toyama, 2003, p. 6). The above discussion is summarized in Table 10.1. This suggests Proposition 3, as follows:

Proposition 3: In the process of subsidiary knowledge utilization, headquarters plays a key role in externalization and combination, while the subsidiary plays an important role in socialization and internalization.

Table 10.1   *The roles of headquarters and subsidiaries in the process of subsidiary knowledge utilization*

	Socialization	Externalization	Combination	Internalization
Knowledge type	Tacit → Tacit	Tacit → Explicit	Explicit → Explicit	Explicit → Tacit
Main actor/locus	Subsidiary	Headquarters	Headquarters	Subsidiary
Activities	New tacit knowledge is created through the interaction between individuals in the subsidiary and their direct experience with local customers, suppliers, and institutions.	Some new tacit knowledge created by subsidiary members is transformed into explicit knowledge through codification and transferred to headquarters for wide use across the MNE network.	Headquarters combine explicit knowledge sourced from subsidiaries with other firm-specific knowledge residing at headquarters, or with knowledge collected from other subsidiaries, to create new firm-specific knowledge.	New firm-specific knowledge created through combination is transferred to subsidiaries and exploited by subsidiary members in the local environment. Subsidiary employees apply new knowledge to practices and make it their own tacit knowledge.

CONCLUSION AND FUTURE RESEARCH DIRECTIONS

This chapter described the complex process of SKU, which involves a series of multiple activities conducted by headquarters and subsidiaries. Much of the literature has focused on the determinants and consequences of various activities related to SKU, such as subsidiary knowledge creation, reverse knowledge transfer, and recombination by headquarters, but leaving the process of SKU as a whole largely undocumented. This chapter provides a comprehensive explanation of SKU by presenting the holistic process model that embraces four sequential processes of new knowledge creation by subsidiaries, reverse transfer of subsidiary-created knowledge to headquarters, combination of subsidiary knowledge by headquarters, and diffusion of newly combined knowledge across the MNE network.

The chapter extended the SECI model in organizational knowledge creation theory. The model has demonstrated that knowledge created through the SECI process can trigger a new spiral of knowledge creation, expanding horizontally and vertically, as it moves through communities of interaction that transcend various organizational boundaries (e.g., sectional, divisional, functional). This chapter described how knowledge can be transferred beyond organizational boundaries in the MNE context and how knowledge from different organizational entities interacts to create new knowledge by exploring the four complementary processes in a SECI cycle that take place between headquarters and subsidiaries.

The chapter provides a more nuanced understanding of MNE knowledge management by suggesting that headquarters and subsidiaries resort to different knowledge management strategies. By incorporating the different attributes of personalization and codification strategies (Hansen et al., 1999) with the respective characteristics of headquarters and subsidiaries, this chapter argued that headquarters are likely to use predominantly a codification over a personalization strategy, while subsidiaries tend to prefer a personalization over a codification strategy. Many studies have noted that MNEs often use a combination of both personalization and codification strategies, assuming that they adjust their strategies depending on the circumstances at hand (Gammelgaard & Ritter, 2005; Imran et al., 2016). This chapter suggested a different approach to using personalization and codification strategies in combination by MNEs.

The holistic process model of SKU and the associated roles of headquarters and subsidiaries have important practical implications. Managers of MNEs need to understand that SKU involves a series of knowledge conversions between tacit and explicit knowledge. In other words, subsidiary-created knowledge can be used across the MNE network through continuous and dynamic interactions between tacit and explicit knowledge possessed by both headquarters and subsidiaries that consistently interact with their own environments. When designing the process of SKU, managers of both headquarters and subsidiaries need to work together to achieve effective knowledge conversion.

This chapter points to several future research directions. First, the chapter provides three testable propositions regarding knowledge management strategies employed by headquarters and subsidiaries, and the holistic process of SKU. Future research may empirically examine these propositions, especially using in-depth case studies. For instance, future case studies may observe how headquarters and subsidiaries in the same MNE organize their knowledge management strategies and examine the difference or interdependence between their strategies. Future research may also explore the entire process suggested in this chapter, by capturing some particular examples of subsidiary-created knowledge (e.g., management policies and marketing practices), and examining how they are identified, transferred back to headquarters, and shared across the MNE network in practice. Future studies that examine empirically the entire process of SKU can provide a deeper insight into SKU by MNEs. Second, this chapter argues that SKU involves four sequential processes of socialization, externalization, combination, and internalization. Future studies may also delve empirically into each process and examine how MNEs implement it during the process of SKU. For example, this chapter showed that the externalization process involves codification of tacit into explicit knowledge. Future research may examine whether and how headquarters and subsidiaries codify subsidiary-created knowledge into explicit knowledge. Finally, the global leveraging of subsidiary-created knowledge has become an important issue in the MNE literature. Many studies have elaborated on how MNEs utilize subsidiary knowledge, but there have been few attempts to study the complete process of SKU. Future studies need to explore the entire process of SKU across the MNE network in various organizational and environmental contexts. These studies can significantly enhance our understanding of the knowledge-based competitive advantages of the MNE.

NOTES

1. In other words, subsidiary-specific advantages (Rugman & Verbeke, 2001).

2. New knowledge is also created through international joint ventures (Inkpen & Dinur, 1998; Pak et al., 2015).

REFERENCES

Ambos, T. C., Ambos, B., & Schlegelmilch, B. B. (2006). Learning from foreign subsidiaries: An empirical investigation of headquarters' benefits from reverse knowledge transfers. *International Business Review*, 15(3), 294–312.

Anderson, J. R. (1996). *The Architecture of Cognition*. Lawrence Erlbaum.

Andersson, U., Björkman, I., & Forsgren, M. (2005). Managing subsidiary knowledge creation: The effect of control mechanisms on subsidiary local embeddedness. *International Business Review*, 14(5), 521–538.

Andersson, U., Forsgren, M., & Holm, U. (2002). The strategic impact of external networks: Subsidiary performance and competence development in the multinational corporation. *Strategic Management Journal*, 23(11), 979–996.

Bartlett, C. A., & Ghoshal, S. (1989). *Managing Across Borders: The Transnational Solution*. Harvard Business School Press.

Birkinshaw, J. (1997). Entrepreneurship in multinational corporations: The characteristics of subsidiary initiatives. *Strategic Management Journal*, 18(3), 207–229.

Birkinshaw, J., & Hood, N. (1998). Multinational subsidiary evolution: Capability and charter change in foreign-owned subsidiary companies. *Academy of Management Review*, 23(4), 773–795.

Bouquet, C., & Birkinshaw, J. (2008). Weight versus voice: How foreign subsidiaries gain attention from corporate headquarters. *Academy of Management Journal*, 51(3), 577–601.

Brown, J. S., & Duguid, P. (1991). Organizational learning and communities-of-practice: Toward a unified view of working, learning, and innovation. *Organization Science*, 2(1), 40–57.

Buckley, P. J., & Casson, M. (1976). *The Future of the Multinational Enterprise*. London: Macmillan.

Cantwell, J., & Mudambi, R. (2005). MNE competence-creating subsidiary mandates. *Strategic Management Journal*, 26(12), 1109–1128.

Chai, K.-H., Gregory, M., & Shi, Y. (2003). Bridging islands of knowledge: A framework of knowledge sharing mechanisms. *International Journal of Technology Management*, 25(8), 703–727.

Chai, K.-H., & Nebus, J. (2012). Personalization or codification? A marketing perspective to optimize knowledge reuse efficiency. *IEEE Transactions on Engineering Management*, 59(1), 33–51.

Chang, Y. Y., Gong, Y., & Peng, M. (2012). Expatriate knowledge transfer, subsidiary absorptive capacity, and subsidiary performance. *Academy of Management Journal*, 55(4), 927–948.

Ciabuschi, F., Dellestrand, H., & Martín, O. M. (2011). Internal embeddedness, headquarters involvement, and innovation importance in multinational enterprises. *Journal of Management Studies*, 48(7), 1612–1639.

Ciabuschi, F., Holm, U., & Martín, O. (2014). Dual embeddedness, influence and performance of innovating subsidiaries in the multinational corporation. *International Business Review*, 23(5), 897–909.

Cowan, R., David, P. A., & Foray, D. (2000). The explicit economics of knowledge codification and tacitness. *Industrial and Corporate Change*, 9(2), 211–253.

Criscuolo, P., & Narula, R. (2007). Using multi-hub structures for international R&D: Organisational inertia and the challenges of implementation. *MIR: Management International Review*, 47(5), 639–660.

Droege, S. B., & Hoobler, J. M. (2003). Employee turnover and tacit knowledge diffusion: A network perspective. *Journal of Managerial Issues*, 15(1), 50–64.

Dunning, J. H. (1980). Towards an eclectic theory of international production: Some empirical tests. *Journal of International Business Studies*, 11(1), 9–31.

Earl, M. (2001). Knowledge management strategies: Toward a taxonomy. *Journal of Management Information Systems*, 18(1), 215–242.

Forsgren, M., & Pedersen, T. (2000). Subsidiary influence and corporate learning-centres of excellence in Danish foreign-owned firms. In U. Holm & T. Pedersen (Eds.), *The Emergence and Impact of MNC Centers of Excellence* (pp. 68–78). London: Macmillan.

Foss, N. J., & Pedersen, T. (2002). Transferring knowledge in MNCs: The role of sources of subsidiary knowledge and organizational context. *Journal of International Management, 8*(1), 49–67.

Gammelgaard, J., & Ritter, T. (2005). The knowledge retrieval matrix: Codification and personification as separate strategies. *Journal of Knowledge Management, 9*(4), 133–143.

Giddens, A. (1984). *The Constitution of Society: Introduction of the Theory of Structuration.* Berkeley, CA: University of California Press.

Gulati, R. (1999). Network location and learning: The influences of network resources and firm capabilities on alliance formation. *Strategic Management Journal, 20*(5), 1172–1193.

Haesli, A., & Boxall, P. (2005). When knowledge management meets HR strategy: An exploration of personalization-retention and codification-recruitment configurations. *International Journal of Human Resource Management, 16*(11), 1955–1975.

Håkanson, L. (2007). Creating knowledge: The power and logic of articulation. *Industrial and Corporate Change, 16*(1), 51–88.

Hansen, M., Nohria, N., & Tierney, T. (1999). What's your strategy for managing knowledge? *Harvard Business Review, 77*(2), 106–116.

Harzing, A.-W., Pudelko, M., & Reiche, S. B. (2015). The bridging role of expatriates and inpatriates in knowledge transfer in multinational corporations. *Human Resource Management, 55*(4), 679–695.

Hedlund, G., & Nonaka, I. (1993). Models of knowledge management in the West and Japan. In P. Lorange, B. Chakravarthy, J. Roos, & A. Van de Ven (Eds.), *Implementing Strategic Processes: Change, Learning and Co-operation.* London: Blackwell.

Hennart, J.-F. (2009). Down with MNE-centric theories! Market entry and expansion as the bundling of MNE and local assets. *Journal of International Business Studies, 40*(9), 1432–1454.

Hocking, J. B., Brown, M., & Harzing, A.-W. (2007). Balancing global and local strategic contexts: Expatriate knowledge transfer, applications, and learning within a transnational organization. *Human Resource Management, 46*(4), 513–533.

Holm, U., & Pedersen, T. (1999). *The Emergence and Impact of MNC Centres of Excellence: A Subsidiary Perspective.* Palgrave Macmillan.

Howells, J. (2000). International coordination of technology flows and knowledge activity in innovation. *International Journal of Technology Management, 19*(7), 806–819.

Huber, G. P. (1991). Organizational learning: The contributing processes and the literatures. *Organization Science, 2*(1), 88–115.

Hutzschenreuter, T., Voll, J. C., & Verbeke, A. (2011). The impact of added cultural distance and cultural diversity on international expansion patterns: A Penrosean perspective. *Journal of Management Studies, 48*(2), 305–329.

Imran, M. K., Rehman, C. A., Aslam, U., & Bilal, A. R. (2016). What's organization knowledge management strategy for successful change implementation? *Journal of Organizational Change Management, 29*(7), 1097–1117.

Inkpen, A. C., & Dinur, A. (1998). Knowledge management processes and international joint ventures. *Organization Science, 9*(4), 454–468.

Jasimuddin, S. M., Klein, J. H., & Connell, C. (2005). The paradox of using tacit and explicit knowledge: Strategies to face dilemmas. *Management Decision, 43*(1), 102–112.

Jensen, R., & Szulanski, G. (2004). Stickiness and the adaptation of organizational practices in cross-border knowledge transfers. *Journal of International Business Studies, 35*(6), 508–523.

Kawai, N., & Chung, C. (2019). Expatriate utilization, subsidiary knowledge creation and performance: The moderating role of subsidiary strategic context. *Journal of World Business, 54*(1), 24–36.

Kim, T. H., Lee, J.-N., Chun, J. U., & Benbasat, I. (2014). Understanding the effect of knowledge management strategies on knowledge management performance: A contingency perspective. *Information & Management, 51*(4), 398–416.

Kogut, B., & Zander, U. (1992). Knowledge of the firm, combinative capabilities, and the replication of technology. *Organization Science, 3*(3), 383–397.

Kostova, T. (1999). Transnational transfer of strategic organizational practices: A contextual perspective. *Academy of Management Review, 24*(2), 308–324.

Kumar, J. A., & Ganesh, L. (2011). Balancing knowledge strategy: Codification and personalization during product development. *Journal of Knowledge Management, 15*(1), 118–135.

Lave, J., & Wenger, E. (1991). *Situated Learning: Legitimate Peripheral Participation*. Cambridge: Cambridge University Press.

Lee, J. M. (2019). Intra- and inter-regional diversification, subsidiary value chain activities and expatriate utilization. *Journal of International Management*, *25*(3), 100668.

Lee, J. M., Narula, R., & Hillemann, J. (2021). Unraveling asset recombination through the lens of firm-specific advantages: A dynamic capabilities perspective. *Journal of World Business*, *56*(2), 101193.

Liu, Y., & Meyer, K. E. (2020). Boundary spanners, HRM practices, and reverse knowledge transfer: The case of Chinese cross-border acquisitions. *Journal of World Business*, *55*(2), 100958.

Meyer, K. E., Mudambi, R., & Narula, R. (2011). Multinational enterprises and local contexts: The opportunities and challenges of multiple embeddedness. *Journal of Management Studies*, *48*(2), 235–252.

Minbaeva, D., Pedersen, T., Björkman, I., Fey, C. F., & Park, H. J. (2003). MNC knowledge transfer, subsidiary absorptive capacity, and HRM. *Journal of International Business Studies*, *34*(6), 586–599.

Monteiro, F., & Birkinshaw, J. (2017). The external knowledge sourcing process in multinational corporations. *Strategic Management Journal*, *38*(2), 342–362.

Monteiro, L. F., Arvidsson, N., & Birkinshaw, J. (2008). Knowledge flows within multinational corporations: Explaining subsidiary isolation and its performance implications. *Organization Science*, *19*(1), 90–107.

Mudambi, R. (2002). Knowledge management in multinational firms. *Journal of International Management*, *8*(1), 1–9.

Mudambi, R., & Navarra, P. (2004). Is knowledge power? Knowledge flows, subsidiary power and rent-seeking within MNCs. *Journal of International Business Studies*, *35*(5), 385–406.

Mudambi, R., Piscitello, L., & Rabbiosi, L. (2013). Reverse knowledge transfer in MNEs: Subsidiary innovativeness and entry modes. *Long Range Planning*, *47*(1–2), 49–63.

Mukherji, S. (2005). Knowledge management strategy in software services organizations: Straddling codification and personalization. *IIMB Management Review*, *17*(3), 33–39.

Narula, R. (2014). Exploring the paradox of competence-creating subsidiaries: Balancing bandwidth and dispersion in MNEs. *Long Range Planning*, *47*(1–2), 4–15.

Narula, R., & Lee, J. M. (2020). The theories of the multinational enterprise. In F. Rivera-Batiz & M. Spatareanu (Eds.), *Encyclopedia of International Economics and Global Trade, Volume 1:1 Foreign Direct Investment and the Multinational Enterprise* (pp. 89–114). World Scientific Publishing.

Nell, P. C., Andersson, U., & Schlegelmilch, B. B. (2010). Subsidiary contribution to firm-level competitive advantage–disentangling the effects of MNC external embeddedness. In J. Pla-Barber & J. Alegre (Eds.), *Progress in International Business Research: Reshaping the Boundaries of the Firm in an Era of Global Interdependence* (Vol. 5, pp. 173–195). Emerald Group Publishing.

Nickols, F. (2000). The knowledge in knowledge management. In J. W. Cortada & J. A. Woods (Eds.), *The Knowledge Management Yearbook, 2000–2001: 12–21*. Woburn, MA: Butterworth-Heinemann.

Nohria, N., & Ghoshal, S. (1994). Differentiated fit and shared values: Alternatives for managing headquarters-subsidiary relations. *Strategic Management Journal*, *15*(6), 491–502.

Nonaka, I. (1991). The knowledge-creating company. *Harvard Business Review*, November–December, 96–104.

Nonaka, I., & Konno, N. (1998). The Concept of "Ba": Building a foundation for knowledge creation. *California Management Review*, *40*(3), 40–54.

Nonaka, I., & Takeuchi, H. (1995). *The Knowledge-Creating Company: How Japanese Companies Create the Dynamics of Innovation*. Oxford: Oxford University Press.

Nonaka, I., & Toyama, R. (2003). The knowledge-creating theory revisited: Knowledge creation as a synthesizing process. *Knowledge Management Research & Practice*, *1*(1), 2–10.

Nonaka, I., & von Krogh, G. (2009). Tacit knowledge and knowledge conversion: Controversy and advancement in organizational knowledge creation theory. *Organization Science*, *20*(3), 635–652.

Nonaka, I., Von Krogh, G., & Voelpel, S. (2006). Organizational knowledge creation theory: Evolutionary paths and future advances. *Organization Studies*, *27*(8), 1179–1208.

Pak, Y. S., Ra, W., & Lee, J. M. (2015). An integrated multi-stage model of knowledge management in international joint ventures: Identifying a trigger for knowledge exploration and knowledge harvest. *Journal of World Business*, *50*(1), 180–191.

Papanastassiou, M., Pearce, R., & Zanfei, A. (2019). Changing perspectives on the internationalization of R&D and innovation by multinational enterprises: A review of the literature. *Journal of International Business Studies*, 1–42.

Penrose, E. T. (1959). *The Theory of the Growth of the Firm*. Oxford, UK: Oxford University Press.

Pitelis, C. N., & Teece, D. J. (2018). The new MNE: "Orchestration" theory as envelope of "internalization" theory. *MIR: Management International Review*, *58*(4), 523–539.

Plourde, Y., Parker, S. C., & Schaan, J.-L. (2014). Expatriation and its effect on headquarters' attention in the multinational enterprise. *Strategic Management Journal*, *35*(6), 938–947.

Polanyi, M. (1966). *The Tacit Dimension*. Chicago, IL: University of Chicago Press.

Rabbiosi, L. (2011). Subsidiary roles and reverse knowledge transfer: An investigation of the effects of coordination mechanisms. *Journal of International Management*, *17*(2), 97–113.

Rabbiosi, L., & Santangelo, G. D. (2013). Parent company benefits from reverse knowledge transfer: The role of the liability of newness in MNEs. *Journal of World Business*, *48*(1), 160–170.

Rice, R. E. (1993). Media appropriateness – using social presence theory to compare traditional and new organizational media. *Human Communication Research*, *19*(4), 451–484.

Roberts, J. (2000). From know-how to show-how? Questioning the role of information and communication technologies in knowledge transfer. *Technology Analysis & Strategic Management*, *12*(4), 429–443.

Rugman, A. M., & Verbeke, A. (2001). Subsidiary-specific advantages in multinational enterprises. *Strategic Management Journal*, *22*(3), 237–250.

Rugman, A. M., Verbeke, A., & Yuan, W. (2011). Re-conceptualizing Bartlett and Ghoshal's classification of national subsidiary roles in the multinational enterprise. *Journal of Management Studies*, *48*(2), 253–277.

Scheepers, R., Venkitachalam, K., & Gibbs, M. R. (2004). Knowledge strategy in organizations: Refining the model of Hansen, Nohria and Tierney. *The Journal of Strategic Information Systems*, *13*(3), 201–222.

Schulz, M. (2001). The uncertain relevance of newness: Organizational learning and knowledge flows. *Academy of Management Journal*, *44*(4), 661–681.

Schulz, M., & Jobe, L. A. (2001). Codification and tacitness as knowledge management strategies: An empirical exploration. *The Journal of High Technology Management Research*, *12*(1), 139–165.

Spender, J. C. (1996). Competitive advantage from tacit knowledge? Unpacking the concept and its strategic implications. In A. E. Bertrand Moingeon (Ed.), *Organizational Learning and Competitive Advantage* (pp. 56–71). London, UK: SAGE.

Szulanski, G. (1996). Exploring internal stickiness: Impediments to the transfer of best practice within the firm. *Strategic Management Journal*, *17*, 27–43.

Szulanski, G., & Jensen, R. J. (2006). Presumptive adaptation and the effectiveness of knowledge transfer. *Strategic Management Journal*, *27*(10), 937–957.

Verbeke, A. (2009). *International Business Strategy*. Cambridge, UK: Cambridge University Press.

Yamin, M., & Andersson, U. (2011). Subsidiary importance in the MNC: What role does internal embeddedness play? *International Business Review*, *20*(2), 151–162.

Yang, Q., Mudambi, R., & Meyer, K. E. (2008). Conventional and reverse knowledge flows in multinational corporations. *Journal of Management*, *34*(5), 882–902.

11. Absorptive capacity, value creation and new service development in multinational enterprises: the role of knowledge flows between customers, subsidiaries and headquarters

Tiina Leposky, Ahmad Arslan, Ismail Gölgeci and Deborah Callaghan

INTRODUCTION

Absorptive capacity has been widely recognised as a crucial element of an organisation's ability to transfer knowledge and utilise it in its customer relationships (Lewin et al., 2011; Winkelbach and Walter, 2015). In fast-changing global market environments, firms are increasingly focusing on their customers to understand their unfulfilled needs and provide services accordingly (Lightfoot et al., 2013; Zimmerling et al., 2017). To gain competitive advantage from these customer relationships, firms must not only be able to source information from the field and transfer it to decision-makers but must also make changes in their service offering to their customers within a reasonable timescale and be able to provide them value.

In international business (IB) contexts, the capacity to absorb external knowledge and apply it for commercial ends is a more complex exercise than in domestic business, due to the varied host locations and the organisational dynamics colouring HQ–subsidiary relationships. This is evident for example in the influence of language for knowledge transfer, as in MNEs, local subsidiaries must use the organisational language to convey their message to HQ, preventing a natural flow of information if language skills on either side are lacking (Peltokorpi, 2017). MNEs must also manage their subsidiaries' dual embeddedness in order to gain most benefits from their international presence (Achcaoucaou et al., 2014), and balance the needs of individual subsidiaries with the needs of the network as a whole (Bouquet and Birkinshaw, 2008a; Weng and Cheng, 2018).

As a construct, absorptive capacity has been used to examine firms' ability to learn from the external environment and capitalise on their learning (Cohen and Levinthal, 1990). It has also been conceptualised as a capability, a dynamic capability, a process, a mechanism, and a stock of prior knowledge (Lane et al., 2006; Song, 2014). This definitional proliferation has caused some confusion in the field, leading to fears of reification of the term (Lane et al., 2006) and, consequently, a need to reconceptualise it by taking into account the wider concept of organisational dynamics (Marabelli and Newell, 2014) as well as internal and external networks (Ebers and Maurer, 2014; Kotabe et al., 2017). Recent academic research has enhanced understanding of absorptive capacity as an embedded element in a firm's learning process. However, a gap still remains in mapping out the path from local customer input to global corporate boardroom, resulting in new service development and new value offers that are applicable at host locations.

In this chapter, we aim to offer a conceptual discussion, where customer knowledge from external relationships in host countries is linked internally with new service developments resulting in value creation with the customer. According to the knowledge-based view (KBV), knowledge is the most essential resource possessed by a firm, and the ability to use it for commercial ends determines the competitiveness and therefore success of an enterprise (Kogut and Zander, 1993). In a bid to enhance competitiveness, many MNEs are attempting to offer innovative services that differentiate them from their competitors and increase their customer loyalty (Javalgi et al., 2014; Zhang et al., 2015). Knowing what customers view as a valued product or service in varying locations and cultures and being able to balance the needs of global standardisation with local adaptation and responsiveness through innovative and transformational processes is of utmost importance to the firms. This chapter applies KBV in the specific context of new service development, arguing that an MNE's absorptive capacity is associated with its ability to offer customers new and valuable services.

By connecting service development with value creation in subsequent customer engagements, our chapter enhances understanding of absorptive capacity not only as a process that transfers intangible knowledge but also as a vehicle that has the potential to change MNE service offers and operations leading to new value offers and revenue streams. The main contribution of this chapter is therefore to the intersection of IB literature focused on subsidiary–HQ relationships, and knowledge transfer through the lens of absorptive capacity. Our novel conceptualisation of absorptive capacity as a process through external and internal relationships provides a further contribution to this literature, as it provides a stepping stone for understanding and measuring the effects of knowledge absorption within the different frameworks of the international firm.

In the following section, we outline the premise of absorptive capacity and how it interacts with the practices of new service development and value creation in the external and internal networks of MNEs. This discussion is followed by theoretical propositions addressing the conceptualisation, organisational dynamics and customer relationships in the context of knowledge transfer and absorptive capacity of MNEs. The book chapter concludes with a discussion of the implications, limitations and future research directions of absorptive capacity.

ABSORPTIVE CAPACITY IN MULTINATIONAL ENTERPRISES

Cohen and Levinthal (1990) are credited with conception of absorptive capacity in strategy and management literature. In their seminal work on absorptive capacity, Cohen and Levinthal (1990: 131–132) state that: "an organisation's absorptive capacity does not simply depend on the organisation's direct interface with the external environment. It also depends on transfers of knowledge across and within subunits that may be quite removed from the original point of entry". Some recent studies have focused on the subsidiary–HQ bond (e.g., Schleimer and Pedersen, 2014; Song, 2014; Ferraris et al., 2017; Weng and Cheng, 2018) and others on the external–internal dichotomy (e.g., Ebers and Maurer, 2014; Zhang et al., 2015; Shaw and Luiz, 2018). In these studies, absorptive capacity has been presented as an innovation that builds on existing organisational knowledge embedded in routines and processes aimed at recognising the value of external knowledge, assimilating it, and applying it for monetary gains. Thus, it has been argued that high absorptive capacity leads to high innovation in firms, including MNEs (e.g., Ferraris et al., 2017: Shaw and Luiz, 2018). However, scant attention has been paid to the dilemma of knowledge acquisition and subsequent decision-making taking place in these vastly different spaces.

The conceptual discussion offered in this chapter follows four phases of absorptive capacity as presented by Zahra and George (2002): acquisition, assimilation, transformation and exploitation. These phases have been widely used since their conception over a decade ago and offer a workable process for absorptive capacity, especially when complemented by a feedback channel which adds a dynamic dimension to the discussion (e.g., Todorova and Durisin, 2007; Leposky, 2017). The discussion offered in the current chapter enhances earlier conceptualisations of absorptive capacity by specifically highlighting the significance of IB context. In doing so, it acknowledges how the external environment influences customer interactions in host country locations (acquisition and exploitation) and how the internal environment between culturally and geographically distant units has an impact upon knowledge integration (assimilation and transformation). Furthermore, our study conceptually highlights the specific context of customer knowledge leading to new service development, thereby contributing to the intersection of literature-spanning knowledge transfers and business models.

The MNE context is especially pertinent for knowledge development as foreign subsidiaries are embedded in their local contexts and they create knowledge-laden linkages with supply chain members, collaborative and alliance partners, and institutions (Giroud and Scott-Kennel, 2009). Foreign subsidiaries can hold a significant role within the MNE if their local knowledge through these linkages provides a competitive advantage for the overall organisation (Birkinshaw and Hood, 1998). Indeed, the access to new knowledge can be an important motivating factor for MNEs to acquire foreign subsidiaries, even when it is widely acknowledged that cultural differences can present significant barriers to gaining integration benefits (Björkman et al., 2007). Therefore, MNEs differ from domestic firms in that they have access to a wider knowledge base, which can be leveraged across a differentiated network (Nohria and Ghoshal, 1994), while at the same time facing complexities and balancing integration and autonomy within a multiplicity of national contexts.

Foreign subsidiaries also hold a strategic position within the MNE network as they implement HQ marketing strategies in their own localities. Standardisation vs. adaptation of marketing strategies is an age-old question within the IB literature, as MNEs seek economies of scale through standardisation but may be unable to benefit from them if the strategy does not fit the local market (Katsikeas et al., 2006). Especially in uncertain conditions that may differ significantly from the home country, understanding the performance implications of strategic fit are important, particularly when local market conditions do not conform to the theoretical expectations formulated in Western economies (Lukas et al., 2001). Consequently, in this chapter, we discuss the MNE context with the stated assumption that it contains unique characteristics relevant to IB. For the purposes of clarity, these have been divided into external knowledge and networks, which are not accessible to HQ in an international structure, and internal network dynamics, which are influenced by cultural differences and distance.

It should also be noted that in the MNE context, direct contact with local customers is done through local subsidiaries (Ciabuschi et al., 2017). MNE subsidiaries tend to have a variety of mandates including customer connection specifically for sales and marketing subsidiaries (Birkinshaw, 2016). MNEs with network structures have long acknowledged the crucial role of local subsidiaries as knowledge sources (Bartlett and Ghoshal, 2002) even though their performance is usually measured in terms of sales and profitability (Birkinshaw, 2016). Moreover, the ultimate strategic direction and apportioning of support resources is often decided by MNE HQ. HQ attention has often been found favourable for subsidiary success in many studies (e.g., Ambos and Birkinshaw, 2010; Leposky, 2017). However, at the same time, other studies have cautioned that if HQ enforces authority, it tends to negatively influence value creation (Foss et al., 2012; Balogun et al., 2019).

As noted earlier, the absorptive capacity of MNEs is influenced by both internal and external sources. External information is generated by market actors and MNEs must be able to respond to the requisition and acquisition of it. (e.g., Iurkov and Benito, 2018). Moreover, internal forces that generate information tend to range from individual preferences to organisational routines assimilated in different knowledge streams (Scott-Kennel and Giroud, 2015; Lim et al., 2017). These internal and external sources of information and knowledge are also referred to as networks and have received significant attention in recent absorptive capacity studies (e.g., Ferraris et al., 2017; Iurkov and Benito, 2018; Shaw and Luiz, 2018). These internal–external networks (sources of knowledge) are found to be useful, if the absorptive capacity of the focal MNE is in line with its learning objectives (e.g., Ferraris et al., 2017; Cenamor et al., 2017). This complementarity is further dependent on relationship dynamics, as external knowledge may not always be readily available from the partner firms (e.g., Kotabe et al., 2017; Ferraris et al., 2020). As a result, MNEs may need to search for this external knowledge from other sources, including customers (Leposky, 2017).

As social interactions are recognised as an essential part of any knowledge transfer activity, the absorptive capacity of MNEs is also influenced by social context (e.g., Hotho et al., 2012; Presutti et al., 2019). Social interaction and integration mechanisms have been found to lower knowledge transfer barriers (Zahra and George, 2002; Presutti et al., 2019), introducing the actors to useful sources of knowledge (Enkel and Heil, 2014) and aiding to establish connections through shared values, norms and formal structures (Lewin et al., 2011; Schleimer and Pedersen, 2014).

A key element of the social context-knowledge transfer discussion in MNEs relates to the subsidiary–HQ relationship; a topic that has already received significant scholarly attention (e.g., Leposky et al., 2017; Ciabuschi et al., 2017). Different MNE subsidiaries, and their HQs, are considered to have unique embedded knowledge sources (Song, 2014; Zeng et al., 2018). Subsidiaries in particular have been noted to hold dually embedded knowledge sources that include specific operational mandates from their HQs, along with localised mandates that are driven by market forces that may sometimes challenge HQ mandates (Schleimer and Pedersen, 2013, 2014; Zeng et al., 2018). The HQ can force normative integration to offset these dual pressures on subsidiaries (Schleimer and Pedersen, 2014), but this integration does not always occur (Ferraris et al., 2020).

Along with the internal network, the subsidiary is exposed to the external environment, which may also be complicated to decipher. A central position in the internal network exposes the subsidiary to knowledge flows from across the organisation (Tsai, 2001; Ferraris et al., 2020), including different markets and cultural contexts adding layers to the information. The immediate external environment is no less complicated to decipher and absorbing the amassed complexity requires continuous effort in order to maintain existing knowledge and to acquire and assimilate a new knowledge base. Understanding, on one hand, the subsidiary's motivation to engage in knowledge activities (Song, 2014), and on the other hand, the power balance that influences the separate phases of absorptive capacity (Marabelli and Newell, 2014) can shed light on the absorptive capacity based on the dyadic internal relationships between subsidiaries and HQs. This can be further linked to new service development and value creation by MNEs, a core premise of discussion in the current chapter.

It should be further noted that absorptive capacity has been conceptualised as a process of four phases where focal MNE, its subsidiaries, and customers exchange knowledge in a dynamic manner resulting in value creation and new service development (Leposky, 2017). These four phases are acquisition, assimilation, transformation and exploitation (Zahra and George, 2002; Leposky, 2017). This dynamic of the relationship between customers, subsidiary and MNE HQ is presented in Figure 11.1.

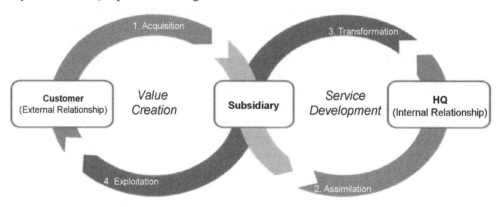

Figure 11.1 The four phases of absorptive capacity in customer–subsidiary–HQ
relationships of MNEs (adapted from Leposky, 2017: 66)

The current chapter builds on the work by Leposky (2017) on the four phases of absorptive capacity, to specifically address new service development and value creation by MNEs based upon internal and external knowledge sources in relation to all the above-mentioned four phases. We present the discussion leading to theoretical propositions addressing all these factors in a step-by-step manner in the next section.

VALUE CREATION, NEW SERVICE DEVELOPMENT AND ABSORPTIVE CAPACITY IN MULTINATIONAL ENTERPRISES

In order to capture the two-way flow of knowledge between external and internal environments of MNE, our focus is only on the relationships between customer–subsidiary and subsidiary–HQ. The inflow from external to internal networks represents the innovation flow, in line with Cohen and Levinthal (1990), with a delimitation on new service development, while the outflow is concerned with value creation. This mapping is presented above in Figure 11.1.

The role of these relationships is further stressed in the development of new services as the process generally requires a higher input of external information or customer involvement compared with selling more traditional products (Hipp and Grupp, 2005; Storey and Larbig, 2018). Moreover, service delivery appears to go through less formal planning than product development, as service propositions can be formulated based on customer needs and wants, rather than what a physical product is capable of delivering (Ettlie and Rosenthal, 2011; Gebauer et al., 2017). The competence of the MNE managers in interpreting the organisational value proposition offers has been referred to as a significant determinant of success for such service offers (Santamaría et al., 2012). Such an offering also enhances the link between the organisation and its external environment through the customer relationship, and the internal links between the customer-facing actors and the enabling actors from support functions and management.

In the absorptive capacity literature, potential absorptive capacity maps a firm receptiveness to external knowledge and a greater potential absorptive capacity prevents a repetitive or path dependent mindset unwilling to consider new information or new ways of doing things (Zahra and George, 2002). The absorptive capacity therefore enhances an innovative approach, especially in the international context since innovations and new ideas are typically not based on completely new knowledge but rather a recombination of knowledge from sources distant to each other (Enkel and Heil, 2014). Considering the recent success of global platform businesses such as Uber or Airbnb, based on service business models utilising existing infrastructures and technologies, novel knowledge constellations combining external knowledge in ways that fit the firm's internal strategic direction can therefore be used to drive service development.

In contrast to the potential absorptive capacity of MNEs, realised absorptive capacity corresponds with the stages of value creation, specifically value in exchange occurring in the enterprise sphere (Cuervo-Cazurra and Rui, 2017) and culminating in the specific point of value delivery through exploitation (Grönroos and Voima, 2013). The original rationale behind Zahra and George's (2002) conceptualisation of potential and realised absorptive capacity centred on the different forces that can affect each of them, the ability to measure them separately, and the insight in understanding MNE absorptive capacity performance. The authors were intrigued by firms' demonstrable skill in some parts of the process but lack of overall success, which they could explain by comparing the levels of potential and realised absorptive capacity and determining the difference as an efficiency ratio. This rationale remains valid even if potential and realised absorptive capacities are viewed as new service development and value creating processes, but further benefits can also be gained from this classification. First, this allows accounting for outcomes for the phases of acquisition and assimilation in the form of the resulting innovation. Using the innovation as a tangible result will help not only researchers in examining absorptive capacity taking place in firms but also practitioners in measuring the success of initiatives. Second, this approach may help clarify antecedents affecting value creation as it is placed in a continuum of knowledge transfer practices and organisational capabilities.

In the current chapter, we posit that absorptive capacity occurs in two distinct relationships, of which one, the external, is value creating and the other, internal, is service innovating. Furthermore, it is argued that the sequential steps of the absorptive capacity process take place in these separate relationships. An interesting feature of this approach is that it coincides with the conceptualisation of potential absorptive capacity and realised absorptive capacity of MNEs as functions of knowledge inflows and outflows. We argue that potential absorptive capacity of MNEs is synonymous with new service development, as it requires the intake and processing of knowledge in a way that leads to the creation of something new through the combination and exchange of relationship- and firm-specific resources. The combination refers to the deployment of resources, in this instance knowledge, in new ways, which generates ideas and insights, while exchange is the mechanisms through which the outcome of the combination is validated (Moran and Ghoshal, 1996). The ability to acquire knowledge, integrate it with existing knowledge – thereby creating inroads to new knowledge - and store and share it effectively with others, is the critical capability of MNEs resulting in a competitive advantage in the market (Kang et al., 2010; Cenamor et al., 2017). Figure 11.2 illustrates the process similarities of absorptive capacity in external and internal relationships.

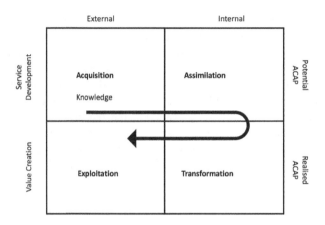

Figure 11.2   Illustration of the absorptive capacity process overlaying service development and value creation with potential and realised absorptive capacity (ACAP)

Categorising the phases of absorptive capacity based on the relationships allows the inclusion of dynamics from different sides of the subsidiary's sphere of influence. After highlighting the importance of phases of absorptive capacity for MNEs, we specifically address them in the context of new service development and value creation.

Dual embeddedness of MNE subsidiaries has been referred to earlier as an important aspect that needs deliberation in the context of new service development and value creation, especially as it is a phenomenon unique to firms operating in an international context. Dual embeddedness and dual direction of knowledge transfer within MNE units (HQ and subsidiaries) have been positively linked to influencing the absorptive capacity of subsidiaries (Najafi-Tavani et al., 2018). Dual embeddedness represents a particular network position of subsidiaries because they are exposed to different knowledge flows (Achcaoucaou et al., 2014). A subsidiary's external embeddedness refers to a network of links to local partners (Ferraris et al., 2020). Specifically, subsidiaries have alliances with local partners that constitute a source of crucial knowledge for reaching a competitive advantage (Cenamor et al., 2017). New knowledge outside the organisation can enhance the development of products, processes, and innovation in the subsidiaries (Ciabuschi et al., 2012, 2017). Thus, instead of being totally dependent on the parent firm, subsidiaries in foreign locations where they have greater access to knowledge than the HQ, can use their external embeddedness to contribute to MNEs' competitive advantage (Zhang et al., 2015).

This access to external knowledge also improves subsidiary standing within the MNE network, and improves its bargaining position (Bouquet and Birkinshaw, 2008a; Birkinshaw, 2016). As a result, subsidiary propositions receive weight in HQs and have more chances on being accepted or adapted (e.g., Bouquet and Birkinshaw, 2008a; Ciabuschi et al., 2017) On the other hand, a subsidiary's internal embeddedness denotes its relationship with their intra-corporate counterparts. In this respect, the subsidiaries can receive strategic knowledge from the parent that may reduce dependence on local contexts and successfully respond to challenges in host environments (Luo, 2003; Najafi-Tavani et al., 2018). This dual embeddedness in external and internal networks offers subsidiaries the potential for learning opportunities that may become the source of competitive advantage (Ghoshal, 1987; Johanson and Vahlne, 2009; Oehmichen and Puck, 2016). As depicted in Figure 11.2, both new service development and value creation must happen in both the external and internal relationships of MNE subsidiaries. This means that, by necessity, both are subject to, at the very least, two different sets of contextual influences for new service development.

Based on the above discussion, we propose Propositions 1 and 2:

Proposition 1: Customer knowledge-based new service development in MNE subsidiaries is conveyed by the inflow of knowledge and takes place in both external and internal relationships sequentially through knowledge acquisition and assimilation.

Proposition 2: Customer knowledge-based value creation in MNE subsidiaries is conveyed by the outflow of knowledge and takes place in both internal and external relationships sequentially through knowledge transformation and exploitation.

It has been established earlier that subsidiary and customer interaction leads to knowledge acquisition (e.g., Ferraris et al., 2017; Zimmerling et al., 2017). For MNEs, this cooperation with customers has been deemed very important, specifically to gain valuable information on local conditions and potential service requirements (Bhawe and Zahra, 2017), given that a foreign customer base requires heightened adaptation needs (Hakanen et al., 2017). In the case of a lack of information or market ambiguity, it might not necessarily lead to increased customer involvement (Zhang et al., 2015). Customer involvement may even decrease unless the subsidiary has a strong willingness to incorporate customer knowledge in service development via a clear absorptive capacity strategy (Najafi-Tavani et al., 2018). Prior research has also revealed that a firm's knowledge acquisition capabilities from its customers are linked to absorptive capacity, and influence overall firm performance (Tzokas et al., 2015; Ferraris et al., 2017). Due to this fact, MNE subsidiaries attempt to develop their relational capabilities to deal effectively with customers including knowledge sourcing (e.g., Rebolledo et al., 2009; Ebers and Maurer, 2014). These relational capabilities also help these subsidiaries to improve their standing and legitimacy in the eyes of MNE HQs (Balogun et al., 2019).

It is important to mention that the customer is part of the broader market and is influenced by market forces like any other market player (Tzokas et al., 2015). As a result, customer willingness to share knowledge or market information with the focal MNE subsidiary is not guaranteed, especially in cases where there is a competing service offering by other players. In such situations, it is pivotal for an MNE subsidiary to be able to create inroads to this external environment so that required customer knowledge gathering can be undertaken (Matusik and Heeley, 2005; Storey and Larbig, 2018). Prior research has signified the importance of relational capabilities of firms (and MNE subsidiaries) to create inroads into the external environment (Ferraris et al., 2020). It should be further noted that this knowledge acquisition is also influenced by the specificities of the external environment, as well as efficiency, scope and flexibility of the acquisition (Van den Bosch et al., 1999; Kazadi et al., 2016). Therefore, we argue that MNE subsidiaries are operating in changing environments and must adapt to their environmental context to make required inroads to acquire customer knowledge to a greater extent than local businesses, where knowledge is more readily available. Based on this discussion, we propose that:

Proposition 3: Foreign subsidiary acquisition of customer knowledge is influenced by relationship-specific factors at the individual level and contextual factors at the organisational level.

The subsidiary's position in the internal network has a significant bearing on the successful assimilation of the knowledge because power dynamics within MNE structures have been found to strongly influence a subsidiary's legitimacy (Balogun et al., 2019). Earlier studies have mentioned that recognition of external knowledge value is a primary condition for absorptive capacity development (Todorova and Durisin, 2007; Lewin et al., 2011; Ferraris et al., 2017). However, this recognition is not guaranteed to take place at every level and part of large organisations with complex structures such as MNEs (Schleimer and Pedersen, 2014). So, in such circumstances, it is highly likely that the MNE subsidiary may value service-specific knowledge from the customers based on customer feedbacks, inputs and overall scoping of market trends (e.g., Javalgi et al., 2014). However, prior research has established that customer knowledge can only be applied in new service design if it assimilated at the organisational level (e.g., Storey and Larbig, 2018). So, in such situations, taking the HQ on board becomes very important. It is also likely that the MNE HQ lacks this specific localised contact with the customer and market specificities due to its cultural and geographic distance, so it may not value service proposition in foreign markets out of sheer ignorance (Ciabuschi et al., 2012) or by either inadvertently or knowingly blocking knowledge transfer efficiency (Birkinshaw, 2016).

Moreover, knowledge appropriability mechanisms may also be different for subsidiaries and HQs, and different appropriability mechanisms have been found to create hindrance (Ho, 2014). Therefore, in such a situation, the MNE subsidiary must possess the means to overcome the HQs' resistance to subsidiary initiatives by wielding sufficient power (Bouquet and Birkinshaw, 2008a; Marabelli and Newell, 2014). This may, however, be difficult for foreign subsidiaries especially in peripheral positions (Gammelgaard et al., 2012) and is dependent on the subsidiary's motivation to engage in a possibly costly and time-consuming knowledge transfer process (Minbaeva et al., 2014; Song, 2014) and its position in the network to be able to do so (Bouquet and Birkinshaw, 2008a; Ferraris et al., 2017).

Along with the subsidiary specific element, there is also a set of predetermined factors, from the point of view of the subsidiary, in the form of social integration mechanisms, which influence the free flow of information between the subsidiary and MNE HQs (Zahra and George, 2002). It should be noted that although a subsidiary can influence its own activity level in social engagements, it can only have a limited impact on other mechanisms that either foster or hinder knowledge transfer. Based on this discussion, we propose that:

Proposition 4: Assimilation of knowledge is influenced by the subsidiary's power, motivation and position in the internal network, and the social integration mechanisms prevalent in the MNE.

In this chapter, focus is on the MNE subsidiary as a focal unit. Therefore, we address transformation in terms of the subsidiary's response to new service development. It has been argued that even when a specific service innovation is customer-led, and its benefits can be clearly communicated, the people responsible for carrying out the transformation may not know how to do it or are intimidated by the consequences of changing their existing patterns of selling and marketing (Witell and Löfgren, 2013). This "inertia" in organisational routines, processes, and strategies has been highlighted in past studies as a major hindrance to change, including new service development (e.g., Lenka et al., 2018). To address this concern a reasonable approach is to decrease the gap between sales and marketing functions, as this can facilitate knowledge exchange leading to better internal buy-in of value proposition changes (Biemans et al., 2010; Lenka et al., 2018). However, a transformation in the business model of the MNE can potentially result in partial organisational support for such an endeavour. However, a true transformation of an MNE's business model is expected to entail the support of the organisation as a whole.

Using a broad definition of a business model, Amit and Zott (2012), state: "A business model depicts the content, structure, and governance of transactions designed to create value through the exploitation of business opportunities." We second their definition by arguing that business models can be examined in the light of service value propositions and their exploitation. Todorova and Durisin (2007) have suggested that social integration mechanisms hold a pertinent position in all phases of absorptive capacity. However, it should be noted that their research viewed absorptive capacity as only an internal phenomenon of a firm. As mentioned earlier, we view absorptive capacity as influenced by both internal and external forces. Therefore, while it seems reasonable that all internal social exchanges are influenced by the context in which they take place, this is not necessarily true for external exchanges in the environment. Hence, the role of social integration mechanisms is limited to assimilation and transformation phases. Based on this discussion, we propose that:

Proposition 5: Transformation in the subsidiary is influenced by social integration mechanisms and alignment of support functions with the business model.

Finally, exploitation occurs in the customer relationship as the subsidiary agent and customer negotiate an agreement of value proposed and value perceived (Grönroos and Voima, 2013; Eggert et al., 2018). The customer alone experiences the service value and realises it in its use (Grönroos and Voima, 2013). However, the subsidiary agent and subsequent customer relationship events (e.g., sales and service events) can be used to enforce the value proposition (Leposky, 2017). The employees or subsidiary agents who directly interact with customers can filter knowledge based on its suitability for exploitation (e.g., Tippins and Sohi, 2003; Storey and Larbig, 2018). These considerations lead us to argue that knowledge application plays a vital role in the creation of customer value since it represents the capability to apply appropriated knowledge to refine the existing services offered by the organisation and to improve its customer value (Bierly et al., 2009; Eggert et al., 2018).

The application of knowledge means that the organisation can quickly respond to resolve problems quickly (Fahey et al., 2001; Winer, 2001). This is expected to help employees to coordinate customer relations across all points of interaction and audiences (Chang and Li, 2007). This response provides a common space of trust between the client and the organisation, restoring customer confidence in the organisation (Cabrera and Cabrera, 2002; Stein and Bowen, 2003). As Kotler (2000) noted, when information or knowledge is not fragmented within an organisation, customer feedback (and, by extension, customer value) is easy to obtain. In the specific context of knowledge exploitation, it has been argued that ambiguity in knowledge exploitation can be reduced by a structured approach to customer interaction during service design (e.g., Storey and Larbig, 2018). Therefore, the exploitation of knowledge is dependent on how the customer perceives the proposition and this perception can be affected by developing relationship-building capabilities in MNE subsidiaries. Based on this discussion, we propose that:

Proposition 6: Exploitation is influenced by customers' perception of value and relationship-specific capabilities.

IMPLICATIONS, LIMITATIONS AND FUTURE RESEARCH DIRECTIONS

Absorptive capacity has proven to be at the centre of innovation and knowledge development. However, less is known about the absorptive capacity as manifested in the customer–subsidiary–HQ interface in the context of MNEs, and how social and relational mechanisms shape its manifestation and leverage. This chapter aims to conceptualise absorptive capacity in relation to the MNE subsidiary's external customer relationships and internal relationship with MNE HQs, arguing that the IB context creates unique circumstances due to the specificity of local knowledge that indicates adaptation needs on the strategic level, and the organisational dynamics inherent in a differentiated structure. Through these two discrete relationships, in which new service development and value creation occur, this chapter attempts to show how absorptive capacity can be used to examine the differences in firms' success in engaging in new service development efforts across borders.

This chapter makes two major contributions to the knowledge transfer and IB literature. First, we examine absorptive capacity within the under-researched context of the customer–subsidiary–HQ interface. We explore the role of absorptive capacity in service development and value creation in this unique context, which both expands the domain of absorptive capacity beyond extensively researched areas of innovation and knowledge management and highlights the active role of customers in learning and information processing procedures in relation to the subsidiary and its HQs. This marks a departure from the dominant view of absorptive capacity as a firm-centric set of capabilities and routines (Cohen and Levinthal, 1990; Lane et al., 2006; Zahra and George, 2002), capturing a better view of the external sources and agents of knowledge and applying it specifically to IB literature in line with Bouquet and Birkinshaw (2008b).

The chapter also specifically highlights the initial role of customers in the very value that is offered to them by the firms. In this vein, absorptive capacity can be viewed as the main underlying capability of the sequential knowledge-related processes and it forms a positive closed-loop of knowledge-centred service development and value creation. Therefore, this chapter contributes to the existing – extensive but fragmented – literature on absorptive capacity by applying it in the specific context of cross-border customer–subsidiary–HQ relationships and to studies on new service development and value creation by using absorptive capacity as a process underlying their inception.

Second, we incorporate the role of social and relational mechanisms into the knowledge management processes underpinned by absorptive capacity. Our propositions explain how each step of absorptive capacity routines (i.e., acquisition, assimilation, transformation and exploitation) is shaped by a unique set of social and relational mechanisms, which are specific to the MNE context due to local embeddedness in the customer–subsidiary relationship, and organisational dynamics exacerbated by cultural and geographical distance in the subsidiary–HQ relationship. In particular, we advance that while relationship-specific factors influence subsidiary acquisition of customer knowledge, subsidiary's power, motivation and position in the internal network, social integration mechanisms prevalent in the organisation influence how subsidiaries assimilate customer knowledge during the service development stage. During the value creation stage, social integration mechanisms and alignment of support functions with the business model influence knowledge transformation at the subsidiary level, and customers' perception of value and relationship-specific capabilities influence the knowledge exploitation. These arguments extend the conversation on absorptive capacity and link the concept to the relational view of the firm within and across organisational boundaries (Dyer & Singh, 1998; Bradbury & Lichtenstein, 2000; Capaldo, 2007; Leischnig et al., 2014). Thus, we contribute to the IB literature by showing that absorptive capacity in MNEs must follow organisational and structural lines of knowledge transfer and is subject to the same forces that influence MNE strategy development.

Our arguments in the chapter also differ from the extant literature in that they consider the directionality of knowledge flows jointly with absorptive capacity and tie these to tangible knowledge outcomes through measurable innovations and value propositions. While many prior studies have considered knowledge transformation as a cognitive process, here transformation is considered from the point of view of changing business models and the dynamics that are at play in bringing the transformation from strategic to the operational level.

The chapter has some limitations in that it is conceptual, so it only proposes possible antecedents but does not empirically verify them. Future studies will hopefully use the foundations laid here to do further testing on the applicability of developed propositions. Furthermore, the chapter takes a narrow view on the networks, consciously limiting itself to a triad of customer–subsidiary–HQ in the context of MNEs. This choice allows for the examination of specific issues around these relationships but does not include knowledge flows from multiple other sources that subsidiaries are in contact with. Therefore, the model does not claim to be all-inclusive or generalisable to other contexts.

REFERENCES

Achcaoucaou, F., Miravitlles, P., & León-Darder, F. (2014). Knowledge sharing and subsidiary R&D mandate development: A matter of dual embeddedness. *International Business Review, 23*, 76–90.

Ambos, T. C., & Birkinshaw, J. (2010). Headquarters' attention and its effect on subsidiary performance. *Management International Review, 50*(4), 449–469.

Amit, R., & Zott, C. (2012). Creating value through business model innovation. *MIT Sloan Management Review, 53*(3), 41–49.

Balogun, J., Fahy, K., & Vaara, E. (2019). The interplay between HQ legitimation and subsidiary legiti- macy judgments in HQ relocation: A social psychological approach. *Journal of International Business Studies, 50*(2), 223–249.

Bartlett, C. A., & Ghoshal, S. (2002). *Managing across borders: The transnational solution.* Harvard Business Press.

Bhawe, N., & Zahra, S. A. (2017). Inducing heterogeneity in local entrepreneurial ecosystems: The role of MNEs. *Small Business Economics*, 1–18.

Biemans, W. G., Brenčič, M. M., & Malshe, A. (2010). Marketing–sales interface configurations in B2B firms. *Industrial Marketing Management, 39*(2), 183–194.

Bierly III, P. E., Damanpour, F., & Santoro, M. D. (2009). The application of external knowledge: Organizational conditions for exploration and exploitation. *Journal of Management Studies, 46*(3), 481–509.

Birkinshaw, J. (2016). *Multinational corporate evolution and subsidiary development.* Springer.

Birkinshaw, J., & Hood, N. (1998). Multinational subsidiary evolution: Capability and charter change in foreign-owned subsidiary companies. *The Academy of Management Review, 23*(4); 773–795.

Björkman, I., Stahl, G. K. & Vaara. E. (2007). Cultural differences and capability transfer in cross-border acquisitions: The mediating roles of capability complementarity, absorptive capacity, and social inte- gration. *Journal of International Business Studies, 38*, 658–672

Bouquet, C., & Birkinshaw, J. (2008a). Weight versus voice: How foreign subsidiaries gain attention from corporate headquarters. *Academy of Management Journal, 51*(3), 577–601.

Bouquet, C., & Birkinshaw, J. (2008b). Managing power in the multinational corporation: How low-power actors gain influence. *Journal of Management, 34*, 477–508.

Bradbury, H., & Lichtenstein, B. M. B. (2000). Relationality in organizational research: Exploring the space between. *Organization Science, 11*(5), 551–564.

Cabrera, A., & Cabrera, E. F. (2002). Knowledge-sharing dilemmas. *Organization Studies, 23*(5), 687–710.

Capaldo, A. (2007). Network structure and innovation: The leveraging of a dual network as a distinctive relational capability. *Strategic Management Journal, 28*(6), 585–608.

Cenamor, J., Parida, V., Oghazi, P., Pesämaa, O., & Wincent, J. (2017). Addressing dual embeddedness: The roles of absorptive capacity and appropriability mechanisms in subsidiary performance. *Industrial Marketing Management.* Available online at https://doi.org/10.1016/j.indmarman.2017.06.002

Chang, W. C., & Li, S. T. (2007). Fostering knowledge management deployment in R&D workspaces: A five-stage approach. *R&D Management, 37*(5), 479–493.

Ciabuschi, F., Forsgren, M., & Martin, O. M. (2012). Headquarters involvement and efficiency of innovation development and transfer in multinationals: A matter of sheer ignorance? *International Business Review, 21*(2), 130–144.

Ciabuschi, F., Kong, L., & Su, C. (2017). Knowledge sourcing from advanced markets subsidiaries: Political embeddedness and reverse knowledge transfer barriers in emerging-market multinationals. *Industrial and Corporate Change, 26*(2), 311–332.

Cohen, W. M., & Levinthal, D. A. (1990). Absorptive capacity: A new perspective on learning and innovation. *Administrative Science Quarterly, 35*(1), 128–152.

Cuervo-Cazurra, A., & Rui, H. (2017). Barriers to absorptive capacity in emerging market firms. *Journal of World Business, 52*(6), 727–742.

Dyer, J. H., & Singh, H. (1998). The relational view: Cooperative strategy and sources of interorganiza- tional competitive advantage. *Academy of Management Review, 23*(4), 660–679.

Ebers, M., & Maurer, I. (2014). Connections count: How relational embeddedness and relational empow- erment foster absorptive capacity. *Research Policy, 43*(2), 318–332.

Eggert, A., Ulaga, W., Frow, P., & Payne, A. (2018). Conceptualizing and communicating value in busi- ness markets: From value in exchange to value in use. *Industrial Marketing Management, 69*, 80–90.

Enkel, E., & Heil, S. (2014). Preparing for distant collaboration: Antecedents to potential absorptive capacity in cross-industry innovation. *Technovation, 34*(4), 242–260.

Ettlie, J. E., & Rosenthal, S. R. (2011). Service versus manufacturing innovation. *Journal of Product Innovation Management, 28*(2), 285–299.

Fahey, L., Srivastava, R., Sharon, J. S., & Smith, D. E. (2001). Linking e-business and operating pro- cesses: The role of knowledge management. *IBM Systems Journal, 40*(4), 889–907.

Ferraris, A., Santoro, G., & Dezi, L. (2017). How MNC's subsidiaries may improve their innovative performance? The role of external sources and knowledge management capabilities. *Journal of Knowledge Management, 21*(3), 540–552.

Ferraris, A., Santoro, G., & Scuotto, V. (2020). Dual relational embeddedness and knowledge transfer in European multinational corporations and subsidiaries. *Journal of Knowledge Management, 24*(3), 519–533.

Foss, K., Foss, N. J., & Nell, P. C. (2012). MNC organizational form and subsidiary motivation problems: Controlling intervention hazards in the network MNC. *Journal of International Management, 18*(3), 247–259.

Gammelgaard, J., McDonald, F., Stephan, A., Tüselmann, H., & Dörrenbächer, C. (2012). The impact of increases in subsidiary autonomy and network relationships on performance. *International Business Review, 21*, 1158–1172.

Gebauer, H., Saul, C. J., Haldimann, M., & Gustafsson, A. (2017). Organizational capabilities for pay-per-use services in product-oriented companies. *International Journal of Production Economics, 192*, 157–168.

Ghoshal, S. (1987). Global strategy: An organizing framework. *Strategic Management Journal, 8*(5), 425–440.

Giroud, A., & Scott-Kennel, J. (2009). MNE linkages in international business: A framework for analysis. *International Business Review, 18*, 555–566.

Grönroos, C., & Voima, P. (2013). Critical service logic: Making sense of value creation and co-creation. *Journal of the Academy of Marketing Science, 41*(2), 133–150.

Hakanen, T., Helander, N., & Valkokari, K. (2017). Servitization in global business-to-business distribution: The central activities of manufacturers. *Industrial Marketing Management, 63*, 167–178.

Hipp, C., & Grupp, H. (2005). Innovation in the service sector: The demand for service-specific innovation measurement concepts and typologies. *Research Policy, 34*(4), 517–535.

Ho, Y. C. (2014). Multilateral knowledge transfer and multiple embeddedness. *The Multinational Business Review, 22*(2), 155–175.

Hotho, J. J., Becker-Ritterspach, F., & Saka-Helmhout, A. (2012). Enriching absorptive capacity through social interaction. *British Journal of Management, 23*(3), 383–401.

Iurkov, V., & Benito, G. R. (2018). Domestic alliance networks and regional strategies of MNEs: A structural embeddedness perspective. *Journal of International Business Studies, 49*(8), 1033–1059.

Javalgi, R. G., Hall, K. D., & Cavusgil, S. T. (2014). Corporate entrepreneurship, customer-oriented selling, absorptive capacity, and international sales performance in the international B2B setting: Conceptual framework and research propositions. *International Business Review, 23*(6), 1193–1202.

Johanson, J., & Vahlne, J.-E. (2009). The Uppsala internationalization process model revisited: From liability of foreignness to liability of outsidership. *Journal of International Business Studies, 40*, 1411–1431.

Kang, J., Rhee, M., & Kang, K. H. (2010). Revisiting knowledge transfer: Effects of knowledge characteristics on organizational effort for knowledge transfer. *Expert Systems with Applications, 37*(12), 8155–8160.

Katsikeas, C. S., Samiee, S., & Theodosiou, M. (2006). Strategy fit and performance consequences of international marketing standardization. *Strategic Management Journal, 27*, 867–890.

Kazadi, K., Lievens, A., & Mahr, D. (2016). Stakeholder co-creation during the innovation process: Identifying capabilities for knowledge creation among multiple stakeholders. *Journal of Business Research, 69*(2), 525–540.

Kogut, B., & Zander, U. (1993). Knowledge of the firm and the evolutionary theory of the multinational corporation. *Journal of International Business Studies, 24*(4), 625–645.

Kotabe, M., Jiang, C. X., & Murray, J. Y. (2017). Examining the complementary effect of political networking capability with absorptive capacity on the innovative performance of emerging-market firms. *Journal of Management, 43*(4), 1131–1156.

Kotler, P. (2000). *Marketing management, millennium edition*. Hoboken, NJ: Prentice-Hall.

Lane, P. J., Koka, B. R., & Pathak, S. (2006). The reification of absorptive capacity: A critical review and rejuvenation of the construct. *Academy of Management Review, 31*(4), 833–863.

Leischnig, A., Geigenmueller, A., & Lohmann, S. (2014). On the role of alliance management capability, organizational compatibility, and interaction quality in interorganizational technology transfer. *Journal of Business Research*, 67(6), 1049–1057.

Lenka, S., Parida, V., Sjödin, D. R., & Wincent, J. (2018). Exploring the microfoundations of servitization: How individual actions overcome organizational resistance. *Journal of Business Research*, 88, 328–336.

Leposky, T. (2017). Servitisation in value creating relationships: Views from headquarters, subsidiaries and customers. PhD dissertation, available online at http://osuva.uwasa.fi/bitstream/handle/10024/7602/isbn_978-952-476-783-5.pdf?sequence=1

Leposky, T., Arslan, A., & Kontkanen, M. (2017). Determinants of reverse marketing knowledge transfer potential from emerging market subsidiaries to multinational enterprises' headquarters. *Journal of Strategic Marketing*, 25(7), 567–580.

Lewin, A. Y., Massini, S., & Peeters, C. (2011). Microfoundations of internal and external absorptive capacity routines. *Organization Science*, 22(1), 81–98.

Lightfoot, H., Baines, T., & Smart, P. (2013). The servitization of manufacturing: A systematic literature review of interdependent trends. *International Journal of Operations & Production Management*, 33(11/12), 1408–1434.

Lim, M. K., Tseng, M. L., Tan, K. H., & Bui, T. D. (2017). Knowledge management in sustainable supply chain management: Improving performance through an interpretive structural modelling approach. *Journal of Cleaner Production*, 162, 806–816.

Lukas, B. A., Tan, J. J., & Hult, G. T. M. (2001). Strategic fit in transitional economies: The case of China's electronics industry. *Journal of Management*, 27, 409–429.

Luo, Y. (2003). Market-seeking MNEs in an emerging market: How parent–subsidiary links shape overseas success. *Journal of International Business Studies*, 34, 290–309.

Marabelli, M., & Newell, S. (2014). Knowing, power and materiality: A critical review and reconceptualization of absorptive capacity. *International Journal of Management Reviews*, 16(4), 479–499.

Matusik, S. F., & Heeley, M. B. (2005). Absorptive capacity in the software industry: Identifying dimensions that affect knowledge and knowledge creation activities. *Journal of Management*, 31(4), 549–572.

Minbaeva, D. B., Pedersen, T., Björkman, I., & Fey, C. F. (2014). A retrospective on MNC knowledge transfer, subsidiary absorptive capacity, and HRM. *Journal of International Business Studies*, 45(1), 52–62.

Moran, P., & Ghoshal, S. (1996). Value creation by firms. In B. J. Keys & L. N. Dosier (Eds.), *Academy of Management Best Papers Proceedings*. Georgia: Georgia Southern University, 41–50.

Najafi-Tavani, Z., Robson, M. J., Zaefarian, G., Andersson, U., & Yu, C. (2018). Building subsidiary local responsiveness: (When) does the directionality of intrafirm knowledge transfers matter? *Journal of World Business*, 53(4), 475–492

Nohria, N. & Ghoshal. S. (1994). Differentiated fit and shared values: Alternatives for managing headquarters-subsidiary relations. *Strategic Management Journal*, 15(6), 491–502.

Oehmichen, J. & Puck, J. (2016). Embeddedness, ownership mode and dynamics, and the performance of MNE subsidiaries. *Journal of International Management*, 22(1), 17–28.

Peltokorpi, V. (2017). Absorptive capacity in foreign subsidiaries: The effects of language-sensitive recruitment, language training, and interunit knowledge transfer. *International Business Review*, 26, 119–129.

Presutti, M., Boari, C., Majocchi, A., & Molina-Morales, X. (2019). Distance to customers, absorptive capacity, and innovation in high-tech firms: The dark face of geographical proximity. *Journal of Small Business Management*, 57(2), 343–361.

Rebolledo, C., Halley, A., & Nagati, H. (2009). The effects of absorptive capacity on operational performance within the context of customer-supplier relationships. *Supply Chain Forum: An International Journal*, 10(2), 52–56.

Santamaría, L., Nieto, M. J., & Miles, I. (2012). Service innovation in manufacturing firms: Evidence from Spain. *Technovation*, 32(2), 144–155.

Schleimer, S. C., & Pedersen, T. (2013). The driving forces of subsidiary absorptive capacity. *Journal of Management Studies*, 50(4), 646–672.

Schleimer, S. C., & Pedersen, T. (2014). The effects of MNC parent effort and social structure on subsidiary absorptive capacity. *Journal of International Business Studies*, *45*(3), 303–320.

Scott-Kennel, J., & Giroud, A. (2015). MNEs and FSAs: Network knowledge, strategic orientation and performance. *Journal of World Business*, *50*(1), 94–107.

Shaw, B., & Luiz, J. M. (2018). The impact of distance (external) and organizational factors (internal) on the knowledge chain of multinational corporations: South Africa as a host country. *Thunderbird International Business Review*, *60*(3), 295–311.

Song, J. (2014). Subsidiary absorptive capacity and knowledge transfer within multinational corporations. *Journal of International Business Studies*, *45*(1), 73–84.

Stein, M. M., & Bowen, M. (2003). Building a customer satisfaction system: Effective listening when the customer speaks. *Journal of Organizational Excellence*, *22*(3), 23–34.

Storey, C., & Larbig, C. (2018). Absorbing customer knowledge: How customer involvement enables service design success. *Journal of Service Research*, *21*(1), 101–118.

Tippins, M. J., & Sohi, R. S. (2003). IT competency and firm performance: Is organizational learning a missing link? *Strategic Management Journal*, *24*(8), 745–761.

Todorova, G., & Durisin, B. (2007). Absorptive capacity: Valuing a reconceptualization. *Academy of Management Review*, *32*(3), 774–786.

Tsai, W. (2001). Knowledge transfer in intraorganizational networks: Effects of network position and absorptive capacity on business unit innovation and performance. *Academy of Management Journal*, *44*(5), 996–1004.

Tzokas, N., Kim, Y. A., Akbar, H., & Al-Dajani, H. (2015). Absorptive capacity and performance: The role of customer relationship and technological capabilities in high-tech SMEs. *Industrial Marketing Management*, *47*, 134–142.

Van Den Bosch, F. A., Volberda, H. W., & De Boer, M. (1999). Coevolution of firm absorptive capacity and knowledge environment: Organizational forms and combinative capabilities. *Organization Science*, *10*(5), 551–568.

Weng, D. H., & Cheng, H. L. (2018). The more, the merrier? How a subsidiary's organizational identification with the MNE affects its initiative. *Long Range Planning*. Available online at https://www .sciencedirect.com/science/article/abs/pii/S002463011730403X

Winer, R. S. (2001). A framework for customer relationship management. *California Management Review*, *43*(4), 89–105.

Winkelbach, A., & Walter, A. (2015). Complex technological knowledge and value creation in science-to-industry technology transfer projects: The moderating effect of absorptive capacity. *Industrial Marketing Management*, *47*, 98–108.

Witell, L., & Löfgren, M. (2013). From service for free to service for fee: Business model innovation in manufacturing firms. *Journal of Service Management*, *24*(5), 520–533.

Zahra, S. A., & George, G. (2002). Absorptive capacity: A review, reconceptualization, and extension. *Academy of Management Review*, *27*(2), 185–203.

Zimmerling, E., Purtik, H., & Welpe, I. M. (2017). End-users as co-developers for novel green products and services – an exploratory case study analysis of the innovation process in incumbent firms. *Journal of Cleaner Production*, *162*, S51–S58.

Zeng, R., Grøgaard, B., & Steel, P. (2018). Complements or substitutes? A meta-analysis of the role of integration mechanisms for knowledge transfer in the MNE network. *Journal of World Business*, *53*(4), 415–432.

Zhang, X., Zhong, W., & Makino, S. (2015). Customer involvement and service firm internationalization performance: An integrative framework. *Journal of International Business Studies*, *46*(3), 355–380.

Index

absorptive capacity 29–30, 114–15, 210–11,
  220–21
  definitions of 65
  and intellectual property (IP) institutions and
    innovation 65–6, 70, 73, 76, 77
  and knowledge exchange 122, 126
  and managerial ties 171–2
  in MNEs 211–14
  potential 215–16
  and R&D 10
  realized 215–16
  and reverse knowledge transfer (RKT) 51, 56
  and value creation and new service
    development 214–20
absorptive capacity and knowledge transfer (KT)
    in small MNEs 26–7
  absorptive capacity 29–30
  acquisition 39–40
  assimilation 40
  discussion and conclusion 41–4
  exploitation 41
  findings 32–8
  framework development 38–41
  knowledge transfer (KT) 28
  methodology 30–32
  theoretical background 27–30
  transformation 40
  visual map 42
Adecco Taiwan 152
affiliate-parent knowledge flows 8, 13, 16, 17, 18,
  19–20

behaviour control 180, 181, 184–5, 188
Bell, M. 6
Benner, Chris 138, 139, 140
Bian, Y. 138
brain drain 137, 144–5, 146, 151
business models 219

capability building in foreign subsidiaries 177–8
  discussion and conclusion 188, 190
  exploitative and explorative capabilities
    178–80
  hypotheses 180–83
  measures 184–6
  methods 183–4
  results 186–8, 189
Carewell 152

China 138, 143, 146–7, 151, 159
  see also intellectual property (IP) institutions
    and innovation, emerging MNCs;
    technological overlap, cultural
    distance and co-location
Chiu, C.-h. 141
Ciabuschi, F. 7
co-location see technological overlap, cultural
    distance and co-location
codification strategy, knowledge management
    198–200, 202, 205
coding, and absorptive knowledge 34–5, 43
collaboration in multi-stakeholder initiatives
    see knowledge exchange within
    multi-stakeholder initiatives (MSIs)
combination see SECI (soc
    ialization-externalization
    -combination-internalization) model
combinative capabilities, and absorptive capacity
    29
communication
  absorptive capacity and knowledge transfer
    (KT) study 32–4, 35, 36, 37, 39–40,
    42–3
  within multi-stakeholder initiatives (MSIs)
    109, 111, 112–13
  and subsidiary knowledge transfer (KT) 202
consultation 125
'consumption-driven commodity chain' 141, 142,
    143, 144, 146, 149–50
control 180–83, 184–5, 188
corporate/organizational culture 98, 182
cultural distance/difference 36, 37, 71
  see also technological overlap, cultural
    distance and co-location
customers
  knowledge flows between customers,
    subsidiaries and headquarters 210–11,
    212, 214–15, 217–18, 219–21
  talent mobility and staffing agencies 140,
    143, 149, 152
  see also absorptive capacity and knowledge
    transfer (KT) in small MNEs;
    social media as knowledge transfer
    (KT) tool (for intellectual capital
    accumulation during international
    growth of small firms)
Cxense 30–31, 32–8, 42–3

Printed and bound by CPI Group (UK) Ltd, Croydon, CR0 4YY

16/04/2025

14658393-0001